DATE DUE

RETURN OF THE BLACK SHIPS

by

Benton Weaver Decker
Rear Admiral, United States Navy
(retired)
and
Edwina Naylor Decker

VANTAGE PRESS
New York   Washington   Atlanta   Hollywood

#5100357
DLC

1-15-82 JK

Dedicated to

those who made the

Occupation of Japan a success

FIRST EDITION

Copyright © 1978 by Benton Weaver Decker,
Rear Admiral, United States Navy (retired)

Published by Vantage Press, Inc.
516 West 34th Street, New York, New York 10001

Manufactured in the United States of America
Standard Book Number 533-03368-3

CONTENTS

FOREWORD

In 1860, the minister of finance of the Yokosuka shogunate asked assistance from the French government in building a shipyard at Yokosuka (YO-KO-SKA—no accent), twenty-six miles south of Tokyo. Leonce Verny, a French naval architect, came to Japan to supervise the construction. In 1866, the keel of the first ship was laid in the Yokosuka Iron Works, and in 1871, the name was changed to "Yokosuka Shipyard." In 1903 a further change was to "Yokosuka Navy Yard."

The base was severely damaged in 1923 by an earthquake. From 1941 to 1945, four aircraft carriers, over twenty-four destroyers and submarines were completed in the yard. The largest was the *Shinano* of 68,000 tons, an aircraft carrier launched October 1944 and sunk by a United States submarine in Sagami Wan the following month.

The U. S. Fleet had anchored in Sagami Wan on August 27, 1945. After a two-day storm it shifted anchorage to Tokyo Bay. On August 29, at 0805, a boarding party took possession of the HIJMS *Nagato*. At 0930 the Fourth Marine Regiment landed on the Yokosuka Peninsula. At 1018 the flag of the United States of America was raised and the area surrendered to COMMANDER TASK FORCE 31, Rear Admiral Oscar Badger, in the USS *San Diego*, moored in the cove. CINCPAC Op-Plan 15-45 established Fleet Activities, Yokosuka, Japan. From an early report:

Everywhere the smell of the bad sanitation and unused structures was awful. Offices and working spaces were in disorder. Civilians had looted the Base. Tugs

v

and small craft rotted in the water. The building-ways were cluttered with parts of midget submarines. Roads were rutted with many rusty and burnt out trucks scattered along the edges. The Base was a crudely built monstrosity in total decay.

On September 8 Task Force 31 was dissolved, and Commodore O. O. Kessing assumed command of the base. On November 23 he was relieved by Captain H. M. Briggs, as Commander Task Group 53.4 and Fleet Activities. Another report stated: "Rats, lice, fleas, flies, and other vermin were everywhere. There were open cess pools and unflushed sewers. Dysentery was prevalent. A 200 bed hospital was quickly renovated."

The U. S. Navy had present seven battleships, twelve large carriers, three small carriers, twenty-nine destroyers, and nine destroyer escorts, as well as hundreds of small craft. The British had eleven ships.

The first commanding officers of the base, upon relinquishing his command, stated on November 25, 1945: "Don't forget this—the Jap has not changed a bit! He is still the slimy, sneaky, treacherous animal who was doing his best a few weeks ago to kill and torture you. . . ." This was indicative of the attitude of many of the officers and men on the base.

I assumed command of the base on April 10, 1946, and was relieved on June 30, 1950. I returned home for retirement and became a speaker for the Redpath Bureau, supporting the Japanese as our friend and ally and praising the outstanding accomplishments of General MacArthur in the Occupation of Japan.

INTRODUCTION

When I was ordered to command Fleet Activities, Yokosuka, Japan, I was surprised and not enthusiastic. I was in command of three battleships: the *Maryland, Colorado,* and the *West Virginia,* moored to Pier 91, Seattle, Washington. They were being "mothballed," a boring task. Those ships would never move again under their own power. The war was over—battleships were has-beens. My career was coming to a close. Then, I received orders to Yokosuka.

I was not happy about them, but anything was better than "mothballing" battleships. My two sons were ensigns in battleships at the surrender ceremony and had considerable knowledge of Yokosuka and the Naval base. They reported that the place was a wreck and the personnel demoralized.

Later I was to find that Yokosuka was my chance to justify my existence. My tour was to be the most productive part of my naval career.

The former Japanese arsenal extended for five miles along the western shore of Tokyo Bay. It included two airports, a seaplane base, aeronautical research center, optical laboratory, gun factory and ordnance depot, torpedo factory, munitions and aircraft storage, tank farms, supply depot, shipyard, training schools and hospitals. During the war seventy thousand civilians and fifty thousand naval ratings worked or trained at this base. It was administered by three vice admirals and six rear admirals.

Machinery and materials had been indiscriminately placed in twelve hundred caves. In these caves, men at machines had been working in poor light, squatting on dirt ledges, and transporting the materials by manpower. School-children were working in the aircraft factory.

The hysterical urge to dig caves in the soapstone hills started in 1943, the terrain being ideal for this purpose. For the last two years of the war, no maintenance of buildings had been undertaken. There had been some strafing by our carrier planes and minor bombing. The Japanese looting prior to our arrival and the natural pent-up reactions of our troops left the base in a shambles.

Credit for the success of our Navy in revitalizing the base in Yokosuka during the Occupation must go to many people. First, I acknowledge that of my seniors who in succession occupied the office of ComNavFE—Commander Naval Forces, Far East and allowed me the freedom of action necessary to accomplish so much in so little time. These outstanding vice admirals were Robert M. Griffin, Russell S. Berkey, and Charles Turner Joy. I could never have remained in command for over four years had they not approved of my actions.

But of all to be praised is General MacArthur, the Supreme Commander of the Allied Powers. He it was who established the first benevolent Christian Occupation in the history of the world. By his wisdom and his courage he transformed a vicious enemy into a friendly ally, an accomplishment which has given us over thirty years of peace in the Pacific. It promises decades of harmony to come. The hatreds of former generations will not be passed on to future generations. It was a new philosophy.

History was made in Yokosuka. Because we were but a small part of the Occupation, we were able to move fast with little opposition, to establish many precedents under the policies of the general's first two directives. This required many capable and enthusiastic subordinates. These were limited in number but not in abilities. Even the wives did their share, which I certainly appreciated. It is useless to give directives and announce policies' if you do not have the manpower to execute them. To those under my command during four fruitful years and to their wives I give my sincere thanks for their wholehearted support.

I have delayed giving credit to the Japanese people, without whose cooperation little could have been accomplished. At first the men were reluctant—they were demoralized and hungry. But they never resorted to violence or to sabotage. For this we can be grateful.

Without the Imperial influence, the Japanese might not have accepted defeat, nor willingly rebuilt along democratic lines. The Occupation would have been long, costly, and violent.

In Japan there were two philosophies—that of the male and that of the female. They were entirely different. Of the two, the women thought more along our lines. They were kind, quiet, hard-working and cooperative. I decided to build up the importance of women relative to that of the men.

In 1945 many Americans wanted no part of Japan. They could not envision the need for Japan as our ally if our world was to enjoy peace. Our people had to be informed or we might have abandoned Japan, to our great sorrow. The press did a thorough and complete job of informing the American public.

It is timely for me to introduce the coauthor, my wife, Edwina. If you knew her, you would like her, she is so feminine. And you would forgive her frequent inclusions of "Benny" in her writings. During our four years in Yokosuka I pled with her to throw away the many letters, papers, and clippings. Being Edwina and a woman, she always agreed and continued to add to the clutter. Now at long last she is able to justify her "refusal to obey orders" by this book which requires constant reference to her "files"—a seachest full of papers.

Our duty in Japan was the most productive period of my Naval career. We had always been happy no matter where we lived or under what circumstances. But these were more than happy years. They were years in which we served our fellow man. They justified our lives.

Arriving in Yokosuka on April 3, 1946 I found the Japanese people unemployed and hungry. Also, I found the naval personnel under my command demoralized. The base was a junk pile. Everyone wanted "home," and no one was in the least interested in the civil affairs of the Japanese. This was during the disastrous demobilization period in which some of our best officers and most competent and experi-

ix

enced men were returned so hastily to the United States, leaving behind too few to handle the stupendous disposal of Japanese war materials, as well as the salvaging and identifying of millions of dollars of United States surplus equipment and supplies.

Even the forces afloat were at loggerheads with the Navy ashore. The fault was mainly with the base. It had failed to recognize that it was justified only as it served the forces afloat. Also, it had failed to meet the friendly advances of the Army. Edwina and I spent all of our time as well as our income in changing this attitude. And we enjoyed every minute. The many social affairs I considered not only as pleasures, but also as "lubricants." It paid off. The base soon was known for its friendliness. My officers and men went out of their way to engender goodwill. They enjoyed doing so. We felt that our efforts were well repaid by the number of friends we made among the services. We all cooperated for the good of the United States. Wives were important in the playing of their part. Mrs. Decker never failed to do her share.

I have quoted a few of the congratulatory letters, for I believe them to be pertinent. By their remarks the writers, of all ranks and positions, showed that they approved of what we were doing. We weren't dreamers! The letters of thanks to me were actually thanks to the people under my command.

> B. W. Decker
> Rear Admiral, U. S. Navy
> (retired)

RETURN OF THE BLACK SHIPS

Chapter I

WE OPEN THE DOOR

In 1853 Commodore Matthew Calbraith Perry, U. S. Navy, in the "Black Ships" arrived off Tokyo Bay and forced Japan to open her ports to the world. He brought to Japan two great gifts—modern industrialization and democracy. Unfortunately Japan accepted industrialization but rejected democracy, remaining a totalitarian nation, limiting the freedoms of her people. She became a powerful nation without a conscience, threatening other nations. This culminated in the ruthless attack on Pearl Harbor.

In 1945 our "Black Ships" returned to Tokyo Bay and forced open the door once again; insisting that Japan accept a democratic form of government.

At the end of World War II, Japan was thoroughly beaten. The people were hungry, shelterless, and depressed. Their government was powerless, unable to oppose communist intrigues. The fallen foe was ripe for rape or for help from a good samaritan.

In 1945 I was on many high-level committees, including JCAC—Joint Civil Affairs Committee in Washington, D. C. There was considerable discussion on a high level about dividing Japan among the Allied powers. China would get Kyushu; Russia, Hokkaido; and we would get Honshu. When it failed to jell, other suggestions were forthcoming. The Supreme Commander in Japan should be controlled by an Allied council. The Emperor system should be destroyed and the

1

Emperor exiled. Their major industrial combines should be broken up into many small companies.

All this would have assured us of the hatred of the Japanese for years to come. Most of us did not accept these "planted" policies which would have encouraged the growth of communism. The Occupation had a good policy, winning the friendship of our former enemy; but most important, the policy had to be implemented by the right man as Supreme Commander of the Allied Powers. This was the key to the future of Japan.

He had to be an American of special qualifications: courageous, immune to innuendoes and social gossip, intimidation, and outright slander, a great leader. He should know the Asian mind. President Truman selected General Douglas MacArthur. There was no better choice. This important decision resulted in the winning of Japan as a firm ally and bringing peace to the Pacific.

In April 1946, many Americans still advocated the complete withdrawal of our forces from Japan and in addition wanted to wreck its economy. A few communists in the Occupation were most active. Also, there were many of Japanese extraction, trained in Russia as agitators and brought into Japan by our transportation from Korea. The Soviets knew what they wanted, even though our government did not. They got an early, aggressive start.

If we had abandoned Japan, she would have become a Russian satellite, against the will of the Japanese. The Chinese feared this, as it would have isolated them. For us, it would have broken the continuity of our Asian island frontier. California would then have become our first line of defense. It was essential that Japan prosper and ally herself with the United States.

Our Navy played an important part in the Occupation of Japan. The Navy's area of jurisdiction was but 2 percent of the whole and its personnel about 1 percent. Sasebo and Yokosuka were our only zones. Being small we were able to move fast and lead the way in carrying out the general's directives. We became the showplace of the Occupation for visiting VIPs.

Because of the Emperor's attitude, the Occupation was

nonviolent; but the Japanese military had spread terrorizing rumors about the brutality of the Americans. The Japanese people were obeying the Emperor's wishes but they had reservations because of the lies spread by the military. They were reluctant, but cooperated to a degree.

The governor of Kanagawa Prefecture, Mr. Uchiyama, informed me he never visited Yokosuka, as the Japanese Navy discouraged it. The Navy controlled the city in all respects and the entire Miura Peninsula was secret. No foreigners were allowed. There was no industry and no commerce. Christianity was suppressed and all Bibles confiscated and burned. The people were destitute, without hope.

I was in Seattle when I received orders to Japan. I had been selected to command the Naval base at Yokosuka. This was where the action was and a far better job than remaining in the states, mothballing battleships.

In crossing the Pacific to Japan, I had stopped by CINCPAC's—Commander in Chief Pacific office in Pearl Harbor to find out what the policy of the Unites States was, so far as Yokosuka was concerned. There was none! Thus I arrived in Japan in a policy vacuum. In the Yokosuka files I found two letters from an earlier commander who advocated blowing up the base and returning all hands to the United States. From the newspapers, I learned that there were some in high positions who advocated abandoning Japan, which would leave her prey for the Russian bear. Later the chief of staff of COMNAVFE several times asked me when I was going to blow up the dry docks. My answer was, "When I get written orders!

My duty in China and in the Pacific before World War II had convinced me of the need for a complete base in the Western Pacific. In 1945 we had given the Chinese one hundred million dollars to build a U. S. base on the Whangpoo, near Shanghai. We never got a dime's worth of repairs out of that investment. Our base in the Philippines was and still is the subject of the whims of Filipino politicians. The base in Guam was weak, for there is no back country, no large harbor, no natural resources, and no large supply of water or power, and no skilled labor. If we couldn't hold it in the last war, how could we defend it in the next?

But Yokosuka was ideal. Here we had an entire nation from which to draw unlimited supplies of labor, power, and water—and it was situated on a large, easily protected bay. Furthermore, it was already constructed—a six hundred million dollar complex. There were building ways, hospitals, warehouses, and twelve hundred caves. Here, too, was one of the world's largest dry docks where we could easily dock our largest carriers. This was what we had always wanted.

I not only knew of our great need for this base in the Western Pacific, but also of the equal need to keep it out of Communist control; therefore, I filled the policy vacuum. As

Captain Decker, with drydock #6, used as a wet basin, in the background.

4

Energetic Japanese women assist in cleaning the Base.

nature abhors a vacuum, so does man. This was the "purpose" needed to restore morale of my officers and men.

At our first "weekly" conference, I announced, "We are going to stay in this base for fifty years. Now, clean it up!" The tone of the base immediately changed.

The press supported me with generous publicity. A letter from the states stated: "Benny Decker is the best known American other than General MacArthur." However, my policy was not sanctioned by Washington. One of the many assistant secretaries of the Navy questioned it. The Russian ambassador to the United States also complained. Admiral

Griffin, after talking to me, evidently fended off the first complaint.

Years later I found that our State Department had had severe reservations about the Japanese and fully expected the military to regain control of the Japanese government. But I felt that the situation in Japan was quite the opposite.

Peace in the Pacific depended on two things: Japan's being a democracy and its having an alliance with the United States. But no democracy can exist unless the people believe in Christian principles; therefore, we should encourage Christianity and emphasize the teachings of that religion. And to counter communism, we must build prosperity. Hunger begets communism.

An alliance depended on friendship between the two nations. The press had to educate the American people to accept and reciprocate the friendship of the Japanese. If we were to be allies, we must be friendly allies! There were some who "wanted out" of Japan. I had heard this expressed in the Navy Department when I was Navy's representative on the JCAC (Joint Civil Affairs Committee). There was a minority of vocal appeasers and a few revengeful military, but many weren't talking—just waiting for developments.

To have blown up that base would have been a major blunder, if not a criminal act. It would have made destitute many Japanese and eventually would have helped to bring about the Russian enslavement of the great Japanese nation. Had I been ordered to do so, I would have had but two courses of action—either obey and destroy, or be relieved of command. I would have elected the latter. But the fact remains that I never received any such orders. I did realize that a few in political office wished this. But, without orders to the contrary, I was dedicated to making Yokosuka our naval operating base.

We had won the war . . . now we had to win the peace! To this end, we did our utmost to develop friendship with the people of Yokosuka.

I had arrived in April by Navy Air at the Kisarasu airfield, across the bay from Yokosuka. The next morning, after an informal tour of inspection, I was driven ten miles to Tokyo in order to report to my immediate senior, Vice Admiral

Robert M Griffin. Tokyo was a mass of ruins. Of 345 square miles, two-thirds were completely burned out. For miles, one passed only rubble, rusty auto and bicycle frames, and stark chimneys. The Japanese had collapsed only after there was nothing left but lost hopes. I reflected that it would be a long, long time before Tokyo could be rebuilt and its population returned to normal, but I was mistaken. I did not yet realize the great willpower of the disciplined Japanese nation.

Yokosuka, twenty-two miles south of Tokyo, on the far side of Yokohama, was in better shape. In order to reach the city we passed through numerous tunnels on a narrow asphalt road that had not been built to withstand the heavy traffic of the Americans. It was badly maintained and full of chuckholes. The poor, crowded town of small, flimsy wooden houses gave stark testimony to the poverty of its inhabitants who numbered about two hundred and thirty thousand. Many of the homes could be reached only by foot; few streets were wide and fewer were paved. There were many firebreaks where houses had been removed during the war and the ground left bare. Every foot of this exposed soil was now used for vegetable gardens. It was not uncommon to see yellow squash vines growing over the roof of the Japanese dwellings. Although there was no fertilizer, there was an abundance of "night soil," and the stench was terrific. One grows accustomed to it over the years, as had the Japanese.

The inhabitants were hungry, but were kind and polite. Each day people would crowd into the electric trains, headed for the rural areas where scraps of food might be found. A potato was a prize to be brought home to a thankful family for the evening meal. There were no overfed Japanese in Yokosuka. The cold nights were endured with no heat, as the Japanese were rugged. They wore heavy clothing when they could, but it also was in short supply. There was no charcoal, and a piece of wood to heat a frugal meal and blunt the edge of the winter's cold was a luxury.

I wrote Edwina:

This country is a lesson! We must never let an

enemy carry a war to our shores. It is unbelievable how poor these people are and what a terrific cost this war has been to them. We must always have a Strong Navy to keep such devastation from our cities.

I would not have believed the Occupation could be so free from acts of violence. Had the situation been reversed, would we have been so cooperative? The Japanese are well disciplined, and not accustomed to the freedoms we enjoy. Their actions are tempered with obedience. They are conditioned to complacency by a culture going back to 500 A.D.

But we had to play it safe. Even though seven months of the Occupation had passed without opposition, my military training prevented me from assuming that the harmony would continue. After I took command, I ordered my Marine colonel to prepare a defense plan and train our forces, holding a defense drill once a week. He used his 400 marines with 400 sailors. It was reassuring to see these men running over hills in a mock battle. Thus, they became thoroughly familiar with the terrain.

But if the worst occurred, we would have to depend on the First Brigade of the First Cavalry with their tanks at Camp McGill. The road was unpaved, and in rain and under the heavy traffic, it would soon become impassable. The army paved it for me. My captain of the yard, Robert Paton, who had the gigantic task of cleaning up the base, set up a concrete ramp for our landing craft to load the tanks. We also put the LCTs (Landing Craft Tanks) and LCMs (Landing Craft Motor—for a single tank) into operating condition. We were prepared for the worst—which, therefore, never happened.

When I arrived we had 3,500 marines, which were immediately reduced to 1,200. Within a few days this was reduced to 400 and shortly thereafter, orders were received limiting us to 100! I reacted, reporting that the security of the base would be jeopardized and that 400 marines were necessary, whereupon the order was canceled, and a colonel was ordered to relieve Lieutenant Colonel Bruno Hochmuth. Again, I insisted that Lieutenant Colonel Hochmuth was capable of commanding my Marine unit to my complete satisfaction, so again, Washington canceled an order.

Bruno was sharing the Tadodai residence with me and was compatible as well as efficient. I couldn't have asked for a better Marine. He was destined to lose his life in Vietnam, as a Major General.

In a letter to Edwina, I wrote:

> I walk through the town and up the crowded alleys with no fear. The people are most friendly and the children, with their charming smiles, call out in one breath, "Hawrow—goodbye!"—a heartwarming greeting. Their parents must be friendly! Little would I have thought I could walk through these streets, day or night, unescorted—unarmed. I was advised to always appear with a large staff and to have side arms, but if General MacArthur could land at Atsugi on the first day of the Occupation without arms and with only a small staff I see no reason for me to do otherwise! Furthermore, I ordered the red light and siren removed from my official car.

I wanted none of the arrogance of a conqueror!

My predecessors had all lived less than a mile from the base in the Tadodai residence, which was by far the best residence in town. Although I was offered one of the wealthy Japanese homes in Kamakura, I decided to live in the Tadodai near the base.

It was a large house, half European and half Japanese. There were several acres of grounds, beautifully landscaped. The ancient plum trees announced the end of winter with their delicate blossoms, and then in April, the cherry trees dominated the gardens. Spring had arrived and we fell in love with Japan. The views from the mounds surrounding the house were inspiring. One could see the bay to the east and Fuji to the west. Fuji, in all of its majesty, was ever present, ever changing. It is said that, when leaving Japan, you will return if you see Fuji. It has a great power of attraction.

The house had twenty-one rooms, some very small, including servants' quarters. It had been built in 1913 for the base commander by Vice Admiral Baron Sotokichi, a graduate of our Naval Academy, Class of 1881. The first occupant was Vice Admiral Prince Higashi Yorihito. The occupants that followed included Vice Admiral Kichisaburo Nomura (twice), Eisuke Yamamoto, Osamu Nagano, and Admiral Nutemasa Yonai. I knew all of these men, having met them in 1939 when I was navigator of the *Astoria*, which returned to Japan the ashes of Hiroshi Saito, the former ambassador to the United States. I admired them as naval officers, particularly Admiral Nomura, who was a good friend of mine. It was Yonai whom the *Los Angeles Times* quoted on April 20, 1946:

> (AP) When the cruiser Astoria returned the ashes of Ambassador Saito to Japan in 1939, Admiral Yonai toasted the American Naval Officers, "One day you shall return to Japan." Yonai was right. Navy Captain Benton W. Decker is now living in Yonai's house, and Yonai is a prisoner awaiting war trials.

The outside of the house was camouflaged with black and brown paint, as were many other buildings, both on the base as well as in town. I objected to their forlorn, depressing appearance. By repainting the commandant's house and those on the base we might make the place a bit more cheerful. The manager, thinking that he would surprise me, painted the trim white. On being praised, the following day he painted the remainder battleship gray! What a monstrosity! So it received another coat of paint—white. The servants were proud that Yokosuka now had a "White House," the same as Washington.

Our servants were plentiful and good, though now and then Colonel Hochmuth (USMC) who shared the residence with me would be displeased with the cooking. His method of getting results was effective. He merely sent word to the cook to scramble him some eggs—a mortal insult. The cook improved rapidly, mainly by using spices and sugar that had not been available in Japan during the war.

The servants required a few restrictions. First, Japanese eat daikon, a huge radish which has a pungent, penetrating odor which we found quite disagreeable. Therefore, I banned the cooking of daikon in our kitchen. Another problem was the use of camellia oil for hair pomade by the girls. In Japan, the seed pods of the red camellia trees were collected and crushed for oil, which has many uses. During the Occupation it was difficult to obtain, and what they had was rancid, strong, and had a sickening, sweet smell.

One of the girls broke out with the ugly sores of beriberi, which was caused by eating nothing but polished rice. On questioning her, we found that her father had a great store of rice, probably looted from the base before we took over. As they loved polished rice, she had eaten nothing else for a long period of time.

The Tadodai was poorly furnished. Admiral Totsuka stated that he had insisted that nothing be moved after the surrender; yet the people of the town had looted the residence that very night! I slept on a mattress placed on a piece of plywood over two sawhorses. I felt every little earthquake and was practically thrown out of my shaky, improvised bed. The chairs in the living room were small and cramped for overfed Americans and the room was lighted by a ghastly chandelier, drooping with faded green velvet. One day, after my friend from *Life* magazine, Eisenstadt, and I had lunch, we decided to redecorate. His solution was simple—remove the chandelier and replace five of the ceiling panels with glass, through which a light shone. The room now took on a better appearance.

After the first party, the battery of toilets in the guest restrooms proved disastrous. Apparently only for show, they were not connected to a cesspool! The hot water system was jerry built, and there was no heating system, but we did have open fireplaces. One cold day, Bruno started a roaring fire in the dining room fireplace. Heavy smoke rolled down the steps from the attic where the chimney emptied. Evidently, the fireplace was for a charcoal brazier, with the fumes heating the attic as well as killing any bugs. In Japan many houses had beautiful bronze radiators, but no piping. The apparent connecting pipes were painted wood! Before Edwina arrived, I had to have some steam heat installed. It took six months, as it was such a strange idea to the Japanese.

Our five gardeners were good workers and meticulously plucked the needles, one by one, from the ancient pine trees. The results were beautiful, but I thought some of this labor could be better directed towards growing flowers and vegetables. There was a garden, hidden from sight, where flowers were grown for arrangements. I soon learned that Japanese gardens could have flowering shrubs and trees, but that flowers were taboo. When asked to grow vegetables, the men were quite upset, saying that they were gardeners, not farmers. I therefore found it necessary to replace one of them with a farmer. On the opposite side of the estate, hidden behind a bunker, a vegetable garden was started. Yokosuka is famous for its spinach. Soon we had the best spinach I had ever eaten—and I'm no spinach lover. The garden was a great success!

Now we had to insist that chemical fertilizer be used instead of night soil. This greatly improved the fragrance in our formal garden. It was necessary also to supply the home upwind of us to complete the cure. I had not been in the Orient long enough to ignore those pungent odors.

One hundred feet to the east of the mansion was a mound in which was the command bunker, from which Admiral Totsuka could observe the bay from Kawasaki to Sarushima Island and north. It was a three-storied cave. On its top, I had a flagpole erected and each morning my Marine orderly raised the stars and stripes. I was in doubt as to the reaction of the townspeople to this flag over their city. That day I received a delegation to thank me for this honor, for now they had a flag like that flown over General MacArthur's residence in Tokyo!

I wrote Edwina in June:

This noon I had luncheon at Marine Air Group 31 with my Marine aviators. I was shown thirteen large wind tunnels. It was a large air base.

I have just returned from a visit to the Twelfth Cavalry at Hayama where the Emperor has a summer palace. Colonel Labrot invited me over for dinner and to show me the place.

I was delighted with the high caliber of the Americans assigned to the Occupation. The Army generals were all capable, cooperative, and pleasant to deal with. The people of the United States should have been proud of the type of Americans carrying out their wishes. I found it very efficient to attend social functions as so much could be accomplished in such a short time. We became a team, all hands working together for the good of the Occupation. Had it not been for the many dinners we gave, and those given so generously by others, we would have met but few people and would have accomplished so much less.

Admiral Griffin requested that the Bureau of Personnel spot promote me to commodore, as had been done for my predecessors. The bureau replied, "Not at this time," and was then forced to relieve my chief staff officer, Captain Milton Anderson, belonging to the Class of 1911. Captain Toni Rorschack, a most capable and likable officer, relieved him.

One pleasant surprise was finding my old friend, Ichiro Yokoyama, former Japanese Navy captain, in the Second Demobilization Bureau. He had been chief of staff to Admiral Nomura. I asked him to several luncheons and discussed with him some of the problems. His advice was excellent. He knew many officers of the Japanese Navy, as well as those of the United States Navy. Mr. Totsuka, who is mentioned in the following letter, was a former admiral, the last Japanese base commander, and thus the last Japanese occupant of the Tadodai. I appreciated Ichiro's frankness and returned the favor.

Admirals Yonai and Nomura were also good friends. Nomura was the Japanese admiral in Washington at the time of Pearl Harbor. The attack had been as much a surprise to him as it was to us. Yonai had been heavily involved in the Pearl Harbor plot, though I believe he had misgivings. We had become friends when I came to Japan in the *Astoria* in 1939. I saw much more of Nomura than I did of Yonai. The latter died in 1949. I asked Captain Owsley to help him and furnish the scarce drugs needed to prolong his life. He was very grateful. Nomura, far senior to me before the war, promptly called on me on January 1, 1947, to pay Nomura's respects.

After the peace treaty, on my return to Japan I then promptly called on him, and was happy to do so.

I asked my friend Yokoyama to bring the former occupant of the Tadodai and their wives to call at his convenience. On that occasion I had cocktails served during their af-

13

ternoon visit. Shortly after I received the following letter, showing the gratitude of the Japanese for small favors. Ichiro Yokoyama wrote:

My dear Captain Decker,

I hasten to convey to you our thanks for your kindness in inviting former admiral in command of the Base, Mr. Michitaro Totsuka, my wife and myself to your cocktail party yesterday afternoon, and for all the thoughtfulness and hospitality you showed us.

Mr. Totsuka was astounded by the vast improvements made in your official residence and was deeply touched by your kindness in letting him see all parts of it under your personal guidance. As he does not feel equal to writing you in English, he has requested me to convey to you his heartfelt appreciation.

My wife and I can hardly find words with which to express adequately our appreciation of your constant friendship. In addition to enjoying such a delightful afternoon yesterday, I particularly appreciated the opportunity you afforded us yesterday to discuss with utter frankness and numerous problems of mutual interest. I am afraid that I indulged in a degree of frankness that I would not have permitted myself in speaking to any other member of the Occupation Force. If I went to excess, I trust it will be excused on the grounds of personal friendship. Hearing from your constant concern for the future prosperity of Yokosuka (my birthplace) under the construction of the new Japan, I am made to realize how inadequate and puny are the efforts of the Japanese themselves.

With best wishes for your good health and continued success.

Yours sincerely,
Ichiro Yokoyama

My predecessors had ignored their social obligations and had no contacts with the Army. They didn't even know the names of the generals. This was no way to operate a joint endeavor. Social life is the necessary lubricant that reduces conflicts to a minimum. Lieutenant General Robert Eichel-

14

berger, in command of the Eighth Army, invited me to dinner just before I assumed command. I found him most amiable and we became close friends. I was to find the Army senior officers to be capable and friendly, creating in me, and my command, a great admiration for our sister service.

As it was conducive to harmony and lubricated the wheels of cooperation, we gave many parties in our quarters. This was no strain upon Edwina or me. All I did was to give my chief petty officer, Gene Wilson, who acted as my secretary, the date and guest list. Everything was automatic, and experience made the organization perfect. The generals all wanted to know who was my superb flag secretary.

Our guests would be escorted from the border of the Navy's zone of responsibility to the Tadodai residence by a Marine escort. The visitor's car would be greeted at the entrance by a Marine who opened the car doors and directed the drivers to their dining room. The guests would be met at the house door by Wah Chan, my steward, and several pretty Japanese girls in kimonos. "What will you have to drink, Sir?" (The bar was in the hallway) Usually the answer was, "Old fashioned!", for Wah was well known for his excellent old fashioneds. With a drink in hand, the guest would be ushered into the reception room to be greeted by Edwina and me, and perhaps a guest of honor. This way the party would get off to a fast start.

To assist our servants, we had the "flying squad" from the Officers' Club. This group was available to anyone—officer or enlisted man. The host would inform the club of the hour, date, and number of guests. A portable bar with assorted liquors, glasses, and ice would be set up in the host's home, and the bartender would give expert service, well supported by four to eight pretty Japanese girls in kimonos. For this beautiful and effective arrangement, the host had only to pay the corkage.

Our guests were delighted with our system and soon called the girls by their nicknames—Cherry Blossom, Bamboo, Cutey Pie, Moon Beam, and Studebaker. Our own girls were called by their first names—Chieko and Yoshii. They were all generous with their smiles.

When I arrived on April 3, Captain Hank Briggs was in command. He was of the USNA Class of 1913 and had been promised a commodore's commission. This had been withheld by Admiral Towers, who was most unhappy about the base. Hank was suffering from an ulcer and was not up to coping with the gigantic confusion and chaos that characterized this command.

That week, Hank found himself host to a half dozen Russians from the Embassy. They arrived at about 1400 for lunch. Hank had invited two for lunch at 1200! This was the typical Russian response to an invitation. You never knew if one or a dozen would arrive, or at what time they might appear. Never did they give warning to the host. Whether it was rudeness or ignorance, I do not know. Perhaps it was a late attempt to meet and sound out the new commanding officer. If so, it failed, for I refused to attend. It was five that afternoon before they finished their heavy drinking and returned to Tokyo. Both Hank and his ulcer took a licking; he was sick for several days thereafter.

The day before assuming my command, I had dinner with Admiral Griffin. I found him good company and was happy to serve under him. I concluded that a change in the Yokosuka Naval base was in order and that my boss would support me.

On April 10, the day of the first Japanese election of representatives, under the Occupation, I assumed command. At the ceremony there were fifteen U. S. Navy captains and six Japanese ex-admirals and captains on duty with the Second Demobilization Bureau. After dispensing a few medals, I went to my office. What a dismal place! The Japanese liaison officer and the Demobilization Bureau officers called.

I had also been assigned Commander Task Group 964 and had many miscellaneous duties including two airfields as well as Sasebo base and many surface craft under my command, scattered here and there. I ordered the craft moored in the inner cove where I could see them. My sons, as boat officers, had reported the dangers of small boats colliding at night with the numerous large battleship mooring buoys and with heavy, watersoaked logs. Most of the buoys and anchors were removed to a buoy yard, and the few left were painted white. The harbor had long been secret, and no one had been allowed to collect any of the tremendous amounts of driftwood that had collected there. By declaring the end of secrecy and removing the restrictions on the harbor, anyone could gather all the driftwood he wished. It was cold and firewood was scarce. The harbor was cleared of debris in a matter of days. A salvage program was initiated to pick up the many LCMs and twenty-one LCTs abandoned along the shores of Tokyo Bay. These were not on charge, so they became a part of the General's Navy when North Korea struck South Korea in 1950.

My office was on the third deck of the Administration Building. Upon my arrival each morning, I always found the decks wet from recent swabbing. Finally I asked why and was told that this was the Japanese way of honoring me. Wet decks meant cleanliness. Thereafter, I ordered them swept only, and my feet stayed dry. In addition, the parquetry would last longer.

On my desk were thirteen general courts-martial awaiting action from the base commander. My legal officer, Captain W. S. Heald, was worrying himself sick trying to get action. The work load had been piling up in spite of his dedication to the cause of justice. With no leadership, the men were getting into trouble, and the number of courts-martial were more than our limited personnel could handle. With "Shorty" Heald at my elbow, we broke the log jam. The records were reviewed, then signed, and the men were soon on their way to the West Coast, where their cases would be reviewed further.

There were many cases of rape. The Japanese women had been so subdued that if one of our sailors propositioned a girl, she would comply and later charge "rape." Our courts gave severe sentences, which I approved. This satisfied the Japanese honor. I expected the sentences to be greatly reduced, as they were, in the United States. The sooner these men were returned home, the better for all hands, including the Japanese.

I initiated weekly afternoon conferences with all officers. Later it included nurses, Red Cross workers, schoolteachers, even some wives. Captain Toni Rorschack, my chief staff officer, labeled them "Brownie meetings". This was because of the "pats on the back" we gave our people to encourage them to produce. Attendance was voluntary, but was excellent, for the bar was free until I walked in. All hands were on time!

With my announcement that we were keeping the base,

17

the proposed destruction of the giant dry docks and cranes was forgotten. The task of cleaning up Yokosuka began in earnest. Indeed, this was no small task.

On the base I found chaos. Things were much worse than my sons had told me. Dirt, filth, and dilapidation abounded, yet nothing was being done to improve conditions. Officers were in dungarees and stood in line with sailors at combat messes. The food was poor and there was no difference in appearance or behavior between the officers and men. This resulted in little pride and no discipline. The lack of positive leadership was evident. Officers and men were "shacked up" all over the base. Girls were found in the most unusual places, at the most unusual times. No effort was being made to salvage valuable property, and all hands were solely interested in the "points" which would entitle them to return home. The men of a Construction Battalion (CBs) had hurriedly left their barracks for home, leaving spoiling food in the pans and unwashed dishes. Rifles, pistols, shoes and equipment were scattered everywhere; no one had lifted a hand. Never before had I ever seen anything as bad as this.

The attitude of some of the men toward the defeated Japanese was poor. They treated them as if we were still fighting the war. There were garish wartime posters depicting ferocious buck-toothed Japanese soldiers with swords drawn. Large headlines over these posters proclaimed, "Remember—these are the bastards who raped Nanking." Sometimes our men cursed the Japanese to their faces. Another unkind act was committed by one senior officer who liked to race his jeep through crowded streets with the siren screaming. The objectionable posters were torn down and the men were persuaded not to curse the Japanese. Traffic laws were established that put an end to speeding.

We turned over the Japanese railroad stock on the base to the Japanese government for civil economy. For our own economy, we had the Japanese maintain the spur tracks. The sailors who were living with Japanese girls in a few of the passenger and freight cars lost their happy homes.

We were forbidden to have dollars. The rate of exchange was firmly fixed at fifteen yen to the dollar by Washington. This was totally unrealistic, thereby creating a black market and corrupting our youth. Washington was penalizing our forces. The result was many expensive courts-martial which branded our men with bad conduct discharges from the Navy. The exchange rate should have been left to the Supreme Commander. As years passed, the yen rate was increased step by step, each change one step behind the realistic rate. Finally it was set at 360 yen to the dollar.

The poor exchange rate caused petty thefts on the base. This could not be stopped except by erecting link fencing. On a visit to Guam, my sharp supply officers had found a large supply of useful surplus materials, including eight-foot-high link fencing. The fencing went up, and the Mikasa Bridge came down, thus ensuring that the base had but two entrances. One of these was kept locked and the other was guarded by Marines, who replaced sailors.

A young officer tried to pass through the main gate. He was wearing a raincoat on a hot, sunny day and appeared to be rather bloated around the waist. The Marine tried to stop him, but the officer ran toward the town, with the Marine in hot pursuit. Upon his capture he was found to have six cartons of cigarettes tucked under his belt. On the black market each eight-cent pack was worth over one dollar!

In another black market case, a chief petty officer, the custodian of the stores of the Officers' Club, had found a boon companion. She was a pretty Japanese girl who, at first, asked only for a cigarette or two. As the relationship progressed she wheedled a few additional items which were becoming ever more desirable on the black market. Finally, the chief had to face the music. He had to steal bags of sugar in order to buy silence. Captain Bill Kirten, who was on the inventory board of the club, was alert. There were far too many bags of sugar for a club, and they had a suspicious appearance. Opening one, he found it full of flour. Sacks of flour were being carried "on the books" as one ton of sugar. The roof fell in on the chief, ending a promising career.

One day, I received a letter from an ex-ensign in New York. He was irate and demanded immediate action to obtain redress. It appears that the young man had stopped in at Tiffany's and had asked the jewel expert what he would offer him for his "diamonds." He was informed that they didn't deal in glass baubles.

The complainant wanted satisfaction. He sent me the address of the merchant who had "sold" him those "diamonds," and wanted me to do my duty as commandant and get his money refunded.

Obviously, he had not cleared his treasure through customs. Further investigation revealed that he had drawn no pay while attached to the base. We had extensive records tracing every dollar (in yen) drawn by a man for pay, as well as a record of money orders received or bought. This man had sent funds home by mail, but received none. As he was no longer in the service, no action could be taken. Case closed.

The most unusual case was that of Private Brown. This Marine believed in doing things on a big scale. He pinned lieutenant's bars on his collar, strapped on his .45 pistol and drove to Yokohama in a "liberated" truck. There he stopped at the first bank and demanded to speak to the president. A Marine in the Occupation had authority. He demanded to see the books, saying, "General MacArthur has ordered me to inspect the bank." The books were in Japanese and the Marine pronounced them suspicious. He had to count the bank's funds. But that had to be done in Tokyo, so Mr. President was ordered to put all the funds (Y 585,000) in the truck. Insisting on accompanying his cash, the President, in a cutaway and high silk hat, rode into town on the tailgate. Just outside of Tokyo, Brown informed the banker that he had gone far enough, and left him standing on the curb. Ten days later, Brown was picked up by a roving patrol. He was living high, and was splurging beyond the limited means of a private in the U. S. Marine Corps.

Brown was put into the brig to await a general court-martial. Soon, he developed a stomachache and had to be taken to the base hospital. Here, he asked to use the head, which conveniently had a window. Brown promptly used this exit to reach an entrance to the twenty-eight miles of caves under the base.

My Colonel took positive action. No liberty was given to any Marine until Brown returned to the brig! Brown was back in two days.

During the first month or so, many Japanese claimed to know where great wealth was buried. I soon found that these reports were spurious and were guesses based on rumors among the townspeople. Perhaps they were to create distrust of those reliable people who tried to help. I finally received a curt letter from an Army officer in Tokyo who believed a report stating that I was holding a vast treasure in one of many caves. The informer said he was a worker on the base. I made this a test case, proving the man a liar. Further, he had never worked on the base. He was sentenced to jail (though placed on probation). This effectively stopped vicious rumors.

There were many remnants of original combat units landed on VJ Day. There was no reason for their continuance, and we needed the personnel for other assignments. We reduced these to heads of departments under the one base command. The major savings was in the reduction of three officers messes and six enlisted messes to one of each. The Marines objected, so we put a Marine officer in charge of the enlisted mess. The Navy would supply the rations and all personnel except the officer in charge and his assistant. It couldn't have been a better arrangement. Captain McNeill, USMC, was the best I have ever seen. All hands ate in a large concrete mess hall with excellent facilities. The service was at the tables by Japanese girls. There were flowers, Japanese china, and excellent food. Music was played at one meal each day. The men never had it better. In this way I was able to save on personnel.

The men were moved into a few well-located concrete barracks, making another reduction in maintenance. Quarters were held for muster and inspection. Officers wore ties and were no longer permitted to wear "simplified" uniforms. Beards were out. At the main gate, sailors had been posted for security, leaving the Marines idle. The security of the base, as well as the town, now became the function of my Marines, in whom I had great confidence. Colonel Bruno Hochmuth was in charge of all such functions.

On June 15 I went to Tokyo for a conference with Admiral Badger and Admiral Griffin. A dozen captains attended. First, Admiral Badger commended me on the improvement in the base and was profuse in his praise for what had been accomplished. My personnel allowance was to be 115 officers and 1750 men, plus 15 Marine officers and 350 marines. The Marine fighter group was closing, as well as Oppama Air

Field, and the air transport base at Kisarazu. Many small outposts were being closed. A year later I suggested to both Admiral Badger as well as his chief of staff that the Naval base at Sasebo could be used as his base instead of Tsingtao, China. The former Japanese Naval base at Sasebo was on a good harbor close to the China coast. But I was told that it was feared that General MacArthur would take over the Navy if it based in Japan. It was true that any ship or unit of troops had to report to the Supreme Commander when they entered Japan. This was not an unusual requirement, and I knew that the general never interfered with me or any other Navy unit. We came under Vice Admiral Griffin. I thought that Admiral Badger would prefer Sasebo. Maybe he did take it up with Admiral Griffin and for some reason rejected the plan. It was a deterrent to the Chinese Communists to have our ships in the port of Tsingtao, but finally we were forced to evacuate that harbor, at considerable loss.

A most fortunate change occurred among the officers. Two months after I assumed command, a new medical officer reported for duty. He was Captain John Q. Owsley, from the Samar Hospital, which had just been decommissioned. It was a pleasant surprise, for John Q was a live wire. He had had the command of that large hospital and I had known him for a number of years. He was a top notch medico. I said, "John Q, we don't need officers on my staff, but we do need you to build up our hospital and to improve sanitation of the base as well as that of the town. We need you to clean things up!" He did, and in a hurry.

Time was of the essence! I wanted action and I wanted it now! I kept the pressure on my officers, for a tour of duty of two short years was hardly enough to accomplish the terrific task facing us. This wasn't the time or the place for fine adjustments and exactness of actions. The base was a monumental cleanup job in which we had to take giant strides. It wasn't a case of polishing, but of cutting deep to remove useless parts. My colonel of Marines, when he became Major General Hochmuth, commented, "You taught me the value of time!" Now I had a medical officer who caught the virus, and away he went.

Of course, John Q's first responsibility was to set up a first class dispensary. I always called it a "hospital," for that is what I wanted. He did a beautiful job, as only a capable medical officer could. The Navy had taken over a group of concrete single-storied buildings, making a 200-bed dispensary. In other areas there were flimsy wooden hospital annexes of the Japanese Navy. They had a total of 3000 beds. Actually three patients slept across two beds. The Japanese doctors weren't all graduates of a medical school, and many were not as advanced as our chief pharmacist's mates. Some were only high school graduates. Bandages were used and re-used until worn out, and medicines were scarce and of unsophisticated types. Penicillin was unknown.

Thus, John Q had little to start with. He set up a nurse's school and trained many civilian doctors at the base.

I was proud of our "hospital," for when the dependents arrived, we were ready. The Army used our hospital, and many Army juniors saw the first light of day in that splendid establishment. When the Korean War broke out, we were well repaid for John Q's efforts and those of his successor, Captain J. B. Butler.

Shortly after I arrived I was informed that a Japanese ex-vice admiral had committed seppuku (hara-kiri) and his wife had killed their two children and then herself! The Military had been purged and also ostracized by their neighbors. They had no way of surviving. It was a great shock to me. These men were well educated and dedicated, yet we could not use them. Some should have been sentenced to prison, but the vast majority had a right to live and support their families. They could be used to rebuild Japan under our firm direction. I ordered my liaison officer, Mr. Takaoka, to provide me with a list of every former flag officer in town and to indicate those who needed jobs. We immediately hired a number of them.

We were having petty thefts from our warehouses. We put a Japanese ex-admiral in charge of the Japanese civil police and a wire fence around each warehouse building or group of buildings. A marine patroled outside, and a Japanese security guard on the inside. There were no more thefts. If anything had been missing, the Japanese ex-rear admiral in charge of the civil police would have lost face, and that wasn't going to happen. These former naval officers were loyal and intelligent; I valued their services highly.

Our Navy ships entering Yokosuka obtained their pilots from the Army in Yokosuka, but this was unsatisfactory. The pilots would only answer on call between 10 A.M. and 3 P.M., causing many costly delays. We established our own pilots' association by hiring four ex-admirals, and one civilian. They were experts, better than those from Yokohama, and they willingly answered any call, day or night. Further, they were paid the usual 3500 yen, while those from the Army were reported to have been paid 100,000 yen per month!—more than the prime minister received!

Many outgoing personnel dispatches ended, "Lovely Yokosuka." What was lovely about Yokosuka? It was then explained to me that Lovely was the last name of our Red Cross worker. He was a man. Why not female workers? A former commander of the base had facetiously answered an offer of female workers by "Send one for each man or none at all!" He got none. Not surprisingly, the Red Cross hierarchy was unhappy with the Navy. It now took a number of dinner parties at my house to melt the ice. I had to convince those in charge that I needed the girls and that I had always appreciated their help. By April 2 we had three assigned, and finally we had as many as a dozen. These girls did a big job of morale building. Besides taking over the routine tasks of Mr. Lovely, they worked in the hospital and in the Enlisted Men's Club.

One evening, the girls, many of my young officers, and some seniors were our guests for dinner. We gave them a tour of the grounds of the residence. On the top of the commandant's command cave or bunker, I had placed a pair of captured 25-power binoculars. The girls were entranced by sweeping the glasses around the town, seeing the people so close up. I had discovered some black marketing by finding our Navy trucks in parts of the town where they shouldn't have been. These girls were now discovering other things. One was a female bath house with no shades, typically open to view from without. The powerful glasses brought out every detail. Everyone seemed entranced by this personal glimpse of life in the raw. They named it "Benny's etchings," which became a subject for future VIPs. But after four years, a tree grew in Yokosuka and my etchings were obliterated.

I wanted some of the girls to work in my EM Club. This

huge cement building of three floors had been used by the Japanese as their Enlisted Men's Club. We had taken it over at the beginning of the Occupation. It was capable of handling a thousand men at a time, but it was not being used to capacity. For one thing, the men were patronizing the dirty cabarets and beer halls in town. We imposed sanitary measures that drove many cabarets out of business. The next step was to make our club more attractive. This took time but was helped by putting pretty Red Cross girls in the club to remind the boys of girls back home. At first they insisted on taking over the entire club. I refused, but said that I would give them two choice rooms near the main entrance. Here the girls set up writing and reading rooms which were particularly attractive to the homesick youngsters. They also brought in two doughnut machines that were most popular. Later we had to supply the raw materials. They also advertised and arranged trips throughout Japan. These were most interesting, but many sailors did not realize their worth. I was most happy with the Red Cross and their assistance in raising morale.

Dependents would soon be en route from the United States, so we asked for nurses. The Navy was prompt in ordering seven from Samar, where they were no longer needed. Women are important in raising the standards of the men.

On my walks about the base I visited the HIJMS *Mikasa*, the flagship of Togo at the Battle of Tsushima Strait, May 27, 1905. It was a permanent memorial surrounded by ten feet of concrete. Our men had demolished the museum and littered the ship with rubbish. It was so disgraceful that Commodore Kessing had been ordered by higher authority to post a Marine guard, Although this was no longer necessary, a Marine was still patiently guarding it. I couldn't spare this manpower and removed the guard.

We were instructed to demolish all military monuments, so I ordered her masts, bridge, stacks, and fake guns removed. The guns had already been removed and used in coastal defenses. We never inspected to see that these articles were destroyed. I expected they were "stashed away" for a better day.

We then gave the hull and grounds to the city to be a park and playground for the children. They put tanks filled with fish outside the portholes. From inside the ship, it looked as it would from a submarine. Swings and a baseball diamond were set up on the land surrounding the ship.

On the base all buildings not occupied by the American military had large signs on them reading: "Property of the Imperial Japanese Government. All Others Keep Out." MacArthur's directive ordered all buildings not used by our forces to be returned to the Japanese. But we went to an extreme, showing poor judgment. I ordered the signs removed and reported through the chain of command that I had ordered these buildings returned to the Naval jurisdiction, for this was necessary for the security of the base and the health and welfare of my men.

In town I noted that most buildings were of poor construction, but there were a few that were concrete, and superior to others. These were undoubtedly ex-Navy buildings that had not been surrendered. My civil affairs officer investigated these buildings and those belonging to the ex-Japanese Navy were ordered turned over to us. One warehouse was filled with thousands of rifles. This had been returned to the Japanese without an investigation of its contents. Fortunately, the Japanese were cooperative.

There had been massive destruction of materials and equipment by our forces when they first landed. It was hard to justify this waste. The laboratories were filled with glass shards and broken instruments of precision. On the entire base I found but one instrument of precision undamaged. It was worth about one thousand dollars. We gave it to one of the schools. Japanese workmen were still breaking up 1½-meter parabolic mirrors for destroyer searchlights. Since radar, searchlights were not as important, but we had paid about fifteen hundred dollars per mirror in 1925. I hated to see such destruction. I stopped it and we used them for home decorations. We were in need of anything to brighten up our houses.

In the caves we found hundreds of paint drums punctured at the bottom, the paint had run onto the floors of the caves. We needed paint badly. The civilians were allowed to loot the base just prior to our Occupation. The machinists had cleverly removed the same gear from each machine tool, making them inoperative. Later they voluntarily returned these gears. During the first seven months of the Occupation, huge quantities of material were removed by the Japanese with no record on the base. I was suspicious that the Saibatsu (the five major companies) were hoarding much of the raw materials. They had been purged and had no yen, but those who had accumulated a stockpile of raw materials would have a head start when the peace treaty was signed.

The summer was about to begin, and with it our first group of dependents would arrive, thanks to Admiral Holloway's (CNO)—Chief of Naval Operations enthusiastic assistance.

Chapter II

DEPENDENTS

Admiral Griffin had word that the Navy dependents would soon be on their way. But the people in Washington dragged their feet. It was just as well, for I had plenty to do before we would be ready for them. However, we agreed that if the Army dependents were to arrive, ours should do so a bit sooner. Admiral Griffin kept the pressure on Washington, and the Navy dependents did arrive first.

I wrote to Edwina:

We have heard that thirty wives will arrive on a ship leaving San Pedro on the tenth of June. I have asked that it be put into Yokosuka. We are all looking forward so much to your arrival. We will have accommodations for you even though they will not be perfect. Each officer is "expediting" his own house and we expect the wives will like them. Of course, we have big plans for better places to live, but that will take time.

Just today, a contractor came in to see me and we

had a talk. He seems to think he can produce what we want—a community all our own, on our peninsula. By March 1947, we will have it. The first apartments will be ready, the first of September this year.

In Hayama (where the Emperor has a summer palace) and in Kamakura, next to it, the Army had many houses. The First Brigade of the First Cavalry under General Bradford invited me to dinner and I discovered that some of these houses would be available for our dependents. But I didn't want housing off the base. The peace treaty would be signed some day and then the Japanese would want their houses back.

New dependent housing on the Base, with concrete barracks in the rear, altered into apartments.

I visualized fifty years of use of dependent housing, so we started to build on the base, using a small number of Japanese houses temporarily. The Ninetieth Sea Bees had abandoned some concrete buildings. My civil engineer changed these into sixty dependent apartments for enlisted men. We planned to build four hundred quarters. The first officers were to move into the former Japanese officers' houses on Halsey Road. In April I had walked into this area and found them all occupied by bachelor officers with Japanese girls—supposedly servants, but not acting the part. The houses were dirty and ill kept. I had no doubts. I stopped this and turned the houses over to officers, according to rank, who had dependents coming out. They were to fix up their own places and they did a good job with little help. Halsey Road became VIP quarters.

I spotted from our garden a well-built house adjacent to the Tadodai residence. It had been the Japanese aide's house. I sent my orderly to investigate. He returned with a story that a commander was living there with a Japanese woman. The fact that he would not give his name caused me to make inquiries. It was hurriedly deserted by the commander. I assigned it to my Japanese liaison officer, Mr. Takaoka. He was doing a good job and his wife was priceless in dealings with the Japanese women. I owed them much for their services and hoped that this would continue. Their excellent command of the English language and their willingness to cooperate made me want them nearby. Mrs. Takaoka's letter is of interest:

June 19, 1946

Captain B.W. Decker
Dear Sir:

It was so kind of you to extend such cordial hospitality to us on Sunday. Thank you very very much.

Your house and your gardens are so cheery now. They have "Welcome!" written all over them, and will be a nice setting to welcome "home" the most important First Lady Yokosuka has ever had or probably will ever have.

I think you understand just how that house problem stands. We should like so much to know how you and Mrs. Decker feel about it.

29

Mrs. Decker might probably find it convenient to have a sort of interpreter advisor at hand to help her in whatever way that I can in a strange country. I am thinking of accepting your kind offer of a house on your compound if it meets the approval of Mrs. Decker and yourself.

You have done and are doing so much for our people that I would consider it a privilege to be allowed to help Mrs. Decker.

I am looking forward to Mrs. Decker's arrival and hope and pray that she will be very happy here.

Very respectfully,
Aiko Takaoka
(Mrs. Teiichiro Takaoka)

In the meantime Edwina, in San Diego, was fighting red tape—she tells the story:

On a bright and sunny afternoon in San Diego, on June 6, 1946, the telephone rang. It was a call from the port director's office at Terminal Island in San Pedro.

"Mrs. Decker, your passport hasn't arrived. As the transport *Charles Carroll* is scheduled to leave day after tomorrow, shall we take your household effects off the ship?"

"No," I said, almost in tears. "Isn't there something I can do?"

"Yes," he replied. "Call the port director's office in your hometown of San Diego. He may have some information. Without a passport you will not be able to sail on the *Charles Carroll*, and your household effects will have to be taken off of the ship."

I was almost hysterical. For weeks I had been preparing for this voyage. Everything my husband had instructed me to do had been done. I had applied for a passport in plenty of time, and I couldn't understand why it had not come. As I sat there by the telephone in a daze, my older, son, Ben, advised me to call the local port director's office. I was told to "pull strings." Otherwise, it was hopeless.

Benny, my husband, had told me when we were first married that wives of military men have no rank and that I was never to expect special privileges or ask for them. Remembering this instruction, I wondered what to do next.

Just then, the doorbell rang. Ada Lucking, wife of Commander Lucking, had come to hear the latest news about my passport. She and I were planning to go together to Long Beach the next day. When I told her the sad news, she said, "If you don't go, I won't go."

"Ada, you must go. When we talked to your husband over long distance, you said that you were going, and when I spoke to him I told him to tell Benny that I was coming too. If I can't go, it is just my bad luck. You must not disappoint Tom."

I remembered that pleasant evening, and how we had waited until almost midnight before the long distance call had come in from Tokyo. I thought how little we realize the truth of that saying, "The plans of mice and men often go astray."

Ben said, "Mom, you must call Washington right away and I think that you should call Admiral Holloway. He is in the Navy Department Bureau of Personnel."

"Son, I can't do it. What will your father say if I should?" I answered.

"Admiral Holloway is a friend of Dad's and I am confident that he will help you," Ben answered.

I picked up the receiver and dialed long distance. The call was put through, and I was able to talk to the admiral. After I told him about my plight, he said words that I can't repeat here. It was the first time in my life that I did not object to such strong language. It was like beautiful music to my ears. He called to a commander near him and said, "Go over to the State Department and get Mrs. Decker's passport, and the other seven passports for the rest of the Navy wives slated to go to Japan on the same ship. Then fly them out to San Pedro."

My thoughtful son had reminded me to tell the admiral about these other wives who were in the same situation.

"You go ahead and plan to sail on that ship, and I hope that the passports will be delivered in time."

I tried to tell him how grateful I was and thanked him for the other wives. Mother, Ada, Ben, and I were jubilant. Ada bid us goodbye and I returned to finish my packing.

The next day Ben took Ada and me to Long Beach where we spent the night at the Huntington Hotel. While at dinner,

I was called to the telephone. Mother was on the other end. She said that word had come from Washington that we wives could sail even if the passports did not arrive in time. They would be mailed to us in Japan. She bid me bon voyage and wished me happiness in my new home.

The next morning, Ben took us over to Terminal Island, where we checked in with the port director. After attending to all necessary details, we went over to the dock to see the transport that would be our home for the next two weeks. It was a beehive of activity. Provisions were being placed on board, and the passengers were busy finding their staterooms. The dock was crowded with many spectators, as well as relatives and friends of the passengers.

"Ben, though I have been told that I can sail without my passport, please don't leave the dock until you see that the ship is well under way." I said as I kissed him good-bye. He promised me that he would. As he turned away and started down the gangplank, my heart seemed to sink into the bottom of my shoes, All of the passengers rushed to the rail where we could see our loved ones. We waved to them as the ropes that held the ship were untied (Edwina is a landlubber! says Benny). The ship moved gracefully through the water and we were under way. I remained by the rail until the dock was out of sight and then went to my stateroom. Captain Weiss's wife, Charlotte, was my roommate. We shared a roomy stateroom with two large bunks, a long window seat under three portholes, two clothes closets, and a private bathroom. I thought It very attractive and comfortable.

There were twenty-two wives on board, including one admiral's wife, Anne Momsen, whose husband invented the lung for submariners. She was an old friend of mine. Her husband was a classmate of Benny's at the Naval Academy and I was delighted to see her again.

There were only two children. Michael was a handful. He was always into some kind of mischief, except when he was safely tucked into bed and sound asleep. Susan was adorable. She was a pretty child with soft brown curls and had a very winning personality.

Secrecy still surrounded the sailing of Uncle Sam's ships and I did not know which route the *Charles Carroll* was going to take. I hoped that we would sail via the southern route and stop in Honolulu. Instead, we sailed via the great circle route, past the Aleutian Islands. It was disappointing, but it was the shortest route and the Navy had to beat the Army!

News came that the first Army transport, the *Ainsworth*, would sail from Seattle on the tenth. We wondered if the Army dependents would arrive before we did.

Anne, Ada, Marion Paton, Charlotte, and I would play bridge in Anne's sitting room off her stateroom. There was a large map of the world hanging on the wall. Each afternoon, Ensign Lee Stark would come to this room to inform us of our position at sea. He used a pin to mark our present location, and also marked that of the *Ainsworth*. We called him our "pinup boy."

We had movies out on deck every evening when the weather permitted. As we traveled further north, the wind and rain increased, and we had gray days. The trip was uneventful, except when flying fish or an occasional whale came into view. In spite of the foggy weather and rough sea, this was a pleasant voyage. The skipper, Captain Butterfield, the officers, and the crew made it so. The wives were congenial and good sports. Captain Butterfield often sent his steward down to the dining salon and recreation room with a tray of cookies or little cakes. Occasionally, small groups of the wives were invited up to the captain's stateroom for afternoon tea.

The twentieth found us busily packing our suitcases in preparation for our arrival at Yokosuka early the next day. I was jubilant when Captain Butterfield informed us that the ship would land there instead of Yokohama. The sun was shining and I felt it a good omen.

Early the next morning, most of the wives went out on deck and watched the beautiful, rugged coastline of Japan come into view. Fujiyama (wisteria mountain) towered above the other mountains and was breathtakingly beautiful. Now I understood why the Japanese people worshipped it.

The ship neared Piedmont Pier, which was named after a U. S. Navy ship which was moored there for such a long time that some Navy men thought it would never sail away. I looked for my husband and soon saw him. Standing beside him were three Japanese women dressed in their native kimonos, beautiful obis (sashes) were tied around their waists

33

and on their feet were wooden *getas.* They were crying. I wondered how I would feel if the situation had been reversed. After all, we were the first of the conqueror's wives to arrive. I felt sorry for them and smiled at them. Noticing me, they wiped away their tears. They pointed to my hat and showed their approval. I had purchased this perky little hat at Marston's Department Store before I left San Diego. It was of blue straw trimmed with a darker shade of blue taffeta ribbon. A bunch of purplish pink grapes and a small bunch of flowers decorated the front. This little hat "broke the ice." When my husband escorted me down the gangplank these women greeted me warmly.

I was delighted to see Captain Owsley again. There were newspapermen and photographers on hand to interview the passengers and take pictures of dependents. After expressing the first flush of excitement and joy, I asked, "Has the *Ainsworth* arrived?"

"No, darling, it has not," Benny replied. "The Navy beat the Army this time."

He threw his arms around me and exclaimed, "How I have been missing this," as he kissed me. "Just once more for the newsreels."

Kanagawa Shimbun—26 June 1946
40,000 Members of Yokosuka Women's Club Welcome Mrs. Decker

Mrs. Decker, who arrived on the 21st, sent a personal note of thanks to Mrs. Mabuchi, President of the Yokosuka Women's Club, for the bouquet of flowers which was presented upon Mrs. Decker's arrival. In his meetings with Mrs. Mabuchi, Captain Decker has repeatedly said, "When my wife arrives in Yokosuka I want her to become a member of the Women's Club."

All members are happy indeed to welcome Mrs. Decker, according to Mrs. Mabuchi, who said, "Captain Decker has been offering his sympathy and assistance in the rebuilding of Yokosuka, and we are more than happy to hear that Mrs. Decker will live in our city. If possible we would like to have her as advisor of the Club, so that we could ask her direct guidance."

The people, who are suffering under the acute food

shortage, express their sincere thanks to Captain Decker for the distribution of surplus U. S. food through the Yokosuka Women's Club. The children in particular are overjoyed over the chocolate and candy. The first distribution of peanuts was a can per three persons. On the 24th, the remaining candy was given to children under seven years of age. Tasty biscuits of flour mixed with candy and chocolate were made by the Koyabemachi Bakery, and starting the 25th these will be given to every child in the city.

Benny, the other officers, and the men of the Naval Base had arranged to have a luncheon for their wives at the Officers' Club. On our way there, I was impressed with the panorama that unfolded before me. The Naval base of Yokosuka stretched before my eyes, and I saw gigantic cranes, tunneled hills, and open flatcars on which tons of coal had been piled. Benny said that he hoped to have the streets paved soon. As it was hot and dusty, he was eager to tell me that conditions would soon be improved. My happiness at our reunion was so great that no small thing like dust could bother me. Yet I was interested in hearing about the past and future of the base, and listened attentively to what he had to say. He pointed out certain buildings, saying that the Japanese had used them for gun factories, laboratories, ship ways, repair shops, warehouses, etc. Soon we arrived at the club.

The Officers' Club was similar to any in the United States, except that it needed to be completely renovated. Some work was even now being done to improve it. Benny had hoped that the painting would have been finished by the time the *Charles Carroll* arrived, and was disappointed that it was not. I was impressed with the doll-sized furniture. It was so small. The flower arrangements throughout the club were beautiful.

The Japanese waitresses were attractive young women. Benny told me that each one had been given a nickname because their real names were too hard to pronounce. He told me the names of each one and how she was given her name. There was "Moon Beam," named because her face was round and full. "Cherry Blossom" was pretty and petite. "Bamboo" was tall for a Japanese woman. When the other waitress smiled, Benny said, "We call her 'Studebaker.'" I understood perfectly because I saw that her teeth were covered with silver. It looked like the grillwork of an auto.

Benny said, "All these girls are off limits. Look—see—no touchee! The Occupation required that all female food handlers be examined once a month. When I received a report, I sent for the doctor, who told me that these girls were all virgins. I stopped the examinations."

We drove through the gate into town. Children smiled and waved to us as we passed them. Some said, "Herro," as they could not pronounce words with "el." The elderly looked so old. Some of them were almost bent double and were carrying large bundles of sticks on their backs. They were a pitiful sight. I was surprised to see so many people dressed in Western-style clothes. Small children wore kimonos, as did most of the old folks. Schoolgirls wore middie blouses and skirts to match.

On the corner, I saw a sign that I thought most amusing. It was over the entrance of a small building that had once been a gas station. It read, "Wellcome Sir, Round Trip by this omnibus Cheerfully." There was a rickshaw parked there, and the attendant was waiting for a customer.

We passed the Saikaya Department Store. I was surprised to see so few pieces of merchandise in the windows. They were almost bare. Many young women had babies strapped on their backs, and as they went into the store I marvelled at how the women could shop, carrying such a load. I saw them on the street, the babies' heads bobbing back and forth in the strong sunlight. I wondered why Japanese people weren't blind and didn't have broken necks. The next winter, I saw a young man in a kimono playing baseball in two inches of snow. A sleeping baby was strapped on his back. As he ran to first base, the baby's head gyrated alarmingly.

The shops were like small shacks and few were painted. There were no screens at the doors or windows. At each entrance, hanging like a short curtain, was a gay piece of cloth in some bright color. On some of them were designs or Japanese characters to advertise what lay inside the shops. I was fascinated as we passed them. The shoe shops, with their wooden *geta* (shoe) and *zori* (shoe with a divided toe strap), the little notion shops, lantern and toy shops, and flower stalls impressed me.

After driving up a hill whose narrow roads left my heart pounding, we passed a shabby Buddhist temple. The gate was off its hinges and the paper at the doors and windows was torn. The grounds were in such a dilapidated condition; it was a most depressing sight. I was glad when we passed by it.

Nearing the top of the hill, we passed a sentry box. A Japanese man dressed in a dark blue uniform saluted Benny. We entered the driveway leading to our house. On either side were large stone pillars connected to a stone wall. On the left were a garage and servants' quarters, a low rambling house, something like our ranch-type houses in the West. Between the servants' quarters and our house was a large sump.

The driveway circled around a small formal garden which faced the front entrance. It was a large, rambling, white shingled house situated in a sort of hollow. The front part was something like an old Southern plantation mansion. The back half was Japanese, with a side entrance.

The servants were standing on either side of the doorway. They smiled and bowed low as I was introduced. The Navy steward, Wah Chan, was Chinese. He was in charge, and it was evident that he wanted them to make a good impression. There was Mr. Imamura, the house manager; Takashi Kuge, the assistant house manager; and Itsuro Tanaka, the chief cook, who looked quite impressive with his white cook's cap on his head. Rekichiro Neshizawa, the baker, was next in line, and was followed by six others whose duties varied from flower arranging, to pressing, to waiting on our tables. After the introductions were made, the door was opened and we walked up the steps into the entrance hall.

Wah Chan had been taken prisoner by the Japanese when he was on Corregidor and he was in the death march. When he was released, he became Commodore "Scrappy" Kessing's boy. He came to Yokosuka when our U. S. forces first landed, and he had been there ever since.

He had been in our Navy for fourteen years and had many ribbons. When asked why he had joined the U. S. Navy, he would say, "Me cabin boy on ships. One day Captain he say 'Wah raise right hand' I raised my right hand. When ship she sail, I try to go ashore, captain he say 'no can do, you in the Navy now.' This was in Shanghai, I think.''

When I asked what his ribbons were for, he replied, ''I don't know, I just follow the captain.''

His enlistment had expired and Benny discovered that he had been a civilian for two years without knowing it. Benny fixed that by having Wah reenlist in a hurry. He received a lot of back pay.

He wanted to have his wife and sons join him in Yokosuka. This was arranged after cutting some red tape. We had been happy to help him obtain his U.S. citizenship. Now he had to get citizenships for his wife and sons.

As I entered the reception hall, I was impressed by the profusion of flowers arranged in all sorts of containers, vases, and baskets. Attached to each one was a card with a message of greeting and welcome from a leading citizen. I was touched.

In the living room I wondered at the magnificent mosaic peacock which perched above the fireplace. On the floor was a Japanese rug of geometric design. The background was beige and the design was in colors that blended with the peacock. A cherry blossom lay at its center, and it was bordered with a wide band of ultramarine blue.

''Benny, I like this room, all but the color. Why did you have it painted this ugly shade of chartreuse green?'' I asked. Benny called it ''pooped out chartreuse.''

''I did not have much choice, because there is very little paint on the base. One day after lunch, Lieutenant Colonel Hochmuth and I were sitting here and I asked Wah Chan to bring in the cans of paint available. Colonel Hochmuth and I mixed this color. I am sorry that you don't like it. But after two cocktails, it doesn't look bad!''

I walked through two sliding wooden doors into the dining room. It was a large, rather long room dominated by a huge banquet table made of cherry wood. The table seated thirty-two people and was attractive, though it had obviously been abused. The chairs had white covers to protect the leather upholstery.

On my right were two French doors which led to a porch. At the end of the room was an alcove surrounded by high windows. In its center was a dining table which seated ten people.

The formal garden was magnificent, and was typically Japanese. It was hedged in by single- and double-blossom cherry trees. I was impressed by the gravel-colored walks and the small pool which was filled by a stream cascading over picturesque stones. Almost directly across the walk was a large ishidora (stone lantern). To the left, on a raised flat rock, was a potted dwarfed pine tree. The obvious patriarch of the land was an ancient plum tree, so old that it was propped up with crutches. At the heart of the garden, on a

Mrs. Decker, with two Navy nurses, strolling in the garden of the Todaido.

low, sloping mound, was a white rose bush. The profusion of roses was far too heavy for the spindly, weak stems to bear. As with the others, this mound was carpeted with a velvet lawn and was surrounded by the gravel walk.

I again reentered the house and walked down the hallway. This led back to the Japanese section, to the reception hall, and branched into corridors which led to dressing rooms and bedrooms. Formerly the geishas had entertained the Japanese admiral's guests here. The hallway was closed off by a swinging door which divided this section from the servants' quarters and the kitchen.

A wonderful mahogany staircase led to our apartment. Tatami (mats) completely covered the floors. They were two inches thick and measured approximately three by six feet. These were covered by finely woven grass mats made of fresh reeds. Sliding partitions of cream-colored paper and black lacquered wood divided the room in half. These could be lifted out altogether to make one large room.

At the far end of the bedroom was a *tokonoma* (alcove) and a *tana* (niche). In the companion recess adjoining it was a *chigaidana,* two shelves arranged stepwise in order to hold art objects. There was a small cupboard with gold paper doors above them, and a larger matching one below.

On the right of the *tokonoma* was a low bay windowseat with sliding, frosted glass panes covered with lattice frames. When slid back, you could see past the narrow passageway to the garden below.

The rooms were decorated in green and white dotted silk, which matched the spread on the large double bed. I thought them charming. As I looked out of the window, above the romantic balustrade, I was seeing a bit of the Garden of Eden.

"Do you like it?" Benny asked.

"I love it!" I replied.

The garden beckoned me once more with a siren's call. At its end was a flat promontory which overlooked the city and the Miura Penninsula. The view was magnificent and reminded me of Point Loma.

There was a bench and a large pair of Japanese 25-power binoculars. I was fascinated by the world which they revealed. I could see the townspeople, the fishing boats in the harbor, and the island of Sarushima.

"Sarushima means monkey island," Benny added. After a few minutes we continued our exploration of the grounds. We walked up rustic log steps bordered by cherry trees and azalea bushes. After passing through a narrow tunnel, we came to a vegetable garden planted with lettuce, parsley, tomatoes, and string beans. We saw terraced gardens, small wooden houses, and a beautiful waterfall fringed with lush ferns. Everything was so lovely, and I was filled with happiness.

Two days later, Benny and I had our first "At Home" to welcome all of the wives and their husbands, enlisted men, and officers. As it was a beautiful day, we entertained in the garden. The servant girls wore kimonos. The serving men wore white jackets. As they had all been well trained, everything went smoothly. For some of our guests, it was the first time that husbands and wives had been together at a party since the end of the war.

One day, Colonel Bruno Hochmuth and I decided to explore some of the Japanese barracks. Perhaps we could find something of use to us.

Silence shrouded everything, and a feeling of hurried abandonment hung over the rooms.

We were able to salvage three medicine chests, a wardrobe, some tables, chairs, and other useful items. In one room I found a bottle of ink. When I picked it up, it splattered all over the floor.

"My Scotch inclinations got me into trouble this time. I guess that this was my booby trap."

We discovered that there was a hole in the bottle just above the ink line and that the slightest movement made the ink spill out of it.

As we returned to the car, I thought of the movie, *Beau Geste*. Ours were the only sounds besides the gentle rustling of the wind through the curtains and doorways of the forlorn buildings.

A few days after my arrival, Mrs. Takaoka, with Mrs. Mabuchi, the president of the Women's Club, called on me. Four of the officers of the organization came with them. Mrs. Takaoka acted as interpreter, as she was the only one who spoke English. I was impressed with the sincerity and eagerness of the ladies to learn about the women of the United States. They invited me to attend one of their meetings, which was to be held soon. Mrs. Takaoka told me that she would come to the house to accompany me and act as my interpreter.

"I was born ten months too soon," she said, "or I would have been a citizen of the United States. My parents went to New York when I was that age and settled. My father was a doctor, as were my brothers. I thought that I would like to be one too, but while I was a student at Barnard College, I met Mr. Takaoka, who was in the Foreign Services of Japan. We fell in love and were married. Since then, I have lived in South America and Europe. I have lived only eleven years in Japan.

"When the war started, my mother was so grief-stricken, because she loved Japan and the United States, that she died of a broken heart. Do you know that when the news came that the war had started, most Japanese thought that we were at war with Russia? We were stunned when we found out that we were at war with the United States. I want to help to bring about a better understanding between the two countries, and anytime I can be of service to you, I shall be happy to do so. I will go with you to help you to shop, and I shall be pleased to accompany you to official as well as civic affairs. The Japanese women are trying to take their place in this new democratic Japan, but they have been suppressed so long that it will take time to become adjusted to their new freedom.

"Japanese names are hard to remember sometimes, and my name sounds a little like tapioca, so if you think about the pudding you won't forget my name," Mrs. Takaoka said.

We both smiled, and I thought that she was charming. We had Coca-Cola, vanilla ice cream, and little cookies. After the refreshments, which they seemed to enjoy very much, they departed.

The following Friday, Marion and Commander Bob Paton joined us for an auto trip to Miyanoshita, a famous mountain resort. Here we planned to spend the weekend at the Fujiya Hotel.

Traffic in Japan passes on the left, as it does in England. It was difficult for me to get used to this. A great number of people were pedaling bicycles, some with little trailers attached to them. We passed many people pushing something on foot or hauling carts. Occasionally there were some ox-drawn "honey bucket" carts. As we passed these carts, the odor was terrible. How the poor coolies who walked beside them could stand it, I don't know. Human waste was collected from city dwellings, put in buckets on the carts, and was then sold to farmers for fertilizer.

It was a beautiful drive. At Odawara we left the seashore and started climbing up into the mountain. It was all so primitive, and the scenery was entrancing. The higher we went, the lovelier it became. The villages seemed to hug the steep sides of the mountains with their thatch-roofed houses. The streams, a rustic mill, the luxuriant, wooded slopes, the Hayakawa River, bridges and the trees all added to the unforgettable panorama.

We arrived at Miyanoshita after an hour's ride. Turning sharply to the left, we drove up the steep driveway to the entrance of the Fujiya Hotel.

Benny had been to Fujiya when he was navigator of the *Astoria*. As he stated earlier, the cruiser brought Saito's ashes from Annapolis, Maryland to Japan as a gesture of goodwill. Saito had been a man of peace and former ambassador to the United States. As part of the hospitality, half of the officers were taken to Lake Hakone.

The Foreign Office had planned a party for fifteen officers to see Nikko. When he heard of these plans, Admiral Yonai felt that the Japanese Navy would lose face if the Foreign Office was more hospitable than they. So, on the spur of the moment, they arranged this party for fifteen at Hakone. Captain Ichiro Yokoyama was in charge, with Lieutenant Commander Dan McGurl, Benny, and thirteen junior officers completing the party. An orchestra and fifteen very pretty dancing girls, well chaperoned and outfitted with American evening dresses, were brought from Tokyo for the occasion. In 1939, dancing by couples in Japan was most unusual, and Captain Yokoyama informed them that this would be a "wild" party. They could dance until 3 A.M. if they wanted to. But by eleven, they noted that the captain and some other Japanese were getting nervous. He was worried that young Japanese fanatics or the Black Dragon Society might disapprove and make a scene. Diplomatically, Benny suggested calling it a day at 11 P.M., much to Captain

Yokoyama's relief. The officers retired to their rooms, which were designated by a picture of a flower. Benny and Dan had the Pansy Room.

Fujiya was situated in the loveliest of surroundings, and I was impressed with the luxuriousness of the hotel. It was Oriental in every detail. Nestled in front of a thickly wooded mountainside, it was embraced by a garden filled with pools and waterfalls. Quaint bridges and flat rocks spanned these waters, completing the picture.

The Fujiya Hotel itself was a large, rambling, wooden structure about five stories high. I still remember large plate glass windows, the many curved lines in the design of the tiled roof, and the prominent projection of the eaves.

Because of the scarcity of housing, most of the best hotels had been requisitioned by the Eighth Army as billets for the families of the Occupation personnel. Often, they were used as rest and recreation areas for the men on leave. The Fujiya Hotel was set aside for the officers.

After entering the lower hallway, we climbed a fantastic stairway. The railing was carved like a serpent whose head rested on top of the newel post at the front of the staircase. When we reached the top, we saw a lovely, glass-enclosed sunroom which overlooked a waterfall and pool. Outside, people were feeding the carp little pieces of bread. These fish opened their mouths and almost stood up and begged for the food. It was quite a sight. Of course, we wanted to feed the fish too, so we obtained some bread and threw small pieces to the beggars. Returning to the hallway, we passed a large frame with pictures of men with long, curled, clipped, and waxed mustaches. I hadn't known that there could be so many different kinds of mustaches!

Our room was in the "Flower Palace" where Benny and his command had stayed so long ago. Ours was the "Camellia Room." (As Benny grew in esteem, he was given the Chrysanthemum or the Emperor's Room!)

The view from the large window encompassed the entrance driveway with the garden below it, the main street, and the mountains which rose across the deep valley beyond the village.

The room was spacious and well furnished with rather small-sized furniture for Americans. Off to one side was a tiled bath. Because soap was scarce, the Army furnished some. Guests would leave behind a slightly used bar of soap as a tip for the servants.

Later that evening, as we wound our way through a long hallway towards the dining room, we passed the glass roof of the "Mermaid Bath." Goldfish swam around in the pool which formed this roof. I had been told by one of my friends, who had bathed here, that she could gaze up and see the goldfish swimming overhead. As the side of the hallway was completely of glass, we had an excellent view of this extraordinary roof and pool combination.

At the entrance to the large dining room, we passed a round pool and a fountain. A small white ball was kept in the air by the pressure of the water. Spacious windows provided a wonderful view of the surrounding grounds and the distant mountains. The hand-painted flowers in the squares of the ceiling and the grotesque, masklike, carved faces at the base of the supporting pillars gave the room a surprising contrast.

The next day, we drove over to Long Tail Pass. While we were enjoying the splendid view of Fujiyama, a little Japanese girl came toward me. I offered her a chocolate bar which I had placed in my coat pocket. She was very polite and thanked me. After she walked away, I asked Benny if he had noticed her bloated stomach.

"She is starving, Edwina."

I felt terrible, but was glad that I had been able to give her that little bit.

On our way to Lake Hakone, we passed a colony of Nazis awaiting their return to Germany. If looks could kill, we would have been exterminated on sight. I shall never forget the hatred in their faces. What a pity we have had to have so many wars, and that people should harbor such animosity! How different the Japanese were. If they resented us, they did not show it.

At the lake, a young German came over to talk with us. He said that he had never been to Germany but had been born and raised in HongKong. He was a citizen of Germany, so he had been drafted and forced to fight for his country. We were glad that there was at least one friendly person in the colony.

The following day, we again took a short ride to Long Tail Pass. We were well rewarded, for "the shy lady," as the sacred mountain of Fuji is often called, came out from behind her mists. This day, we beheld her in all her glory.

Upon returning to the hotel, we took a swim in the outdoor swimming pool. The large, tile pool was fed by a natural, continuous flow of water at an agreeable temperature (chlorine had been added, however, by the Army). Overhead was a gorgeous trellis of wisteria in full bloom.

That afternoon we returned to Yokosuka.

Another day, Benny took me to Yokohama and Tokyo. I had read and seen pictures of the devastation wrought by the war, but it was beyond my imagination to visualize the terrible damage done by our aviators.

"Don't be too sympathetic, Edwina, remember that war is war, and if the Japanese could have bombed us this way, they would have," he wisely counseled me.

"Yes, I know, but look at the children, the poor little things, and look at those pitiful hovels made from scraps of corrugated tin roofs and whatever other pieces of wood the people could salvage. It is awful! I hope and pray that there will never be another war."

When we arrived in Tokyo, we went to Commander Naval Forces Far East headquarters where Benny introduced me to Admiral Griffin and his staff. As he wanted to talk privately with the admiral, he left me with his chief of staff who exclaimed, "Did you ever hear of such an absurd request as your husband has made? He wants to have a Navy band sent out here for the Naval base at Yokosuka."

"Why, I think it would be wonderful for the morale of the men stationed there," I said, remembering the phonograph which the men had rigged to welcome the *Charles Carroll.*

"I could have had your husband's job. I was given the choice of Commander Fleet Activities or this one. I chose this one, as you can see. I consider it a better job. The different activities under Benny's command are going to be gradually whittled down."

I was quite pleased when I was finally able to bid Captain Bard goodbye.

Dennis McEvoy, of the *Reader's Digest,* had invited us to

dine with him that evening at his home, which he shared with Mr. Chamberlin, a banker. We met James Monahan who was also with the *Reader's Digest*. The evening was a most enjoyable one. The host was very hospitable and entertaining. The dinner was excellent. Dennis played some classical music on a grand piano and the evening passed all too quickly. A few days later we had them to our house for dinner.

Dennis McEvoy had casually mentioned that the Japanese edition of the *Reader's Digest* might be delayed—no printer's ink. "What makes printer's ink?" he was asked, and was told lamp black and linseed oil.

On the base Benny had found a large shed filled with loose lamp black, and this created a problem; the wind, through the openings and cracks, made piles of soot. He also had barrels of linseed oil. Here was a solution to his problem to dispose of this material. Dennis, as well as others in short supply of printer's ink, requested the materials through the Japanese government and everyone was happy.

On the Fourth of July, we went to Yokohama. Benny had been invited, with other top-ranking officers, to be in the reviewing stand. Brigadier General Weible, commanding the Yokohama base, was the reviewing officer. We had a Marine and Navy contingent in the parade, which was the first to be held in Japan. Mrs. Weible and I were extended the courtesy of joining the officers in reviewing the parade, and we were pleased to be with our husbands.

The Japanese who lined the streets to watch the parade seemed interested and showed no animosity. In fact, they seemed to enjoy it. I was happily surprised and impressed by their attitude.

Afterwards, Benny and I went to Tokyo to attend a luncheon given by Major General William C. Chase at the Imperial Hotel. There had been a parade in Tokyo too, and we caught a glimpse of the tail end before we reached the hotel. I met General and Mrs. Robert L. Eichelberger, General Paul Mueller, and other distinguished officers, wives, and newspaper correspondents. That evening, there was a fireworks display on the athletic field on our base. The welfare department was responsible for the show, and all of the Naval base personnel and dependents enjoyed it immensely.

The following Friday evening we attended a dinner party given by Major General Paul Mueller, chief of staff, at the Imperial Hotel for members of the presidential commission. Some of the honored guests were Postmaster General Robert Hannegan, Senator Millard E. Tydings of Maryland, Assistant Secretary of War for Air Stuart Symington, Lieutenant General Gael Sullivan, and Lieutenant General John R. Cannons of A.A.F., air training commander.

The Imperial Hotel was to be the scene of many such affairs. I thought it was a strange, rather gloomy place. It had been designed by the famous architect Frank Lloyd Wright to withstand earthquakes. Built in about 1920, one wing was damaged during the war. Benny said, "In rebuilding this wing, army engineers wondered how it ever stood up under the 1923 earthquake. They couldn't believe that Wright had approved the engineering design." It is difficult to describe, as it was so different from any classic style. The nearest I can come is to compare it with a Mayan temple. Two stories high, it was built in a U-shape with three sides facing a large pool. The prominent projection of the eaves, the many straight lines and absence of curves, and the straight and slanting tiled roof completed the peculiar style of the building.

On the ninth we went to Tokyo to a dinner party that Admiral Griffin gave in honor of Secretary of the Navy James V. Forrestal and the congressional delegation. Again, the party was held at the Imperial Hotel. We had previously met Mr. Forrestal when Benny was the executive officer on the battleship *South Dakota*. We were pleased to see him again. The other members of the delegation were: Senators Allen J. Ellender (Louisiana), Owen Brewster (Maine), and Hugh Butler (Nebraska); and Congressmen C. Jasper Bell (Missouri), J. W. Robinson (Utah), George P. Miller (California), Eugene Worley (Texas), Fred L. Crawford (Michigan), and Karl M. Le Compte (Iowa). Secretary Forrestal seemed so serious at the party. Benny and I could not get him to smile. He looked worried. The next day, he and the other members of his party left for Bangkok, Siam to continue his world tour. Benny tried to convince him to visit Yokosuka, but Forrestal said that he would see it as he flew over Tokyo Bay!

We went to a buffet supper party that evening at Scajap

Manor, formerly the home where Benny had been entertained in 1939 when he was in the cruiser *Astoria*. It was in this house that Admiral Yonai toasted the Naval officers, prophetically saying, "One day you shall all return to Japan." The party was given by Rear Admiral and Mrs. Momsen, and Captain and Mrs. Donald F. Weiss. U.S.N. My dinner companions were the French amabassador, General Peschkoff, and General Schilling, on my right. Needless to say, I had a wonderful time. Both gentlemen were charming and very interesting to talk to.

On July nineteenth, we attended in Yokosuka the ceremonial destruction of the Wall of Secrecy, which had veiled the top-secret waterfront of the base from the Japanese people. This eight-foot wall was smashed by a bulldozer

Mrs. Decker being assisted over the rubble of the Wall of Secrecy.

driven by a sailor. It was thrilling to see that barrier crumble like a stack of cards. Now the Japanese people had a view of their future waterfront park. Beyond it lay the trim United States Navy, amid the hulks of the once-proud Japanese Navy. It was one of the most impressive events. Many dignitaries from Tokyo and Yokohama were present. No longer would the waterfront be denied to the people; it belonged to them. The secrecy was ended at last. It was one of the most important symbolic acts in the city's history.

The following day after the greetings were exchanged, the mayor led the way to the platform. We were escorted to our seats and the program commenced. The mayor gave a short speech, and then introduced Benny. A Japanese interpreter stood a little behind.

"I am very happy today. For several months I have been watching with great interest the energy of the city officials and the diligence of the workers in creating this park out of unsightly rubble. Today we can admire the magnificent results of their coordinated efforts.

"For years we fought a long, hard war which neither you nor I wanted. It was forced upon us by your arbitrary and unscrupulous military, drunk with power and reckless of life and property. This clique fostered suspicion and ill will by erecting between Japan and the United States a wall of secrecy.

"To me this park is symbolic of the Occupation. At long last the wall is down, and this land has been returned to its rightful owners—the people.

"Just as our bulldozer tore down the wall that surrounded this park—just as this land has been returned to you, the people, and just as you now have opened to you vistas of freedom, so is the Occupation, under the able and inspiring leadership of General MacArthur, striving to tear down the restraining walls between our two countries and give back to you your rightful freedoms.

"It is up to you, the people of Japan, as to what you are to do with your freedom. As this park has been beautified and made useful, as this land has been changed from war to peace, so can you make Japan into a beautiful, prosperous, and peaceful land.

"It is my fervent prayer that this city of Yokosuka will

50

lead in this movement. You have a city ideally situated for industrialization and commerce. Your harbor, as you can see, is splendid and well located. Your buildings and homes are intact after a disastrous war. You have electric power and water. You have labor. It remains for you, the people, to supply the will power, the drive, the enthusiasm required to make this a prosperous, well balanced community. The Occupation forces and the good people of Yokosuka now join hands in making Yokosuka a model city."

The throng of Japanese people showed their approval with thunderous applause and waved their hands shouting, "Banzai!"

We walked over to a place chosen for a tree planting ceremony. They called these "friendship trees." Benny put a shovelful of dirt around the base of one small tree, while I poured some around another. Mary and Colonel Bruno Hochmuth followed suit, each performing the same rite.

The Mayor then made a few closing remarks, after which we left the platform. Just before the close of the ceremony, two lovely young Japanese girls gave Mrs. Hochmuth and me a beautiful bouquet of flowers.

The decorated automobiles and floats, with their moving theatricals, passed the Seaside Park. We were surprised at these attractive floats, as they were so different from any we had seen in the United States. The entertainers were dressed in gay costumes and seemed to enjoy themselves as much as the onlookers. One float in particular impressed and amused us. It represented an Oriental restaurant with pretty lanterns hanging from the roof. In large letters, on the sides, were the following words "Heart Felt Thanks For Great Benefaction of America So That We are Getting Fat." Another one was a small replica of a ship with "Miss Yokosuka" printed in large letters on the sides of this vessel on wheels.

A woman, dressed as a bride and carrying an umbrella, sat astride a hooded horse. It made one think of the days of the feudal lords. Directly in back was a horse-drawn phaeton. This horse also had a short hood of white over its head, a fancy throw on its back. The driver was dressed in an attractive outfit and wore a large hat. Riding in the rear seat, I presume, was the bride's family.

The float representing one of Commodore Perry's black

51

ships was simply out of this world. Four Japanese men were dressed in white sailor suits and caps such as those worn in Commodore Perry's days. Under these caps were blond, curly wigs. As you can imagine, the contrast was startling. The old sailing ship was most interesting, too.

The parade ended with a beautiful float representing the world. Over it was a roof supported by columns. Over these columns were doves of peace. It was quite impressive, and was a wonderful finale.

The following Friday we gave a buffet supper party in honor of Mrs. Bledsoe, the wife of the rear admiral in command of the forces afloat (cruisers and destroyers). At each end of the long dining room table was a half-meter mirror reflector filled with floating flowers. On either side of the reflectors, near the center of the table, were square battery jars containing live goldfish. Eight weighted, gimballed candlesticks were placed between the reflectors and the battery jars. Frosted glass globes on each candlestick threw out a lovely soft light.

During the dinner, General Eichelberger, a real friend of the Navy, was fascinated by a fish which was giving him a cold steady "fish eye."

Benny had salvaged the weighted, gimballed candlesticks from one of the Japanese warehouses. The other officers had not recognized them, but he had known what they were because his father, Rear Admiral Benton C. Decker, had brought home a similar pair from the Spanish flagship in Santiago in 1898, after the war with Spain. Our Navy used similar ones about fifty years ago. The battery jars were salvaged from the Japanese electrical stores. All of this salvaged Japanese Naval equipment was used as makeshifts with which to decorate our poorly furnished houses.

Near the bar we had a one-meter parabolic mirror, an ex-Japanese destroyer searchlight reflector. It took several parties to develop this idea. At first we filled it with water and placed a goldfish in it. The fish saw a monster directly beneath him, and no matter how fast he swam, the monster was always there. Finally, in desperation, the goldfish leaped clear of the mirror. Scratch one idea and one goldfish. Next, we filled the mirror with blue colored water and floated yellow chrysanthemums on the surface. Beautiful, but not practical. After two of Wah Chan's old fashioneds, a guest would attempt to rest his glass on the surface of this attractive table. The resulting splash was sobering.

Finally, it was decided to cover the mirror with a glass top. In it, our house boy would make a beautiful sand picture. The guests could admire this and still use it to rest their drinks.

We never bothered about the menu. It would usually be a buffet, thus avoiding the usual protocol and allowing each guest the opportunity to escort the partner of his choice. In Tokyo, they submitted their guest lists to the representative of the State Department. This usually resulted in a guest having the same dinner partner over and over. Our system was to mix the ranks—generals could dine with young wives, and junior officers with the mature ladies. It was a popular arrangement.

Sometimes, to make things more interesting, we tried a different sort of meal. We had the time-honored Navy dinner of "rice and curry." With a good imagination, it was possible to have as many as twenty condiments, each served separately. This drew out the meal and created many surprises. The Army was entranced by this menu. As soon as dinner was over, you could watch a movie—the latest from the states, or the guests might gather around the piano for the usual songfest. Among our guests, both from the Army as from our base, we had many piano players and guitarists. One "musician" would hesitate to play alone, but when many were gathered together the competition was stiff. The lyrics became so well known and liked that everyone joined in for a song.

A Japanese artist of ability took our large paintings of the Dowager Empress of China (1907) and her consort, and changed the faces to resemble our own. We called these our "ancestors." The ladies' room was designated by Edwina's "ancestor" while the gentlemen's was indicated by Benny's.

It was fun to hear a "well oiled" guest searching for the restroom to find it marked by Benny's face draped in the Chinese regal robes of the consort.

I had an excellent Navy photographer. At our parties, he roamed through the gathering taking individual photographs. His work was outstanding. After a party, my secretary sent prints of the guests to them, and this proved popular.

Headquarters Eighth Army
United States Army
Office of the Commanding General
APO 343

Yokohama, Japan
6 August 1946

Capt. B. W. Decker
Commander, Fleet Activities
Yokosuka Naval Base
Yokosuka, Japan
Dear Captain Decker:
The first thing I want to do this morning is not only thank you for the very nice time Mrs. Eichelberger and I had last night but also to extend to you our appreciation for the fine glass net balls and batteries which we are delighted to have. I don't know how you get all these excellent ideas of yours but you are one of the best sources we have had so far for decorating the house with novel arrangements.
With renewed thanks for your kindness and with warm regards,

Sincerely,
/s/ Robert Eichelberger
P.S. Please tell Mrs. Decker how much we enjoyed her grand dinner.

After dinner, a movie was shown on a screen in the garden. We saw *The Bride Wore Boots* with Barbara Stanwyck and Robert Cummings. It was very good, and the setting was perfect. Later, the guests gathered around the piano which Captain Owsley played to the accompaniment by Admiral Bledsoe on his accordion. Sometimes the two would exchange their instruments, which both played equally well. There were about fifty guests present, and they all seemed to enjoy the music.

On Sunday, the fourth of August, following a quiet luncheon at home, Lieutenant Fromke, Benny, and I decided to take a walk. Although at the start I was enthusiastic and full of energy, the steep, unpaved paths full of ditches and stones soon tired me out. We visited a Buddhist temple and went through the priest's home. On our way there, we passed some small boys with little cages and nets. They were catching cicadas. The males make a shrill note by vibrating membranes of special sound organs on the underside of the abdomen. In August, this is a popular pastime for the boys. When they have tired of this amusement, they set the insects free. It makes them feel as if they have done a kind deed.

The Japanese, by their grapevine, had notified our household of our location. The driver picked us up and took us home in the car. We were all grateful for their thoughtfulness.

The next evening, we gave a dinner party in honor of four-star Admiral Richardson, who was in Japan to testify at the war crimes tribunal. There were twenty-two guests, including General and Mrs. Eichelberger, Vice Admiral Griffin, Rear Admiral and Mrs. Bledsoe, General and Mrs. Byers, and Major General Casey.

Admiral Richardson was the commander in chief of the Pacific Fleet prior to the Pearl Harbor sneak attack. He told us about the situation that caused his relief of command. He wanted to keep the fleet cruising at sea, but the merchants and politicians wanted them in port. He blamed the politicians, not Kimmel.

We went to the war crimes tribunal and sat on the stage facing the balcony. To the right of our seats were the judges: Jaranilla, from the Philippine Islands; Northcroft, from New Zealand; Bernard, from France; Zaryanov, from Soviet Russia; Mei, from China; General Cramer, from the United States; Lord Patrick, from Great Britain; McDougall, from Canada; Roling, from the Netherlands; Pal, from India; and Sir William Webb, the presiding judge who was from Australia. The defendants sat on our left. From the stage to the balcony, in the front row, were: Doihara, Hata, Hirota, Minami. In the back row of this box were: Hashimoto, Koiso, Nagano, Oshima, and Matsui. In the middle box sat Tojo, Oka, Umezu, Araki, Muto. In the back of these men were Hiranuma, Togo, and Shigematsu, with whom years later Benny would become a good friend. In the last box, in the front row, were: Hoshino, Kaya, Kido, and Kimura. Sato, Shimeda, Shiratori, Suzuki, and Itagaki sat in the rear. Members of the families of these men sat in the balcony.

The large courtroom in the war ministry building was a most impressive place. I shuddered at the solemnity of the drama that was being enacted before me, but I could not forget that these men had fought for their country. According to our standards, some of them had been cruel. Now they were on trial for their lives. Tojo was particularly interesting to watch. He seemed somehow bored and uninterested.

General Matsui, who was in command of Nanking during the rape of that unfortunate city, was on the stand. His defense rested in the fact that he had not been close enough to his troops to know of their actions. He also claimed to have been ill at the time. The Japanese ambassador to China, at that time, testified that he couldn't remember to whom he had sent his report. Sir William said that he thought he could be pressed to remember, which he did. Kido, who had been in charge of all the information printed in Japan, was also on trial.

The Panay incident was reviewed in spite of the defense protests that it had been closed. Sir William was elegant in his reply. The incident, as far as the United States was concerned, might be closed, but the judges sitting with him from the other nations wanted to be informed. Therefore, the case would proceed.

At the time, many of the Occupation personnel questioned the value of these trials, as they were most expensive and drawn out. However, they were avidly attended by the Japanese, and thus informed the people of facts that had been withheld from them. The Japanese were shocked. I doubt if they would have ever believed the reports if not for these trials. Most Japanese despised Tojo but felt less strongly toward many of the others.

Much information was also obtained by the Allies. All papers had been burnt by the Japanese on the fourteenth and fifteenth of August, 1945. The trials uncovered the few surviving copies of some of the papers, thus rescuing from oblivion many historical facts. For this, historians should be grateful.

Benny was particularly interested in a dozen heavy volumes of the testimony of Admiral Toyoda's trial, which was held in Yokohama. It was the only record of that officer's command in Yokosuka, and it gave my husband much valuable information. Toyoda was acquitted.

Benny was opposed to the principle of the war crimes trials. He had been involved with the original plans in Washington at the time when Assistant Justice Jackson had pushed the idea in order to punish the Germans. The fact that these trials were not in accord with American laws caused Benny to agree that the Navy neither supported nor opposed them. The trials made retroactive laws against conspiracy and held subordinates responsible for the decisions of their seniors.

Though much has been said of these trials, they tried to be fair. When Japan regained her sovereignty, it was to be expected that many officers would be pardoned, or at least paroled. We accomplished our purpose, and there must be no revenge in our hearts.

The United States "ambassador," George Atcheson, and his wife gave a large dinner party at their lovely home in Tokyo. Although we were invited to spend the night, we had already accepted an invitation to stay at the embassy. Colonel Wheeler had invited us to take a trip to Nikko the next day. That morning, we rose early and drove to the Ueno Station, where we met General MacArthur's staff, their wives, and the rest of the party of officers. We boarded the finest private train in all Japan, called the foreign diplomat's train.

The interior of this train was really magnificent. The woodwork in the club, or observation, car was mahogany inlaid with mother of pearl designs. At one end of the car was a satin, hand-embroidered picture of chrysanthemums, and over each window were lovely, embroidered pictures of birds. Under these, on top of each window, were exquisite wood carvings. In addition, the bedroom and compartment walls were all covered in satin brocade.

After a wonderful breakfast, we retired to the club car, where most of us remained the rest of the journey. Air conditioning had been installed by our engineers, making this the only car in Japan so equipped. Even so, there was no safety glass or double glass windows. The gauge was narrower than ours, and the rails were badly worn, especially on the curves.

The kaleidoscope of scenery which passed our windows

was fascinating. We flew through quaint villages, rice paddies, and picturesque railroad stations. There were always six or seven uniformed men on each station platform to greet us and salute as we passed.

We arrived at Nikko at eleven o'clock and were met by an elderly Japanese man, Mr. Aoki, who was to be our official guide. Filing into the waiting cars, we started on our trip up into the mountains. As we left the town and began climbing up the steep grades, the road became very poor. It was full of chuckholes and rocks. There were twenty-six hairpin turns before we reached the summit. We passed beautiful Lake Chuzenji and several inns on our way to the fish hatchery at Shobugahama beach. This is the best and largest trout hatchery in Japan. After looking in all the pools filled with fish in different stages of growth, we waited for one delinquent car. Just before Colonel Wheeler left to try to find it the missing party arrived in a Nikko Kanko Hotel bus. Their car had struck a boulder, which had pierced the floor board. Hailing a passing truck, they had been taken to the hotel where they had chartered this bus.

We returned to the hotel for luncheon. Afterwards the party drove to the entrance of the Kegon Falls. We took an elevator down a shaft bored through solid rock. A stiff breeze blew up this shaft, and the water dripped from the ceiling of the short tunnel leading to the outside. Walking down some very worn and uneven steps, we reached the lookout point and saw the Falls. This is the outlet for Lake Chuzenji, a 330-foot drop. Our guide said that it was a favorite place for frustrated lovers to commit suicide. Many people had ended their lives by jumping to the rocks below. To think that such a beautiful spot had been used for such tragedies! In spite of this, we enjoyed the view, which was magnificent!

We then drove to the cable car station. During the war, the Japanese had dismantled the upper section of the cable car system in order to obtain scrap metal. But all of the parts were still piled nearby. They had never been used. This was the case all over Japan. On the base, 150,000 tons of scrap iron had accumulated for thirty years. This, with metal from damaged ships, was returned by us to the Japanese for local civil economy. It helped the people and gave us elbow room.

At a lookout point, we had a fine view of the mountains

and valleys. Some tried their skill at skimming little disks down the mountainside. The Japanese peddlers were selling these disks for a few yen. At the station, we boarded a cable car on a single track. It was a thrilling ride down the mountain. About half way down, we passed a cable car coming up the mountain. The officers all laughed when I gasped, "If either car had not been exactly on time as we met at the switch, it could have been disastrous!" My heart was in my mouth for a few seconds.

When we reached the foot of the mountain, we found our automobiles and rode over to the Toshogu Shrine or mausoleum. Started in 1624, it took fifteen thousand workmen twelve years to complete. A very sacred spot, this shrine was dedicated to Ieyasu Tokugawa, the founder of the Tokugawa shogunate (1603–1868).

The stone torii (gate) at the entrance was most impressive. On its left was a vermillion-colored five-storied pagoda, one of the finest in Japan. We passed the sacred stable where we saw the famous carving of the three monkeys, "See no evil, hear no evil, and speak no evil." The Yomeimon Gate, which stood at the foot of the stone steps in the courtyard, was magnificent. It is supposed to be the most elaborate and skillfully constructed edifice ever built by the ancient Japanese craftsmen. It is very ornate, decorated with carvings and metal fittings, and covered with gold leaf.

Beyond this gate was the Karamon Gate, very Chinese looking. It was the formal entrance to the *haiden* (oratory) and the *honden* (holy of holies) which were elaborately decorated buildings. We entered them by a side entrance after removing our shoes. In one of the buildings, we were told to stand in a certain spot and clap our hands. This caused many reverberations throughout the structure.

The famous "sleeping cat" carving reclined over a gateway which led, via 200 stone steps, to the mortuary chapel and the tomb of Ieyasu. We, however, did not go beyond this gate.

A tale was told to us about the carver, Hidari, which means "left-handed." He was so clever that his carved cats scared away the mice. Out of jealousy, the other artists cut off his right hand. Undiscouraged, he developed the use of his left hand, and carved this sleeping cat.

59

We visited the Rinnoji Temple, the largest wooden building in Nikko. It contains three large images of Buddha. The cherry tree in the front courtyard is supposed to be over three hundred years old.

At the foot of this temple is a house where President Grant stayed when he visited Japan in 1879. The Japanese are very proud that a president of the United States had honored Nikko by staying there.

We saw the crescent-shaped Sacred Bridge, used only by the Emperor, and rode along the avenue where beautiful cryptomeria trees, similar to our huge California redwood trees, were growing on both sides of the road. There is an interesting story about these trees. Years ago, all *daimyo* (a minor ruler) gave gifts to the temples. One *daimyo* was very poor. He finally decided to plant cryptomeria trees as his gift. Of all of the gifts, today his is the most beautiful and valuable.

When we returned to the train, we were very hot and tired. But all agreed that we had had a wonderful time and had enjoyed the day immensely. That night, Benny and I returned to Yokosuka.

It seemed to me that the workmen were very slow in fixing our house. Benny had ordered the bathroom in April, shortly after taking command of the base. Yet it was still not finished. One day, I was so exasperated with the slowness of the plasterer that I decided to shame him into action. I took the trowel and, though I had never tried it before, proceeded to apply plaster on the wall. The worker was frustrated and began to suck his breath between his teeth, an Oriental mannerism showing great chagrin. He finished the job quickly and smoothly.

This was fortunate, as we were to do a great deal of entertaining. Bathrooms and well-plastered walls were absolute necessities.

Soon afterward, we gave a luncheon for Walter Simmons of the *Chicago Tribune*, Victor Boeson of the *Liberty* magazine, and Sid Whipple of Scripps-Howard. These gentlemen were interested in what Benny had accomplished in Yokosuka.

One day, Benny suggested that we ride over to Kamakura to do some sightseeing. We visited the Hachiman Shrine, which is situated on a wooded hill. An avenue of cherry trees lies on either of its sides, and its approach is decorated by a thirty-two-foot stone *torii* and many picturesque bridges.

The middle one is a curved, Oriental bridge called Taikobushi (Drum Bridge) because of its graceful shape. Ponds filled with red and white lotus blossoms completed the scene.

The shrine was dedicated to the Emperor Ojin (270–310 A.D.) and his parents. The existing buildings date from 1828. A giant gingko tree was to the left of the long flight of stone steps leading to the main shrine and colonnade. It measured twenty-three feet in circumference and seventy feet in height. This tree marks the spot where Shogun Minamoto no Sanemoto was assassinated by his nephew, Kugyo, the chief priest of Hochimangu who waited behind the original tree for him to arrive from a visit to the shrine. When the original tree died, the present tree was planted. The tragedy took place in January 1219.

The buildings of the shrine are painted vermilion. On either side of the entrance to the main building are the Nio, fierce armored guardians of the shrine. These grimacing warriors are supposed to scare the *oni* (devils). Many ancient national treasures, palaquins, drums, bows and arrows, and suits of armor are kept there. At the foot of the stone steps, to the right, is a minor shrine called Wakamiya (junior shrine) which is dedicated to the Emperor Nintoku, son of the Emperor Ojin, and three other deities. This building was built in about 1624. In about the center of the compound is a pavilion which is visible from almost all vantage points. The grounds were filled with picnickers, some of whom were taking naps, while others rowed boats around the small islands. The *ishi dori* (stone lanterns) scattered throughout the compound and on the small islands added to the atmosphere of this fascinating place.

The large, bronze Buddha called the Daibutsu (great buddha) was very impressive. It was originally enclosed in a large building which was damaged by a storm and finally carried away by a tidal wave in 1495. The image was cast in 1252 by Ono Goroemon, one of the leading sculptors of that era.

The Buddha stands forty-two feet, including the pedestal. The circumference of the base is ninety-six feet and five inches. The length of the face with its half-closed eyes, expressing perfect repose and calm, is seven feet eight inches, while each eye is three feet three inches long. The estimated weight of the image is just short of 103 tons. The silver boss on the forehead weighs thirty pounds. We were surprised to see that the hair was covered with snails. An elderly Japanese, who was basking in the sun, told the story that the snails had covered Buddha's head to protect him from the sun. As we walked around the image, the water marks from the flood could still be seen.

To reach the Hase Kannon, we had to climb many steep and uneven stone steps to the top of a hill. The original temple was destroyed and only the remains of the foundation were left. Here the gilt image of Kannon, goddess of mercy, was inside a small makeshift building at the rear of the foundation. The place was shabby looking and was cluttered with rather worn-looking images. The magnificent gilt statue was framed by heavy curtains and looked greatly out of place in its poor surroundings. The image was supposed to have been carved by a priest named Tokudo Shonin from half of a tall camphor tree which washed ashore at Kamakura in 721 A.D. From her throne, Kannon views the seacoast extending from Yuigahama Beach to Hayama. It is a divine view indeed.

On Thursday, the twenty-second of August, we went to Tokyo to a dinner party given by an American silk expert, Mr. P. F. Magana, who was attempting to rehabilitate the Japanese silk industry. We met Countess Maeda, wife of Lieutenant General Marquis Toshinari Maeda, her daughter, Prime Minister Yoshida, and his secretary. The countess fascinated me. She was very attractive and wore the most beautiful jewels. Prime Minister Yoshida was interesting to talk to. At that time, Benny felt that Yoshida was very conservative, and didn't approve of my husband's emphasis on the importance of women in Japan's political and economic future.

We had all been looking forward to Navy Day and were not disappointed. The morning of October twenty-seventh was bright and full of promise. The celebrations started with religious services in the Mikasa Chapel. At 2:30 P.M., Benny and I stationed ourselves in the reviewing stand that had been erected in front of the main gate to the Naval base. Vice Admiral Griffin, his wife and daughter, General and Mrs. Paul Mueller and their daughter, Major General and Mrs. William Chase, Brigadier General and Mrs. Courtney Whitney, Brigadier General and Mrs. Hugh Hoffman, all of the Navy captains and wives attached to the base, and some commanders and their wives joined us in the reviewing stand to watch the parade.

Eight hundred sailors and marines proudly marched past us. The Japanese showed great interest, and I noticed no signs of animosity on their faces.

After the parade, we all went to Kurihama, where, on the eighth of July 1853, Commodor Matthew Calbraith Perry made history. Here, on the western shore of the Bay of Yedo, the "Black Ships," the *Susquehanna*, his flagship; the *Mississippi*, and the sloops-of-war *Saratoga* and *Plymouth* dropped anchor. On the fourteenth of July, accompanied by his officers and an armed escort of marines and sailors (in all, about three hundred men), the commodore went ashore and presented President Fillmore's letters addressed to the Emperor, and his own credentials to the Shogun's special commissioners. A few days later, after exploring Tokyo Bay and anchoring off Yokosuka, the American Fleet sailed for Hong Kong with the understanding that Perry would return the following spring for the Emperor's reply. On the eleventh of February 1854, he brought his "Black Ships" farther up the bay, nearly opposite the present site of Yokohama, and within the sight of Yedo (Tokyo) on a clear day. The Japanese protested the selection of this anchorage, but Perry ignored the protest. On the thirty-first of March, the first treaty (ratified at Shimoda on February 21, 1855 and proclaimed on the twenty-second of the following June) between the United States and Japan was concluded. Uraga, a historical place, seemed most fitting to celebrate the first Navy Day to be held in Japan by our victorious Navy after the surrender. We went to the Perry monument, which the Japanese had pulled over during the war. After the surrender, Admiral Halsey ordered that it be restored within twenty-four hours. Vice Admiral Griffin gave a speech and laid a beautiful wreath on the monument.

Over the entrance to the monument, they had placed an

arch upon which were crossed the flags of the United States and Japan. A correspondent took offense at the crossing of the flags. Later, another complained about the words of the historical song, "The Black Ships." But Benny chose to ignore the complaints; the war was over!

James Young, a newspaper correspondent, had arranged a touching presentation, which was a complete surprise. Captain Winfield Scott Cunningham, a Naval Academy classmate of Benny's, was presented with his class ring, which had been torn from his finger while he was aboard the *Nitta Maru* being shipped to Japan as a prisoner of war with 1200 other American captives. Captain Cunningham was governor of Wake Island when the war started, and was captured when the island was taken by the Japanese.

The story of the ring is a fascinating one. Toshio Saito's home was being searched on October fifteenth. Legal section investigator George F. Getty and his interpreter Paul M. Hayami, with a detachment of Japanese policemen, conducted the search of Saito's home at Gamayori, Honshu.

Saito was suspected of having in his possession valuables confiscated from the owners who were taken prisoners on Wake Island. A Mr. Tripp of San Diego had enquired about his ring in the letter and so the investigator was suspicious of Saito, who was to be placed under arrest for complicity in alleged war crimes committed aboard the Japanese transport *Nitta Maru*.

Sergeant Hayami saw Mrs. Saito place some objects in her kimono sleeve, which she had taken from a small cabinet while he and the Japanese policemen were conducting the search. Mrs. Saito was asked to show what she had put inside her kimono sleeve and the rings were discovered. The third ring belonged to Colonel George H. Potter, U.S.M.C.

Captain Cunningham had escaped three times from Japanese prisons in Shanghai, and his thrilling experiences were covered in a book written by Quentin Reynolds called *Officially Dead*.

When "Spiv" Cunningham was presented with his ring, he had tears in his eyes. I had a hard time to keep from weeping, too. The presentation was made by Alva C. Carpenter, Fort Wayne, Indiana, Chief of S.C.A.P.'s legal section; and Lieutenant George F. Getty, iiI, Los Angeles, California, who had conducted the successful search.

"Spiv" Cunningham had asked Benny to assist a woman who had helped the POWs in Shanghai while he was a prisoner of the Japanese. We contacted this woman and promised to assist her in a few ways available to us. But Benny's dedication cooled as time passed. "Spiv" had already sent thirty dollars and the promise of more funds if they were needed. She was not hungry and her extravagant request for help far exceeded our means to assist her. This was but the second case of a Japanese whom Benny sincerely wished to help becoming unreasonable. All others were more grateful, and inspired him to increase his efforts. There is really no way to fully repay one for human kindness. This is one of the functions of heaven, and to expect to receive full repayment on earth is unrealistic.

When the ceremony was over, we drove to Kurihama Hall, where we looked at some museum pieces pertaining to Commodore Perry's landing in Japan. All of the Japanese families who had anything reminiscent of this historical event were asked to contribute to this display, and it was most interesting.

We took our seats in front of a stage and prepared to enjoy a program that Captain Heald had arranged, through the courtesy of the Japanese Actors' and Actresses' Union. The program was: (I) music selection (Fuji dance band); (II) modern Japanese dance; and (III) Song of the Kurofune (Kurofune means black ships, the designation of Commodore Perry's ships by the Japanese at the time of his landing)—"Otsue," sung by girls of Yokosuka. The Fuji dance band played "Anchors Aweigh." Following this piece, Miss Toshie Fujikake and her troupe put on a skit called "Handball and Lord."

The next act was an attractive Japanese singer, Miss Toshie Yamaguchi, who sang three songs. One, written by Dr. Inazo Nitobe, was composed at the time of Commodore Perry's visit to Japan. This song had become very popular among the Japanese people.

> Through a black night of cloud and rain
> The black ship plies her way,
> An alien thing of evil mien
> Across the waters gray.

Down in her hold, there labor men
Of jet black visage dread,
While, fair of face, stand by her guns
Grim hundreds clad in red.

With cheeks half in shaggy beards
Their glance fixed on the wave,
They seek our sun-land at the word
Of Captain wolfish-grave.

While loud they come—the boom of drums
And songs in strange uproar,
And now with flesh and herb in store
And slowly floating onward go
These Black Ships wave—tossed to and fro.

Upon our arrival at home, we found Mr. James Farley; Judge Joseph Keenan, of the war crimes trial; and Mr. Malone, assistant prosecutor of the war crimes trial. Mr. Davies, who was the Coca-Cola representative in the Far East, was also waiting for us. Yokosuka was the place to see in Japan.

That evening, as a finale for Navy Day, we gave a large dinner party. The distinguished guests including our guests of the afternoon, Lieutenant General and Mrs. Eichelberger, Mr. George Atcheson (our ambassador), General Peschkoff (French ambassador), Major General and Mrs. Paul Mueller, Vice Admiral and Mrs. Robert Griffin, Major General and Mrs. Clovis Byers, Major General and Mrs. William Chase, Rear Admiral and Mrs. Albert Bledsoe, Brigadier General and Mrs. Hugh Hoffman, Brigadier General and Mrs. Frank Besson, and Mr. and Mrs. U. Alexis Johnson (our American consul).

It is interesting to note that Commodore Perry, Major General Chase, and Benny all came from the state of Rhode Island.

Chapter III

YOKOSUKA

Yokosuka was a demoralized community. The Japanese people were hungry, and thousands of civilian men prowled the streets. They were jobless, and their families needed food and fuel. There was no sewer system, and sanitary conditions were appalling. There were no public toilets. We should be grateful for our service stations and department store facilities.

First in order was to clean up the flies, mosquitoes, and fleas. A jeep with a dusting attachment dusted the base and the town with DDT. In April, the tree trunks in our garden were covered by large black flies, which evidently came out of the bark in the spring. It was unbelievable. The spraying was effective except in the narrow valleys and alleys of the town. In these areas, which were inaccessible by jeep, fleas and flies would still be a menace. Fortunately we had a solution. Our Marine fighter group 31 in Oppama, under the command of Colonel Munn, had received orders to return to the States, but in the meantime they wanted to continue flying. They needed a reason, so we asked them to spray our narrow valleys, encrusted with small houses and innumerable cesspools. Daily, these young, daring flyers would zoom up the hills following the pathways, dusting with DDT. The children loved to run out into the open, throw wide their jackets, and become hidden momentarily in the clouds of DDT. It was fun for them and it helped us in delousing the city. We also had a rat patrol. This had been in effect prior to my taking command and was evidently doing a good job. The Navy was afraid of typhus and needed no encouragement.

The next problem was our water supply. It is unbelievable that there was water pressure on the base as well as in the town for only three hours a day. After that, the reservoir, owned by the Navy, would be dry because of the many, many leaks. Everywhere on the base were lead pipe water risers, which were easily punctured and spouted water. The city was worse. Because of this, it was impossible to properly chlorinate the water. Quantities of chlorine were fed into the water by our Navy, but it was not effective. When the water pressure was reduced to zero, a back suction or vacuum was created which brought into the system contaminated fluids. We had to keep the water pressure on continuously. Although our people stopped the base leaks, the town was another matter. This was our first collision with the mayor. It was finally necessary to get a new man to cooperate. I had even considered cutting off water to the city if they did not speed up their repairs. In the end it became possible to keep the reservoir filled and thus keep pressure on the system for twenty-four hours a day. John Q now removed all lister (drinking) bags. That was a giant step.

The city billed me $24,000 for water. First, it wasn't their water. Second, there was no water. They were only guessing and hoped to get some funds for the asking. It did, however, open the door for me to take another step. I gave them the entire system. Thereafter, they were responsible for its proper maintenance.

The real answer to our civil affairs' problems was woman power! The men were reluctant. When victorious, the Japanese male was overbearing—when defeated, he was subservient. The women had a more even disposition. They took life's ups and downs in stride. They had had little to say concerning matters outside of their homes, but it wasn't ever thus. Women had been important and powerful in the early history of Japan. In 1008 A.D. Lady Murasaki, a very talented woman, wrote *The Tale of Genji*, the first Japanese novel on record. Only after 1930 were women reduced to a menial position.

I decided to change this. It was the only hope we had to alter the thinking of the Japanese nation. We couldn't change the men, but we could support the women, who were more democratic. Much of our success in this area was due to the help of my Japanese liaison officer's wife, Mrs. Takaoka. She had been educated at Barnard College and spoke excellent English. I asked her to organize a woman's club. In a few days she appeared with five of the most distinguished ladies of Yokosuka. The leading woman was Mrs. Kazu Mabuchi, wife of a prominent citizen. She had been the head of a club

Dedication of the Shinsei Yokosuka Women's Society Club House.

under the auspices of the Navy. This had been an organization created to maintain control over each block in the city during the war. Evidently it was not satisfactory, for the Navy disbanded it in 1943. Mrs. Michi Fukuda, Mrs. Tanakawa, and Mrs. Toshi Tanaka were also present.

As usual, another group heard of my request and tried to cut in by calling on me with an offer to help. They said they already had eighty thousand members (seemed exaggerated!) and that they would inform me of the police and city officials who had stolen goods. This was a bad approach. Though four women were present, a man did all of the talking! I concluded it was the extinct Navy Club.

I trusted Mrs. Takaoka, and her selection of older women led me to believe these ladies were what I needed. I was not disappointed. As they sat in my office, I asked them how many members they had. Although only a few days after I had approached Mrs. Takaoka, they already had two hundred members. But I said, "That is nowhere near enough. I want thousands. Then I will support you to the limit!"

As I looked at these distinguished ladies, I thought of another problem we had. My supply officer had asked me about the disposal of a warehouse full of chocolate candy bars which had accumulated during the war. They had been in tropical areas for several years. They were not in good condition, many rancid or wormy. I recalled the furor that developed when the Navy dumped thirty tons of rancid butter at sea. The folks back home wanted no waste. In addition, we had huge stocks of peanuts and other supplies which were unfit for issue to our men. I had directed my officer to leave a box of chocolates on my desk. Now I had an idea. Perhaps the women would be able to use this candy.

In the Solomons, many captured Japanese diaries included a paragraph stating, "Today I received a piece of hard candy from the Emperor. Before I enjoyed this great luxury, I bowed toward Tokyo and gave thanks to his Imperial Highness for this great gift to me."

Taking a chocolate bar, I then handed the box to the ladies. "Would you like a candy bar?" I asked, as I knocked a weevil or so from mine. They hungrily ate one apiece and started to cry!

"We haven't tasted chocolate since the war began. No one ever gave us candy but you, the conqueror."

"I have a million of these. If you will enlarge your women's club I will give you the distribution of our surplus food for the hungry, the children, the aged, the sick, and the poor."

With this, the club rapidly grew to ten thousand and then to a peak of fifty-three thousand members. Practically every woman in town was a member. My strength was founded on this club.

We were having trouble with the garbage collectors. Their carts were hauling far too many cans of garbage through the gate.

I asked the Women's Club to take over this concession. The racketeers had been robbing us by bribing the "help" to put whole hams, roasts, and canned goods into the barrels. This would now stop. Behind each horse-drawn cart walked a woman inspector. The garbage cans were delivered to the Women's Club where the "substandard food" was then given to the hungry. (Edwina had insisted that I call this "substandard food") We had no more trouble after one minor misunderstanding, the first day.

The women had suggested that they could salvage more food it they were allowed to clean the dishes themselves and scrape the different kinds of food into separate cans. I willingly agreed to this and went to the mess hall to observe the system. It was working well, but the four women were neither young nor pretty. I did not think that they added anything to our superb mess. When I objected, the women explained, "We didn't want to arouse the passion of your men!" The next meal the women salvagers were more attractive. Thereafter, the men left a bit more on their plates.

I realized that today's new generation of Japanese will be repelled by the idea of their elders eating "substandard food." They must realize that when a person is hungry, even a parboiled boot is better than nothing. Those good people knew better than any of us what it is to be starving. We did the best we could to help them. We gave them, in addition, tons of "K" rations left over from the war which were excellent, but no G.I. wanted to see another such ration. To be sure, the cigarettes were spotted, the chewing gum hard, and the tins cans a bit corroded. But I never heard a complaint— only sincere thanks.

On the twenty-eighth day of May, an interesting message was received from headquarters, Marine Aircraft Group 31.

A stack of letters and cards have been received thanking us for the refuse food which we have been delivering to the Yokosuka Ladies' Association for charitable distribution. The following is a translation of one of them.

A Letter of Thanks

I am writing you a letter but in my mind are the

71

smiling faces of the MPs patrolling under the fragrant leaves of early summer.

We thank you very much for the food you have given us.

Year after year
How gratefully the wild pinks,
Blooming on the moor,
Accept the day.

The women of Japan, looking backward toward the past, have been dreaming under the beautiful cherry trees without paying any attention to the advancements in foreign countries. Although we are honest women, looking after our own homes in accordance with the teaching that all women should be brought up to be "good wives and mothers," we simply did not care what was going on in the rest of the world.

It is too late, altogether too late, yet we cannot help regretting and feeling ashamed of having been left in ignorance for such long ages.

How can we but respect and admire the American Occupation Forces for their courteous and gentlemanly attitude. Why had we to fight such a kindhearted people? We were too far from understanding.

We heartily beg your pardon for the sin we committed against America. We have been deeply impressed by the sympathy and help extended to us.

Wounded, stricken to the ground
We've been cared for;
These our tears,
Are tribute to your mercy.

Only by your kind aid can Japan, though treading now the stony path of travail and disaster, be born again a happy nation.

Very sincerely yours,
Kou Misono

My officers and men who read this message were profoundly affected. How well Misono described the feelings of her countrywomen. God bless her and may all Americans and Japanese remember her words.

16th, August, 1946

From
Mrs. K. Mabuchi
President of the Shinsei
Yokosuka Women's Society

Our Dear Commander B. W. Decker—

In reflecting upon the hardest time we had since the end of the Pacific War, we, S.Y.W.S., cannot help of appreciating your kind and warm hearted help to the Yokosukan people to get rid over the sad and disastrous life, especially with regard to the food shortage in Yokosuka.

No one know what a disastrous thing would happen if there was no help from the Commander of the U.S.A., because food problem was the most acute in that time. And so we can't find any suitable word to mention the gratitude to you kind help.

Our Society was established 30th, April this year. Since that time we were much obliged to your kindness and love forwarded to our Society and Yokosukan people, as if you were the hen to the Yokosukan citizen as the hen to her youngsters.

Yokosukan people say that you were the Goddess to save the people in Yokosuka at the edge of starvation. All the things which was given to us by your American Navy were distributed to the poor and disastrous people in Yokosuka, according to your rules and instructions. All fathers, mothers, boys and girls, old and young, especially those who were sick, children and war orphans received your hearty presents with tear of thanks.

The people in Yokosuka are very happy to have such a benevolent COMMANDER in Yokosuka. Shinsei is the name of our Society. It means Newborn. The word Newborn would be applicable to the people in Yokosuka nowadays because of the thousand helps of your Yokosukan people could never forget the precious name B. W. Decker, the Commander, for hundreds and thousands years.

We, again, appreciate very much your kind help and wholehearted support to our Society and beg your unchangeable help to our Society. We Sincerely swear to follow your instructions and do our best at any cost.

Yours Truly
K. Mabhuchi
Representing the Shinsei
Yokosuka Women's Society

To build up the prestige of the city police, the first step

Captain Decker, Colonel Hochmouth, and the Chief of Police inspect the Yokosuka Police Force.

was to give them good shoes. On the base we had a storeroom full of field or campaign shoes left by our men who were in a hurry to return to the United States. They left heaps of clothing and gear in their barracks. Those shoes were good shoes. We gave them to the local police. But they were sizes ten and eleven, while the Japanese wore sizes three and four. They solved that problem—they arrested some local cobblers and released them after they had reduced the sizes of the shoes and had turned them inside out so they would take a high polish. Our police looked proud and well dressed. Our prisoners were also well dressed, as Lieutenant George T. Wolf, U.S.M.C., in charge of the police, issued them the salvaged and abandoned dungarees. Several major city police chiefs visited us to see what we were accomplishing.

There was no way for the citizen to identify a specific policeman. We corrected this by issuing numbered badges.

We also issued the police tropical helmets from our surplus. Helmets would not be needed in peace times—we were out of the tropics for good. We had them painted white and a police emblem was placed on the front. I thought they looked great, but this summer uniform was dropped after I left in 1950.

A policeman was usually standing in a police cubicle at the gate of the Tadodai residence. He was a friendly old man who faithfully saluted me, whether I was coming or going. At first, there also were two Marine orderlies, but later the number was reduced to one. I really had no need for a Japanese policeman, and so suggested to Captain Wolf that he be assigned to a more important post. The captain informed me that this man was too old for any other duty, and that to discharge him would be a hardship on a faithful officer of the law. I agreed, recognizing that there was a limit to frugality. Off and on, I would see the old man in his box. His salute became a friendly greeting of welcome.

A big step for the women occurred when they took places in the police force as matrons. This was a revolutionary idea in Japan. The chief of police wanted none of it. The uniform he presented was entirely different from that of the males, and was most unattractive. I insisted that it be similar to that of the regular police. Mrs. Gonzales, wife of our senior

Women are commissioned as police.

dentist, did a beautiful job of designing a uniform. We had given the police numbered badges for identification by the citizens. But the chief of police issued smaller badges to the matrons. When questioned, he said large badges didn't go well on bosoms. Just the same, I insisted that the smaller ones be replaced.

The matrons proved very successful in directing traffic, for example at the main gate. As they were pretty, they made a good impression. The only problem was that they would often be married within three weeks of taking the job. The turnover rate was a problem.

My medical officer also had plenty to do in Yokosuka. We had thirteen hospitals in town, ranging from a few beds to several hundred. All were unbelievably unsanitary. Our medical personnel was limited in number as were all other branches, but though it required additional time and effort, they produced. In the next few years they were able to do big things for Yokosuka, contributing greatly to building a friendship between Japan and the United States.

Cholera broke out in the Otsu area, where some Japanese, newly repatriated from Korea, were living. It was like a three-alarm fire! The Army and our medical officers, under Captain Owsley, closed in on the area from all sides. It was immediately quarantined and massive steps taken to inoculate everyone that moved and fumigate the rest! The outbreak could have been caused by refuse drifting ashore from incoming repatriate ships. Therefore, the beach was swept clean. In a short time, the disease was under control, and no new cases developed. We could all be proud of our Army and Navy medicos!

I had one Protestant and one Catholic chaplain. These also came into the picture, for this was a Christian Occupation, and I wasn't going to let them forget it. While roaming about the base. I found an abandoned Quonset hut which had formerly been used as a chapel. It was a shambles, with hymnals and Bibles scattered everywhere. I had the chaplains on the carpet and gave positive orders to clean that chapel. Then I asked them to recruit all the missionaries they could, for I had need of them. Yokosuka had no active Christian while under the Japanese Navy, but with a little encouragement I could see possibilities for Christian growth. My missionaries worked with enthusiasm, and Christianity soon grew in the town.

My civil affairs officer had been directed to investigate a large concrete structure just outside of the main gate. I had spotted it from my office window and thought it looked like ex-Navy which had not been surrendered. He returned with a report that several ex-Japanese Navy officers had taken over this Japanese Navy Hospital, Kai Jin Kai, 120 beds, and were planning to sell it on the black market. In the meantime, it was used as a cheap rooming house. The proof lay in a photo of an official graduation of Navy nurses with admirals handing out diplomas. Now it was a disreputable mass of filth. Pointing to this building, I told the chaplains, "That was a hospital, and I want a missionary to make it into a first-class civilian hospital with help of our medical department."

Though a Protestant, I admire the Catholic organization. They move fast and decisions are made through a chain of

In our garden Bishop Breton receives a medal from the French Ambassador, General Pechkoff.

78

command. Chaplain Boguslaus T. Poznanski returned in three weeks with the report that the Catholics would accept the challenge. He had found a bishop in Fukuoka with an organization capable of operating a hospital, but which was in need of one. When Bishop Albert Breton came to Yokosuka, I invited him to dinner. He was a most interesting man of sixty-five, and had spent forty years in Japan. Though a French national, he spoke Japanese. His dancing eyes, pink cheeks, white beard, reminded us of Santa Claus, for he not only looked the part, but also he brought Yokosuka and me a wonderful Christmas present. He told me that he was willing to open this former hospital as Saint Joseph's Hospital. He had a keen mind, a wonderful sense of humor, and a flashing smile. During the war, the Japanese had interned him as a dangerous character. While placed in solitary confinement, he sang hymns to keep up his morale. After four months of this, the Japanese released him because, as he said, "They couldn't stand my singing any longer." What a man! Upon his release, he continued to preach and work among the Japanese people.

It took a while to bring him and his nuns, the Visitation Sisters, to Yokosuka, but in the meantime my priest and Lieutenant Commander Bernie Ehrenberger (M.C.) proceeded to clean up the mess left by the Japanese Navy. Seventy-one truckloads of trash were removed from the area and twenty loads were also removed from the corridors. The squatters were evicted and the nuns busily cleaned up the interior, while workmen cleaned the cesspool filled with six years' accumulation.

Bishop Breton wanted to paint the hospital, but we had no white paint. One day, while visiting, Captain Owsley found painters busily painting the interior white.

"Where in this world did you get the white paint?"

"Not in this world," replied the bishop. "This paint came from heaven!"

The next visit, Captain Owsley noted that the basement had not been painted. He asked the Bishop, "Why didn't you paint the basement?"

"No more white paint," the bishop replied wistfully.

"What happened to heaven?"

"We lost contact!" said the bishop.

October twenty-first, the hospital was opened with a suitable ceremony. Our doctors advised them on operations and even assisted on some. They raised standards and removed the trundle beds on which the patient's wife slept, sometimes with the entire family. These families had to prepare meals in the sickroom. Doctors had little anesthetic under the Japanese regime and had used a dull hypodermic needle on as many as twenty people without sterilization. We changed all of this. John Q even established a Japanese Medical Association to raise requirements, and frequent clinics were held. All this was to return tenfold in the first days of the Korean War.

One day we received a letter from a distraught mother. Her child needed ice or he would die. Would I help? Under the Japanese Navy there was no ice in town, but the base had tremendous refrigeration plants for high altitude aircraft tests. We immediately sent ice to the hospital (not Saint Joseph's) then sent an observer to check. The ice was used by the doctors and nurses—not for the sick child!

That hospital was told, "Times have changed!"

Catholic chaplain Poznanski also brought in Father Bitter and Father Voss of the Jesuits. They volunteered to open a Boys' School in the torpedo area in Taura. The school was to be started with the sixth grade, as both sexes in Japan attended the same school only prior to this grade. Each year thereafter, they planned to add another grade until they had a grammar and a high school. They also planned to receive Jesuit missionaries, fifty at a time, for language studies. I was delighted to have this group interested in Yokosuka, as it would be a big contribution to local education and Christianity. In Japan, the school year begins in May, so it would be opened May 1947 as the Eicho School.

Poznanski then brought in six nuns from Nagano. He was a real ball of fire. These sisters were penniless and wanted to start a girls' school. They were delightful people, especially Mother Ernestina Ramalo, who was of the Handmaids of the Sacred Heart of Jesus. I have never met a more spiritual woman, nor one so charming and so dedicated to helping others. They founded the school on the base, using some excellent concrete buildings which they later bought from the Japanese government. They had twelve hundred girls who would someday be a great asset to the new Japan.

The sisters were without funds of any kind. I asked Mother Ernestina how they expected to survive. "God will provide!" she said, and she was correct.

At first they visited both my home and my office, but soon this was discontinued. She explained that they would be forgiven for relaxing their vows when destitute. Now that they were well established, they must obey those vows. I often walked through their compound, with my German police dog, Cherry, which the girls admired very much. It was a joy to see such happy children, so grateful to the sisters and to us for their education. It was also a great inspiration to be in the presence of such a noble woman as Mother Ernestina.

The school opened in 1947 and grew rapidly. The sisters were well received by our people. I did have one small request from Mother Ernestina. They needed a bell. We had a large bell cast and installed. As the belfry was close to the Officers' Club, when the bell was rung at six o'clock in the morning to awaken the sisters, it also awakened the officers, some of whom had gone to bed rather late. This did discourage late sleepers.

Our Protestant chaplain was not loafing, but he had to work under a handicap. The Catholics were centrally organized and well directed. But the Protestants were divided into many groups, which were controlled by the democratic processes of presbyteries, committees, and area organizations, which met perhaps once a year. Father Voss laughingly summed up the situation, "Protestants are protestors!"

Chaplain Ricker did get some answers. The Methodist missionaries, Mr. Thompson and his wife, were given the concrete buildings in Taura that had been used by some ex-Naval officers. They were filthy cabarets. It was a menace to my men as well as to the town. I had the buildings returned to us and assigned to these missionaries. They purchased the property and expanded the group to include a very successful Christian activity center. It started as a sewing school, then added a soap factory as well as a dormitory for bachelors. Then the Protestants, as well as the Jesuits, protested the presence of a red light district in Taura. I asked them to wait six months and see what developed. The prostitutes couldn't take it—they moved. My two missionary groups had won a victory over sin!

The Aoyama Gakuin, a Methodist engineering college,

had a formal opening on the twenty-eighth of June. This school was located on the Naval base in former Japanese barracks. It was amazing what the Methodists had accomplished in such a short time. Three big concrete buildings and several other small buildings had been assigned to them for this college. The rehabilitation of these buildings was almost finished.

The program was opened with a prayer, then "The Star Spangled Banner" was sung. At my request, the Japanese national anthem followed. The American missionary had not planned to have this song on the program, as he was under the impression that it had been prohibited by the Occupation.

A few days before, we had heard that at one of the local schools they were singing the "Internationale," the Communists' anthem, at their daily exercises. Inquiry revealed that the principal was probably a communist and had convinced the other school authorities that General MacArthur had banned the Japanese national anthem, "Kimigayo." Therefore, he said, their anthem now was the "Internationale."

The Japanese professors and the students at the Aoyama Gakuin College were visibly touched. They had more than misty eyes! I believe this was the first time their anthem had been sung since the Occupation.

Edwina had high hopes for the future of the school and the students. In my speech I said that I expected this school to bring about a better understanding between our peoples. It would be a strong influence for a lasting friendship between Japan and the United States.

The many activities in Yokosuka were in good hands, and many improvements had been accomplished both on the base and in the city. We were combining the old with the new—the best of the Japanese culture with practical, democratic Americana.

Edwina picks up the story—in Yokosuka Benny asked me to visit a public school. I was shocked by what I saw. The windowpanes in the school were all broken or missing. The faucets in the washrooms had been literally ripped out of the walls, and water leaked from the pipes. The few toilets were very unsanitary, and the odor was sickening. The long corridors were full of drafts, and not a room had been painted. Desks and chairs were terribly shabby.

The teachers and pupils were very polite and seemed pleased to see me. I was warmed by their smiles and friendship.

Next I went to the Koishi Hospital, which was much in the same shape. As we passed the operating room, a patient was carried out on a stretcher. Her bare feet were sticking out from under a shabby light cover. As the long corridor was drafty, I feared that she might catch pneumonia. Evidently, she had had her appendix removed.

When one member was taken ill, the whole family went to the hospital with the patient. The nurses were mainly janitresses, so if the husband was ill, it was usually up to the wife to take care of him. She slept in a trundle bed, while the children slept on the tatami mats. There were no central kitchens, and all of the cooking was done in each room over hibachi (small charcoal stoves). Even the laundry was done in the room on an individual basis. The wards were so crowded, and I felt great sympathy for the patients and families alike.

Though the Japanese had a supply of rubber from the Dutch East Indies, they never used rubber gloves. They knew nothing of penicillin or blood plasma. The Japanese medicine was patterned after that in Germany, and, after the Second World War started, medical publications stopped reaching Japan.

Although my visit to the Koishi Hospital had been quite depressing, I still wanted to see the jail. Much to my surprise, it was better.

Marine Captain George P. Wolf, a veteran of the Guadalcanal battle, assumed the supervision of the Japanese police department. He quickly taught these men that they were the servants, not rulers, of the people. Salaries were raised and the policemen received new uniforms of khaki and shield-type badges for their blouses and caps. Their shabby shoes were replaced with American made ones.

The police headquarters and the police boxes around the city were scrubbed out and disinfected, then painted green with white trim. The harsh treatment given some of the prisoners was stopped, and the old Navy dungarees were provided to clothe them. Showers, a tailor shop, and barber shop were innovations.

It was a strange sight to see groups of prisoners squatting

on the tatami mats inside their cells. Two women were in a separate cell. I was told that one was there for black marketing, while the other was serving a sentence for vagrancy.

Later that afternoon, Benny asked me if I had enjoyed my visits to the school, hospital, and jail.

"It was very interesting," I replied. "If I were Japanese and had to choose between one of the three places to go, I would choose the jail. It was in the best condition."

A few days later, Benny inspected the police headquarters and jail and was well pleased. The chief and the police force were very flattered.

Benny resumes: the only large department store in town was on the main street and was heavily camouflaged with black and brown paint. We had painted the administration building and the Tadodai residence white to brighten them. It was a big improvement, and we hoped that the town would follow suit. Mr. Okamoto was the first to paint his department store, and I was well pleased with his cooperation. But before it was half painted, all work was discontinued. After a week of no progress, I decided to investigate. A Japanese government official from Tokyo had ordered the improvement stopped. He told Mr. Okamoto that he had to have a permit from the Japanese government in order to paint his building. They were determined to show who was boss. I directed the painting to be completed, stating that if anyone interfered again I would have him tried by military court.

Before the war, there were few difficulties with orphans or older people. Both were absorbed by the family system. Now, orphans and old folks from families destroyed by war were destitute. Many were arriving as repatriates. They were in dire need, and created a problem new to the Japanese. The Shinsei Women's Club founded a war orphanage and an old folks' home. It was an excellent solution. On the outskirts of the city was a Navy barracks where they housed the 120 orphans. To support this activity, they made the Japanese baths into a commercial laundry and then opened a soap factory.

We gave the Women's Club salvage rights to empty beer cans. This kept the base free of litter. From cartloads of these cans, the orphanage manufactured toys, utensils, and gadgets to be sold for a few cents. The home soon became self-supporting. Mrs. Kaoru Sano, widow of a Japanese Naval officer, was the matron in charge.

Raincoats made from fire balloons.

Ensign Hahne dispatching a load of empty beer cans from the E.M. Club to be made into toys.

I was shocked by the huge accumulation of waste paper on the base. The Japanese never threw anything away. Blueprints filled the rooms. Apparently they had retained all construction plans for all ships built since opening of the yard. As there was an old paper mill on the base, we directed the Japanese to make it operative and to use this scrap paper. "What kind of paper do you want?" "Toilet paper!" Within a week we were swamped with it. "Make wrapping paper." Again we had to stop the mill. So we gave the plant to the Japanese, provided they would use our scrap paper first. Thus a new industry was born in Yokosuka.

My civil affairs officer encouraged the formation of a chamber of commerce. Mr. Kay Sunoda was the head, and did much to bring industries to the city, as also did the Industrial Club. Industries were new to Yokosuka. The furniture factory was one project, as was a silk industry and several spinning mills for cotton.

On Tokyo Bay shoreline, the Japanese grew seaweed as a crop. It is now popular here, on Japanese hors d'oeuvres. One would see the harvesters wading between the stakes to pick the leaves, which would be dried and marketed. But ships, passing up and down the channel, would pump residue oil into the Bay, killing this vegetation. Normally, it would have required a long time to enact environmental laws and enforce them, especially in view of the divided responsibility between the Occupation and the Japanese government. I was asked if I could stop this. Easy—I wired to the Hydrographic Office in Washington a local notice to mariners, stating, "Pumping of bilges in Tokyo Bay is a $50 fine." It was broadcasted to all ships. There was no more oil.

I now began to see the possibilities of building Yokosuka into a prosperous town. But I needed an approved plan within which I could work. Therefore, I drew up a brief and general plan for the "Re-Industrialization of Yokosuka." I personally carried it to General Marquat, Head of the Economic & Scientific Section of SCAP. He directed me to his young civilian OPA economist, who hurriedly read it and then announced, "You are to destroy Yokosuka! You are to move the people out of that town!"

He might not have known it, but this was just what the Communists wanted. I replied, "I have no such orders, and I don't believe that is the policy. I am going to see General MacArthur." That did it. He recommended approval to General Marquat.

I filed my plan with a feeling that I was now on firm ground. Under this shelter we started the "Miracle of Yokosuka."

Chapter IV

THE NAVAL BASE

The waters surrounding the base were cluttered with wrecks; some were sunk by bombs and others by scuttling at the end of the war. It was necessary to remove them, in order to make the harbors and coves accessible. Under our supervision, the Japanese diligently accomplished this during the first three years with no urging on my part. The immensity of this task is best judged by two of our weekly progress reports, as follows:

Interim report of harbor clearance X six wrecks to be salvaged from Nagaura Ko and six from Yokosuka repair basin includes one old German submarine outer hull only and one Japanese destroyer broken X above salvage work now estimated to be completed September 1947 X Green Bay now under survey to determine the amount of salvage operations in that area X total wrecks removed to date two seven three.

and

Report Harbor Clearance X Nagura Ko cleared with exception repairing or scrapping of some vessels once salvaged X four sunken wrecks remain in Yokosuka Ko, one destroyer cut into twelve 150 ton pieces, one bucket dredge cut into six 150 ton pieces, one cable ship cut into seven 150 ton pieces, one wooden patrol boat X two pieces of cable ship have been lifted X work may not be completed until end of current year due floating crane going into availability for complete engine overhaul X total wrecks removed to date three six six.

In cranes, we were wealthy, though all were in sad condition. None could lift its rated capacity. The Japanese mechanics had not repaired them since 1943. Now they promptly put them into excellent condition. Inside our buildings, we had seventy-eight cranes, three of which lifted 100 tons each. There were thirty railroad cranes, two of which could also lift 100 tons each. We had six stationary cranes, one of which could lift 350 tons! There were an additional thirteen on our shipways, and four floating cranes, two of which were self-propelled. Many Americans had urged the destruction of this vast wealth.

The base had six dry docks. One, which was 1120 feet long, was capable of docking any ship in our Navy. The pump rooms were flooding, and in the matter of a few months, the machinery would be ruined. We soon put them into operating condition. What a prize for any navy! Again, there were some who had advocated blowing them up!

There were three building ways, which we would not need. We cleared them of the rubble and miniature submarines, and placed them in reserve. There were tons of welding rods stored on these ways, but as the rods did not meet our standards, they could not be used.

When the Korean War commenced, all of this salvaged equipment was of great value in the support of our forces afloat.

Our repair officer's job was to transform this tremendous wealth of machines and the almost unlimited supply of labor into a department capable of repairing small craft and making voyage repairs to visiting ships. As ComServPac—Commander Service Force Pacific increased our mission, we would stay one jump ahead, until we were finally repairing major ships, except for "restricted" repairs. The work forces became intensely loyal to the base, and the workingmen took pride in their jobs. An inspecting officer remarked that stateside labor would raise an objection to us doing so much. They never did. I think they saw the common sense in our actions, as well as the need for developing our capabilities. They also knew that there was just so much money for repairs, and that we were making it all available to them. And Comdr. Danielski, followed by Lieutenant Commander Sly, Commander Day, and finally Captain Burzynski all played big parts in keeping the forces afloat happy.

One of our policies was very welcome to the visiting ships. A group of 100 unskilled Japanese laborers, under a native crew boss, reported to each ship for any job, such as scraping the bottom or painting the ship. They also chipped bilges and cleaned fuel tanks. I told each skipper that all we asked in return was that they feed them a good noon meal! The Japanese men were splendid workers, but were hungry.

The base was littered with 241 completed or partially completed two-man and three-man submarines. The first were suicide submarines and the latter were midget submarines. Several three-man subs had been towed to Pearl Harbor and were involved in the sneak attack. These hulls had to be scrapped. I had the last one, a cutaway model of the three-man sub, mounted near the gate as a relic of the late war. As a display it was of much interest to visitors.

We closed 1200 entrances to the many caves on the base. They were being used as hideouts, making petty thieving very convenient. At first we were unhappy about the numerous caves—reported to be twenty-eight miles overall. But should war occur, they would be invaluable. We did use some for the storage of ammunition after lining them with cement. The headquarters cave, just in the rear of the Administration Building, had been used by the Japanese for overall command of air defense. It could be used by General MacArthur should the bombs start falling again. Three officers from SCAP did inspect it, after it was made habitable. Until needed, I used it as a "tourist" attraction, and later we grew mushrooms in it.

Construction of this cave was started in the fall of 1943. It was tunnelled out of sandstone with seventy feet of rock overhead and was part of a series of many tunnels connected by stairs. Some were lined with concrete and some with cedar, or fiber board. A few were not lined at all. It not only contained offices, but also bunks, messing facilities, and combat control rooms. It even had a room for "consoling women."

The main room of the cave was 200 feet by 60 feet by 40 feet. The air defense of the Yokosuka District, which included central and southern Honshu, and a complete communication center were housed in it.

In November 1946, there were 241 wooden buildings still standing in the base proper—that is, on the Yokosuka Peninsula alone.

Our Secretary of Defense inspects the former Japanese headquarters cave.

We were having an average of three fires a day. Japanese workmen would hide out in unused "wooden buildings" to keep warm and heat their tea. They built fires in the middle of the wood floors, forgetting sometimes to cool the ashes. These abandoned buildings and shacks, being both fire and health hazards, had to be removed. Women laborers were good at this, and the people had need of the firewood.

We were using 139 concrete and structural steel buildings, totaling 5.4 million square feet, with 118 in reserve. In the other areas under our jurisdiction were hundreds of other buildings.

There were three power plants on the base. The steam plant had two 5000 kilowatt generators. This plant was made ready for any emergency and we fully stocked our coal storage. In the caves were two diesel generators, each having a capacity of 1750 kilowatts, which were released for reparations, to be shipped to China.

Under the Occupation all unused buildings and materials were to be returned to the Japanese for their use. There had been waste and improper supervision during the first half year. I had to reform our processing and tie strings to our approvals. We worked out a viable procedure for the return of these unused buildings and materials. The Japanese would initiate a request for a building or certain material, often at our suggestion. The request would be considered, and, if approved, a letter was prepared in our office. The Japanese would then process it through their own channels. The Japanese government would establish a cost which was to our satisfaction. When the letter came to us, it would be promptly approved. This not only saved time, but also reduced misunderstandings. In addition, we also checked a number of the projects after six months to ensure that there was no fraud.

On the Miura Peninsula, south of Yokosuka, was a storage for old Naval guns which had been removed from ships long demolished. The Japanese used many ex-Naval guns for coastal defense. Even the guns from the historical monument, the battleship *Mikasa*, Tojo's flagship, had been removed for this purpose. On the base we had nine 18.1-inch guns for replacements in the *Yamato* and the *Musashi*, the largest battleships in the world. These huge guns were wire wound.

We had the Japanese cut them with torches. The wire, under great tension, sprang open like the petals of a flower.

The tools to make these guns had been made in Germany and were housed in Kure. These included a 118-foot horizontal lathe and boring machine. To make the roller paths of a turret, a five-storied high vertical milling machine was needed. These roller paths were made in six sectors which were welded together and milled on this milling machine into a highly accurate circle. In Kure, during the war, the workmen who ran these machines had been confined for secrecy. Now the Army was shipping one of two 30,000-ton hydraulic presses from the Yokohama area to China. I asked for it, but was too late. The bridges and roads had to be strengthened, for we were to load it from our base at Taura. This press was of no value to the Chinese, but they did want the wood crating! As the Army wouldn't let me have it, I asked for the one in Kure, hoping to save it for the free world. Two weeks later, the Army blew it up!

In the Oppama area, there were thirteen wind tunnels. These we demolished, but salvaged the machinery. There was one mach 1.1 for testing air models at greater speed than sound. It was one or two stories high and about fifty feet by fifty feet. This was ordered destroyed. Previously, the War Department had ordered several cyclotrons which were of no military value demolished. This order came in spite of strong recommendations from some scientists to save them for scientific purposes. It caused quite a furor. Being forewarned, I saved our mach 1.1 by boxing it in with wood walls. The Japanese were given the large concrete building in which it was situated for use as a cotton mill. About a year later, the Air Force called me on the phone. They were in difficulties as they needed a mach 1 wind tunnel to send to the United States for instructional purposes in some college. The one held by the Air Force in Japan had been demolished so effectively that not one part was left. Did I have a few pieces left for shipment? No. I didn't have any pieces, but I did have my entire unit intact except for some demolished gauges. They could have this with our blessing.

My long experience as a navigator paid off when it came to naming points and places on the base. The Japanese names were unsatisfactory, so we marked a chart with our selection of names and sent it into the hydrographic office. One hill was named Edwina Hill at the insistence of my officers. It made my wife very happy. The next charts carried these names instead of the former Japanese designations.

This action was more successful than a similar attempt made in a joint chief of staff paper during the war to standardize the names of islands and bodies of water in the South Pacific. This paper was routed, not to the hydrographic office, but to the Department of the Interior, which controlled the naming of geographical places. It stayed there until the end of the war.

The yacht club was flourishing, thanks to Margaret Walker. She was the founder, the promoter, and the first commodore. Margaret had come in from Kamakura to visit the Hovatters. She and Doris Hovatter were the only women to attend the organization meeting for the yacht club. I asked for volunteers, and soon got more than I could have hoped. Before Margaret knew what was happening, she was elected to the job.

Building the yacht club was no easy task. We converted a large wooden building which the Japanese Navy had used to train for identification of ships and aircraft. The high overhead allowed small boats to be housed without unshipping their masts. It was also conveniently located for boats moored in a small harbor, while being most inconvenient for any other activity. This was the only use which I could imagine for such an odd building in such a poor location. Here, Margaret was the answer. She was always game to try something new—such as operating a bulldozer or sailing boats. She had ability, courage, and stamina. She was our lucky charm.

The Japanese workmen had never seen a woman with so much drive. They were amazed at her skill in handling a bulldozer. These men soon had an entirely new view of womankind. And, believe me, they produced under her supervision. Margaret was a good scrounger too. The origin of many of the materials obtained was doubtful. We used to call this a "midnight requisition." No paperwork—just results. When Margaret was making a turn in her bulldozer, it was good judgment to give her a wide berth.

The sailing of small craft was popular with all hands,

and especially with me. I was a registered Star boat measurer. This was the forerunner of our small boat industry in Yokosuka, which built yachts up to fifty-four feet. Today, thanks to Margaret Walker's spadework, the yacht club is still active.

The day came for the Marine fighter, Group 31, to depart. On January fifteenth, they left the air station and landing strip at Oppama vacant. During an inspection of the deserted air base, I found five thousand barrels of av gas abandoned. It was undoubtedly overage, and therefore too risky to use in planes. But it was an answer to our prayers. Our gasoline was Japanese, less than seventy-two octane. At the end of the war the Japanese used a small quantity of high test gasoline to get their planes into the air, then switched to low octane. This was made from pine tree stumps. Scattered over the countryside were many uprooted pine stumps, awaiting distillation into seventy-two octane gasoline.

Low octane gas was not suitable for our motors, but was all we had. We could mix this 110 octane av gas, gallon for gallon with the Japanese gasoline and obtain an excellent fuel, charging the same price. Our gas station soon became popular with the Army as well as the Navy. Uncle Sam got $75,000 salvage out of that abandoned gasoline!

In Oppama, I also found several thousand drums of napalm. This, mixed with gasoline, was used in the fire bombs and flame throwers which were so successful in the war. As we had no further use for it in Japan, we reported it to Washington and were ordered to ship it home. It evidently had salvage value.

The Marine Air Group 31 had left Japan and the Army wanted the Oppama Air Field, which was restricted in its approach, as well as on takeoffs. They wanted it for the storage of thousands of motor vehicles which were to be rehabilitated by the Army in the Oppama area. We would retain many of the buildings, later to be used by our seaplanes. I insisted that, in exchange, the Army turn over to us the Atsugi air Field, which they had previously abandoned. There we had an important radio transmitting station. We had released our field at Kisarazu and were now to give up the one at Oppama. I wanted a field, should our aviators need it in the future.

The Army and Navy used the "unit" system during the

war. We ordered stores by the unit. Now that war was over, the unit system was still being used by the Occupation for the PX (gift shop). The contents of a unit were all identical. It depended on what was available, and on what the merchants wanted moved. I looked over the PX and found that the goods displayed there were mostly junk. It was so bad that I challenged the officer in charge. He maintained that he had nothing to do with the selection of items. He explained that he was forced to receive stores from the Army in units, each unit being a cubic yard box of assorted items, most of which he couldn't sell. His storeroom was filled with old brown ashtrays, pipes, cigars, small pieces of silk, cheap handbags, etc. For a few desirable items we had to store quantities of unsaleable items.

"No more units! You order what you want and nothing else. If necessary, we go to Hong Kong and buy our own supplies."

We went to Hong Kong!

We soon had the best PX in Japan. Even the generals bought from us, as did Mrs. MacArthur. We had Chinese rugs, furniture, camphor wood chests, ivories, as well as imported woolens.

I was allergic to "lines." If five people were waiting at a counter, I expected the officer in charge to take action to move that line. We used dependent wives as clerks and they were excellent.

Another unit system was the liquor unit. The Navy handled ours, which was better than that of the Army, who wisely bought from us. But we weren't happy. For a case of good Scotch or bourbon you had to order so many of "cooking whiskey." In every unit we had so much Sunset gin and other unheard of brands that we knew we were being taken. We had to insure also each shipment with a company selected by the Navy in Hawaii. Captain Bill Kirten, my chief staff officer, was quite knowledgeable, and I took his advice. No more "tie-ins"—no more insurance. Our losses were nil, so why pay five thousand dollars to cover them?

The supply officer, in Oakland, said he would not fill our order (with no tie-ins!), so we bought from Hong Kong— cheaper and better. They soon found that the war was over and tie-ins were discontinued.

For meat we had also to buy by the unit. The result was

a ton of roasts and a ton of hamburger. When the Army found that they could buy direct from Argentina, they thoughtfully invited us to share with them. Having a tremendous cold storage capacity, we ordered a half a shipload, at twenty-seven cents a pound! While it was en route, the Army became scared. Someone in the States cried "hoof and mouth" beef, so they asked us to take it all. Averaging the price and selling it mixed, we did a land office business in roasts and steaks. But we still had a plentiful supply of hamburger.

An early directive forbade us to eat Japanese food or feed the Japanese people. These were good restrictions, for we were not to rob them, nor allow a black market to develop for our food. But conditions had changed. I decided to use the excess hamburger to make the EM Club more attractive to sailors and their girls. We opened a hamburger and soft drink counter where a sailor could treat his dance partner to a luscious hamburger and Coke, all for a reasonable price. Soon, we rid ourselves of the excess hamburger, and made the club a big attraction for the better type of girls.

As our storerooms were filled with the unsalable leftovers from the Army's PX units, we gave them away for Christmas presents. Each man received a handbag for Christmas. It was filled with odds and ends, a safety razor and lotion, cigars, plug tobacco and a pipe, as well as ashtrays and many similar undesirable items. We authorized a sailor to give these to his Japanese friends, who found them of great use. That cleaned our shelves and our books, and spread goodwill far and wide.

The Navy Department had directed me to send to Washington all of the profits from our stores. They would then return to us what they thought we needed. Someone must have really worked hard to think up such a confusing and roundabout system! I sent them two hundred thousand dollars which had been made by the first men of the Occupation and told them that unless I received further orders, the money made from then on would be used on the base where it was needed far more than at home. No answer was received and we sent no more funds to support the recreation of those at home. It proved a good decision, as we used our profits to make the base a most attractive place for the men and their families, as well as for the forces afloat. Washington also wanted us to charge between 14 and 15 percent profit per item in our stores. This was unreasonable, and we didn't have the bookkeepers. We averaged but 4 percent and made plenty of money so I did not change the rate. All this ended after I was relieved, and prices went up.

Being a "bull" captain had advantages. Sometimes I would have to resort to another defense. I would be told, "Benny, you can't do that!" If from a Naval officer, my answer was, "I come under MacArthur!" If an Army officer made the challenge, I replied, "I'm in the Navy!" I couldn't lose.

We stored black oil in the ex-Japanese tank farm on the Azuma Island near the base. During the war the Japanese had spread the rumor that poisonous snakes infested the island, scaring off trespassers. On close examination, we found none. On Azuma Island, we had excellent magazines and torpedo storage, as well as oil tanks. Many large and long lines from the tanks ran under the bay to the distant battleship mooring buoys in deeper water off Yokohama. We closed the cutoff valves. But there was a black market in oil. We weren't losing any from our tanks. Where did it come from? We finally found out. The boats were draining the huge pipe lines under the bay—probably thousands of barrels had been left in them.

Our refrigeration storage was located in Taura, which is adjacent to Azuma Island, just across the inner harbor from the base proper. We had so much space that we released some of the buildings to the whaling industry. They used every bit of the whale to feed the Japanese people. Though invited to all of their functions, I was too busy to worry about such a successful operation. Commander Higgins attended in my place.

Henry Walker replaced four inoperative phones on my desk with one phone that worked. He had to run a new cable to Tokyo to do it. Also, he installed all new switchboards in the telephone exchange. Then he ran an underground gas-filled cable to the dependent housing. The Japanese telephone system had been unbelievably bad.

Throughout the base there were festoons of wire from innumerable short telephone poles—and none of the wires was being used. Some hung so low as to be a menace at night, catching the unwary under the chin. The whole was unsightly. Father Voss needed money to renovate the old buildings of his Eicho High School. I gave him the concession for removing all wire above ground. The base was greatly improved, and the Japanese received a good supply of salvaged copper. But, always, somebody doesn't get the word. Our dependent housing telephones went dead. The underground cable had been cut by Father Voss' Japanese. They had run out of above-ground wire, and so, on their own, dug up our new gas-filled cable to the dependents.

The cable to Totsuka, our radio station, was cut by thieves. It was soon repaired and the city, being greatly embarrassed, saw to it that it never happened again.

The public works officer used every bit of salvaged asphalt that the LSTs (Landing Ship Tank) could load out of our abandoned base in Okinawa. The drums were ruptured in the tropics, and melted asphalt ran over the decks and had to be chipped out on arrival in our colder climate. There was an asphalt plant on base that we put into operating condition. Ensign Ludovici put in the first road, from the Officers' Club to the Administration Building, along the new wire fence. It was such an improvement that we named it Ludovici Lane—just an ensign, but worthy of the recognition.

My corner on the coal market was paying off. We had anticipated the shortage of coal, as the Korean forced-labor was abandoning the Kyushu mines. Our large storage area had been depleted. Without coal, our power plant would be of no use in case of an emergency. Thus, all the first summer, when nobody wanted coal, we were able to stockpile it. Now that winter had come, coal was scarce and many homes were cold. We had coal and willingly shared it with others. I had remembered my Boy Scout motto—Be prepared!

In Tokyo, Admiral Griffin and his wife were enjoying Christmas at home when their houseboy entered.

"Madame, I know today is your happy day and I must tell you nothing that will make you sad. But tomorrow I must tell you—there is no coal!"

That day, we had several tons delivered to their home, the Fujiyama Palace.

Admiral Francis Denebrink, ComServPac, inspected the

base. He was a longtime friend of mine. In fact, he had recommended me for this command. Now he told us that we were to become an operating base. This was in recognition of our work in Yokosuka. Our previous mission had never been spelled out, and we had enlarged our ability until it was now being recognized. We were happy to be so designated, and were going to continue to grow. We had the largest dry dock, and many machine shops capable of building or repairing the largest ships. Our work force was unlimited, both in size and in ability. Our Japanese workmen were loyal and capable. They were proud of the "can do" spirit.

Our Navy had taken excellent inventories of machines and buildings, but the only inventory of materials and stores was that taken by the Japanese. We found it highly inaccurate. When they burned their files before the surrender, it became a matter of memory of the individual storekeeper. No one knew what or where. I insisted another inventory be taken. It didn't even resemble the first. So I ordered another, and found that I would never get a reliable one.

It was hopeless. Even during the war they didn't know what they had. In addition, they evidently never threw away old bottles or old shoes. Judging from what I saw, it was the world's worst supply system.

On February 12, 1947 I wrote my friend, Roland Smoot:

Capt. R. N. Smoot, USN
Bureau of Naval Personnel
Washington 25, D. C.

Dear Roland—

As you probably have heard, this Base has been accumulating additional missions and at the same time losing personnel. This is not unexpected. As time goes on and we consolidate, we become more efficient. It takes fewer men to do the job. The latest is that we are to handle all logistic afloat as well as ashore, including repairs. We welcome the opportunity to work with the Japanese and use their equipment for our support. This all adds up to a big saving in forces afloat—29 officers, 780 men, one repair ship, and one LST spare-part ship.

This Base has changed considerably. We now have 125 families living on the Base. Our men are in two excellent fire proof, steam heated barracks and the Marines in another. We have an efficient supply set up, a splendid hospital, and sufficient recreation and athletic facilities to make this one of the most compact and desirable stations.

We have been getting orders transferring officers with dependents to distant duties. Shipley and Carlson are cases in point. Both have lately had their wives transported to Japan. It appears desirable (at least in future cases) and economical to move those without dependents instead of those with them. I believe consideration should be given to this point.

Also a CPO, Knight had his wife brought out and had agreed to stay one year. Six months thereafter he received orders to shore duty. This looks like a waste of transportation.

We should furnish you with this additional information. Would the enclosed list of dependents be of value?

Edwina and I are having an enjoyable stay out here. The Army is most cooperative and considerate. We find them tops. The social life is equal to that at Annapolis with many parties and outstanding guests. The "visiting firemen" from the States keep us informed on the price of butter and hamburger at home, which makes us more contented with our lot. Of course the lack of rank makes the job more difficult for me with the Japanese and the Army. I had expected a spot and had hoped for selection, but failing in both the four stripes will have to bear up under the strain.

Sincerely,
Benny

I had failed in selection to the rank of rear admiral. Usually, after being skipped by the selection board, an officer requests a change of duty, hoping for a different judgment by a new board, a year later. My past record was excellent and the present assignment was important. General MacArthur had warned me, "Serving under my command is the kiss of death." Yet, to serve under him was a great inspiration, and in Japan, we were making history. Anywhere else would be dull and less productive in comparison. Many of the generals of the Occupation, including General Eichelberger and General Ned Almond, were upset over the selection board's decision and had written letters. I had many friends, and was content in this. Promotion was secondary to my job.

In another letter to Captain R. N. Smoot:

At present everyone is happy. They are working hard and long, but that is what keeps them from trouble. The dependent's housing is excellent. We lead the Army because of our better layout and planning. Any man (third pay grade and above) or officer who wants to bring his wife out may do so as there are plenty of houses and servants. Any person reporting, who desires to accompany his wife out here should request of Com-NavFe, information Com Flt Act Yokosuka, permission to bring his dependents. We say yes on the house and ComNavFe authorizes the transportation. This place should make a good recruiting story.

Our Repair Unit of 9 officers, 68 men and 576 expert Japanese will be operating 15 April. We have taken over all logistics ashore and afloat except tanker control which is still hanging in the bight. It must be settled by 1 May as the U.S.S. Frontier leaves for the States. This includes the disposition of M.I.O. #10.

I have discussed with Admiral Griffin my status. He advises staying out here until after the next Selection Board in November. I am happy here and very busy. It would be to the interest of the Occupation (and the Navy) to keep the C.O. here for two years. Stability in officers connected with military government is also desirable. It takes six months to acquire knowledge of the Japanese and their ways and also the high level contacts with the Army is a "must."

Sincerely,
Benny Decker

On the twenty-ninth of March, I wrote to Major General Almond requesting a "procurement demand" (P.D.) as we were short of personnel to accomplish some repairs:

1. The Navy has done its best to carry out SCAP and 8th Army directives and was careful not to abuse the privilege of P.D.'s. We realize, however, that there have been abuses by others, that forced a change in the procedure and general closing down on P.D.'s. However, we feel that the pendulum has swung to the other side and that now we are too much on the defensive.

2. We have a number of important P.D.'s in the mill. Three of them are for the renovation of Japanese buildings for the use of our Repair Base. If the holes in the roof (caused by strafing) and the glass windows are not repaired, our U.S. machinery will be damaged. Without the electric wiring our repair work cannot be accomplished, and with the present dirt decks our work will be little better than that of the former Japanese Navy.

3. The three afore mentioned Repair P.D.'s were submitted on 7 February 1947. These were hand carried by one of my officers through all the steps, and all means available were used to expedite these P.D.'s. After almost two months the repairs have yet to be started!

Respectfully,
B. W. Decker

As it rains frequently in Japan, the dirt floors in the buildings were always muddy. The wind whistled through the broken windows and those buildings were not only unfit for use, but hazardous to health and safety.

On April the twelfth, General Almond wrote the following answer to our Procurement Demand:

. . . On the construction project to which Captain Decker makes special reference, a project which amounted to considerable. . . The project reached G-4 from the Chief Engineer without there being any evidence of consideration or recommendation by ComNavFe. The C & P Division of the G-4 office was directed to secure the comments of ComNavFe with respect to the project. It was intended that this be done informally; however, instead the division functioned the paper back to the Chief Engineer's to obtain such comments from ComNavFe by indorsement. General Casey quite appropriately phoned G-4 and asked if it would be agreeable to this office if he had Captain Dunning of Admiral Griffin's office confer with the Chief Engineer's office on the project and indicate his concurrence thereon by his initial. General Casey was informed that this would be entirely adequate. . . .

Morale on the base was dependent on a number of things. One was the presence of dependents. Early in 1946, I planned to have all housed on the base. This would require four hundred houses or apartments. We could foresee that housing in Kamakura would not remain for long. The Japanese would be unhappy if we continued to occupy their homes for any duration. After modifying some concrete barracks into apartments, and having the Japanese build some small homes, we had to resort to other means, as the Army was restricting procurement demands on the Japanese.

Our policy was to authorize housing even though none was available at the time. This allowed our dependents to accompany their husbands, saving about six months. When they arrived, if no house was available, we would double up. Or if previously agreed to, we housed them in temporary rooms with communal baths and general mess for their meals. No doubt, in comparing our delays with those of the Army, we were at an advantage. But this was only because the Army's size made a similar reduction in the time interval impossible. Our men and officers would supervise the preparation of their new homes, sometimes reducing the vacancy to zero! The beds would be warm when the new occupants moved in.

We had to stand by our guns to defend our Navy personnel, who had shorter tours of shore duty than the Army, and who had looked forward to this shore duty after years of sea duty. The Army generals were willing to give us as much of a break as we could justify.

When I arrived in Yokosuka I found that the local authorities had confiscated all swords as directed by the authorities in Tokyo. These swords were turned over to me and were most interesting. There were 300 of them. The Occupation directed that all of museum worth should be sent to SCAP in Tokyo, which I did, The remainder, some 280 swords, were then distributed to commanding officers who visited Yokosuka. I wrote to my wife, before she left for Japan:

I was invited to Kamakura to see how the ceremonial swords are made. It was most interesting. I didn't expect to see such a gathering of people. Four ex-Japanese Admirals and one Navy Captain, plus all kinds of businessmen were there. We had a Ceremonial Tea. Then, they told me how the swords are made. At the peak of the war, they were making thirty thousand swords per year. At the end, they had eight thousand being manufactured. So as not to throw men out of work, until they could find other employment, General MacArthur gave permission to finish the swords for G.I. souvenirs.

The Japanese sword is a marvel of workmanship. Over five hundred years ago they made swords as they do now. It is a combination of an iron back and a steel cutting edge. The iron keeps it from shattering while the steel maintains a hard, sharp edge. This was what we learned only one hundred years ago in the making of the armor. Also, the sword is laminated. Again we learned that this made strength about seventy-five years ago.

A small block of pure iron, red hot, is refolded about sixteen times, rapidly reaching one hundred thousand laminations, and is welded into a straight iron blade. The back is covered with a protective paste, grey in color, and the edge is left exposed. The straight blade is now heated by a cutting motion in a bed of burning charcoal. Thus, the edge only becomes steel. It is then, with a quick, expert blow, cut into a pan of water. The exposed steel becomes highly tempered and the back remains soft iron. The blade, because of the differences in the coefficient of expansion and contraction of iron and steel, is now a gracefully curved sword. The edge shows a design left by the paste, between iron and steel.

This is a "signature" identifying the maker. Also, in the shaft of the sword blade is the stamped name of the maker. The blade is then sharpened and polished and fitted with sword "furniture," a case, and a dress scabard with suitable "mon" (crest).

It takes great skill not only to make but also to use a sword. The Shinto Priests make the swords, and in this case one demonstrated its use. With feet well apart, he slowly raised the sword with both hands. Then with a leap up and a shout to contract his chest muscles, he swiftly brought the sword down with excellent coordination and follow-through. He chopped through two bundles of bamboo (which represent two human necks) at a stroke, and chopped a three-inch bamboo pole clean through. He was excellent—the blade perfect. But I thought it poor taste, so I refused to try my hand. The two Japanese ex-admirals had their fun. I wonder, if they saw anything incongruous in admirals, in civilian clothes, defeated and disarmed, playing at beheading people. They ruined the sword!

Chapter V

THE GOOD SAMARITAN

On arrival in Japan I called on the General. In Japan, the General was MacArthur! As Supreme Commander of the Allied Powers, he lived in the Embassy and had his office in the Dai Ichi Building. There I found him always accessible. We had many pleasant talks. But before I met him, I had some doubts. In the Solomons, I was on Halsey's team, and we strongly resented the Southwest Pacific communiques in which MacArthur's name was bandied about. We felt that his air force, under General Kenney, hadn't cooperated with us. But as I look back, I now think that much of this feeling was inspired by those who wished to destroy this great man. Politics, in and out of the services, could be blamed for much of it. I was naive then, but now I recognize the sly innuendo which, if repeated many times, destroys the reputations of many good Americans. When I was ordered to Japan to serve under General MacArthur, I asked myself the question, "Why?" I left my first meeting with him thoroughly sold. My attitude changed completely, and to this day I recognize General MacArthur as the greatest American of our time.

The General never gave me an order. These would be transmitted through my naval chain of command. His directives were complete guides, and any success we enjoyed in Yokosuka was due to his great leadership and wisdom of administration.

Upon her surrender, Japan was left defenseless. Washington had ordered the immediate release of "all political prisoners," thus freeing many communists and bringing additional members in from Korea. They created turmoil and unrest until General MacArthur stopped them. The Russians had seized the Habomae Islands just northeast of Hokkaido. Next, they were planning to land a division of troops on Hokkaido.

I was told by a general on the SCAP staff that General Derevyanko had informed General MacArthur that he was bringing in a division of the Russian Army. General MacArthur thanked him and stated "when they arrive have them report to me and I'll assign them an area." Whereupon General Derevyanko replied that no Russian troops could serve under a foreign commander. Thus, General MacArthur prevented the Russians from seizing Hokkaido.

I asked the General where he planned on stationing the Russians, if they reported to him. He answered, "Shikoko!" This is an island of farms, the least of the four main islands. The Russians would have been isolated.

With the Russians taking over Hokkaido they would outflank Okinawa, Formosa, and the Philippines. And Russia would not stop there—communism is never satisfied, never contented, but always aggressive.

The transformation of Japan from a violent enemy into a

friendly ally was an unprecedented accomplishment. Our benevolent Occupation of Japan was truly unique in history. Free of revenge or retribution, the United States not only poured hundreds of millions of dollars into the reconstruction of Japan, but also furnished expert assistance to guide that battered nation into postwar affluence.

Instead of stomping in as a conqueror, General MacArthur arrived unarmed and unescorted at Atsugi airfield, the former Kamikaze base. With his natural poise and regal bearing in his unpretentious, war-weary khaki uniform, General MacArthur impressed them. He never doubted the wisdom of placing his trust and his life in the hands of the Japanese. The conqueror became the trusted friend. Winston Churchill said that this was the greatest accomplishment of any commander in the war!

The General understood the Japanese. No other man could have handled the situation so well. Commodore Matthew Calbraith Perry, when he opened the doors to Japan in 1853, had held himself aloof and insisted on rigid protocol in all dealings with the Japanese. The General did the same. His tall, imposing figure was both handsome and distinguished, and held great charm. Though older, by many years, than his generals, admirals, and advisors, he was easy to talk to. He never talked "down" to his subordinates. Although his age and terrific work schedule forced him to conserve his energy, he usually worked late and was always busy. His social life was limited to a luncheon from 1:30 to 3:00, after which he would take a siesta.

I thought him shy with strangers. With people he knew and trusted, he would talk fluently on a large range of subjects. I enjoyed my visits to his office, and the luncheons to which I was invited. I never felt uncomfortable in his presence. Although a busy man, he always had time to answer my questions. On one of my first calls, I asked him about the invasion of Japan. In the Navy Department, I had participated in the planning of Olympic and Coronet. His reply was candid and most interesting. Here is my letter concerning his discussion. I sent it to my former skipper, the wartime commander of the amphibious forces in the Pacific, Admiral Turner.

Admiral R. K. Turner
General Board
Navy Department
Washington, D. C.

Dear Admiral,

Two of your old friends have asked me to convey to you their best wishes. I called on General MacArthur. He was most pleasant and spoke of you in glowing terms, closing his remarks with a request that I send you his best wishes. I told him of your present duties and good health.

The General spoke at some length about the invasion of Japan. He had been informed of the weather conditions on the planned D days and had his intelligence officers report on the Japanese troop disposition.

His opinion is that the invasion of Kyushu would have been accomplished with little loss of life and would have moved along smoothly until D plus 18 when the Kyushu volcano blew its top. After that all movements would have stopped. He stated all large units of Japanese troops were being brought into positions to oppose a Kanto Plain landing. Therefore, there would have been little opposition in Kyushu.

The Kanto Plain operation as planned by JCS—Joint Chiefs of Staff would have been disastrous, for 23 Japanese divisions were within 48 hours of the area, and also the weather on the proposed D day was very bad, which would have destroyed our boats, making the landing south of Chosi. He stated that he had not made any final plans but that he had made general plans for a landing well north of the Kanto Plain, then coming south, while a smaller force in reserve in Sagami Wan, acted as a threat, to keep the Japanese divisions pinned in that area.

Another former friend sent you his regards. He is ex-captain Yokoyama whom you knew in 1939 on our visit to Japan and again in 1941 in Washington. He is well and not in jail! Mrs. Yokoyama and his three daughters and his Tokyo house all came through without harm. The eldest daughter was married last week in Tokyo. Yokoyama has a position with the Second Demobilization Bureau in Tokyo where he is number 2.

Please give my best regards to Mrs. Turner and with best wishes to you.

As ever,
/s/Benny
B. W. DECKER

25 June 1946

Dear Benny,

Thank you very much indeed for your letter of 13 June, which arrived yesterday. It is very pleasant indeed to receive the kind wishes of General MacArthur, and to know that he took the time to talk to you about our projected operations for invasion of Japan.

That was an exceedingly interesting point that he made about the interference from the Kyushu eruption which occurred on our intended D plus 18. However, probably we could have found some way to have overcome the difficulties. I agree with him, and have told many people, that I believe the Kyushu invasion could have been made with smaller loss, certainly on the percentage scale, than we had during the Okinawa operation. The whole plan looked good, and preparations were going forward extremely well.

His remarks about the Kanto Plain operation are also very interesting, and I thoroughly agree with him as to the probable difficulties. Undoubtedly, there would have been a very strong troop defense by the Japanese. In addition, I was always very chary about the possibilities of ensuring continued operations across the beaches during the spring of the year. The scheme we had in mind seemed to be about the best that we could think up at the time, but I always expected that a better one would be developed, particularly because General MacArthur was very clearsighted in his appreciation of the difficulties.

If you see General MacArthur again, please give

him my very best wishes and thanks for his thoughtful message.

Thanks also for the news about Yokoyama. I am glad he is not in jail! I saw him across the deck of the MISSOURI during the surrender ceremonies and he looked very sad. However, I always liked him, and thought very highly of his family. If you see him, please give him remembrances.

Thanks ever so much for your letter, and your kindness in sending it. I imagine your duty has a lot of interest in it; you now have been away from home duty for such a long period.

Very best regards to you and to your family.

Very sincerely,
Kelly Turner

The General and Mrs. MacArthur invited Mrs. Decker and me to luncheon many times. The routine was easy to follow. Upon their arrival, the guests would be cordially greeted by Mrs. MacArthur, who was a model hostess. Fifteen minutes later, the General would enter the room. After shaking hands with each person and saying a friendly word, he would lead the female guest of honor to the dining room. Mrs. MacArthur would be seated at one end of a long table, with the General at the other end. He would have a lady on each side, while Mrs. MacArthur would have a gentleman on either hand. Edwina would be nearer Mrs. MacArthur, while I would be closer to the General. His conversations were always most interesting, but did require an initial question. One time a lady broached the subject of babies. The remainder of the meal was devoted to related subjects, with the General contributing little. I found it convenient on several occasions to alert the ladies to pick a subject more suitable to the General's experience, and then to sit back and listen. He would fill the meal hour with memorable words.

One lady asked, "Do you think the Russians are bluffing?"

His reply was long and interesting. I remember, "A bluffer is most dangerous. His actions unpredictable."

But, in spite of the many contributions of this great man, the Occupation still encountered opposition and political problems. Even now, I still find it difficult to understand the opposition of the former secretary of state, Mr. Dean Acheson. Though he had visited Europe eleven times, he refused the General's invitation to visit Japan, claiming to be too busy. He even refused to see me when I called on him shortly after I retired. This attitude did not mirror that of the State Department's professionals, many of whom I knew and found most friendly both in Japan and in Washington.

History will not forget nor ignore the noble American who guided Japan from the age of tyranny into that of democracy in five short years. And we must never forget that, but for MacArthur, Japan would now be communistic, and a threat to the United States.

The Supreme Commander of the Allied Powers was guided by the SWNC (State, War and Navy Coordinating Committee) paper 230 which took over from a JCAC (Joint Civil Affairs Committee) paper. Working with the Navy Department months prior to the surrender, I had participated in the preparation of the JCAC paper. I took a firm stand against the exile or the trial of the Emperor as a war criminal. The status of the Emperor should be decided by the Supreme Commander of the Allied Powers. There was a plan to shackle the commander with an Allied council, which we advocated to be advisory only. The final wording made it possible for the General to appear at the first meeting of the Allied council and then turn the chairmanship over to his political advisor, George Atcheson.

Edwina remembers:

On December the fourteenth Benny and I went to Tokyo to the French mission's Oda House. Mrs. MacArthur and her son, Arthur, along with about eighty generals and prominent religious, civil, and diplomatic officials were present. From glassed-in porticoes to the right and left of the veranda, the guests gathered to watch the presentation of the highest French award, the Grand Cross of the Legion of Honor, to General MacArthur. Benny and I were seated on the right side of the veranda where we had an excellent view of the ceremony.

The affair was most colorful. At 10:30 A.M. the Supreme Commander stepped on to the veranda with General Peschkoff. It was a bright, sunny morning. In the attractive rock garden below, a section of French Marines came to present arms.

The First Cavalry Division band struck up the French national anthem, which was followed by the "Star Spangled Banner."

Above the veranda hung the flags of the United States and France. Behind General MacArthur and General Peschkoff stood ten French and American officers—holders of lesser degrees of the Legion of Honor.

In presenting the decoration, General Peschkoff read the citation first in French and then in English: "Miraculous leader who, during the implacable Pacific War, rendered himself illustrious in his capacity as Commander-in-Chief of that theatre. By his magnificent victory over Japan he was one of the principal artisans of the success of the Allies."

In a low, soft voice, General MacArthur slowly answered in French: "I thank you with all my heart for this great distinction. This will add another link to the long chain that binds our two countries. May this friendship never diminish. Once again, General, I thank you."

Instead of the traditional French salutation of bestowing a kiss on each cheek, General Peschkoff shook General MacArthur's hand with his left hand, as General MacArthur placed his left arm across General Peschkoff's shoulder (General Peschkoff had lost his right arm).

At the conclusion of the ceremony, MacArthur turned again to Peschkoff and said, "My dear old friend, may it ever be thus."

The guests assembled in the drawing room where we were served champagne and drank a toast in honor of the occasion. This affair was attended by one of the most distinguished Allied gatherings ever assembled in Japan.

Chapter VI

ALL IN THE DAY'S WORK

Commander and Mrs. Walter Gray were staying with us while their house was being finished. When we arrived home late that afternoon, Mrs. Gray informed us that her son, Bill, was still fighting the war. In a small back bedroom, a hole had been cut in the floor to allow workmen to install pipes under the house for steam heating. At the end of the day, as the workmen came out of the hole, Bill met them with his squirt gun and shot them with water.

The next day, not to be outdone by her brother, the daughter snapped the padlock and locked the gardeners inside of the toolshed, then the children picked up some pebbles and hurled them at the improvised prison.

Wah Chan hurried to inform me of the situation. "Missy, the gardeners, they quit! Children lock up gardeners and no can get out. Marines rescue, but no stay."

The Grays, Benny, and I gathered in the living room to discuss the matter.

"I think it would be a good idea to have the children eat in one of their bedrooms tonight to discipline them."

"Wah, tomorrow, the Marine orderlies will take the children outside and have them apologize to the gardeners."

The next day the children did make their apologies. The gardeners, having had their wounded pride soothed, went to work as usual. The children were finally convinced that the war was over.

It would have been a disappointment if the gardeners had gone, but Benny said that there really was no danger, as they would have lost face if they left us to work for anyone of lesser rank. This was fortunate, as the head gardener was presently arranging the patio.

When I arrived, there wasn't a plant or a shrub in the patio. I ordered a large (two-meters diameter) parabolic Japanese searchlight reflector artistically placed on top of some rocks in the patio's center. A riverlet flowed over some small black stones into the searchlight mirror, which was

113

filled with water lilies. It was most attractive, and I was very grateful to our gardener.

One day, a distinguished geologist from the Ueno Museum called. When he saw our patio he was shocked, and called our attention to the haphazard grouping of rocks and stones of different geological periods! The poor man was quite upset by this unforgivable oversight.

Benny had been under the impression that Yokosuka was free of gangsterism. But, one day, one of his sailors observed a Japanese man approach a bootblack who handed the man some yen notes. Upon further investigation, the sailor found that this was a form of gangster tribute for protection. Several days later this same sailor grabbed the Japanese man as he was accepting another tribute and turned him over to the M.P. To the surprise of the Japanese authorities, their prisoner turned out to be a woman in disguise. She was a member of a notorious Japanese gang headed by Mr. Hata, a citizen of Yokosuka. Benny insisted upon a complete report from the M.P.s.

The report revealed that this group also collected *denki* money. This was a system by which a gangster demanded so much yen from each storekeeper or homeowner for each light bulb. In return he paid their electric light bills. In addition, these gangsters had taken over a local market area on the main street and had demanded exorbitant rents. This market area had been formed in a vacant lot by the small merchants who had formerly maintained sidewalk shops.

Benny had given these merchants notice that the unsanitary, unlicensed, and uncontrolled merchants' booths, which had squatted on the pavements of Yokosuka, would be closed down. The shopkeepers had then moved to the vacant lot where they soon fell under the domination of the gangsters.

Benny held a conference with the mayor and demanded that Mr. Hata be put in jail and that gangsterism be stamped out in Yokosuka.

Two days later, somebody entered our unlocked house and stole one Navy tablecloth and five matching napkins. A beautiful bowl that Admiral McConnell and Commander Thornton had given us was removed from the dining room table and placed on the floor in the center of the dining room. Mayor Ota said that this was to "pin prick" Benny, saving face for Mr. Hata's gang.

The governor and the leading men of the town and prefecture then called on Benny to plead for Mr. Hata's release. These men said that Mr. Hata had signed an agreement in blood giving up gangsterism in Yokosuka, and had gone before his ancestral shrine to renounce his life of crime.

The prefectural officers pointed out that Mr. Hata was a very fine man of high character and was one of three directors of the prefectural police. In addition, he had been of great help to the Japanese during the war. Labor would have been difficult to obtain for the war industries and the Navy yard if it hadn't been for Hata's very effective methods of persuasion. The fact that he was head of the gangsters made it easy for the government to deal with them. If Benny kept Mr. Hata in jail it would be necessary to deal with many smaller gangs rather than with Mr. Hata's unified and well-organized group. Mr. Hata went to jail.

The following Friday, Admiral and Mrs. Bledsoe, Captain Michelet, Benny's new chief staff officer, and Captain Heald came to lunch. Plans for the new flag officers' quarters constituted the bulk of our conversations. Benny said that he would ask that five houses be built.

"I know that we cannot hope to get this request approved, but we may be able to secure approval for at least one or two new homes. The time is coming when the Japanese houses, in Kamakura and other places, will have to be returned to their owners. The senior officers should have quarters on the base."

Florence Bledsoe said, "Let's call the hill where the proposed flag officers' quarters are to be built, 'Unnecessary Mountain.' " And it was so named.

Now the trees were dressed in their gayest colors and Yokosuka reminded me of autumn at the Naval Academy in Annapolis, Maryland. The evenings and mornings were becoming progressively cooler.

Tuesday morning, September twenty-fourth, Benny and I drove to Tokyo. After a short conference with Admiral Griffin, my husband joined me for lunch at Brigadier General and Mrs. Hoffman's house. The other guests were Major General and Mrs. Ned Almond, Major General and Mrs. Clovis

Byers, Mrs. Hunter of the American Red Cross, and the host's aides. Following a delightful meal, we split up and agreed to join forces at the Imperial Palace grounds. From there we drove through one of the side gates. Here 250 acres are surrounded by willow-fringed moats which serve as the boundaries of the enclosure. It seemed much like a beautiful park. In the Emperor's hothouse, we saw his wonderful collection of bonsai, (dwarfed trees). Some were from three to five hundred years old. Next we passed the Emperor's laboratory and then drove on to the music hall, which was built around on enclosed courtyard. In the center was a large platform supporting two enormous drums on either side. They were covered with gold leaf and painted with black and red lacquer trim. Jujitsu meets, concerts, and royal plays were presented there for the Emperor, members of the royal family, courtiers, members of their staff, and guests. A balcony extends around the gravel-covered court on the second story of the building. The court itself reminded me of a California patio. The roof was of glass. In one of the rooms, we saw all of the royal musical instruments. There were many different kinds of elaborate *samisens* (three-string mandolins), other kinds of Japanese stringed instruments, lutes, etc. In another room, we looked through a beautiful hand-painted picture book of the special Japanese dances that were staged for the Emperor and his royal parties.

Leaving the music hall, we went to the royal stable where we saw the Emperor's famous white horse, "White Snow." He was a beautiful animal. We stroked him and had our pictures taken standing beside him. Nearby in the carriage house was the Emperor's coach, which was similar to that of the King of England. The black lacquer exterior looked like glass, and the gold leaf trimming and trappings were gorgeous. The interior was made of hand carved sandalwood and the upholstery was of gold satin brocade. The Empress', Princes', and Princesses' carriages were similar, but not as elaborate. I had never seen so many magnificent saddles from all over the world. In large glass showcases were three stuffed horses that had been used by the Emperor.

The Imperial Palace and some other court buildings had been destroyed by sparks from some nearby structures which were burned by air raids in May 1945. A seventy-mile gale was blowing when the fire bombs were dropped, and the sparks flew everywhere. Our men had not intended to destroy the palace and other structures. The Emperor and Empress lived in a part of the Imperial household office which was used as a temporary palace.

The inner enclosure is open to the public only on New Year's Day and the Emperor's birthday (April 29). The public is allowed to go as far as the first bridge, called Neganibashi, which means "Spectacles Bridge," which extends to the front gate. The Imperial Palace is directly in front of this bridge. It is immaculately maintained and very impressive. It extends northeastward through a short boulevard to the Tokyo Central Station. The second bridge is within the granite stone wall. Ancient pine tree branches hang over it. The Sakurada Gate, to the south, was formerly used to enter the shogun's castle.

From the carriage house, we motored to the Akasaka detached palace grounds. After a short walk, we came to the main entrance of this most imposing building. It reminded me of pictures I had seen of the Palace of Versailles in France. We were met by the staff of the Emperor's caretakers. On entering the main reception room, I was awed by the grandeur of this spacious room. There were two large marble mantels at each end of the room, with gorgeous hand-embroidered satin fire screens in front of them. The pink marble pillars were simply "out of this world," they were so beautiful.

The inlaid parquet hardwood floor was composed of intricate designs and was so highly polished that it looked like glass. The furniture was all covered with gold leaf and was of the Louis the XVI period. At the back of each chair, in the center near the top of the elaborate upholstery, was the Emperor's seal, the sixteen-petaled chrysanthemum.

The walls were all covered with gold satin brocade, and were magnificent. The ceiling was hand-painted, or frescoed. Drapes were of satin brocade, the same lovely gold color of the walls, and the curtains were made of white lace.

In an adjoining room, the Emperor's chef, Tokuzo Akiyama, served us tea and French pastry.

When we finished eating, we continued our tour of the palace. I do not know how many rooms there were, but we must have walked at least a mile, and we did not even enter all of the rooms. We saw the Prince's sitting room, but not his bedroom. However, we were shown one bedroom suite which gave us an idea how the others must have appeared. It was very elaborately furnished in the French style. A heavy satin canopy stood over the bed, or I should say, where the bed should have been. It had been removed from the room.

The main dining hall was enormous and could easily seat fifty people. Around the walls were beautiful hand-painted birds on porcelain. Dark-paneled wood complemented these lovely pictures. The furniture was dark, hand-carved, cherry wood.

The family dining room was a miniature of the main dining room.

The smoking room was decorated in the Egyptian style, and was startlingly unique.

The ballroom was magnificent with its huge crystal chandeliers, high windows framed with rich brocade drapes, French gold chairs, and its white concert grand piano with gold trim. Above the piano was a lovely balcony.

The library was rather Victorian in its appointments. The walls were paneled in dark wood, and the bookcases were filled with hundreds of sets of books.

When we returned to the main entrance of the palace, we thanked the staff of the Emperor for the delightful visit and then thanked Brigadier General Hoffman for the lovely luncheon and tour of the Imperial Palace grounds. We reluctantly returned to our automobile and drove back to Yokosuka.

By September twenty-sixth, the Japanese workmen had still not finished the installation of the steam pipes and radiators in our home. That afternoon, Commander Gray and his wife and family called. Fay Gray told us of her battle to have her bathroom tile properly installed. The Japanese idea of bathing is so different from ours. Instead of having shower stalls with the drain inside, there is usually a large drain for the entire room. Fay finally succeeded in having a shower wall made to her specifications. One day, upon returning from the commissary, her Japanese cook met her saying, "I fix." He could speak very little English, so she did not know what he meant. He led her to the bathroom and proudly pointed to a hole that he had persuaded the tile man to bore in the center of the low retaining wall. The cook beamed with pride, but poor Fay almost cried. The next day the hole was plugged up.

James Young, a newspaper writer and author of several books on the Far East, and Captain Carol Tyler came to lunch. Jimmy Young was a great help in discussing Navy Day plans. He also informed me about Captain Cunningham's class ring, which was to play a prominent part in our ceremonies.

Mr. Young, Benny, and I walked to the top of Pilot's Hill to see the monument to Pilot Will Adams or Miuri Anjin, as he was later called. He landed in Japan a shipwrecked British sailor whom Tokugawa kept as an important instructor. On the way there, I slipped in the clay mud many times. It was a steep walk and I wondered if I would be able to reach the top. The recent rain made our walk even more difficult. When we finally reached the top, Wilson, Benny's driver, took some pictures of the triumphant mountain climbers standing beside the monument. Miuri Anjin and his wife were cremated and buried there.

James Young said that he had been chased up that hill by the Japanese police before the war. His friend was caught and imprisoned, but Jim escaped. They had been attempting to get a view of the base.

Not far from the monument was the ruined foundation of Miuri Anjin's home. Before the war, the house had been a shrine. During the war, the Japanese looted and destroyed the place.

I was impressed with the wonderful view from the top of Pilot's Hill. The walk down the hill was almost as treacherous as the walk up the hill. I was relieved to reach the foot of the hill.

Sunday afternoon, Commander Wally Higgins and we had a most interesting adventure. We took a boat ride over to the island of Sarushima, where we went ashore to explore. Ever since my first glimpse of the island from our garden, I had a desire to see and explore it. This island had been a fortress, and there were antiaircraft gun emplacements. The guns had been dismantled, and the former barracks were just a shambles. Numerous caves were filled with abandoned, worthless gear. Benny had wanted to see the island to deter-

119

mine if it could be used by the people for picnics, boy scout gatherings, etc. The island was overrun with weeds, ruins, and trash, but nature had endowed it with a beauty that the war marks could not obliterate. It had possibilities. Soon, it became a boys' camp.

That evening, Benny and I motored to Tokyo to attend a large dinner party at Lieutenant General and Mrs. Whitehead's (Air Force) home. The mansion, formerly the Maeda House, was second only to the American Embassy in beauty and grandeur. When the Countess Maeda, wife of Lieutenant General Marquis Toshinari Maeda, had lived there, there had been between sixty and one hundred servants. The house still belonged to the Countess. After having met her at Mr. Magana's home in 1946, I was interested and duly impressed. It was the largest home that I had ever seen, and seemed more like a hotel than a house.

We were introduced to a couple of blank-faced Russians, but we did not catch the names. They were so aloof that we paid them little attention. Later, we found that one was General Derevyanko, the Russian ambassador, and the other his high ranking interpreter (Commissar to watch the ambassador).

The future of Yokosuka depended ultimately upon its economic stability. Benny wanted to introduce industry to provide work for the unemployed. There were many deserted buildings which might be converted into the needed factories. He hoped to interest Japanese businessmen in manufacturing products needed for peacetime consumption by offering them these facilities. Mr. Katsuo Sakuma, an executive of an electrical concern, proposed that the old broken-down buses be rebuilt and propelled by electricity rather than gasoline, which was very scarce and expensive. As motor transportation was acutely needed, a new factory was started at once. The former Japanese ordnance plant was selected for this company's use. Later, it was to grow into a Toyapet auto plant.

Agricultural implements were desperately needed. Mr. Kazuo Tajimi asked to use certain idle machine tools and furnaces to melt down guns, shell casing, and torpedo parts to make plows, rakes, hoes, and shovels.

In the morning of the nineteenth, Mrs. Takaoka told us

about the Yokosuka peoples' festival. Benny was surprised at the amount of money that was to be spent on this festival. When he questioned the wisdom of this, he was told that the Japanese people were depressed and needed a wonderful festival to improve their morale.

On Saturday morning, October nineteenth, I went to Captain Michelet's office to attend a meeting to plan the Christmas festivities. Admiral Bledsoe's wife, Florence, Miss DesBaillets, Chaplain Ricker, and Ensign Marshall were the other members of the committee. We discussed plans for a Christmas party for the dependent children, various activities for the enlisted men, etc.

Following the lunch, Florence and I took Miyoko Yokoi to see the peoples' festival parade, and then motored over to Seaside Park for the Japanese entertainment at the open-air bandstand. We enjoyed the colorful Japanese kimonos, obis, and fans that the entertainers wore. The music, typical Japanese, was played on the *samisens*. The musicians in the background made an attractive picture and lent native atmosphere. I really enjoyed the show and was impressed by the happy throng of Japanese people gathered in front of the bandstand. They looked as if they were enjoying the entertainment immensely.

As we started to walk toward our waiting automobiles, a young girl came out of the stage door at the side of the grand stand. She carried two large bouquets of flowers, which she presented to Florence and me.

That evening, Benny and I drove down to the city hall and watched the people gather to march in the lantern parade. It was quite a sight. We were told that two thousand people were going to be in this parade. I had wanted to wait for the participants to arrive at our house, but Benny had said that the Japanese people used to stage such parades for the Imperial Japanese Navy. He did not think that it was fitting for the United States Navy to accept the same kind of homage. The procession started as soon as it was dark enough to see the lanterns. It was a magnificent sight.

On the thirteenth, Benny and I went to Tokyo to attend a luncheon that General and Mrs. MacArthur were giving at the United States Embassy. Mrs. MacArthur had greeted us in the drawing room, and we were chatting when the General's arrival was announced. After greeting Mrs. MacArthur, the General greeted each one of the guests in a most cordial manner. I was impressed with his wonderful speaking voice, his dark, penetrating, friendly eyes, his handsome face, and his strong personality.

Luncheon was announced and we followed our host and hostess into the large dining room. Mrs. Griffin sat on the General's right and Mrs. Bledsoe sat on his left. I sat on the right of Vice Admiral Griffin, who sat on the right of Mrs. MacArthur, a very gracious and vivacious lady. Mrs. MacArthur kept the conversation from lagging at our end of the table. I was not able to hear what the General had to say, although I heard a word now and then. When the luncheon was over, we walked slowly past a tiered stand of black lacquer. On this stand were silver salt and pepper shakers of every kind and description. These silver replicas of Japanese life ranged from lanterns, fans, drums, and jin rikishas to bathtubs. We did not loiter, however, for we understood that we should depart as soon as the meal was over. Following luncheon, the General always took a nap before returning to the Dai Ichi building. We thanked Mrs. MacArthur and the General for a delightful time and departed.

All Hallow's Eve found the Deckers at a Halloween dinner party at the Officers' Club on the base. Almost everyone wore a costume. Mrs. Kawabata had borrowed the most beautiful kimono that I had ever seen for me (it belonged to a princess). She obtained a wig, and came over to the house to dress me. It took one hour to put on the under kimonos, tie the numerous cords and sashes, fix the outer kimono, and tie the obi. The wig, with its many ornaments, was quite heavy, and I knew now why most Japanese girls, who wore these hairdos bowed their heads. The zori nearly killed my feet, so I was forced to wear a pair of Japanese embroidered bedroom slippers. I was disappointed, as were Mrs. Kawabata and our servant girls. But it was a case of being dressed correctly or be able to walk. I chose to walk.

The Japanese people had a friendship coat designed for the American Friends Association in honor of Commodore Perry's visit to Japan. It was made of the same material as a coolie coat. On a black background, in the center of the back, was a mon (family crest) with a cherry blossom. This Imperial Japanese Navy insignia was outlined in blue on a white background over half of the rising sun. On the right side of the coat, inside the shield, were two white stars on a blue background above five alternating red and white stripes. This design was a symbolic union of the Japanese and United States flags. Across the back of the coat, starting at the left wrist, were these words, "American Friends Association." This extended to the end of the right sleeve. Seven alternate white and red stripes circumscribed the bottom of the coat above a three-inch black hem.

Mrs. Kawabata, who had gone to so much trouble to get my costume, had lost her husband recently.

Ex-Admiral Kawabata, when a flag officer during the war, had observed that the new overpass being built near the base during the war would allow people to see over the wall and into the base. He had the work stopped, and the traffic continued, as before, to cross the electric train tracks. Shortly after calling on us he was killed at this crossing.

Shortly after Admiral Kawabata's death, Mrs. Kawabata called on me with an interpreter. She said: "My husband ordered all the people in Yokosuka who owned Bibles to turn them into the Naval Base. In a public square they were burned. I feel so badly about this terrible deed that I want to make up for it by devoting the remainder of my life to helping you, to help the Occupation and to help to bring Christianity to the people."

The assistant Secretary of the Navy, the Honorable W. John Kenny, arrived in Japan and came to visit the Naval base on the morning of the eighth. At the Naval hospital, he presented a silver cup to the first American baby born in Japan since the Occupation started. Chief Petty Officer and Mrs. Durgas were the proud parents. The dependents' ward was greatly improved since my last visit, and I was delighted to see that so much work had been done.

On the day before, a tragedy had occurred in Kamakura. Marion and Bob Paton's home caught on fire due to a defective flue in the chimney. The Japanese workmen had failed to put metal around the space between the flue and the roof.

Bob had already left for the Base at Yokosuka. As it was raining that morning, Bob wore his old suit. Marion was upstairs having a cup of coffee when her maid, Tamoya, ran up to warn her. The smoke was already coming up the stairs. Marion decided to take time to call Bob. When she finished and started for the stairway, it was a blazing inferno. She ran to the clothes closet and picked up a pair of I. Miller shoes and threw them out the window, and then jumped after them. Fortunately, the earth was soft from the rains, and she only sustained a few bruises and scratches from a rosebush. Florence Bledsoe, who lived nearby, had seen the fire and had rushed over to help. All Marion saved were her shoes and the clothing on her back.

When Benny and I heard about the fire, we invited Marion and Bob to come and stay with us until they could find a new home. They were delightful house guests and we enjoyed their company.

Admiral Richardson came to lunch at our home. Afterwards Benny went to work in the office, while some other officers' wives accompanied us to Mrs. Nagaoka's home and woodcarving factory in Kamakura.

Benny was most disappointed in not being with the admiral, whom he admired greatly for his courageous opposition to the political pressure that made the Pearl Harbor surprise attack so possible. An officious Army colonel, an assistant to General Crawford Sams, was on the base threatening Captain Owsley for having supervised the cleaning up and reforms in the hospitals as well as small civilian establishments, a health menace to both the Navy and to the Navy's zone of authority. Benny had ordered this work done. Captain Owsley was energetically and wholeheartedly doing a better job than could be found anywhere else in Japan. Benny did not know Crawford Sams at that time. He had to oppose the colonel's attack upon Owsley. Sams supported Benny's position, and there was no further interference. Later he and Sams became good friends.

In the thirteen hospitals in Yokosuka, our medical department was enforcing reforms such as standard visiting hours and centralized kitchens and facilities. The patients' families were no longer allowed to move in with them. Also, our doctors helped to train nurses and laboratory technicians. These measures went a long way towards a complete program of better health for the city.

Both Captain Owsley and his successor, Butler, were

angels to the Japanese. When the Korean-Chinese War casualties arrived in Yokosuka, the bread cast upon the waters by our medicos was returned a hundredfold by the civilians who helped in our base hospital.

To return to Kamakura—and our trip with Admiral Richardson—a little background information on the days of Kamakura Era (1192–1333) might be helpful. "Kamakura carving" has held a very special place in Japanese fine and industrial arts. Looking back to such remote times, the exact origin is somewhat obscure, but it is said that it was first learned from Chinese artisans of the Sung Dynasty (960–1126 A.D.). There is no doubt, however, that this art is strongly influenced by the masters who sculptured the early Buddhist statues which became characteristic of the culture of this period. The secrets of this art have been jealously guarded and handed down over the centuries from generation to generation. Many descendants of these artists still live in Kamakura today.

Mrs. Nagaoka took Admiral Richardson and the group of Navy wives through her factory. First, we saw carved pieces with an outline design traced upon the wood. The maiden hair tree, the Japanese judas tree and other such hard wood of fine-grained texture are used for the carving. The entire surface is then covered with an aged black lacquer and dried. This is followed by layer upon layer of rich vermilion lacquer. We did not see this process of repeated lacquering as the technique is a closely guarded secret. This work was done in a separate, glass-enclosed compartment in the large room. The artist left his lacquer pot, brushes, and carvings on the floor. He evidently had been told to stop work while the visitors were there.

The Japanese flower from which the lacquer is obtained is perfectly beautiful. It looks like a vermilion chrysanthemum, with long, curly petals. The first time I saw these flowers growing wild along the roadside, I thought them magnificent. When I returned home, I questioned the servants about them.

"Ah, madame, they are poisonous! You must not touch." Miyoko informed me.

I was so disappointed. I understood now why lacquer poisoning was rather common in Japan, although the people who work with the lacquer seem to have built an immunity to it.

After the tour of the Kamakura Bori factory, Mrs. Naga-oka invited us to her home. We saw some beautiful finished pieces of Kamakura Bori bowls, trays, plates, etc. Mrs. Naga-oka's daughters served us tea, and we had a very pleasant visit.

On Thursday, the fourteenth of November, Mrs. Takaoka and I attended a meeting of the Shinsei Women's Club executive committee. This was held in one of the schoolhouses nearby.

I was very interested in the manner which Mrs. Mabuchi conducted the meeting. She asked the club members if they were in favor of such and such proposition, but never asked if there were any opposed to it. It would have been rude in the Japanese code of ethics for women to have openly shown any opposition. These women had a great deal to learn about democracy.

It was my privilege and pleasure to present a gavel made of hard wood with a silver band around the head of the mallet. Engraved on the band were the words, "To Shinsei Yokosuka Women's Club from Fleet Activities."

The honor of presenting this gavel to the Shinsei Women's Club of Yokosuka from Fleet Activities gives me the greatest pleasure.

Since my arrival here, I have watched the results of your wonderful work in cleaning up the streets and vacant lots. The efficient way you have fed the poor, by your food salvages, has brought you the greatest respect and admiration from all of the people who have heard about it, here in Japan and in the United States. You have set an example for other women to follow in Japan and in other countries.

I had the pleasure of visiting the Yokosuka Girls' High School recently and I was impressed with it. It is a good school. However, I visited a grammar school near our home, not so long ago, and it was in a deplorable state. The future of any nation, for good or evil, depends on the education of its children. Without good schools and playgrounds, these children will grow up disil-

126

lusioned and discontented. Some might become delinquents and these delinquents, if strong willed, might sow the seed for future wars.

The most important thing for everyone to work for these days is for an everlasting peace. The orphanage you have started for the destitute women and orphans is a great step toward that goal.

I congratulate you for the wonderful work you have done and I wish you the greatest success in the future.

I handed the gavel to Mrs. Mabuchi, who thanked me and began to speak in Japanese. Mrs. Takaoka interpreted her speech.

It is a unique and great honor for us to be presented today with this beautiful gavel especially made in America for this club, and presented to us by the United States Navy, through the kindness of our esteemed and beloved Mrs. Decker. We are very deeply moved and most grateful for this gracious gift.

We shall always cherish it. And in the years to come, pass it on to those who follow us in our work, as a symbol, not only of the power and leadership for which this gavel stands, but also for the warm hearted good will and helpful understanding so generously showered upon the efforts of this club. It shall be ever present, to increase the efficiency of our meetings and to give us encouragement and moral support in our work.

We, the women of Yokosuka, will do our utmost to build up a truly peace loving and democratic new Japan, and do our utmost to make our country worthy of winning back the trust and the friendship of all nations. In this way we will repay our gratitude to you for your generous kindness and understanding thoughtfulness in so honoring us today.

On behalf of the Shinsei Yokosuka Women's Club, I express our most heartfelt gratitude and thanks.

Several days later, Mrs. Takaoka and I visited the Shinsei Yokosuka Women's Home for Orphans and Destitute Women.

127

The home was located at the edge of the city off of the main thoroughfare to Camp McGill, on the road to Hayama. The club had converted former Japanese Army wooden barracks into this refuge. It was a forlorn-looking group of buildings with most of the windows broken or cracked. Everything was in need of repair.

The members of the executive committee were on hand to meet us and the women and children of the home lined either side of the walk leading to the entrance. The women bowed low and the children smiled as Mrs. Takaoka and I stepped out of the automobile. The members of the executive committee escorted us to the doorway, across which was hung a ribbon. Mrs. Mabuchi handed me a pair of scissors and I ceremoniously opened the orphanage doors. Mrs. Mabuchi and the other members of the executive committee then took me on a tour of the barracks.

We walked into a large, barren room which was used as a reception hall. Off of this room was a classroom with small, crudely made chairs. We returned to the long hallway and walked down the corridor to the kitchen and dining room. Outside, against the wall, was a pile of old lumber which had been gathered by the women from the vacant lot near the entrance to the Naval base. This wood was to be used for fuel. The former Japanese baths were converted into the orphanage and a general public laundry. The profits were used for the upkeep of the establishment. In a large back room was the factory, against a wall in a corner was a huge pile of tin cans that the club members had collected. The trash concession had been turned over to the Shinsei Women's Club because they had been so successful in handling the garbage disposal and distributing substandard American food to the needy people in Yokosuka.

The club employed seventy-five people, ten horse-drawn carts, and four motor trucks. The horse-drawn carts were used to collect the empty tin cans from the Navy clubs. The trucks were used to collect rags and waste paper which was sold to pulp mills. Bottles were also collected, as were other discarded articles which could be of use. The women made a profit of about 400,000 yen each month from the sales of this assortment of odds and ends.

The empty tin cans were used to make toy automobiles,

The Women's Club made our empties into toys.

airplanes, clips for the Japanese *geta*, and canteens for the schoolchildren. The women made a model of an acrobatic racing car which flopped over on its back in realistic spills. This cute little toy became their most popular manufactured article. One single order that the club received for the United States was for one hundred and forty-four thousand such cars.

This toy factory was quite interesting, and I watched the women work for a few minutes. It was fascinating to watch the transformation of a lowly tin can into an object which was both useful and attractive. Considering the equipment and machinery that the women had, I thought they they were ingenious.

From the factory, the members of the executive committee escorted us to the dormitories. One destitute woman was assigned to each room, where she took care of one or two orphans. This was an excellent arrangement. The rooms were all alike, and were quite small and bare. About one hundred and twenty orphans and destitute women occupied these rooms. There were seventy-two rooms in each of these double barracks.

When our tour was finished, we were escorted to the automobile. Many of the women and orphans followed to bid us good-bye. My memories of the home will always center around the friendship and warmth of those whom it sheltered.

On our first Thanksgiving Day in Yokosuka the Shinsei Yokosuka Women's Club sponsored a citizens' mass meeting of "Thanks to America and Allied Forces." Benny, Commander and Mrs. Paton, our good neighbor and interpreter, Mrs. Takaoka and I motored to Seaside Park. We were met by the mayor and other city officials who escorted us over to the grandstand where Colonel and Mrs. Hochmuth were awaiting us. The program consisted of speeches of thanks and a beauty contest.

After Miss Yokosuka had been selected, the lovely girl presented Mrs. Hochmuth, Mrs. Paton, and me with beautiful bouquets of flowers.

We attended a dinner party at Vice Admiral and Mrs. Griffin's home in Tokyo for the members of the Naval Affairs Committee who arrived in Japan the previous day. Our congressman, the Honorable Ed Izac from San Diego, was the chairman. The other members of this committee were the Honorable Andrew U. Biemiller, Honorable C. W. Bishop, Honorable Ned R. Healy, Honorable Mike Mansfield, Captain

F. N. Kivette, U.S.N., and Lieutenant William G. Campbell, U.S.N.

Work on the base was humming and improvements were a great boost to the morale of the officers, enlisted men, and dependents alike. Benny was looking forward to the time when all the personnel and their dependents would be housed on the base.

The Japanese houses assigned to the Navy were located in Kamakura. These had been requisitioned by the Army and the occupants ordered to move. All of the Navy personnel and their families were given houses according to their needs. Most of the houses were large, two-story places.

A typical example was the house assigned to Warrant Officer and Mrs. Henry Walker. They had an eleven-room, two-story house with an American toilet in the bathroom. As American toilets in Japan were scarce, the Walkers appreciated this luxury. During the first summer, the Japanese servants insisted on closing and locking all windows and doors each night and as the Walkers had a Japanese double bed to sleep in, which was about the size of an American single bed, they were extremely uncomfortable in the hot, humid climate of Japan. Japanese windows are always in threes. First, a sliding door on the outside like a storm shutter. Then a glass window, followed by a paper window on the inside. In the wintertime this window arrangement acted as satisfactory insulation against the cold weather. The Walkers finally convinced the servants, before the end of the summer, that the windows should be left at least partially open. This the Walkers were soon to regret, because the mosquitoes swarmed into the bedroom and had a feast on two unsuspecting Americans sleeping without a net. Screens were nonexistent.

Benny and I went to Tokyo to the home of Brigadier General and Mrs. Hoffman. When their guests had all assembled, the Hoffmans instructed us to get into our waiting automobiles and proceed to the Emperor's duck preserve, which was situated in the lowlands at the head of Tokyo Bay. It was quite chilly, and we were delighted to see small charcoal fires arranged in narrow, shallow dugouts not far from the hunting lodge. We walked over to this inviting spot, where we were greeted by Japanese officials, Mr. (formerly

Viscount) and Mrs. Yoshitami Matsuidaira, Minister and now the Grand Steward. Hot tea was served in the Japanese handleless tea cups. The steaming liquid warmed us up and was very welcome.

The master of the hunt passed out instruction pamphlets on duck netting. This Japanese sport, or entertainment, was to amuse foreign guests. After we read our instructions, we were each given a white tag with a number on it. Some had black numbers, while others had red ones. Some of these numbers were in circles, and the rest were enclosed in squares. We were told that we could go duck netting in teams.

The master of the hunt instructed those with circled numbers to follow him. The other guests were to await the return of the first team; each would have its turn. As I was given a "square," I had to wait. Large nets with long handles were given to each person who was to participate in the first hunt. The guests lined up in pairs according to their numbers, a red number paired with a black one. There were ten people in all. With their nets jutting over their shoulders, they walked along the grassy lane and were soon out of sight in a dense bamboo thicket.

The time went by quickly, and soon I was standing in line. When all ten members of our team were assembled, we too began to walk toward the bamboo.

The pond was hidden from view, but there were canals leading from it to the different mounds of screens. Here, we were to await the Japanese signal to follow the master of the hunt to the banks of our canal. It was interesting to watch the signal man, who was looking through a small opening in the screen. He intently watched for the ducks, and enticed them by putting food into the canal by a sort of bellows that he worked with his right foot.

When he signalled, showing as many fingers as there were ducks in the canal, we ran to our places as quietly and as quickly as possible. The hunters holding the red numbers were assigned to the left side of the canal; those with the black numbers were on the bank facing them. The ducks were attracted from the pond and down the different canals by flightless, tame white decoy ducks. When the wild ducks started to fly up out of the canal, we all swung our nets in their direction. I caught one, which the attendant removed from the net. Before placing it in a bamboo basket, he put the duck's head under its wing. It all happened so suddenly, and I hoped that the bird had not suffered.

When all of the wild ducks in the canal had either been caught or scared away, the master of the hunt signaled us to withdraw from our positions. We lined up again and walked along the grassy path to the next mound. We repeated the same procedure as before, and I caught another duck.

There was a great deal of excitement when we returned to the lodge. On the tables in front of the pavilion we saw the ducks. The guests were looking at the limp mallards and teal with a mixture of sadness and admiration. When the last team returned, the rest of the ducks were displayed, and our scores calculated.

Benny caught five ducks and had a better score than I. However, I was on the winning team.

Benny winked, "Those poor drakes didn't have a chance with the 'blond' decoys leading them down blind alleys."

Our hosts beckoned to the guests to come into the lodge. A long table in the center of the room was set up for luncheon. In front of each guest was a little sukiyaki stove with red hot charcoal under the flat skillet. On our right were small plates with slivers of raw duck meat, the previous day's catch. Mr. Tokuzo Akiyama, the Emperor's chef, showed each guest how to dip the pieces of duck meat in a small dish of soy sauce. They were then placed in the skillet and cooked. They were delicious! Besides the duck, there were dishes of cold cuts, pickles, olives, and bread. We were served sake in the tiny Japanese sake cups. It was a most unusual and enjoyable luncheon.

As we prepared to return to Tokyo, each guest was given some ducks to take home. We thanked our hosts and walked to our waiting automobiles.

One Saturday, we drove to Tokyo to have luncheon with Admiral Griffin and the Bards. Afterwards, we motored up to Karuizawa, a beautiful mountain resort. Here, we visited Brigadier General Maris' home, which was the former residence of the aircraft manufacturer, Mr. Nakajima. It was an imposing place, but the plumbing was poor, and the heating nonexistent. General Maris and the officers who occupied the house dubbed it "the ice palace." The summer home of the general was in Karuizawa in a picturesque spot next to an excellent golf course. The general told us of the international colony of political exiles who were waiting repatriation. From the recreation hall balcony, we were able to watch them as they danced. There were Germans, Swiss, Swedish, Turks, Russians, and Chinese. A few of our military men were also present.

The next day, all of the men except Benny played golf. He and I had decided to go sightseeing. We ate luncheon at the clubhouse and asked that a Japanese guide accompany us on our jaunt. Lieutenant White, General Maris' young aide, secured Gozo Kawamura. As we left, Lieutenant White told us that Gozo was making a plaster cast bust of General Eichelberger, commanding general of the Eighth Army.

"I would like to see it very much. Can't we visit your studio, Gozo?" Benny asked.

"I live in a very humble place and if you don't mind the clutter I shall be very pleased and flattered to have you visit my house," Gozo replied.

We drove along the picturesque road dotted with country homes. In the distance we saw the second largest active volcano in Japan, Mt. Asama. There was a plume of smoke coming from the summit, and it was an awesome sight.

"There is a superstition among the Japanese people that when Mt. Asama erupts, there will be a catastrophe. It is smoking now, and it looks as if it will erupt again soon," Gozo told us with a sad, resigned expression on his face.

Finally, we arrived at his house. On a pedestal in the center of the living room, we saw the plaster cast of General Eichelberger. It was a striking likeness and seemed so alive. We thought it excellent.

Benny speaking, "How would you like to have a studio in Yokosuka, Gozo? I will give you a place all your own, and you will be able to cast your work into bronze. We will let you use the foundry for this work."

"Sir, I am overcome with emotion and gratitude. All during the war, I have not been able to cast any of my sculptures into bronze and I can't finish my work without being able to cast them. There is one very important matter that I must take up with my wife. She is a seamstress and she has some customers. She is making dresses for them and I don't know how she will manage and if she will want to leave Karuizawa. I shall have to talk to her first," Gozo replied.

"Let me know when you are coming, Gozo, and I will have everything ready for you."

We left Gozo's home and went to see the studio of a famous woodblock artist, Paul Jacoulet. The Frenchman, who had turned native, wore a Japanese kimono. He had a rather athletic build and appeared to be about fifty. On his face was powder, rouge, and lipstick; women's bracelets and rings adorned his hands. I believe that a great deal of this eccentricity was merely executed for effect.

He was very pleasant and showed us his famous Manchurian collection. We were enchanted with the lovely pictures. The colors were so soft and beautiful. There were many other woodblock prints, and we bought two of them.

One casual remark concerning the overabundance of projects caused me to pause in my planning. I had kept no record of these projects, and things were moving so fast that I began to think that I might be "biting off" too much and leaving too many loose ends. I took an inventory. At the end of the first year, I had a list of two hundred and five projects—some completed and some still in the mill. Five of these I had dropped, as I considered them failures. I regret that I didn't keep this list, as it would now be invaluable.

But I do remember my failures. With outstanding assistance from both the Japanese and the Americans, my failures could only be due to overly ambitious planning. One was the sewer system. It grew into a monster with which I couldn't cope. First, a large amount of pipe was needed, then a disposal plant, and finally a fertilizer plant. Also, the large number of honey-bucket drivers who would lose their source of income all caused me to forget the affair after a slow start.

Another failure was my fishing fleet. When our craft came back empty, I realized that our neighboring town of Misaki should be the fishing port—not Yokosuka. Then, there was the yeast plant. It produced quantity, but not quality. I decided to continue importing yeast from the United States, as my chemists were limited in their ability. A newspaper started well, but soon lost the drive necessary to become the voice of the people.

The fifth project concerned the placement of a bronze figurine on a boulder in the harbor. It was to be similar to the mermaid in Copenhagen, Denmark, and hopefully would have been as beautiful. But neither my sculptor, Gozo Kawamura, nor I, could conceive of a statue different from the mermaid, but with the same appeal. The idea was foreign to Japanese thinking, and I was of no help.

In June 1948, I expected to be detached, so I needed the coming year to see my plans to fruition. I had to finish what I had started.

The Occupation had ordered that the Japanese revise their textbooks for the public schools. But some of the Americans in charge of this important project allowed the Japanese to insert many anti-American thoughts and much Communist propaganda into these texts. As the books did not come off the press until just before the beginning of the fall term, it was too late to re-revise them. The Catholic priest, Father Voss, who was a Japanese linguist and was alert to the situation, came into my office in September to show me the English translation of some of the offending paragraphs. These books were being used in the schools under Naval jurisdiction, and I objected. We immediately alerted the Marine major in charge of education on General MacArthur's staff. We ripped out the pages and continued to use the mutilated books.

To remove the offending militaristic Japanese propaganda, our Americans had allowed many crude changes which included communistic propaganda. It seemed to be a clever plot, as it would take one year to revise the textbooks again.

June twenty-sixth 1947 was Griffin Day in honor of Vice Admiral R. M. Griffin, Commander Naval Forces Far East. When the admiral and his staff arrived at the Administration Building, the sailor and Marine guard of our defense force gave a fifteen-gun salute. Two Japanese saluting guns had been salvaged and installed near the signal tower to answer salutes. We weren't a saluting station—but we were ready if that designation should be made. The admiral inspected the guard and then motored to the Marine parade grounds.

There, he was joined by Admiral and Mrs. Bledsoe, Colonel and Mrs. Fellers, and other senior officers of the base and their wives.

The admiral first inspected the defense force of four hundred Marines and four hundred sailors under Colonel Fellers, and then inspected the Marine barracks and Barracks A, where part of our enlisted force lived. Included in the inspection were the laundry, the dry cleaning plant, the swimming pool, and the building site for our chapel. Here, he laid the cornerstone of the chapel during a ceremony given by Chaplain Ricker. Next, he visited Griffin Park, the new housing area, where our dependents lived in 146 houses, duplexes, triplexes, and 96 apartments in former barracks. We had 26 houses on Halsey Road for senior officers. The admiral also inspected our new schoolhouse and the new gas station.

At noon, there was a reception held at the CPO Club. Admiral and Mrs. Griffin, Admiral and Mrs. Bledsoe, and Edwina and I were in the receiving line. Soft drinks, sandwiches, ice cream, cake, and other refreshments were served. At twelve-thirty the officers and their wives went to the Officers' Club for luncheon, ending an important day in our history. Admiral Griffin was well pleased.

The Secretary of the Navy wrote:—

10 July 1947

My dear Captain Decker:

Father Flanagan of Boys Town and Mr. Byron Reed, his secretary, who was with him on his trip to Japan, told me of the extremely courteous treatment that they received while visiting on your station, and reported on the splendid work you were doing. I was particularly gratified to learn of the effort you were making in the field of education and health for Japanese children.

When you return I hope you will come in to see me and tell me something of your experience.

Sincerely yours,
James Forrestal

Unfortunately I never had the opportunity. I admired the

137

secretary very much and would have enjoyed supporting him in any way.

After VJ Day the Japanese military had spread alarming lies about our men, stating that they ravished women and that the virtuous women of Yokosuka should take to the hills. Unscrupulous men set up brothels to subdue the American lust. To fill them with talent, they encouraged farm girls to perform their patriotic duty by protecting the virtue of Japanese womanhood!

Shortly after VJ Day, a magazine had published an article in which a chaplain complained of the base commander authorizing two red light districts in the city. Elsewhere during the war, similar districts were policed by our military without complaint. As much as we might abhor it, the facts warranted it. But now that the fighting was over, the chaplain thought it his duty to publicize the commodore's action. The district was under the control of a Navy guard at a gate. A man entering it would leave his I.D. card with the guard. On his departure, he would receive treatment before his card was returned to him. This was an effective control.

The hue and cry from stateside forced the commodore to close the districts. The VD rate went through the roof. One day I inquired the rate of the doctor. No one knew, as they now kept no records. I ordered that a report be compiled. When it appeared on my desk, it was startling. In all my days, I had never seen such a high rate. Some men were being reinfected.

To fight this disabling and demoralizing disease, many weapons had to be used. Emphasis was put on recreation facilities. On the base, more clubs were established, and the Enlisted Men's Club in town was improved. Athletic teams were also encouraged. Here, many junior officers were invaluable. It was important to make the base a desirable place for duty. It soon got around that a second case of VD would mean a transfer to a tanker on the Bahrain run—six months at sea. This form of "aversion therapy" was effective.

Every case of VD on the base was restricted until the man had made out a form stating when and where and with whom. The police picked up the girl and one of the civilian hospitals would treat her.

If one of these girls was from out of town, steps were

taken to return her to her home. One girl was from Kyushu. They sent for her father, who quickly arrived by train to escort his wayward daughter home. When she told him what her earnings were, he promptly refused to interfere in such a profitable profession.

To clean up VD we needed the people's help. The powerful Women's Club was to play an important role. They had the use of the large EM theater on Saturday morning for movies or talks. There were some colored VD movies which I wanted used as part of our campaign. The women held a VD meeting at which Captain Owsley and I talked.

"You and I are meeting today in a common cause—the betterment of the people of Yokosuka. Since last April when I took command, I have planned with you to make Yokosuka the number one city in Japan. Where Yokosuka leads—others will follow.

"We have gone a long way on this road to improvement. It is timely that we now take another forward step—one of the most important and progressive steps taken by any city in the world. Yokosuka is about to prove that she is progressive, that she can lead in the crusade against venereal disease. This disease has long been one of man's great enemies. It has taken a huge toll in the health and wealth of all nations alike. It has been able to do this only because we have blindly and foolishly protected it by a false sense of shame.

"Venereal disease is no different from many communicable diseases. It is curable. Stigma is attached to it when it is allowed to remain uncured.

"During the war, because of economic reasons, Yokosuka had to endure it. This meeting is to end that. We are here to plan our attack upon VD—to stamp it out in Yokosuka.

"Thanks to the Yokosuka hospitals and to her splendid doctors, there are now six free clinics supplied with necessary drugs through our military government. Your duty is to create public opinion that will popularize the needed physical examinations and encourage those who have VD to submit to treatment.

"No longer will Yokosuka be known for its high rate but instead it will be known for its cleanliness.

"Yokosuka is cleaning house."

The VD rate in town was 457 per 1000! We ordered every workman on the base to take a VD test. Unfortunately the Japanese didn't have preventatives, nor had they taken VD seriously.

We had a tremendous supply of condoms—enough for an army. These were made available to liberty parties, but no one took any. The Women's Club was happy to receive our entire supply for distribution throughout the town. That was one way to skin the cat!

Reminders of "home and mother" were encouraged. American girls, such as the Red Cross, Navy nurses, and dependents, all made for stable conditions. Knowing that men needed female company, we made it possible for them to take their girls to the EM Club, where they could buy hamburgers and cokes. All Japanese were hungry, so our men became popular with the best girls. It was possible to dance in one of three dance halls in the club, or to see a movie. We didn't give the men much time to dawdle on the way home, for liberty expired thirty minutes after the last dance.

The officer in charge of the EM Club had been detached, so I replaced him with Ensign Tim Hahne. This was a most important assignment, and Hahne was a splendid choice. Tim would make that club into the best in our Navy. One day, I had asked him, "Tim, what do you know about running a club?"

Tim always answered by bragging about his father or his uncle, "My father was the best club manager!" he replied.

"That's great, Tim, for you are now the EM Club manager.

A few days later, Hahne came into my office. He was disturbed.

"Captain, do I have to inherit the former manager's mistress?" he continued, "A Japanese woman came to the club and demanded a list of supplies. When I asked why, she said that the former manager had told her that I would look after her needs. When I laughed at her, she said she would report me to you."

She must have had some good qualities, for the wives on Halsey Road knew her. But this blackmailing of Occupation personnel was out! I banned her from the Navy Yard.

Soon there was a noticeable improvement in the morale and appearance of our men. It was not long before the VD rates both in town and on the base dropped to 67. I gave Tim Hahne full credit for making the club so attractive to "good" girls and off limits to "bad" ones. Fraternization on the streets of Yokosuka was not to be seen.

The mayor showed initiative by planning a nationwide showing of our VD films. He came into my office with his plan.

"We would like to use the EM Club theater for a convention. The women will come from all over the nation—from Hokkaido to Kyushu. It will be a great boost for Yokosuka."

"That sounds great, Mr. Mayor, but who are these women?"

"They are the leading prostitutes of Japan."

Wow! I could see *Time* magazine with that for a story. "I am sorry, Mr. Mayor, but our Navy would not like me to hold a prostitutes' convention. You must cancel your plans."

"What can I do? They are on their way now."

"Sorry, but I will stop the train at Zushi."

The convention was held in army territory.

One day while casually inspecting the supply department with Commander Gray, I asked, "Walt, what's in that building?" pointing to a detached brick security-type building.

"Matches—VD matches. I wish I could get rid of them. This is our flammable storage, filled with ten tons of trouble."

During World War II some Brain Truster, just out of college, dreamt up the idea of VD matches. A sailor propositioning a girlfriend would light up a cigarette with a VD match. When he saw those warning letters on the match cover, he would be reminded of the terrible consequences and would be saved. Did it work? No way! No sailor would be caught afloat or ashore with a pack of VD matches in his pocket. Seldom does a man going on liberty have that in mind, and if he did, he wouldn't be stopped by a little pack of matches. It might stop the girl! So we were stuck with ten tons of matches.

I violated one of my rules. I wired Washington for permission to dispose of ten tons of VD matches. In reply I got ten tons more! Evidently they too wanted to get rid of theirs.

141

I gave all twenty tons to the Japanese, as part of my VD program. The Japanese were very short of matches, so these were most welcome. Every schoolchild got a carton. Every workman on the base got a carton, as did every woman in the Women's Club. The distribution was perfect. I loved those hundreds of colored pictures with notes from the school children, thanking me for the "beautiful VD matches." Maybe Washington knew what they were doing when they sent me their ten tons of matches!

We ordered electric chimes for our beautiful church. When they arrived we played well known hymns from 4:30 to 5:30 each day, just as the men on liberty were leaving the base. I called them my "VD chimes."

Edwina continues: Victor Boeson's article, "Thanks to the Yanks," was published in the December 14 issue of *Liberty* magazine. This was a story about Yokosuka under the Occupation. Benny was very pleased with the article and wrote Mr. Boeson the following letter:

19 December 1946

Mr. Victor Boeson
Dear Vic—

Your article was excellent. On the 16th I received the 14th December copy of Liberty Magazine which you so thoughtfully sent me. Not bad mail service! Immediately it became Yokosuka's most popular magazine. The people here all praised the article and join me in saying, "Thanks to Vic!"

Fan mail is now coming in. One letter suggested teaching the Japanese a new international language! Several old shipmates have written. Your command of the printed word has given us a big boost and encouraged us to keep the ball rolling.

The Women's Club has had its election, which was self imposed purge in keeping with the times. Printed ballots, locked ballot boxes, and telephoning of the count gave the women a big day. Mrs. Mabuchi would not run again, as she could not spare the time. The new president is Mrs. Fukuda, the elderly woman in the picture you printed. She was elected by 35,516 votes! (Enclosed is a picture of the relieving of the watch!)

142

The losers were crest fallen and felt great humiliation. I gave them a half hour's talk on the continued need for their services, and explained that Americans did not lose face when they lost office. If every person who was defeated committed hara kiri we would have no Republicans! They got the word and are now very happy.

The Taura Hospital deal went our way. The Japanese lost another fight but sooner or later they'll even the score by slipping a fast one over some unsuspecting junior officer in SCAP.

Syd Whipple comes in frequently to see us. This coming Saturday I am having him over for a big affair. . . . Dennis McEvoy, Mr. & Mrs. Tom Lambert, Mr. & Mrs. Miles Vaugh will be down. Mr. & Mrs. Crane and Mrs. Handelman can't make it.

Good luck and seasons greetings to you and yours.

As ever,

B. W. Decker

We had anticipated Christmas by ordering many Christmas trees, one for each dependent family, as well as many large ones for the clubs and activities. With each tree, the base issued ornaments as "presentoes" from the welfare fund. The people in town soon caught the Christmas fever!

We had a few language difficulties. I suppose the Japanese had as many laughs at our misuse of their language as we had at theirs.

Commander Hal Green, a dentist who lived on Halsey Road, was rushing to attend a Christmas party at our quarters when his tree arrived. Hurriedly, he turned to his house boy, "Boy san, you savvy trim tree?"

"I savvy trim tree," so Hal left. The houseboy then took out his pocket dictionary and looked up the word *trim*, and proceeded to trim off all of its branches.

During the war, the Japanese government had banned Christianity, and many Japanese did not know anything about Christianity. Benny believed that they should know something about the basic religion of the conquerors. This might help them to understand some of the reforms that General MacArthur was trying to bring about in the Occupation. The Japanese Christians were delighted that they could once more practice their religion openly, and many more were converted to Christianity.

Gozo Kawamura had established himself and his family in the large rooms in back of the stage of the Enlisted Men's Club. For weeks, with the assistance of his wife and daughter, he had been making life-sized nativity figures. A manger was erected on the corner of the vacant lot near the main gate. Soft lights focused on this lovely and awe-inspiring scene. An explanation was printed in Japanese on a sign at the side of the manger. This was to ensure that all who stopped to gaze would have some idea of the miraculous story.

We were happy to see large groups of people reverently

Christmas display at the main gate of the Base; the sculpture is by Gozo.

admiring this beautiful scene. The children brought bouquets of flowers to place before the manger. What a magnificent display of the true character of the Japanese people!

On Christmas Eve, Benny and I joined other Naval officers and their wives to sing Christmas carols on the Naval base. It was a thrilling sight to see the generously illuminated Christmas tree in the circle in front of the Administration Building. Miss Yamaguchi, a marvelous soprano who had sung at the Perry Monument Navy Day, sang once more for us. On top of the roof of the Administration Building was a large electric lighted star.

Christmas Day, after breakfast, our entire household and the outside workers, twenty-four in all, and our next door neighbors, Mr. & Mrs. Takaoka, assembled in the living room. Standing by the tree, Mrs. Takaoka handed me each package. As I read the name, the person came forward was given a present. The children were adorable.

At the invitation of the United States War Department, nine American publishers and editors arrived in Japan. They were: Roy Howard, President of the Scripps-Howard chain of newpapers; Carroll Binder, editor of the editorial page of the *Minneapolis Tribune*; Sevellon Brown, publisher of the *Providence Journal*; Erwin Canham, editor of the *Christian Science Monitor*; Wayne Coy, assistant publisher of the *Washington Post*; E. Z. Dimitman, executive editor of the *Chicago Sun*; Ralph J. Donaldson, chief editorialist of the *Cleveland Plain Dealer*; and Thor Smith, assistant publisher of the *San Francisco Call Bulletin*. They came to Japan on a far eastern inspection tour. On January thirteenth, Vice Admiral Griffin gave a luncheon for them at his home in Tokyo.

On February the second, 1947, Benny took these distinguished guests on a tour of the Naval base. Afterwards, these visitors were entertained at luncheon at the Officers' Club. The newspapermen were very favorably impressed with the Naval base, and Benny was quite pleased.

Chapter VII

TOURING JAPAN

Jeff Barnett, who operated the railroads for General Besson (chief of the transportation section), was to make an inspection trip. We were invited to go, and so on February twenty-second, we motored to Helm House to meet the colonel and Miss Mary Jose. From there, we proceeded to the Yokohama railroad station and boarded a private car, the Portland, where Colonel Wheeler greeted us. On the same train were Colonel and Mrs. Shonzi, and Major and Mrs. Smith. During the night their car was separated from ours and they went to Kyushu, while we continued on to Kyoto.

Early the next morning, we arrived at this famous old city, which had been the capital of Japan for more than a thousand years (794–1868). At the railroad station, we were taken through the Emperor's reception room. It was furnished in the style of Louis XVI and was very attractive.

Kyoto was not bombed during the war, for it was famous as a cultural and religious center. There are libraries, museums, the Kyoto Imperial University and Dishishia University, some smaller universities, and many other organizations. There are hundreds of Shinto and Buddhist shrines which are famous for their beauty and age. Unfortunately, time did not permit us to see everything.

We drove up a narrow road called, "Tea Pot Lane." Small stores lined the sides of the road. They reminded me of small booths at a county fair. We continued up the road until we came to the Kiyomizu (Clean Water) temple. This temple was dedicated to the eleven-faced Kan-non, the goddess of mercy. The first temple was built in 805 A.D., but present buildings date from 1633 A.D.

The main temple was built on the edge of a cliff. In front of it was a wooden platform. We walked to the railing and looked across the valley to the hills. At the foot of the cliff was a small pavilion, a light, ornamental building which housed the "needle shrine." Pious believers are often seen here offering prayers to Fudo-Myo-O, who is supposed to have the power to punish wicked beings. Through the early morning mist, the pagoda, with its magnificent, panoramic view of the city and mountains in the background, reminded me of some hanging scrolls (kakemono) that I had seen. I felt that what I was seeing was something that I had been looking for all my life. I had fallen in love with Japan.

We visited another temple, then we went through Yamanaka's museum and store, where we saw many tantalizing art treasures. On our way there, we passed through Maruyama Park. This park is famous for its 400-year-old cherry tree.

We stopped at the old Imperial Palace, which is surrounded by a high wall. It is situated on a large tract of land and we took quite awhile to walk around the grounds. The buildings were simple and attractive. The Coronation Building, the Emperor's private gate, and the Empress' garden were lovely reminders of centuries past.

After leaving the palace, we toured a brocade factory. Walking from loom to loom, we watched the skilled weavers comb their threads into position with their long, serrated finger nails. Many beautiful obis were being made. Later, in the display room, we saw many finished obis, magnificent tapestries, and other exquisite pieces.

After a delightful visit to the home of Mr. and Mrs. Hayashi, where we had a delicious luncheon, we returned to the railroad station and boarded our train.

In Osaka, Major General and Mrs. Mullens and the general's aide met us at the station. Colonel Wheeler was given a message from General MacArthur and had to return to Tokyo. The rest of our party crossed the channel that night.

The next day, after traveling through beautiful, snow-covered mountains which embrace the Yoshino-gawa Valley, we arrived at Kochi. The military government sent two jeeps to meet us. The drivers were very cordial, and we looked forward to our tour of the city.

Kochi is located on the South Coast and is one of two important cities on the island of Shikoku. The inhabitants are mostly farmers and fishermen, and rice is the principal crop.

A short distance from the station, I noticed a sign over a small shop. On it was crudely painted, "Peace Tea and Cake."

I was distressed with the poverty I saw. The streets were filled with shabbily dressed people, and even the best stores were little better than shacks. I had to admire, however, the friendliness and cheerfulness of those poor people. If they could ignore their sordid surroundings, we should too.

The damage done by the war was terrific, and what had been spared by that holocaust was finished off by a recent earthquake which was followed by a tidal wave. I have never seen such devastation in my life. The pavement looked like ocean waves and railroad ties were twisted and broken. One building was just a heap of rubble. Another was missing one whole side wall. The rice paddies were completely covered with salt water; there would be no crop that year.

We drove up a hill that had somehow escaped the disasters. At its crest, we joined our friends and the driver of the other jeep and walked over to Kochi Castle. This was built by a feudal lord, Yamanouchi, some time in the sixteenth century. Now the castle was deserted and run down. We went inside the musty old building and ascended the stairs to the tower. The view of the city and surrounding country was well worth the effort.

As the streets were full of chuckholes and the jeep seats hard, we were all pretty tired when we finally returned to the train. It was pleasant to sit back in the soft seats of our car and relax. It was about ten minutes of four when our train pulled out of the station.

That night we arrived at Todotsu. Our car was detached from the train and we spent the night on a siding near the station.

Early the next day, we traveled on to Matsuyama. As the city was under British command, we were met by the British Royal Welsh Fusiliers. After Benny and Colonel Barnett paid their official call on the commanding officer, we started out to see the city. It is situated on the inland sea and has a fine harbor. We explored the port area and then drove past the former Japanese fighter air field. Here we saw the synthetic gasoline factory.

After lunch we drove to the famous Dogo Hot Springs. Due to an earthquake, the springs were dried up and the place was no longer a tourist mecca. This was a great pity as it was one of the oldest hot springs in Japan. At about three, we left Matsuyama.

The next day, early in the morning, we arrived at Hiroshima which had been demolished by our first atomic bomb. Two jeeps were furnished and we started out to see the town. I was surprised that the people did not show any resentment toward us. I had thought that they would be seething with hostility. If there was any resentment, however, the people kept it to themselves.

Unless you saw Hiroshima as we did, you could not comprehend the terrible destruction. The city was a mass of rubble and twisted metal. Misshapen skeletons of buildings reared their ugly silhouettes over the silent town. We found pieces of broken china twisted with melted glass. A white jar, which we presumed to be a cold cream jar, was as flat as a pancake. Many of the buildings which were left standing were but hollow shells. The interiors were completely destroyed. Everywhere we looked, we saw visions of hell.

We wanted to see the famous Shadow Bridge, but could not find it. They say that a honey-bucket cart was going over the bridge when the atom bomb fell. The flash acted like a camera and the shadow of the man walking beside his ox was photographed onto the bridge.

The mayor stressed the fact that Hiroshima was the first city ever to have been atom bombed! No doubt it gave the city a unique place in history, but I am sure that his enthusiasm was not generally shared by the population. It was a dubious distinction!

The next stop on our trip was Matsue. After the grim testimony of Hiroshima, this city was like a breath of fresh air. The war seemed to have completely forgotten it, and we walked down the streets of Old Japan. After visiting an imposing old castle, we toured the house where Lafcadio Hearn, the famous writer, lived.

We left Matsue on the afternoon of February the twenty-seventh and arrived at Maizuru the next morning at six o'clock. Maizuru was the repatriation center for Japanese from all over the world. We went through the wooden buildings and saw many of the repatriates who were waiting to be either quarantined, inoculated, or questioned. Others had either been left behind, or were waiting to be released to return to their homes. It was an interesting but pathetic sight.

That evening, we arrived in Kanazawa. In some places, the snow was piled so high that it touched the second story

149

of the houses along the road. The dinner had been arranged by a prominent Japanese bank president and his vice president. The inn was attractive and our hosts were most cordial. Our waitresses were very attractive Japanese geisha girls who were dressed in beautiful kimonos. During the meal, we were entertained by dancing girls and Japanese music. It was a very pleasant evening.

The next morning we visited a silk factory and the Kutani Pottery factory. Later, we took a bus to the Hakaunro Hotel, high in the mountains in back of the city. This hotel was run by the Eighth Army as a rest camp for the men. We lunched in a private dining room and were served in the European style. I was attracted to the beautiful centerpiece, which was made of roses in ice.

Instead of the bus, we rode back to the railroad station in a weazel, a wartime tracked vehicle for land or sea. The ride down the steep mountain grades was exciting.

The evening of the second, we arrived at Nagano, an inland city. The next morning we went shopping and sightseeing and visited the famous Buddhist temple, Zenkogi Shrine, which was run by priestesses. Inside of its peaceful walls, all memories of the war faded into the shadows of the temples. We were ushered into the main reception room, where the high priestess greeted us most cordially. A middle-aged woman with a great deal of dignity, she wore a purple robe with a white neckpiece edged with green, white, and yellow brocade. Covering her shaved head was a fez-like hood which tapered off to a point just above and between her eyebrows.

There were two women attendants dressed in dark and simple attire. Their shaved heads were uncovered, and it would have been impossible to tell whether they were young boys or girls.

One of the priestess' attendants beckoned and the interpreter asked us to find a *zabuton* (cushion). We sat down Japanese fashion around a *chow* bench (low table). The high priestess sat on a beautiful *zabuton* on a slightly raised dais in front of a low, gold screen. We were served tea and little sweet bean cakes. While we were enjoying the refreshments, we took the opportunity to ask many questions.

The name of the temple was Zenko-ji! It was founded

thirteen hundred years ago and was rebuilt eleven times due to fires. The present temple was three hundred years old.

The high priestess' family name was Omekyo, which was changed to Gyokuyo (which means "precious stone"). With her attendants and her interpreter, she traveled all over Japan. In April, she planned to visit Nagoya. Here she wished to preach in the temples. This sect of the Buddhist faith was "dedicated" to charities and to educate the children in "good direction" and was one of the most popular sects in Japan, having one million followers.

At sixteen, the high priestess came to Zenko-ji from the Kyoto School, where she had prepared herself for this religious life from the age of thirteen. Now, at sixty-three, she had spent almost fifty years at Zenko-ji.

There were fifty male priests in the cathedral area. They have the right to marry, but the priestesses may not.

I was pleased that the high priestess believed that the Japanese women should have the right to vote. Though a member of the Imperial family, she approved of women from all walks of life joining the sisterhood.

Every morning from five o'clock to seven there is a religious ceremony for the members of the temple. When this is over, they all have breakfast, which is followed by another service. The high priestess reads religious books between these services. No meat, wine, or tobacco is ever partaken by the members of this Buddhist order. The next high priestess, who will succeed Gyokuyo at her death, is called the vice president.

Delinquent boys and girls are encouraged and taught farming and straw manufacturing by the sisters and priests. The Japanese government paid the boys and girls one yen per day (about three cents in our money) while learning. The results were usually good.

When we finished eating, the high priestess gave me a string of beads similar to a Catholic rosary. In the large center bead was a small picture of Gyokuyo. I had to close one eye and hold the bead to the other to see the picture. We were also given a white china cup on three legs, which was very small like a sake cup.

We thanked the High Priestess for her kindness and bid her good-bye. Her attendants and the interpreter took us through the temple. Everywhere there were beautiful *kakemonos* (hanging scrolls) depicting the life of Buddha and other religious leaders. In one room there were gold engraved tablets and little shrines dedicated to departed Japanese.

The trip from Nagano to Yokohama was short and we arrived at the Higashi station at about ten o'clock. Benny's driver was waiting for us. We thanked Colonel Barnett for arranging such a pleasant trip, bid him and Mary Jose good-bye. Though it was quite late when we arrived home, the servants were waiting for us. They welcomed us in such a warm and friendly way that we were quite touched. It was good to be back home.

On March the fifth, Benny and his staff officers entertained members of the Chinese press at a cocktail and luncheon party given at the Officers' Club.

The note of appreciation was typewritten on creamy satin brocade with a gold border framing a parade of Chinese chariots followed by men on foot. On one side of the note, at the bottom of the left hand corner, was printed in gold lettering, "The Chinese Press Party to Japan." On the other side the same message was written in Chinese characters. Inside, the note read:

July 1, 1947

Dear Capt. Decker:

This brief note is to express to you the deep appreciation of the members of the Chinese Press Party to Japan for the kindness you accorded to them during their stay in Japan from March 26 to April 14. It was a great privilege to enjoy all the facilities of your office where you were good enough to place at the disposal of the Press Party. It was largely due to these facilities that our tour of Japan and Korea was such a tremendous success.

The Press Party has instructed me to send to you a few small mementoes from China (pillows). They will naturally not fully express our appreciation, but we hope show in a small measure the warm sentiments of all the members of the Press Party toward the pleasure

of meeting you and enjoying your hospitality.
With kindest regards,

I remain,
Yours very respectfully,
Chen Posheng
in charge of
the Chinese Press Party to Japan

The Yokosuka Girls' High School held their graduation exercises at the school on the eleventh. The governor of the prefecture, Mr. Uchiyama, and the mayor of Yokosuka presided, and I was asked to say a few words. Mrs. Takaoka accompanied me to the exercises and interpreted for me. Commander Higgins and Lieutenant Huggins were also among the guests.

At the end of the exercises, the entire graduation class started to weep. I asked Mrs. Takaoka why they were crying. She said that during the war they had been drafted, and their education had stopped. These girls were sent far away from their homes to work in defense factories. Now, after all that they had been through, they were finally graduating, and their emotions got the better of them.

On March the fifteenth, the Sea Scouts, a newly organized group of teenage daughters of Army officers stationed in Yokohama, came to Yokosuka on their maiden voyage. Benny and I met them at the pier when they arrived. A luncheon was given for them at the Officers' Club, and afterwards we took them on a tour of Yokosuka. We visited the old battleship *Mikasa* and then explored the headquarters' cave. The girls were enthusiastic about everything and were delightful guests.

Springtime in Japan is perfectly beautiful. Our garden commenced to show signs of life as early as the first week in February, when the plum trees began to blossom. The plum blossom is prized in Japan as a symbol of perseverance, because it is the first flower to appear after the winter's cold.

The budding activity in our garden mirrored the activity on the Naval base. Streets and curbs were being laid out for the best housing area for the service personnel in all of Japan, and construction of some single duplex houses had already begun. Spring was a time of rebirth and rejuvenation for the Yokosuka base as well as for the surrounding countryside. Benny and the officers and men under his command were like the plum blossoms. They persevered.

On April tenth, the clubs celebrated the first anniversary of Benny's command in Yokosuka. My husband attended the party at the Petty Officers' Club where he gave the following speech:

A year ago I reported to this station. In that year great changes have taken place. These improvements were created by you—the officers and men of this command. Many officers returning to Yokosuka are amazed at the improvements—they congratulate me on what they see.

The credit is yours. From today, we will accomplish twice the task of last year. We fully support the forces afloat and ashore. We repair and dock the ships—we feed them—fuel them—and give them recreational facilities—all with a smile. You are the people who have created a reputation of friendliness as well as efficiency from California to Korea.

Today you wear the uniform and conduct yourselves like men of war. You render the military courtesies as confident and able blue jackets. Your conduct, far above last year's standards, is above reproach. Your VD rate is low. Black market activities in Yokosuka are the lowest in Japan. I am proud to be your commanding officer.

Today at the close of my first year in command I thank you all for the part you have contributed to the success of this Occupation—and for your help in building our peace time Navy reputation. Everyone in the Pacific has heard of Yokosuka—a bit of the True Navy.

I feel confident that with your backing the next year will continue to see Fleet Activities leading the way.

Benny returned to the Officers' Club party where a decorated cake was wheeled into the dining room. He cut the cake with the sword.

As I gaze at the menu with Benny's picture on the cover, I am quite nostalgic about that evening, and it would not take much to make me cry. How I would love to see all of those wonderful people again!

The officers and their wives gave me three orchids. Bella and Al Dunning (Naval captain on Vice Admiral Griffin's staff) had also given me two, so that evening I was "dripping" with orchids.

The fifteenth was a beautiful day filled with the fragrance of cherry blossoms. It was the perfect time to have a party honoring Mrs. MacArthur.

We had invited this wonderful lady to inspect the Yokosuka Naval Base and attend a garden party luncheon in her honor. Here she would meet all the officers and their wives. As a part of the preparation for her first visit, Ensign Millard Carlson was asked if it would be all right to show Mrs. MacArthur his new apartment as a typical example of the housing provided on the base for Navy families. Delighted, but somewhat apprehensive, Ensign Carlson agreed. He and his wife had only recently moved in, and had not yet completely settled. One bedroom was being used for storage, no drapes were up, and only the essential items of furniture and furnishings were in place. Unfortunately, Benny was not aware of this.

When he arrived home that evening, Millard told his wife, Edna, "Mrs. MacArthur is coming to see our place tomorrow."

"What—Mrs. MacArthur!"

Their excitement at the imminent visit slowly mixed with bewilderment as they surveyed their apartment with new eyes.

"But, I haven't finished our drapes yet! And the bedroom is full of boxes!"

"Oh well, honey, don't worry too much about it, Captain Decker said they might not have time to stop—and if they aren't here by eleven A.M., they probably won't come."

Edna and Millard spent the evening arranging and rearranging furniture. This was as much to help quell their ex-

155

citement as to make their home presentable. In some inexplicable manner, the news of the imminent visit traveled through the immediate neighborhood. Friends offered drapes, vases and flowers, rugs, and anything else that might improve the appearance of their abode.

When Millard came home the next day, just before noon, he was shocked to find Edna in her housecoat, with her hair up and no makeup!

"Well, did they come?"

"Did who come?"

"Mrs. MacArthur and Captain Decker!"

"No. You said they'd be here *after* the luncheon!"

Millard insisted he had told Edna the correct time for the visit, eleven A.M., *if* they came. And Edna just as firmly denied it.

"It doesn't matter now, honey, because it's almost noon. We might as well get ready to go."

As they started dressing, Edna cried in a startled voice. "Millard—they're here!"

"What!"

Edna grabbed her robe as the doorbell rang and told Millard to duck into the bedroom.

"The bathroom is cuter than the bedroom!"

As Edna answered the door, Millard, clad only in his scivvies, scurried into the bathroom, which he assumed to be the safer place.

Edna's apologies and explanations for her appearance were most graciously accepted by Mrs. MacArthur. She put the embarrassed woman at ease by saying that, under similar circumstances, she would be reluctant to show her house. Edna, however, insisted.

As they moved into the hallway, Millard locked the bathroom door. Edna tried the knob, but it wouldn't turn. She just knew that Omiko, the little Japanese maid, had hidden there.

"You can't come in here!"—a quiet voice from Millard.

"I'm sorry, Mrs. MacArthur, but my husband is in the bathroom."

Mrs. MacArthur again laughed off a second embarrassment. Edna was reassured when she glanced at Captain Decker and found him still grinning, apparently pleased with

156

the spontaneous informality of the visit.

As the entourage drove off, Millard emerged from the bathroom. He had not even met Mrs. MacArthur.

The group left the Carlson's home and proceeded to our house, where the guests, including Vice Admiral and Mrs. Griffin, were waiting. Seventy-seven officers and their wives were waiting to greet Mrs. MacArthur. Many Japanese dignitaries, such as Mayor Ota; Mrs. Kawabata, president of the Japanese local Red Cross; Mrs Mabuchi, president of the Shinsei Women's Club; and Mr. Murata, president of the Uraga Shipbuilding Co., were also present. The Japanese

Mrs. MacArthur receives in our garden the floral tribute from the City of Yokosuka.

bowed low and presented her with a beautiful bouquet of flowers.

Mrs. Carlson was chosen to pin an orchid on Mrs. MacArthur, who jokingly greeted her, "I see your husband finally got out of the bathroom!" This started the party in a gay mood.

Everyone present at the party seemed to enjoy the affair and was impressed with Mrs. MacArthur. She is indeed one of the sweetest women I have ever met. This delighted our officers and their wives and ensured that the Navy met this charming and friendly First Lady of Japan.

Tokyo
April 16, 1947

Dear Captain & Mrs. Decker,

I feel sure you both realized how much I enjoyed my day with you in Yokosuka. Everything I saw was of such great interest and everyone I met—so delightful. The General has been very interested in hearing about it all. It was so thoughtful of you to plan this for us and I can't begin to thank you enough.

Hope to see you in Tokyo before too long. Best wishes to you both.

Sincerely,
Jean MacArthur

Admiral Louis Denfield, chief of naval operations, and his staff came to Japan to inspect the Naval facilities afloat and ashore. This was the first visit of one of the joint chiefs to Yokosuka.

The twenty-sixth was a wonderful day for Benny. This was the day that the Admiral inspected the Naval base. He was favorably impressed and agreed with Benny's hope that the United States should keep this base.

The next day, we went to Yokohama and boarded the private railroad car, the Portland at 8:10 P.M. Jeff Barnett was going to make his last inspection trip before leaving for the States, and we were again invited to accompany him. His other guests were Colonel Herbert Wheeler, who was on General MacArthur's staff, and Colonel Wilson.

The next morning, early, we arrived at Toba. Mr.

Mikimoto's grandson met us, and we boarded the most ancient little train that I had ever seen. Fortunately, we did not have a long ride, or I would have been frozen by the time we arrived at the Pearl Farm. A very old boat was waiting at the dock, and soon we were put-putting over to the island where the factory was located.

Tatoku Island, the home of Mikimoto pearls, is in Ago Bay, off the coast of Shima Peninsula, which juts out into the Pacific from the middle of Japan proper. Tatoku means "many virtues," and it was given the farm by Arasuke Sone, Minister of Agriculture and Commerce. In January 1896, Mr. Mikimoto obtained a patent from the government to start his pearl farm.

Upon our arrival, we were given a startling exhibition of pearl diving. Three Japanese girls, dressed in long white mother hubbards and goggles, dove off a small boat about one hundred feet away. Each girl had a basket in one hand. Before diving, the girls took long, deep breaths. It sounded like they were whistling. In an instant, they disappeared from sight. It seemed to be ages before they finally bobbed to the surface with their baskets full of oysters. The divers repeated this performance several times. It was very cold, and we all felt that they had had quite enough, and so signaled them to climb back into the boat. Much to our surprise, they took off their only garments, which were used to protect them from jellyfish, and began to wring out the water. I was so startled that I am afraid that I lost my composure. The divers were stark naked! My face, I know, must have turned all shades of scarlet. I walked away and turned toward the building.

Shortly after the Occupation started, the Army had ordered that the divers wear a garment when diving. The Occupation would not permit them to dive naked. Therefore, they wore the white cotton slips.

We toured the factory and saw how the oysters were piled and sorted, then opened. The pearls were graded for color, perfection, and size. We were given knives and shown how to open an oyster. Benny and I were each given three to open. The pearls were to be our gift from Mr. Mikimoto. We acquired four or five lovely specimens. I found three in one oyster! Two were cultured pearls, while one was a natural.

The naturals were small, but the others were one-fourth inch in diameter. We were also each given a lovely string of pearls.

The most interesting part of our tour was watching the skillful Japanese girls seed the oysters. Using their surgical instruments to partially open the shells, they placed small clam shell beads inside the oysters as irritants and then quickly closed them again. These oysters, with their unwanted house guests, were placed in a closed basket under floating rafts. Here they were left for four years, as it takes that long to make a pearl of commercial size.

After leaving the factory, we were introduced to Mr. Koichi Mikimoto, who had gotten out of a sickbed to greet us. A fine old gentleman of ninety years of age, Mr. Mikimoto wore a little black derby hat and a long black cape. He had been given a similar hat by Thomas Edison in 1926. Being a great admirer of Mr. Edison, Mikimoto had worn this hat on special occasions ever since.

When Major General Lester visited the pearl farm, he decided that he would give Mr. Mikimoto a new derby hat. This was the one that the old gentleman now wore.

After we were all introduced, Mr. Mikimoto gave us each a toy diving girl on a stick. There was a tiny pearl in the hands of the girl, who was suspended from a string attached to a U-shaped stick of bamboo. When the bamboo was squeezed, the little figure made a diving motion.

We thanked Mr. Mikimoto for our wonderful visit and for the toys, then bid him a fond farewell. Time had flown all too quickly.

We putted back to the mainland in the little boat and returned to Toba on the ancient train. We boarded the Portland, and were soon on our way again.

The next day, we arrived in Nagoya. This city had been about 60 percent destroyed. The few remaining buildings were modern in appearance, and we enjoyed seeing the largest torii gate in Japan. We visited the famous Noritaki china factory and the Ando cloisonne factory.

Cloisonné enamels are called *shippo* in Japan. It is the name for the Sanskrit "Septa-Ratna" or Seven Heavenly Treasures in Buddhist Sutra. These treasures are gold, silver, emerald, agate, coral, crystal, and pearl, and are well exemplified in the *shippo* enamels.

The oldest specimen of cloisonné dates back to the third century A.D. Modern cloissoné, however, was initiated in the early 1800s by Mr. T. Koji, whose grandson, Mr. Sataro Koji, founded the Ando Studio in 1880. Today Ando enamels are the best specimens of *shippo* to be found.

Cloisonné has a metal base, either copper or silver, upon which ribbon-shaped wires of those same materials are glued. These wires outline the artist's design and are soldered in place by firing. Enamel pastes of different colors fill in the cells formed by the wires. Three layers are necessary, as the paste shrinks when fired. The surface is then ground and smoothed with several graded whetstones, after which it is hand polished. Finally, metal (usually silver) bands are set to cover the top and bottom edges of the piece.

The tour of the factory was fascinating, and I was very impressed with the patience of the men who squatted on the floor, carefully applying the wires to the intricate designs. The afternoon passed all too quickly, and we once more returned to our train.

We arrived in Kyoto about five in the evening and had dinner in Hayashi's house. The next day, we saw the famous Heian Shrine and the Silver Pavilion (Ginkakuji) and the Niju Castle. We visited the Kawashima silk-weaving factory where we witnessed the creation of stunning obis and tapestries. The Nishimura lacquerware factory was even more interesting. We motored to Nara where we fed some deer with bran crackers bought at a wayside stand.

Nara was the first capital of Japan (709–784). The first written histories of Japan were compiled here in the eighth century. Fire and time have levelled some of the old structures, but this city is still considered the cradle of the rarest cultural heritages of Japan.

On our way to the Kasuga Taisha Shrine, we passed about eighteen hundred stone lanterns on both sides of the walk. We had to climb a few steps at a time, ever forging upward, and I was glad when we finally reached the vermilion-lacquered sanctuary. There were 1000 metal lanterns hanging from the rafters along the balcony. The beautiful architecture and the enchanted setting of this famous shrine gave it a fairytale quality. The surrounding garden was beyond description. The so-called backyard had a tree whose trunk had been grafted with six different kinds of trees—

camellia, wisteria, mandarin, cherry, maple, and elder. This tree is known to the Japanese as an emblem of constancy.

As we stood in front of the shrine admiring the entrance, we were told to look up at the roof. There, we saw a monkey.

"Don't get any closer," said our guide, "if you do, the monkey will throw a tile at you."

We thought it very kind of him to warn us. Then he added, "The roof will be ruined if many more tiles are thrown."

The Todai-ji (Great Eastern Temple) was the next temple we visited. The imposing pillars and two gigantic wooden figures of Nio—the guardians of Buddhism, are regarded as the best existing examples of the sculpture of the Kamakura Period (1185–1333).

We saw the Big Bell, which is hung from huge rafters in a belfry at the center of the compound. This bell, which was cast in 752 A.D., is used only on special occasions. (For ten yen, the priest let us ring it!) A large log, suspended horizontally by ropes attached to the rafters, is used to sound the bell. I stood under it and looked up into its shadowy cavern. It is enormous, and is reported to be the second largest bell in Japan. Its dimensions are 13.6 feet in height with a base of 9.2 feet in diameter. The walls are 10 inches thick, and the circumference is 27 feet. It weighs 48 tons! We walked over to the Hall of Great Buddha. In Japanese, it is called, "Nara no Daibutsu" (the great image of Buddha of Nara). The large wooden building looked very old and neglected, but had a mysterious air. The sloping roof betrayed its Chinese influence.

As we walked up to the platform, we noticed a carved wooden seated image of Buddha to the right of the entrance. On his head was a tattered scarf, anf he was dressed in rags. It seems that this Buddha was in disgrace.

The great hall was overshadowed by the huge, bronze image of Buddha. It is supposed to be the biggest of its kind in the world. After repeated trials in casting, it was completed in 752 A.D. It is 53.5 feet high. The face is 16 feet long and 9 feet wide. Each eye measures 3.9 feet across, while the ears are 8.5 feet long. The length of the thumb is 4.8 feet, and the image weighs nearly 500 tons.

In a semicircle over the head of the image are lesser

deities. Everything is covered with gold leaf. It was dazzling.

At the bottom of one pillar was an opening. Our guide said that it was considered very lucky to crawl through this hole. As it was not very wide or tall, we decided that only a small person could crawl through. We would have had to have been very lucky to achieve such a feat.

From Nara, we motored to a suburb to see the famous Horiuji (temple). It is the oldest existing Buddhist temple in Japan, and some of its buildings are probably the oldest wooden structures in the world (607 A.D.).

The "Kondo" wall paintings were exquisite, and we were quite impressed by a group of bronze images attributed to Japan's pioneer Buddhist sculptor, Tori Busshi.

This temple was one of the three headquarters of the Hosso sect of Buddhism. There are thirty-three structures inside the compound and twenty-one of these buildings are registered as national treasures. Prince Shotoku, Regent of the Empress Suiko, built this temple. Here is preserved the essence of ancient Buddhist fine arts.

The drive back to Kyoto was pleasant, but by this time we were all pretty tired. We were glad to again board our train.

Early the next morning, we arrived in Yokohama. Mr. Imomara and Burkhart, Benny's driver, met us at the station. We thanked our host, Colonel Barnett, and bid good-bye to the other guests.

The servants greeted us with wide smiles, and we were glad to be able to visit with our houseguests, Helen and Bill Costello. Bill, a C.B.S. commentator, was preparing a story about Yokosuka.

May the sixteenth was a very important day for Yokosuka. Prince Nobuhito Takamatsu, the brother of the Emperor, and Prince Tadatsuga Shimatsu and Norizani Ikeda came to our house for lunch. Upon his arrival, Prince Takamatsu surprised us by greeting Chieko, our "number one" maid, with some familiarity. He had immediately recognized her and talked with her at some length. She was the widow of a Japanese Navy captain, Shiba. From the Prince's behavior, it was obvious that Chieko was a lady of quality, which of course we had known from the first.

The Prince was a fascinating man whose friendliness put

our guests at ease. He was renowned for his democratic tendencies and was a well-traveled and extremely intelligent man.

After the luncheon, Benny and I took our royal guests to the Enlisted Men's Club. Upon our arrival, the mayor of Yokosuka, Mr. and Mrs. Ohta; the governor of Kanagawa prefecture, Mr. and Mrs. Uchiyama; and Mrs. Kawabata, president of the newly formed local branch of the Japanese National Red Cross Society, greeted us. After some pictures were taken, we went up the stairs to the auditorium.

When the people saw the Prince, they rose to their feet

Prince Takamatsu opens the Japanese Red Cross in Yokosuka. *L to R*—Mayor Ohta, Capt. Decker, Mrs. Uchiyama, Mrs. Decker, Prince Takamatsu, Mrs. Kawabata, and Governor Uchiyama.

and gave him quite an ovation. We walked to the stage and took our seats. As soon as the Prince and Princess sat down, the audience followed suit.

Mrs. Kawabata introduced the Prince. As he left his chair, all of the people again stood to honor him. The Prince, with his hand, signaled for the people to sit down.

He had come to Yokosuka to officially recognize the first local branch of the Japanese National Red Cross Society. This branch was called the Yokosuka branch of the Kanagawa chapter.

The Prince spoke to more than twelve hundred men and women. He gave them the encouragement that was needed to organize the Yokosuka chapter along democratic lines. Though there were forty-eight established chapters of the Japanese Red Cross Society, the Yokosuka branch was the first unit to serve the needs of a local community. This branch marked the initial inception of a unit founded to serve local residents.

On this opening day, the society reported a paid senior and junior membership of 1645 men and women, with women predominating. It had a treasury income of Y725,000.

When the meeting was over, all of the officials came with us to accompany the Prince and Princess to their automobile. We reluctantly bid them good-bye and watched them depart.

Sir William and Lady Webb came to our house to have lunch with us on Sunday, the eighteenth. Major and Mrs. Place and Captain Kirten were our other guests. The conversation was fascinating, and touched upon the war crimes trial and the future of Asia, as well as many other interesting topics.

General Blake, U.S.M.C., with his chief of staff, Colonel Loomis, and other members of his staff, came out to Yokosuka to inspect the Marine unit. Benny and I gave a dinner party that evening (the twentieth) in honor of the General and his staff. Among these guests was Father Hubbard. After dinner, the father showed colored movies of Alaska, "The Valley of Ten Thousand Smokes." Father Hubbard narrated, and his enthusiasm for Alaska and his wit were most refreshing.

The next day, Benny and I took Brigadier General Blake

on a sightseeing trip. We went over to Kurihama, passed the Perry monument, and drove almost to Misaki. I was disappointed that time did not permit us to go there, for it was such a picturesque fishing village. Unfortunately, we had to return in time to get ready for a dinner party in Yokohama.

It was a pleasure to receive the following letter from General Blake:

Pearl Harbor
30 May 1947

Dear Captain Decker,

Inspection trips at best are usually quite dreary affairs but thanks to you and Mrs. Decker, my visit to Yokosuka was, for me, a most delightful one. So I wish to thank you both again for the considerate hospitality which you extended to me there. I hope that the fine work you are are doing at the Base will not go unrecognized, and that our future policy will not permit it to be lost to our nation's defenses.

With best wishes to both you and Mrs. Decker, I am
Very sincerely yours,
Robert W. Blake

On May the twenty-second, the Yoshi Catholic Boys' School in Yokosuka had their formal opening exercises. Bishop Breton, Father Bitter from Tokyo, Father Voss, General Chevalerie, the Ambassador from Belgium, and other guests were present. Members of the Catholic Women's Guild served refreshments of tea and cake. Both Benny and I felt much like proud godparents.

It was the months of schools. May being the first month of the school year. We were invited to attend the opening of "The Sacred Heart of Jesus School for Girls" on May the twenty-fourth. Mother Ernestina, a native of Argentine, was the Mother Superior. She and the other nuns were so gracious, and the program was very interesting. This school was located in former Japanese naval barracks. The nuns had done wonders for it, and there were about seven hundred students at this time.

Mrs. Takaoka accompanied Mrs. Hochmuth and me to visit the Mabuchi School for deaf and dumb children. The school was located on the outskirts of Yokosuka on the road to Camp McGill. Mrs. Akira Mabuchi and her husband, the principal and founder, met us upon our arrival at the school. I was quite surprised to find such an attractive building. The entrance hall was cheerful and inviting. We visited all of the classrooms and watched, fascinated, as the teachers instructed the children. Old fashioned beanbags were tossed around for sound vibrations.

The children were so friendly and seemed unaware of their handicaps. The dancing class was impressive. The children were taught to dance to music that was coming from a record on an old fashioned phonograph machine. Of course, they could not hear the music, but they kept time by feeling the vibrations.

We visited the hobby shop and watched some older boys make rattan furniture. The Mabuchis invited us to have tea in the principal's office. After a delightful social hour, we thanked our host and hostess and departed. This school had been established long before the Occupation, and was an excellent example of the unusual!

On the evening of the twenty-seventh, Benny and I took the Takaokas with us to Tokyo. We attended a small dinner party at the beautiful mansion of Prince and Princess Takamatsu. The other guests were Prince and Princess Shimazu. Princess Takamatsu was a lovely woman who was a joy to look at. She spoke excellent English and had a marvelous sense of humor. I found her a very cultured and a fine conversationalist. Princess Shimazu was also charming. After cocktails were served in a living-room, we walked into the beautiful formal dining room. A menu lay at each of our places. It had the Prince's mon, or crest, on it, and read:

Consomme Printanier
Ayu fruits au Citron
Boeuf Braise's
Legume
Bavarois Diplomate

I was seated at Prince Takamatsu's right and Prince Shimazu was seated at my right. Benny sat at Princess Takamatsu's right and Princess Shimazu's left. We enjoyed the company and the delicious dinner very much. Following the dinner, we withdrew to the living room for coffee and cordials. It was a most delightful evening.

The next day, the transport *Le Jeune* arrived. We went down to the Piedmont pier to meet the ship. Mrs. Cook, wife of Vice Admiral Cook, was a passenger. She introduced us to Sumner Wells' daughter-in-law, Mrs. Ben Wells. Vice Admiral and Mrs. Griffin and Rear Admiral and Mrs. Bledsoe met the ship also. The Bledsoes gave a luncheon for these distinguished guests and we were invited. The luncheon was given at the Bledsoes' lovely home in Kamakura. Conditions in China were discussed and we heard that they were not too good. We could not let world affairs dampen our spirits and we had a delightful afternoon.

June 7, 1947

Dear Captain and Mrs. B. W. Decker,

There will be a Gratitude to U.S.N. Party at Mr. Mabuchi's estate June 10th, Tuesday from four o'clock to five o'clock in the afternoon.

You are cordially invited to attend this party and to meet the members of our committee.

Ichiro Tajimi, Chairman
Gratitude to USN Committee,
Yokosuka

A soap factory was going to open soon. They wanted to call the soap "Edwina Soap." What a refreshing thought! They were also planning to market a new product, something like DDT. They wished to call this "Decker."

There was never a dull moment in our lives!

That evening, we gave a dinner party for thirty guests. It was an interesting evening as we had Father Flanagan of Boys' Town, Ambassador George Atcheson, and the new Minister to Korea, Mr. George Jacobs, among our guests.

The *Fall River* was to return to the United States. A farewell party was given at the Officers' Club on the evening of the sixteenth, for the departing officers. "Turk" Wirth and Captain Detzer each cut out a piece of a large cake with a Japanese sword. We were sorry to see that Father Flanagan was among those slated to leave in the cruiser.

We had grown very fond of this wonderful man in the few short days he had been in Yokosuka. He was enthusiastic over the Eiko Gakuen Boys' Catholic School that had been recently started by the Jesuits. Benny had assigned some vacant ex-Japanese Navy buildings to this Catholic order to start a school for Japanese boys. With Father Poznanski, Nelson B. Neff (Col., U.S.A.R.) from General Whitney's office in Tokyo and Father Voss and two priests, Benny took Father Flanagan through the buildings. This school was located near Taura.

Chapter VIII

MASONRY IN YOKOSUKA

At the age of twenty-one, I was raised to the degree of Master Mason. I was the fourth generation of Masons of direct Decker descent. My mother's side, however, was Catholic. In my life there had been little conflict between the Catholics and Masons, and there was none in Yokosuka. I firmly believed in the value of Masonry to educate my men. As a young officer, I coached many sailors in their Masonic work, and as a lieutenant at the training station in San Diego, I traveled the Southern part of California performing the third degree initiation ceremony. It was natural for me to encourage the growth of Masonry in Yokosuka. We were fortunate to have on the base Chief Sofield, a Master Mason. I had previously had him under my command on a destroyer in San Diego. He was an inspired Mason, and encouraged the fraternity among the men. He applied to the jurisdiction of California for a dispensation to open a lodge on the Base.

Why the supreme lodge of California turned us down is unknown to me, but it was a blunder of the first magnitude! The lodge on the Philippines, however, was more cooperative, even though the people still had fresh memories of the Japanese Occupation of their land. Thus, our Masonic lodge had its birth. A previous lodge had been located in Yokohama and had been restricted, by the Japanese to foreigners only. When the war began, the lodge was raided by the police. The Worshipful Master promptly recessed the meeting and turned off the lights. The Yokohama lodge once again turned on their lights, only a few days before we opened.

Our lodge was in a former rear admiral's house on Unnecessary Mountain, close to the Administration Building. The house was so inaccessible that no dependents desired to live in it. At first, I had encouraged my Catholics to use it for their Catholic Youth Organization and their Catholic Women's Organization. But they chose to use the Mikasa Building, which was far more convenient, and so the Masons obtained their fraternal lodge. Everyone was happy. This masonic lodge is still active.

I had tried to get the Knights of Columbus to open a unit on the base, but they rejected the opportunity, as they were limited to the continental limits of the United States. This was a disappointment, as they would have been a good influence for my men. All through my naval career, I had found that these organizations gave the officers and men a purpose and an excellent education and kept them out of trouble. I was amazed at the improvement in several of my officers. Although they had had little formal education, their speech improved and their capacity to reason was greatly enhanced. In addition, they acquired a certain polish.

The dependents were soon to form auxiliaries of those societies. Mrs. Gonzales opened the first Eastern Star (the women's auxiliary) in Japan, and we were the first to start the DeMolay, the organization for boys under twenty-one.

Large shipments of surplus food were being shipped from the United States for the Japanese. These would often include food that was novel to the Japanese. In such cases, they would make an unpalatable goulash out of several strange items. One day, the schools had corn, pineapple, and catsup cooked as one dish. When the children refused to eat it, our dependent wives went into the schools and prepared the food in appetizing dishes. In this way, the Japanese learned to eat foods other than their usual rice, pickle, and daikon. Today, because of better nutrition, they are taller than their parents.

A recommended mission of the Naval base was received through the chain of command:

(1) Provide Base services to vessels assigned ComNavFE and vessels on Bahrain-Yokosuka run. Provide similar services to transient vessels as required. Base services include repair, docking, supply, hospitalization, oil storage and issue, boat service, recreation, fleet post office, mail and courier service, motion picture exchange, permanent shore patrols in Yokosuka and Tokyo, and other activities prescribed in PacFlt Letter 21-47.

(2) Carry out occupational duties. These include pratique, military government of U.S. area of responsibility containing a quarter million Japanese, disposal of enemy equipment, and preservation of the plant equipment of the dockyard for reparations.

(3) Maintain custody of U.S. share of ex-Japanese naval vessels until final disposition.

(4) Operate Radio Tokyo transmitting station.

(5) Provide logistic support for naval personnel including dependents ashore in the Yokosuka-Tokyo area and the Coast Guard Personnel (Lorran Station) on Oshima.

(6) Provide transportation and other logistic services for NATS.

CincPac approved this with modifications as follows:—

By separate correspondence. Cincpacflt will recommend long-range requirements and an ultimate mission for Yokosuka. As an interim measure, approval of the mission outlined in paragraph 3 of the basic letter is recommended, subject to the following additional and qualifying considerations:

(1) The number of vessels to be assigned to ComNavFe will not be appreciably increased over the number now assigned. The withdrawal of 3 DE's during fiscal 1948 is planned. Vessels of DE class or larger will be rotated and will not normally require extensive overhaul or replacement of spare parts at Yokosuka.

(2) Repair facilities in excess of those normally avail-

able in a tender will not be required except that docking facilities will be available for routine docking of minor craft and for emergency docking of vessels of the DE class or larger.

(3) Except as required for training purposes, current stocks of ammunition, torpedoes and depth charges will not be replaced.

(4) The number of Marines assigned is considered adequate for performing security duties in the city of Yokosuka and the fleet facilities area.

(5) Stock levels will be promulgated by a separate letter.

(6) The training of Japanese to replace US Naval personnel will be intensified. The maximum practicable and legal use of Japanese is enjoined, consistent with security of classified material.

(7) Facilities in excess of those required to fulfill the approved interim mission, as qualified above, will be inactivated.

This was the first definite mission assigned the base and was a positive step toward the recognition of Yokosuka as part of the Navy's support in the Far East. It encouraged me to believe that the Yokosuka Naval base would be retained after the peace treaty.

Edwina reports:

It was my second summer in Yokosuka, and perhaps my last. My life as the wife of the Commander Fleet Activites was proving most interesting, and Benny assured me that I was of value to the United States in winning friends among the Japanese.

(Benny speaking: I must break in on Edwina's report to assure the world that Edwina was a great help and contributed much to the success of the Occupation of Yokosuka. I thoroughly believe that much of the goodwill and the success I had with the Shinsei Women's Club can be attributed to Edwina, the co-author of this book)

On the Fourth of July, Benny and I went to the Imperial Plaza in Tokyo to attend the big parade. A military parade is always exciting, but this show of the strength of the Allied forces was most impressive.

The Navy men marched in the Army parade, and I was very proud of them. The Indian Gurkhas, however, stole the show. They were stunning with their high turbans, leopard skins, and their batons. I thought it wonderful that the British Army would march with our men in a Fourth of July parade, commemorating our independence from Great Britain.

Prince and Princess Takamatsu, younger brother and sister-in-law of the Japanese Emperor, Captain and Mrs. John Q. Owsley, and the Fellers were our dinner guests on the evening of the tenth. The Princess, as always, was exquisitely dressed! She spoke several languages fluently and was a stimulating conversationalist. The slender, reserved Prince was an ex-Naval officer and was very popular in Yokosuka.

The month passed quickly with many flag officers visiting the base. Rear Admiral Kitts with Task Force 71 arrived on the twenty-eighth of July. Then Rear Admiral McConnell and Captain Thornton were our houseguests, followed by Commodore Keleher, who came to Japan with Vice Admiral Cook from China. We took the commodore sightseeing as well as for a tour of the base and gave a large dinner party.

On the fourteenth of August we attended the opening of the new Yokosuka court house, when Benny gave a speech and was presented with a large bouquet of beautiful flowers. As this was the annual Obon festival, the city was illuminated with many lanterns, so we drove through the streets admiring the festivities. The women were all dressed in their best kimonos. After watching the start of the fire relay races we proceeded up an unfamiliar street and became lost. As the street was very narrow we could not turn around, so we drove on and on. The road soon became a cowpath, ending in the boondocks. We finally ended in Hayama.

This was also the day for the opening of the harbor of Yokosuka to world trade. The harbor under the Japanese Navy had been secret. This was an important step for Yokosuka, even though little seagoing shipping could be expected for a number of years.

The Obon festival continued the next day with a parade of floats. We had missed the one the day before. Mrs. Takaoka and I went to the city hall.

From the mayor's office we had an excellent view of the

streets below. Before each float dancers bowed and danced, always looking up to the windows where we sat. The floats were most unusual and interesting. The Perry float, which depicted the arrival of Commodore Perry in Japan in 1853 won the first prize. It was rather startling to see Japanese men dressed in costumes resembling the American naval uniforms of the period. The blond wigs that the men wore were fantastic. Of course, there was the usual lion, "to gobble up all of the bad spirits so that they could not harm anyone." Several men were inside of this papier-mâché lion, and wiggled the lion from one side of the street to the other. Four young men carried a palanquin in which was a replica of a temple. Their faces were painted white and their hair was held by ribbons in a style resembling that of the American western Indian. The Japanese Buddhists believed that there was a good spirit inside the little temple. This spirit would ward off all evil spirits. In addition, the young men wished to share the fun of the festival with the spirit god. They carried the temple from one side of the street to the other and seemed to enjoy coming close to a person or object as they could without actually touching them.

After the parade, Mrs. Takaoka and I drove to Seaside Park and watched the water carnival, which was presented by fishermen from a nearby village. We watched from the windows of the automobile. The fishermen bowed and put on a special performance. I enjoyed seeing the gaily decorated boats and the fishermen's costumes were so quaint.

August eighteenth was a bleak day. The tragic news of the plane crash in the Pacific which took the lives of Ambassador George Atcheson, Colonel Larr, Colonel Russell, and Captain Boyer (U.S.N.) stunned us all. We reached for straws hoping that somehow the men might be found.

Benny had liked George and found him a most capable and loyal American. His services were of great value to the Occupation, and his death was so unnecessary. He was returning to the United States in an Air Force plane which evidently ran short of fuel—an inexcusable blunder. He gave his life in the service of his country.

That afternoon, Benny and I attended a farewell party given in honor of the officers and their wives who were leaving Yokosuka soon. At this party we saw Miss Swart, the late Ambassador Atcheson's secretary. She said that the ambassador had written about Benny and me in his article about the Occupation of Japan for the *Encyclopaedia Britannica*, 1946, and also for the *Encyclopaedia Americana*. This was one of the last things that he had done before he left on that tragic plane flight.

We attended the first football game to be played in Japan, so far as we knew, between the Marines and the Navy, and was held the afternoon of the twenty-first at Green Beach Field on the Naval base. I was happy that Navy won.

After a great deal of effort and "red tape" Benny had at last made it possible for Wah Chan to be reunited with his wife and sons who had been living in mainland China. On the evening of the twenty-second, Wah brought his wife and sons in to meet us and following dinner, we saw the movie *Deep South*. It was a wonderful way to greet the fall.

We received a nice thank you letter from the Allied Mothers' Association of the Yokosuka Primary Schools.

September 16, 1947

Dear Mr. and Mrs. Captain Decker,

I am writing to you in behalf of the Mothers' League Association to thank you for your kindness and generosity to give us the food and other articles. We have distributed them to all the school children of twenty-eight schools in this city. You should have seen their happiest smiles and their expression of gratitude to you!

Many thanks to you, and to my happiness to tell you that the people of Yokosuka began to notice the work of our "Fukushi Jin Kai" as the executor of your concern for the promotion of the public welfare. How fortunate we are to have such a good understanding commander as you from the bottom of our hearts.

We assure you that the Mothers' League Association will work hard to lead people of this city to become bright and honest citizens who love peace and righteousness in near future.

We also thank for Mrs. Captain Decker's attendance to the opening ceremony of the Association which was great honor for us. You could not imagine how much we did appreciate her earnestness to assist us, and her opinion in regard to future education and its systems which was very valuable to us.

Again we thank both of you for your kind and earnest help, and ask for your assistance spiritually as well as materially.

Yours Respectfully,
Asa Tokunaga
President of Mothers'
League Association in
Yokosuka

Once again the Selection Board would meet. I had been skipped the previous year, and this would be the second and probably the last time I would be considered for selection to rear admiral. The layman cannot realize the importance of this selection. From the day a lad enters the Naval Academy he dreams of being an admiral.

On arriving in Yokosuka, I was a senior captain with no orders or instructions concerning my command. The door was wide open. Had it been otherwise, I would have had to carry out my instructions or request a change of duty. I adopted policies that I thought correct, and were in accord with the policies of General MacArthur, the Supreme Commander. I saw no conflict there. But I did suspect that in Washington there was conflict.

There was considerable political opposition to General MacArthur. He was a possible presidential candidate, and this caused many to be aligned against him. The General was a highly dedicated American, and strongly anticommunist. I could ask for no greater leader. I elected to be on his "team."

In this book there are many letters to support me in my dedication to an alliance between Japan and the United States. Any definite stand brings forth some opposition and unfortunate for me, mine was on a high level and in Washington. The greatest harm this opposition accomplished was to have me skipped for promotion and retired at an early age. To receive letters such as the following indicated that I had friends in high position, maybe not those in control of my destiny. But I was willing to pay the price, to accomplish my purpose. And I was happy while doing so. I didn't dwell on the risk.

In the fall, the House Armed Services Committee inspected the base and I received the following letters:

3 October 1947

Dear Captain Decker:

May I take this opportunity to express to you in behalf of all of the members of our party our sincere appreciation for your hospitality and courtesies extended to us during our visit to your command on Wednesday. All of us were very much impressed by the work in progress in Yokosuka and thoroughly enjoyed our visit with you there. We wish to compliment you and the officers in your command upon the excellent briefing presented and the well organized tour of the installations.

With kindest personal regards.

Sincerely yours,
W. Sterling Cole

Tokyo, Japan
8 October 1947

Dear Decker:

Enclosed is a copy of a letter received from Congressman W. Sterling Cole of the House Armed Services Committee.

I am very grateful for the effort you put forth to insure a favorable presentation of naval activities in Japan to the Committee, and wish to express my appreciation of the many courtesies extended by you and your staff to the Committee members and me on the occasion of the inspection tour of Fleet Activities, Yokosuka.

Sincerely,
R. M. Griffin

W. Sterling Cole   Committee:
39th District, New York   Armed Services
Joint Committee on Atomic Energy
Congress of the United States
House of Representatives, Washington, D.C.

3 October 1947

Vice Admiral R. M. Griffin, USN
Commander, Naval Forces, Far East
Yokosuka, Japan
My dear Admiral Griffin:

May I take this opportunity to thank you in behalf of all the members of my party for your hospitality and many courtesies extended to us during our visit to Yokosuka on Wednesday. We were very grateful that you made it possible for us to visit this installation and were impressed with the fine work being done there. We particularly appreciated the opportunity to see the extent of the Japanese fleet maintenance activities formerly carried at this base.

Our tour was a great revelation to all of us.

We only regret that we did not have more time to devote to the inspection of the Naval activities while in Japan. However, due to the excellence of the briefing, the efficient tour which was arranged, you have made it possible for us to achieve an understanding of the Navy's problems in this area.

With kindest personal regards.

Sincerely yours,
W. Sterling Cole

One incident proved a harsh blow to my confidence. Some months before this visit I received a personal reprimand, the first in my career, from my immediate senior in command, Vice Admiral Griffin. I knew I was exposing myself to criticism, but had hoped it would not come from my own boss. Although I did not hold this against him, it was a shock.

I tried to always talk with the press and express my opinions. One article, however, caused the admiral to blow his cool. Undoubtedly he was under pressure, from Washington, and maybe from his chief of staff. I received a phone call—the admiral wanted to see me immediately. The conversation was all one way, and I wasn't even asked to be seated. It was soon over, and I was on the way out of the office. He stated that Russia could now demand a base in Japan, if we had one. Why did I have to say that our Japanese labor was free? If I continued talking to the press, I would find myself packing my suitcase and on my way home.

During my ride back to Yokosuka I had plenty of time to consider this confusing turn of events. First, I didn't know what article or which correspondent had caused this violent reaction. Two articles, however, gave me a clue:

Keyes Beech on June 22, 1947 reported—Decker thinks we should hang on to it (Yokosuka) even after the Occupation ends.

He pictures it as the Guantanamo of the Orient and believes we should rent it from the Japanese Government as we do Guantanamo from the Cuban Government. After all, we could charge the rent to reparations.

Miles W. Vaughn, United Press, Vice President for Asia, date line July 17—Captain Benton W. Decker, Commander Fleet Activities at Yokosuka thought the United States should retain control of the Yokosuka Naval Base after the peace treaty is signed and make it a permanent station for the United States naval strength in this part of the world, for an indefinite period.

The Captain explained that Yokosuka possessed all the necessary attributes for a powerful base to uphold American domination of the Western Pacific Ocean. He recalled that Yokosuka was one of the largest of the Japanese Naval bases and has extensive installations and equipment which could be duplicated only by spending millions of dollars.

Captain Decker said one valuable thing was the number of trained Japanese workers, some of whom have been working on naval craft for 40 years.

In a conversation with this correspondent after his address to the visiting newspapermen, Decker suggested control of Yokosuka could be arranged in a separate agreement between Japan and the United States after the general peace treaty between Japan and the Allied Powers was signed.

He believes that no other nation could object because of the predominant role of the United States in the defeat of Japan and the acknowledged fact that the United States must be responsible for the Western Pacific Area.

These were accurate. The press was honest and loyal. I considered Miles Vaughn a great man and his article to have been timely and in the interest of the United States.

I might have used the description "free" labor at some-time. Certainly, I had intended to express the fact that Japanese expert labor was available in unlimited quantities and was costing us nothing, as it was charged to reparations, and reduced the balance of payments. No funds were necessary. We were pouring over four hundred million dollars per year into Japan, creating more credit than we could ever use. Why shouldn't we get something in return? And why dodge the issue?

Russia had an ice-free port in Manchuria and no peaceful need for one in Japan. As we had won the Pacific War without Russia's help, she had no legitimate claim. The Russian ambassador in Washington had used my statements to question the actions of the United States. He should have been told off!

Admiral and Mrs. Griffin had been good friends, and I concluded that he was performing a disagreeable duty as directed. He did not forward my fitness report to me, and therefore made no record of this private reprimand. Nor did he state to me at the time that it was a private reprimand. He might have reported it in personal correspondence, but I noticed no change in the admiral's friendship.

I continued my dedication to General MacArthur and to cementing our friendships with the Japanese. It was important that a foundation be laid for a treaty with Japan. I made many speeches to the officers and men of the Occupation and spoke of this to every visitor to the base. An assistant secretary of state, in 1950, called on me for ideas and we did sign a separate treaty with the Japanese, as I had proposed.

On the sixteenth of October, I received an encouraging surprise from the General—a letter of commendation. I knew at the time of my "pass over" in 1946 that Generals Eichelberger and Almond had expressed their disappointment by writing to Washington. But now, just before the board's meeting to select rear admirals for 1947, the General wrote me the following letter:

Tokyo, Japan
16 October, 1947

Dear Captain Decker:

It is with a deep sense of appreciation that I have noted the splendid record of accomplishment at the Yokosuka Naval Base during the period of the Occupation. While this record attests the high caliber of the officers and men under your command, and their unfailing devotion to duty, even more it reflects the fine qualities of leadership with which you have endowed the task and the professional standards which you have established and maintained.

Apart from this, the magnificent manner in which the large civil community of Yokosuka has moved with rare enthusiasm to embrace the democratic concepts which underlie Allied Policy, bespeaks your own sound and patient guidance, the constant application of wise statesmanship, and implicit confidence by all citizens in your leadership and direction.

For these signal contributions both to our country and to the Allied cause, accept my admiration and profound gratitude.

Sincerely,
Douglas MacArthur

It was forwarded to me direct, not through channels. It did receive some publicity in the United States, and I expect that Admiral Griffin forwarded a copy to the Selection Board. I did not. I know of no other instance when such a letter was received from the General. It certainly made me that much more content to wind up my naval career under his command.

I was deeply touched by the following unexpected letter from another source:

Captain Decker:

I told Tom about our conversation the other night

about the promotions to be made November 15th.

The Club is having a meeting this week and Tom wants to suggest some sort of testimonial, and then each correspondent will get the New York and Washington offices of their papers to go on record on your behalf.

The reason I was supposed to see you was to be sure this will not hurt you in any way, we know the correspondents have been anxious to have some sort of recognition for you.

Please call Tom if he can proceed on this.

Thanks for your kindness,
Helen Lambert

I didn't think that such a letter would hurt or help me, but I held the Press Club in the highest esteem and was honored to have them go on record approving my efforts. Of course, I wanted very much to be selected for flag rank, but life would continue with or without those two stars. The General's letter and this indication of the approval of the correspondents convinced me that mine was the right choice, whether or not it ever brought further recognition.

Carl Mydans sent me the following letter, which I am proud to quote:

October 30, 1947

Captain B. W. Decker
Yokosuka Naval Base
Dear Benny,

I am enclosing for your information a copy of a cable which was sent off today to Admiral Felix Johnson, Public Information, Navy Department, Washington. I have never before seen a group of individualistic correspondents so unanimous in their agreement and so eager to sign the enclosed document.

We had at first planned on sending a duplicate cable to Forrestal but then we decided that we might be more effective if we kept it within channels and avoided what might be construed in Washington as a steam roller lobby job. We feel quite confident that Admiral Johnson will place this record, as we have requested, as part of the record for selection.

Best wishes and remember we've all got our fingers crossed.

Carl Mydans

30 October 1947

Admiral Felix Johnson
Public Information
Navy Department
Washington, D. C.

Tokyo correspondents have learned that Captain Benton Weaver Decker Commanding Officer Yokosuka Naval Base is one of number of officers to be considered next month for promotion as rear admiral. We feel you would want to know that correspondents corps this theatre judge Captain Decker as one of the best administrators and one of finest public relations officers they've ever known and they feel this should be made part of his record for selection for Rear Admiral signed George Folster nbc Tom Lambert Associated Press Carl Mydans time and life Horace Bristol Fortune William Carty Paramount News William Costello cbs Richard Ferguson acme Joseph Fromm World Report Richard Hughes British Kemsley Press Walter Simmons Chicago Tribune Hessel Tiltman London Daily Herald Ralph Chapman New York Herald Tribune Burton Crane New York Times Howard Handleman International News Gordon Walker Christian Science Monitor Jack Percival Sydney Morning Herald and London News Chronicle Robert Martin New York Post Massey Stanley Sydney Daily Telegraph Frank Hawley London Times Keyes Beech Chicago Daily News Sydney Whipple Scripps Howard Karl Bachmeyer Newsweek Peter Kalischer United Press Charles Gorry Wirephoto Ray Falk Nana Michel Macdonagh Reuters.

Admiral Johnson was a classmate of mine, but, I never received any correspondence from him. On November tenth, I received the following letter from General Shepherd, U.S.M.C.

Dear Captain Decker:

I wish to express my thanks again to you and Mrs. Decker for the very lovely dinner you gave in honor of me and my officers. It was indeed a most delightful party and I enjoyed so much meeting your guests. I appreciate your courtesy and hospitality very much.

From what I observed during my inspection, you have a very fine and happy command.

I hope that the selection board now meeting will see fit to place your name on the list for Rear Admiral and that I will have the pleasure of returning your hospitality when you come to Washington.

With kindest regards to you and Mrs. Decker, I am

Sincerely yours,
Lemuel C. Shepherd, Jr.

P.S. I had luncheon with the Secretary of the Navy today and personally told him what a fine command you had. He stated that he had heard the same from other sources. I hope that the Board takes cognizance of these reports.

L.C.S.

Up to 1946, when I reported for duty in Yokosuka, I had every reason to expect favorable consideration by the board. My service reputation was excellent. My fitness reports were free of adverse remarks, and I had been specially selected for many unusual and important tasks. Selection by the board is not entirely free from political pressure. Higher authority, right up to the president, the commander in chief of the Navy, influences selection. The war was over. The military fighting had stopped, but the political fighting had just begun.

I had cast my lot the first week in Japan by announcing to my officers that we would remain in Yokosuka for fifty years—an about face for that base. To the press, I softened this by stating that we would be in Yokosuka for five years. A few months later, I lengthened this to ten years. Finally, I boldly announced that we should remain in Yokosuka after the peace treaty.

There were irresponsible remarks that "we should get out of Japan." This was expressed by liberals in many newspapers. Naval officers were reluctant to comment on the subject, though they knew the importance of a Western Pacific Naval base to our Navy.

Normally, a captain is not heard throughout the land, but the American press in Japan had a loud voice. It kept the American public informed. The politicians had to listen to our correspondents. The lack of an announced policy gave the "liberals" the opportunity to advocate the abandonment of Japan.

Without our press we would have lost Japan. Alone, General MacArthur could not have saved it; though he did save Hokkaido when the Russians attempted to gain a foothold by bringing in a Russian division of troops. He also saved Japan from internal strife when, in February 1947, he outlawed a communist inspired general strike. But alone he could not have prevented our government from abandoning Japan.

Japan was defeated. Her people hated communists, but they were helpless. Had we abandoned her, as many advised, Japan would have been enslaved by the Russians and made their satellite on the Pacific Ocean. Thus, China would have been surrounded by her natural enemy. Also, our island frontier of the Philippines, Formosa, Okinawa, and the Aleutians would have been penetrated. The Western Pacific would be dominated by Russia.

Therefore, the future of Japan and the United States depended and still depends on our mutual friendship and alliance. Our Navy had always needed a base in the Western Pacific, but millions of dollars had been spent with little result. Now we had a $600 million complex for the asking. It was the only return we would receive for our huge monetary support during the Occupation. It was for the benefit of both nations.

To help me, I was blessed with a wife who tirelessly worked by my side. Edwina cultivated friends and goodwill wherever she went. In addition, I shall never forget the loyal support of my officers, men, and their wives. We were a team. Most visitors of importance came to Yokosuka, the showplace of the Occupation. Our efforts won their praises and support, and soon this began to bear fruit. In the spring Admiral Denfeld, the first of the Joint Chiefs to visit

Yokosuka, expressed his approval of the work on the base and in town. This was the first encouragement from the Navy top command. During the next summer, Commander Service Force, Pacific, with the commander in chief's Pacific Fleet approval, spelled out our mission for the first time and removed his two repair ships. Yokosuka had won her right to existence. Many senior officers and leading politicians expressed approval in the years following.

Notwithstanding, my name was again absent from the selection list! But I could thank God for my friends! They rallied around me and encouraged me at one of the lowest points in my life. I am grateful to them even to this day!

Thirty years have passed and even now I am thrilled to read again of the generous action which those correspondents took to support me. No man has had more loyal friends.

The Tokyo Shiboura Electric Company (GE) was employing three thousand Yokosuka men. This was a real accomplishment. Our unemployment records, kept in the civil affairs office, revealed a rate of about four percent, which was lower than that in the United States. When it plunged down to 2.5 percent, however, I became suspicious. I found that this could be measured in a number of ways, dependent on the definition of "unemployed."

One evening, on returning home from Tokyo, I noticed that one part of the city was dark. Investigation revealed that this was not a power failure, but a deliberate act of the power company. Calling in the president, I asked for an explanation. As there was not enough power for Tokyo and Yokohama, the company was borrowing from us, blacking out part of Yokosuka. But, the president added, it was fair, because he had ordered that the blackout be rotated among the different sections of the town!

The Japanese base had previously used great quantities of electricity. Now we were using but a fraction of the former amount. I didn't think it was fair. No more blackouts—we were just as important as Tokyo or Yokohama, and we didn't expect them to be calling the shots. The next time the president of the power company did this, I promised to have two of my Marines call on him.

A Japanese homeowner was charged so much per light

or outlet—there were few meters. This method encouraged many methods of cheating. The most common was to have no electrical line to the house. When power was needed, a long bamboo pole was used to reach the bare power lines. In this manner, they would hook into the lines and could cook their evening meals by electricity.

Gratitude to Captain Decker
Yokosuka in Getting a Light City

Since the latter part of October every city, town, and village in this prefecture suffered from continual stoppage of electric current, consequent on unlimited transmission of electricity operated by Densan strikers. However, Yokosuka citizens scarcely had this trouble, and are thankful to Captain Decker for his instructions. On the other hand, Shinsei Women's Society, schools, the Chamber of Commerce, Police Station, Fire-brigade Station, and Kanto Electric Distribution Co. cooperated for active movement as minimum use of electricity, controlled use of electric heater, and electric power, and exterminate of stealthy use of electricity. Employees of Kanto Electric Distribution Co. and policemen organize 20 Exposure Parties of stealthy use of electricity and are to inspect every house in the city through this month. They already exposed a bad offender, and are expected to be successful.

[*Yokosuka Times,* 15 Nov.]

Yokosuka was blossoming. The Jesuits were putting the nine buildings assigned them to good use as the Jochi University. It was always a pleasure to have Father Voss drop in for a chat. He had given me much excellent advice on Japanese matters and I cherished his friendship. In addition, we now had fifty enterprises, including a glassworks factory, a pen-and-pencil factory, a textile mill, an auto factory, one which made bus bodies, and many others. A metalware factory and a furniture factory employed four thousand men, with their goal of more thousands soon to be achieved. Under the Japanese Navy, Saint Joseph's Hospital had one thousand patients crowded into it. Now it had 120 beds and was raising its standards to ours. The chamber of commerce

187

and the Industrial Club were functioning well, as was the Japanese Red Cross. The Shinsei Women's Club was doing a good job and needed little guidance. All in all the future looked very bright.

Our first shipment of reparations required by the treaty of the end of World War II was to be made in December. This required the construction of a special ramp in Nagura Cove to move the heavy pieces of machinery into barges for further movement of ships.

We were having difficulties with the American liberals in the Occupation. They had advocated a law stating that any woman must be given five weeks leave prior to giving birth and three months off after the event. I called the American woman who promoted this law and told her that it was ridiculous. No Japanese woman needed that time, and it would work against her getting a job. It was not in the interest of equal rights for women. No enlightened nation had such a law. She promptly corrected me, "Oh yes they have. All the most enlightened nations have the law."

"I disagree—the United States doesn't!"

"The United States is not an enlightened nation." And that woman represented the United States! She had been assigned to the task by Washington, and soon created several other incidents.

Later this woman from Yokohama civil affairs office was at the Baptist School in Oppama, undermining my authority and spreading communist propaganda. A hurried phone call from the school asked for assistance. I couldn't go up to investigate at that time, but did send my wife. Her report caused me some concern. A few days later, we inaugurated our new chapel. At our invitation, a convention of service chaplains had gathered and I gave the welcoming speech. I pointed out our progress in making the Japanese friends, and said that we hoped they would be allies, as we probably would remain in Yokosuka after the peace treaty was signed. After my address, I left. Later, I was told that this same DAC (Department of the Army Civilian) took over the pulpit to correct me. She said that I was wrong. The Japanese were still our enemies and we had no right to the Yokosuka Naval base (the communist line!). She attempted to turn the religious meeting into a political convention.

I called a general in Yokohama and reported the matter. He assured me that she would never work in the field again.

Benny triumphantly returned from the championship pistol meet for the Far East at Camp Palmer. The Marine team had won the trophy for the highest score, and my husband proudly presented me with his gold medal.

C.W.O. Oderman and his Marine sergeant had evidently taken the Army team for "a ride." While sitting near the firing points, they kept hammering their pistols, changing the sights, and filing the sears. The young Army shooters, impressed by our Marines, adjusted theirs. When the competition started the Marines laid aside their mistreated weapons and brought out their target pistols, which had been carefully guarded from any abuse.

During the match, they were drinking tea from a thermos. One would think they had gone British—that is, until one smelled the tea. While a rifleman must abstain, the man who shoots a pistol must have no nerves—alcohol applied internally is the best medicine!

Benny told me a tale about his medal. I am inclined to think that he was good, but just wanted to "spin a yarn." Anyway, here is his story.

The coach, C. W. O. Oderman had asked Benny to fill in on the team as the necessary fifth member. At Camp Palmer, the morning of the meet, Oderman woke Benny up at four o'clock and insisted that he drink one third of a glass of Old Grandad whiskey. Benny took the "medicine" as directed. At five o'clock, Oderman brought around another one third of a glass of whiskey. He did the same at six and at seven o'clock. At eight o'clock, Benny was on the firing line and Old Grandad was pulling the trigger. Benny asked the coach how he was doing, but all that the coach would say was, "Keep on firing." Benny stood one in the Far East in slow fire. The coach tried to get him to drink some more "Old Grandad," but Benny said that he had had it. By noon, the team was firing rapid fire and Old Grandad was gone. Alone, Benny didn't do so well. In spite of his low score in rapid fire, however, the Marines' team won the trophy.

One of Benny's officers and his wife, Captain and Mrs. David Olney, were eager for us to see the proposed site of their quarters. This was an old cement-block house on top of Edwina Hill, in back of the Administration Building. To get there, it was necessary to use a jeep to navigate the narrow, bumpy, winding road. The Olneys thought that this building could be converted into quarters, even though the two-foot-thick walls would make remodeling difficult. The scarcity of housing forced officers to make do with any available buildings. The view from this highest point on this hill was perfectly beautiful. We could see the city of Yokosuka, Tokyo Bay, Yokohama, and in the faint distance, Tokyo. Although my husband was doubtful about the project. Dave said that he thought that he could convert the building, so Benny gave him the go-ahead.

I received a letter from a Buddhist priest, husband of my maid, Miyoko Yokoi. We had lent him our viewmaster and had provided the family with pictures of our travels.

My dear Madam,

Very much thanks of your kindness for my wife, Miyoko. She is much happy to serve you.

Last night I had pleasant time by Viewmaster that you lent me. The many pictures is very beautiful and wonderful. I think the Viewmaster is very good for education of child. It is regret to have not such clever and skillful thing in Japan. The pictures is fine landscape. My family took pictures what show customs and cultures in America.

I hope you are happy in Japan.

I beg you we are saved for hunger by your assistance.

Yours sincerely,
Ryuge Yokoi

The many dinners we attended were always pleasant affairs, and the food was characteristically good. One evening, however, Benny became quite ill upon our return from such a party. Our crab dinner was fighting back. I awakened in the middle of the night thinking that I was surely going to die. They rushed me to the hospital. I was fortunate, and was able to return home the next day. For the next few days, my battleworn stomach was treated to a diet of tea and consommé.

190

A few days later, I was up and around, and decided to go shopping at the Yokohama PX. When I returned home, I learned Benny had severed his Achilles tendon. On his way to sail his star boat, the *Daiichi* in a Saturday championship race, some wives of Army officers, who had arrived from the states, asked his assistance. Benny took them to our PX and introduced them to our people. In order to catch up with his crew, he jumped a wall. When he landed, it felt as if someone had hit him on the head with a baseball bat. He was somewhat nauseated and could not stand. His foot dangled uselessly, as the Achilles tendon had snapped. Benny was immediately operated on by Dr. Geiss, and a special Army surgeon from Tokyo. After six weeks in the cast, Benny's ankle was as good as new, it was a beautiful job. During this time, he enjoyed the sympathy of all his friends, who sent many flowers and notes, and praised the surgeons!

Saturday, Oct., 1947

Dear Mrs. Decker,

I want to thank you and Captain Decker for your kind hospitality to us Saturday when we were at Yokosuka. We were so upset when we heard about Captain Decker's accident, especially since we felt it would not have occurred had we not chosen that time to arrive.

I would like to think I could have been as gracious a hostess as you were. You were an inspiration to the four of us.

Please convey our best wishes to Captain Decker for a speedy recovery.

Sincerely,
Grace Weaver

We had many war-weary stores which we tried to distribute evenly among the various schools and charitable organizations in Yokosuka. This letter from Sister Howe expresses the gratitude of many for the small gifts which the Navy was able to provide.

IHS
S. Heart School—Yokosuka
16.10.47

Dear Mrs. Decker,

It is with true gratitude that I write in the name of the whole community, as well as the staff of Teachers pertaining to our Japanese School, to thank you and Captain Decker for your most welcome gift of candy and cigarettes. We not only appreciate your gift, but feel very specially touched by the kind thought of wanting to remember one and all of us.

I enclose a card from our children and older pupils, as a small token of their gratitude.

With renewed thanks to both you and your husband.

> Believe me,
> Yours very gratefully
> in the S. Heart,
> Sister Mercedes Ruiz Howe

The mothers of Japanese schoolchildren were reluctant to form an association with the teachers. Their previous reputation was against them. Even a month before this letter, Asa Tokunaga signed "President of Mothers' League Association in Yokosuka." But the following letter was signed "President of the Parents and Teachers' Association." This was a big step and gave me assurance that the Japanese were becoming democratic. We were making progress with no pressure being applied.

> November 5, 1947
> Asa Tokunaga
> President of the Parents
> and Teachers Association

Captain B. W. Decker
Commander of the Fleet Activities
Dear Sir,

It is my honour to have a chance to express our thanks to you, the commander of the Fleet Activity in Yokosuka, for the generous gift of chocolates to our school children. All children were so extremely enjoyed by your presents that I am sending my letter of thanks on behalf of them. Perhaps you can't imagine how much it meant to them.

They have no words to say their gratitude, but they thank you from bottom of their little hearts.

Association of Yokosuka for the kindness you have shown towards us and our children.

What happy we shall be when we recollect having so kind man like you and I believe it is our pride to have so thoughtful commander in Yokosuka. And it is our great hope to have the opportunity to show our gratefulness in future and that is our most important duty to answer your goodness by proving our efforts for the rehabilitation and reconstruction of Yokosuka. The only way we can give in return is to make a vow to offer ourself for democratic Japan.

I hope you will be healthily for ever.

Yours respectfully,
Asa Tokunaga

27 October 1947

Captain B. W. Decker,

Through this great war, we Japanese have lost all wishes in future, but you and your peoples have helped and encouraged us all the time since the war ended. Our city, Yokosuka, had gradually been cleaned in many ways. We are deeply thankful for you.

Our school has also been repaired by your favour. We have a very happy thing that we want to report you. It is the completion of the lecture hall. We have waited and waited the completion of it. Now, by the end of this month our hall will be completed at last, and we are with great pleasure now.

The ceremony of the completion of this lecture hall will be held on 1st of November. We, all students, are eagerly hoping that Mr. and Mrs. Decker will be present at this ceremony.

From now on, everytime we use it, we will feel your kindness and refresh your memory. We earnestly hope that your presence at our ceremony will be greatly expected with honour.

Yours respectfully,
Yokosuka 2nd Girls'
High School
Masako Suzuki

The first sumo wrestling meet was held in Yokosuka. Benny had convinced the Japanese that such a meet would help gain recognition for the city. It was to be a Yokosuka first! One hundred and sixty of the nation's best wrestlers competed. The big expense would be the huge amounts of food and sake needed to feed these enormous men, and their hordes of retainers, geishas, and followers. They consumed an unbelievable amount of rice, fish, sake, and delicacies.

Then disaster struck. It rained, forcing the meet to be postponed one day. A disastrous food bill resulted. Benny felt responsible, so the Navy supplied the sacks of rice. The next day the misfortune was forgotten in the excitement of the gala occasion. Benny was conspicuous among those giants whose girth made him look slim. Yokosuka was now in the big league! Benny picks up the story:

It always gave me great pleasure and encouragement to receive support from the Japanese. The base union sent me a Christmas card from "all members." Of all the cards, this made me very happy. I always felt that I had been fair to labor, and certainly recognized their importance in the growth of Yokosuka, or anywhere else, for that matter. This card indicated that our union officers recognized my support of the working man.

When I reported for duty in 1946 Japanese labor on the base was unsatisfactory. They would drag out a job, fearful that upon its completion they would be without work. At first we had five thousand laborers, the equivalent of one thousand Americans. The Japanese paid them about ten dollars per month in yen. This was credited against the four hundred million dollars, the annual cost of the Occupation. Getting these men to produce a full day's work was a problem. Many were in squads under the supervision of an American sailor. We had young recruits as replacements for the battle-tested old-timers, and the Japanese were able to pull the wool over their eyes. Time would fly while a sailor, after generously sharing his cigarettes with the much older Japanese workmen, would tell them all about "home and mother." In order to regain control, we replaced the sailors by "straw bosses," and gave each Japanese straw boss a bicycle. If he failed to perform, we would take back the bicycle—a great loss of face. Another threat was we might replace our supervision with Japanese ex-military men.

Now things were entirely different. I admired my labor force for its support in all my projects and for its enthusiasm during our annual inspections. The men completed the jobs satisfactorily and on time. They were as loyal as any stateside workers.

A problem developed in the Shinsei Women's Club. Although unpopular with charter members of the ruling committee, a younger woman had come into power. I thought nothing of it until Mrs. Takaoka, in a diplomatic manner, inquired whether I had known this woman in Shanghai. I hadn't been in Shanghai since my early days, and then I had met no Japanese. "No. I never met the woman."

Mrs. Takaoka then informed me that she had come into power because she claimed to have been my mistress in Shanghai and that she had been involved in a shady deal with the Japanese Navy. She had stolen a battleship! Actually, this involved buying a ship for scrap from the Japanese Navy and not paying for it. She was bold, clevor, and had a record.

In the Women's Club, she had diverted wagonloads of old beer cans to some gangsters. She had also obtained donations of potatoes from the local farmers, and had diverted them to her purpose. A wide-awake Japanese policeman had found some of our property in her warehouse. She threatened the officer, "If you value your life you will keep your nose out of my affairs." She then tried bribing him with some twenty thousand yen (four hundred dollars). It took courage for the officer to report her. I ordered the chief of police to arrest her, which he reluctantly did. She was forced to leave town.

We encouraged women to work on the base. Many were untrained and uneducated, but they were most conscientious in their work. We found they were excellent in sorting the mess of spare parts which had been dumped on the base. Each woman would be given a spare part, such as a piston ring. She would then go through piles of similar parts, gathering all of that size. These were then put into bins where the expert from the United States would identify the article. When properly marked, these parts were of value. Otherwise, they were worthless. In this way, our supply department saved millions of dollars.

Our newly organized and trained Japanese fire depart-

195

ment was having more and more time to shine brass, as the hazards were reduced. One of our fire department assignments was to train the Japanese firemen and to make the civilians fire-conscious. With water on the full day, and with frequent inspections, the insurance rate in town was dropping rapidly. We had a problem answering a fire alarm in town, as our base threads were standard U.S. and would not fit their hose which were standard Japanese. We had adapters designed, making it possible for the two services to support each other.

One way in which we built up the morale of the local firemen was by awarding a trophy or emblem to the company passing the best inspection. This emblem was a white flag with a red rooster on it. This idea had been prompted by my memories of the coaling-ship days in the old Navy. The port and starboard sides on a ship coaling would compete for the most coal per hour. At the end of the hour, the rooster would be awarded to the leading side. It had helped expedite matters then, and seemed to work just as well now. The trouble came when they answered an alarm. One morning at three, I arrived at the scene of a blazing temple. But, although firemen were all around, there was no water. Why? I was informed that they were waiting for the "rooster" company to turn on the first stream!

We found that many alleys and paths were too narrow for the engines. We had a jeep equipped with some gear for this purpose and also insisted that fifty-gallon drums of water be kept in some places.

It was of interest that the Russians were always preferring charges against me. Sort of flattering! They said that my firemen were the beginning of a Japanese navy and that my police department, now reorganized, was the new Japanese army. I was also modernizing the base. Fancy that! They always had some complaint, but it didn't slow me a bit.

The real Sunday punch for women came when my Marine commander reported that the jails were overflowing. We had insisted on uncrowded conditions and separate cells for each sex. To solve the problem, we had to parole those who were good prisoners, as most were. I needed a parole board. This duty I assigned to the Shinsei Women's Club.

The men would now have to ask the women for their

freedom from jail. The women were careful about whom they paroled. Any person paroled would be under the eyes of the women of the neighborhood, for all women in the town belonged to the club. No parolee could violate his parole without the women knowing it immediately. The record of violators was zero. The women were in their glory and my problem was solved.

Japan is in the path of many typhoons. During the first year, a typhoon alert would cause us to install wooden shutters outside of the glass windows. This resulted in a darkened, gloomy house, which was most depressing. But after a few typhoons had passed through, we decided to let it blow. We did not use the shutters and we survived. The wind was not bad. It was the rain that flooded low places, and seeped through cracks. In 1946 ships were advised by the Japanese to stand out to sea and ComNavFE had ordered them out at the first typhoon. There was some merit in this, if there were many ships, all moored to buoys; but under existing conditions, I opposed it. Any ship alongside a pier in our sheltered harbor was far safer than it would be at sea, where visibility was limited. A carrier alongside the Piedmont Pier was completely protected by the high cliff adjacent to it. The wind velocity on the deck of the first carrier to ride out a typhoon alongside the Piedmont Pier was about thirty knots, and eighty knots at our weather station. That stopped the landlubbers from ordering salty sailors to sea and into trouble. In the *Chaumont* I had ridden out many hurricanes alongside a pier which was less sheltered than the Piedmont seawall berth.

I was of the school—when in port, double up the lines and secure the boats. In a storm, if protected, stay put!

I was particularly fond of my chief staff officer, Bill Kirten. He had many good ideas and was a distinct asset to the command. He was not selected for flag rank, which was a grave disappointment to me. But I had concluded that we were the "unwashed" so far as Washington was concerned. I had seen just enough of duty in Washington to realize that personal contact with the Selection Board just before it met was a means of greatly improving one's chances. I recall a yarn about a well-known captain when he was coming up for selection to flag rank. It was said that he called on each member, saying, "I know I haven't a chance. It will be humiliating to receive no vote. Will you cast a ballot for me?" He was the only one unanimously selected for rear admiral! True or false, "Pleuvy" was one of the best fleet commanders we had. He always had soup on his blouse and was by no means a teetotaller, but he sure could move that fleet.

Bill Kirten saved us many dollars and ran that base in a firm but friendly manner. He was a great hunter and I enjoyed shooting duck and other birds with him. He was particularly capable at cementing relations with our sister services. A noted singer and guitar player, he could get a party of mixed ranks into a singing mood in as many minutes as it takes me to say it. I envied his ability.

Looking out of my office window on the third floor of the Administration Building, I enjoyed the view of a beautiful tree in the small circle near the front door. It was Bill who told me that it was a magnolia tree, and sure enough the tree finally burst out with fragrant, white blossoms. Bill put that tree under his immediate authority. There was to be no picking of blooms. He rationed them, and I got my few blooms at regular intervals. His Southern love for a magnolia tree protected it and we all enjoyed its beauty.

Bev Reed, my Supply Officer, came into my office and said, "Captain, you aren't going to like this one. My office has really pulled a lulu this time."

"Well, spill it."

"We put in for one hundred cartons of Puffed Wheat, but the storekeeper left out the word "car," so we ordered one hundred tons!"

"Wow! Have we enough warehouses to hold that much? Get a message off cancelling the order."

"We have done that already, but the factory reported that the train is already rolling."

"Inform the Navy Department."

"We have, and they have sent an Alnav for all ships and stations to order their Puffed Wheat from us, but that won't amount to much."

So we waited for the avalanche of Puffed Wheat to deluge us, and it did. We served puffed wheat cookies, candy, cakes, biscuits, and tried it in ice cream, until the men had it coming out of their ears. They were about to rebel, so we had to dream up some other way. We got permission to sell it to the Japanese and then use the yen from the sale to pay our men, in place of yen obtained from official Army sources. But selling it to the Japanese proved difficult. We advised, "Use it for chicken feed." But the Japanese didn't have any chickens. "Educate the Japanese to eat breakfast food like we do." But they didn't have sugar and cream, or even milk. There was no sale.

Some time earlier, the supply officer had reported that he had twenty tons of chocolate syrup dumped on us from the Pacific Islands and ships, from the roll-up after the war ended. It was enough to last us twenty years, but it wouldn't keep. In fact, it was getting moldy already. What now?

We all knew that the Japanese hadn't had any chocolate for years, and sugar was a luxury, so why not sell this to the Japanese in a tie-in deal with the Puffed Wheat? We did, and it went over big. They made candy balls out of it, and they sold like hot cakes. We got rid of our syrup as well as our Puffed Wheat at "cost." We then sold the yen to sailors at the official exchange rate, and the Japanese had a big bargain. That's business!

The CID, when they found out about our sales, investigated us for black marketing, but we had it all in writing. It was legal.

On January twenty-third 1948, the news sheet for the base was launched. It was called the *Sea Hawk*, and was under the management of F. R. Wenners, its managing editor. This was to be a great help in keeping all hands, including dependents, informed. One of the foundation stones of good morale is "passing the word." Our "brownie meetings" were of great value in keeping the officers informed. Now we had a means of reaching the personnel and dependents on all levels. In fact, it is now of use to me, twenty-eight years later, in recalling those full years that fill this story.

The first year our dependents' school used the Mikasa Building and the teachers were from the Japanese Catholic School on the base. It was of limited value in 1946. In 1947 we had to have our own school, which we started under the supervision of Miss Florence des Baillets, a former Red Cross woman who resigned in order to organize our school. It was in its own new building in the dependents' area. We soon

199

obtained the services of Mrs. Margaret Jackson, a retired professional, as principal and teacher of the first and second grades. Ninety children were enrolled in January 1948. All of the teachers were dependents except Mrs. Jackson, a capable lady of matured years. The Army wanted young teachers while I wanted older, more experienced ones. So we were all happy. And our school was a big success. I asked that the day's routine begin with a prayer. This was received well, as I had expected. Later, however, a Catholic mother objected. I wanted none of that nonsense, so I asked Father Voss for advice. Simple, just turn the matter over to him. That ended it. On the base, Catholics and Protestants had no conflicts, and Father Voss was wise enough to kill this one early in the bud.

Our six bowling alleys were from our Navy in Tsingtao. They were most popular. We had asked for them when the Communists were about to take over Tsingtao. Also we bought the Navy's liquor in Tsingtao direct, but they insisted that the alleys had to go to Honolulu first and then be transshipped to Yokosuka! The base finally got them, after a long delay and a wasted voyage. We soon added two more lanes. At the club, Bingo was a nickel a card—the good old days when a nickel was money. The masonic lodge was holding its regular meetings while the Holy Name Club was holding its discussion groups. Father G. C. Voss, S.J., was the spiritual director, QMI Duncan was president, and Ensign Scarafino was vice president.

The twenty-one-piece band that I had requested for the admiral was his band, but was stationed in Yokosuka. He seldom needed its services, and I wanted to use it to dress up our station. The band would be a sure hit at the Marine parades and at football games.

The White Hatters were fully employed playing dancing music at the various clubs on the base. Once a week, they played for the CPO Club, after which they played at the Petty Officers' Club, and then the Officers' Club. They also worked nightly in our EM Club for dances and established a standard of performance for the two Japanese orchestras. We had three dance floors where sailors as well as soldiers could find dancing better than in the honky tonks. This was part of the VD program. Certainly it aided morale. The Japanese wanted to

200

furnish orchestras of thirty to forty players. Or should I say, they would provide a dozen musicians and twenty or more for a free lunch. The White Hatters were in demand. I insisted on but one rule—"Good Night Sweetheart" at 2300. I wanted my people bright-eyed and bushy-tailed the next day. Only once did I depart from this, to my sorrow. It was the anniversary dinner dance in Edwina's and my honor on April 10, 1949. The club had filled a Japanese "meter and a half" search light reflector with punch—thirty gallons! Everyone patronized the bar until it was closed at 2300. My chief of staff officer requested permission to keep the dance going until they drained the punch bowl. I said yes, why waste it! They didn't, but the next day at nine o'clock, not an officer was stirring on that base.

I received the following letter from Rear Admiral Bledsoe of the support group. I am very proud of this letter as it shows that the efforts of my command were appreciated by those whom they served. Otherwise, our existence would have been unwarranted.

Commander Support Group
Naval Forces Far East
care of Fleet Post Office
San Francisco, California
Yokosuka, Japan
30 January 1948

From: Commander, Support Group, Naval Forces, Far East

To: Commander, Naval Forces, Far East

Subject: Commendation of Captain B. W. Decker, USN

1. As you know, the major share of the support of my command during the past twenty months has been rendered by Fleet Activities, Yokosuka. Since my Flagship has based there a considerable portion of this time, I have had almost continuous opportunity for observing the manner of functioning of this Base. During this period that command has developed from a hodgepodge of miscellaneous and uncoordinated units into a well-integrated and efficient Naval Base which would compare favorably with any US shore establishment and in many respects is the superior of any I have ever ob-

served. Ships stopping there, as well as those basing there, have invariably commented on the sympathetic and intelligent attention given to their requirements.

2. I consider that this is due to a great degree to the leadership, industry and outstanding ability of its Commanding Officer, Captain B. W. Decker.

3. I request a copy of this letter be placed on the current fitness report of Captain Decker.

A. M. Bledsoe
Rear Admiral

Copy to:
Captain B. W. Decker

The admiral and his wife, Florence, both were great assets to the Navy in Japan. Their cheerful friendship and musical ability helped to cement interservice ties. His command fitted in well with mine and with those of visiting vessels. There was never any trouble or conflict. It was a most congenial relationship between the forces afloat and those ashore.

February eighth, we watched the start of the marathon relay race around the Miura Peninsula for the Decker perpetual trophy. The purpose of the race was to prove to the people that the Miura Peninsula was no longer a secret area, as it had been under the Japanese Navy. We attended the event as the guest of Shoichi Kowada, president of the Yokosuka Athletic Association. The city of Odawara won.

General of the Army
Douglas MacArthur
Supreme Commander for
the Allied Powers

February 1948

Sir,

We are happy and grateful that Occupation has proved a boon to our city of Yokosuka, producing results which we believe exemplify the benevolent and construction spirit of the Allied policy.

This city, once Japan's naval center, which was completely paralyzed by the surrender, has been transformed into a model community throbbing with manifold activities for civic development along the lines of peace and democracy. And in bringing about this change Captain Benton W. Decker, Commander Fleet Activities, has been directly instrumental. It is his leadership and initiative, coupled with a warm, friendly disposition, that have revitalized the prostrate city and spurred it on to positive efforts. It would be truly regrettable, should the Captain be transferred to a post elsewhere upon the termination of his present assignment this spring.

We, the undersigned, voicing the sentiment of the entire citizenry of Yokosuka, do most earnestly beseech you to see that Captain Decker's tenure of office is extended. It is our fervent hope that this petition of ours will be granted so that our city may, with his guidance and help, continue its march on the road of recovery and reconstruction.

> Most respectfully yours,
> E. Ohta, Mayor

> February 17, 1948
> Convent of Seishin
> Sishikai
> 5019 Fujisawa
> Kanagawa-ken, Japan

His Excellency
Captain B. W. Decker,

We are very happy to send you a letter to express our heartfelt thanks for your kindness shown at the last Christmas.

I am afraid that you may have forgotten it already, because it is so long a time since. But, your beautiful presents were received with much gratitude by the Sisters at Fujisawa. Our surprise and joy at the arrival of the presents were beyond description. When the last Christmas approached, Rev. Mother, who is the foundress of our Order, had been seriously ill. So, naturally we all were occupied with her nursing and were expecting rather lonesome Christmas. The good God was our only hope at that time. Just then, it was a happy truck arrived, loaded with so many nice things; pretty

203

clothes, shoes and toys, etc. At first we are so surprised that we did not know what to do. Then we carried them into a hall and put them in order. First, we made the parcels for two hundred orphans and thirty widows who are living with us. Yet, as the nice presents were still full in the room, we sent them to the orphans in the various places of the country.

Our Congregation was founded by Rev. Mother Theresia, a German Mother, about twenty-eight years ago, at Akita in the north part of Japan. There are seventeen branch houses undertaking various kinds of social works: e.g., T. B. sanatorium, dispensary, orphanage, baby home, widows' home since January 1947, taking in about two hundred and fifty persons. We are using the half part of the place for the education. As we opened the school in May 1946, we have only 1st and 2nd grades and the 1st and 2nd year of the High School.

The landscape is very beautiful here and Mt. Fuji can be seen distinctly. The Sisters and children will be very glad if you visit here sometimes.

We all pray for you and your family.

His Excellency
    Captain Decker!
I remain,
Yours Respectfully,
Sister Justitia for Rev. Mother Theresia
(Mother Superior of the Convent of the Daughters of the Sacred Heart)

The base looked good. We had painted most of it a warm beige. In April we planned to open a new mess hall and shortly thereafter, the new theater with six hundred seats. It was situated close to the barracks area, where I wanted it. After the building had been built and seats ordered, specially planned for about nine hundred capacity, each seat affording a clear and unobstructed view, the Army decided that we didn't rate more than six hundred seats, so when the seats arrived, the excess was assigned elsewhere and our seating plan became a random arrangement.

The recreation building, formerly Barracks A, was adjacent to the Enlisted and the Marine barracks. It had eight bowling alleys, twelve pool tables, and a number of handicraft activities and clubs, including an outstanding railroad club. Paymaster "Walt" Gray was a capable and enthusiastic miniature railroader. In fact he had spent much of his spare time scrounging (salvaging) parts from the old Japanese Air Defense setup in the headquarters cave. He had a great imagination and interest. The outlay filled a room thirty feet by sixty feet with engine controls and a traffic manager. I wondered at it.

The yacht club had five Star boats in the first Star fleet in Japan. As the official measurer, I knew they were up to stateside standards. We had many odd craft, all getting good use.

The new base chapel was opened 14 March. The cornerstone had been laid June 26, 1947, Griffin Day. Our talented Lieutenant Commander John H. Holtom, director of the choir, sang with Mrs. Hazel Cunningham. The choir was outstanding with Chief and Mrs. Fields, CSM and Mrs. Lewis; Ms. McGlothlin, Danielski, Jackson, Beighley, Lawler, Dinkel, Lieutenant Emily Fischer; Musician First Class and Mrs. Metcalfe, Seaman first class Hix, and Sergeant Lanier.

The chapel was a beautiful New England type white wooden building with a steeple, just like I wanted, and located exactly where I wanted it, between the barracks area and the Dependent housing. We had three bells in the tower, one cast by our own repair department. Later we were to get electronic chimes in addition.

During the building of the chapel, I stopped by to inspect the work. I was disappointed in the quality of the wood used in the pews and in the pulpit, and the workmanship was crude. The Japanese are noted for their excellency in woodworking. Something was wrong. I asked Father Voss to look at the chapel. Father Voss pointed out that this was to belittle Christianity, that the contractor was deliberately challenging us. I demanded the pulpit and pews be replaced. The new ones were excellent and I was pleased and thankful for Father Voss's advice. It seemed as if the workmen now had more respect for me. I had one doubt—was this a means of getting those pews for some other place and purpose?

When the theater was completed, the Army pointed out that we did not rate both a theater and a chapel, so one had to be demolished. They had decided that the chapel would go. This was so senseless that I declared anyone damaging property on the base would end up in the brig. They willingly accepted this and the matter was dropped. The Army was always considerate of us, but this childish thinking was so unusual that I concluded that they had wanted a sharp answer to justify a deviation from the policy.

The Bledsoes were leaving to return to the states. We sent the following message, as a statement of the admiration and affection of all hands on the Base:

> FOR REAR ADMIRAL BLEDSOE X THE UNFAILING COOPERATION OF THE FORCES AFLOAT WHICH DATES BACK TO YOUR ASSUMPTION OF COMMAND HAS BEEN SINCERELY APPRECIATED BY ALL OF US ASHORE X ONLY WITH YOUR HELP AND UNDERSTANDING HAVE WE BEEN ABLE TO CARRY OUT OUR MISSION X IT HAS BEEN A PRIVILEGE TO SERVE YOU AND FOR YOU X BEST WISHES AND HAPPINESS TO YOU AND YOUR FAMILY AND SUCCESS TO YOU IN YOUR NEW ASSIGNMENT FROM THE OFFICERS, MEN AND DEPENDENTS OF THIS BASE

> To: COMPFLEACTY
> FOR CAPT DECKER X MRS BLEDSOE AND I APPRECIATE THE PRIVILEGE OF LIVING WITH AND KNOWING YOU AND THE PERSONNEL AND DEPENDENTS OF YOKOSUKA X WE LEAVE WITH REGRET AND A WARM SPOT FOR EACH OF YOU X REAR ADMIRAL L BLEDSOE

MacArthur had thrown his hat into the ring for the presidency, which made me very happy. He made an excellent statement. He was countering Eisenhower's statement that military men should not enter politics. General MacArthur was quoted as saying he would serve, if elected.

I was asked to attend several briefing conferences in SCAP, the first of March. I was able to state my views on Japan:

"The peace treaty should be simple and direct. We should guarantee the internal and the external security of Japan. Japan guarantees us the rights necessary to implement this security and accepts advisors we think necessary.

"Communistic nations will oppose such a treaty, but they will oppose any treaty—so what! Anti-communist nations will be only too glad for the U.S. to guarantee the security of the Pacific. Great Britain can't afford to."

Chapter IX

TOUR OF DUTY EXTENDED

Admiral Berkey asked me to stay for another year. This was in keeping with my wishes to complete the job in Yokosuka. Certainly there was no future for me elsewhere—it was too late to convince the Selection Board that I should be a flag officer. My heart was in Yokosuka. So I accepted the invitation. I received indications that Washington would receive my request favorably. And in June 1949 I would retire. Edwina agreed. She got her mink coat!

Here is another letter. I didn't need to be rewarded for my acts, but it certainly was heartwarming to receive this letter. I found a renewal of faith in the human race. People like Mother Britt can write such kind thoughts. I'll accept her prayers as more than full payment for anything that I might have done:

March 16, 1948

Dear Captain Decker,

What a surprise we had today! I had hoped to get off a word of gratitude for your great generosity in giving Mother Schickel and myself so much of your precious time. It was a great honor to have met you, and a still greater pleasure to find such a very important, busy man so leisurely. The cleanliness, activity, understanding of the people on the part of the officials, left me with the impression that Yokosuka is not only a near-future "A no. 1" Port in the Pacific, but the most perfect haven of peace in the world. I wonder if anywhere such progress has been made in this still war-torn world! Many prayers of thanksgiving have gone heavenward for what you have accomplished and will continue to follow you that God may yet do much more for the betterment of mankind through you.

I had also hoped to thank you for the kitchen utensils Mr. Gorry managed to pull out of the depot to which Commander Holtom kindly directed us. But before I could do that, the priceless pots and pans that Commander Gray got together at your request, so now I must try to express our heartfelt gratitude for all. You simply cannot realize what treasures these are in this land of want. I wish I might thank each one who contributed to the work of locating, loading the truck, etc., but that is not possible. However, prayers defy time, space, and even paper . . . so all may be assured of our prayers of thanksgiving.

If ever you are in Tokyo, do let Mr. Gorry bring you out to see us. We bought a chichirin to take to the new house, and shall cook with that until we find a gas range somewhere. Fortunately it is very cold in Tokyo, so the ice box will not be such an important item for a couple of weeks, but when you visit I hope you will find that we have a kitchen set-up. Should an ice box "wander in" from any of the islands will you keep us in mind?

With renewed gratitude from all the nuns, I am

Yours gratefully,
E. T. Britt
(Mother Britt)

International College
No. 1 Miyashiro-cho
Shibuya-ku, Tokyo

On March twenty-fourth, one of my former bosses, Captain Quiggly, retired, arrived on the base with several business partners from the United States Steel Export Company of New York. He was interested in our 2760.55 tons of steel in 1193 ingots on the base, alone. I thought it a great idea for the Japanese to sell them to the United States as it would be years before the Japanese steel industry could handle those huge ingots. These men walked through the base testing the ingots with magnets. Those of high nickel content would show little magnetic attraction while pure iron registered a high attraction. Many of the ingots were of no interest to them. Others would require more accurate tests to determine their value. They were grateful and I would have thought the Japanese would be too. However, the plan fell through. Bert Crane wrote up an article for the Japanese press about the sale of this material and the sale was disapproved by the Occupation. I thought that the real reason for the Japanese stopping the deal was the Saibutsu's desire to corner raw materials for the future. They had no funds, but he who had the raw materials had the wealth.

12 April 1948

Dear Captain Decker:

His Excellency, Most Reverend A. C. Cicognani, Apostolic Delegate, has forwarded to the Secretary of the Navy a letter from Bishop Thomas Wakida, a copy of which I am enclosing herewith.

The Secretary is gratified to receive such commendation for a Naval officer and has asked me to send his personal appreciation to you.

A copy of this correspondence is being sent to the Bureau of Naval Personnel to be retained in your official record.

Sincerely yours,
(Fitz Lee)
FITZHUGH LEE
Captain, U.S. Navy
Aide to the
Secretary of the Navy

APOSTOLIC DELEGATION   3339 Massachusetts Ave.
United States of America   Washington, D. C.
No. 287/41
This No. Should Be Prefixed to the Answer
April 8, 1948
My dear Mr. Secretary:
I take the liberty of enclosing a copy of a letter which I have just received from the Most Reverend Thomas Wakida, Bishop of Yokohama, in reference to Captain Benton W. Decker.

I sent it to you not with any intention of asking that his orders be modified, but only in the thought that the Navy Department may be interested in having this testimonial of commendation of one of its officers.

With sentiments of highest consideration and kind personal regards. I remain.

Yours very sincerely,
Archbishop of Laodicea
Apostolic Delegate

The Honorable
John L. Sullivan
Secretary of the Navy
Washington, D. C.

Diocese of Yokohama (Japan)
Yamate, 44
March 16, 1948

His Excellency
Most Rev. A. C. Cicognani, Apostolic Delegate
Washington, D. C.
Your Excellency:
In the name of the Clergy and Diocese of Yokohama I have a request to make:

Captain Benton W. Decker, Commandant Fleet Activities of Yokosuka has been in Yokosuka for two years, and has done magnificent work for the people of this city, trying to impress the fact that there can be no real democracy without Christianity. He is responsible for three schools and two hospitals in Yokosuka confided to Protestants and Catholics as well; and has also endeared himself to the non-Christian people of Yokosuka to the extent that they have a petition all over town to have his tour of duty extended.

I, as the representative of the Diocese would gladly join in that petition, asking Your Excellency to use your high influence in the proper channel in Washington, so that we may keep our good Captain Decker for at least another year.

I remain Your Excellency,
Devotedly yours in Christ,
Thomas Wakida,
Bishop of Yokohama

24 March 1948

My dear Benny:

I have just received your letter which covers the points about which I wanted detailed information.

I intend to extract pertinent items from your memorandum and the supporting enclosures for the benefit of the Bureaus and Offices interested. They furnish the best sort of dollar facts in justification of the earlier decisions concerning Yokosuka.

I consider that your handling of that job out there does you great credit, and Yokosuka is an outstanding example of vision and good management.

Best regards to you and all my friends.

Sincerely,
Robert B. Carney
Vice Admiral, U.S.N.

The following is a translation of petition submitted by Hachiro Okayama, President of Yokosuka Municipal Assembly:

26 March 1948

General of the Army Douglas MacArthur,
Supreme Commander Allied Powers
Sir:

It is of the utmost honor to present a letter to your Excellency whom all the Japanese people love and admire. We would like to pay our respects ot your noble character and at the same time express deep appreciation for your warm understanding towards the Japanese people.

At this time I would like to speak of Captain Decker, who is the present Commandant of Yokosuka Naval Base. Captain Decker has given the people of Yokosuka, during their trying periods, bright hopes for the future, through his assistance and encouragement. He is adored and respected by each and every citizen of Yokosuka for his noble efforts. I firmly believe that the confidence and adulation heaped by the people upon Captain Decker is a reflection of your Excellency's high moral integrity.

We have heard recently that Captain Decker is leaving for the United States. We hope that Captain Decker could remain with us for the sake of the City's continued progress.

Yokosuka Municipal Assembly has voted unanimously to draw a resolution based on public opinion to request Captain Decker's continued presence in his present capacity.

We beg of your Excellency from the bottom of our hearts to retain Captain Decker through your good office.

Respectfully yours,
Hachiro Okayama
President Yokosuka
Municipal Assembly

Edwina wrote her mother in San Diego:

These past two years have been the most interesting years of my life and Benny's. We are staying another year. The people of Yokosuka asked for us by petitioning General MacArthur. We feel this job is a big one where Benny can do so much good. We have a good Naval Base here that is costing the U.S. very little. The Japanese government is paying the wages, and we captured the equipment. One of Benny's missions is to protect the U.S. taxpayers. This is one place we get more than we give. As we have disarmed Japan, it is necessary that we protect her. This means a small force remains here, to maintain surveillance and to deny Japan to Russia and Communism. Yokosuka is a good base to support a security force.

With the idea that the Americans would stay here for twenty years, "Benny" has paid great attention to military government of Yokosuka. It is the cleanest and most prosperous city in Japan, the streets are clean and the people happy. Though still hungry, they are not starving. There seems to be a great deal of improvement in dress, from rags to rather plain but warm clothing. The people are with us. But Benny thinks that this means little if we don't change their way of thinking.

This Occupation will fail and peace in the Pacific be of short duration unless Japan is a democracy, but no democracy can exist unless its people understand and practice Christianity. The Golden Rule and the Ten Commandments are necessary to a democracy. There has never been a democracy that was not Christian. First came Christianity, then came from it democracy.

Cardinal Spellman was here recently and we were fortunate to have a word with him and hear his talk. Monsignor Fulton J. Sheen, the famous Catholic radio speaker, was here too. Cardinal Spellman is a fine man, very humane in his dealings. Because Benny is so interested in Christianity in Japan we are invited and included in the functions of the Church. We have initiated the creation in Yokosuka of Protestant and Catholic hospitals, two Catholic schools, two Protestant activities, a Catholic Church and several Protestant churches. Also there are monthly revival meetings for the Japanese. We hope that Yokosuka will be an important city in Japan. Our little chapel on the Base was completed recently. It is a bit of old New England. We have a full set of electric chimes so every day from 4:30 to 5:15 p.m. we have hymns played on them. The men in their homes can hear them, all are touched by the beautiful songs recalling memories of home. The Church holds 200 people. It is white with a steeple, green shutters and beautiful shrubs around. The altar is impressive and so are the pews with their red plush cushions. The music is a Hammond organ. Sunday before last, 18 U.S. children were baptized, 12 of whom were babies born here. We attend Church every Sunday if we are here. We practice what we preach. If Benny isn't selected for Rear Admiral next October, he will have the satisfaction of a job well done. This chapel is used by both Protestants and by Catholics.

Edwina

Our social life kept us busy. General and Mrs. Paul Mueller held a reception on January first. We attended with hundreds of other senior officers and wives to pay our respects to an outstanding officer who was the chief of staff to General MacArthur. Benny knew him as the General of the Eighty-first Division which captured Angaur. Now he was an important part of the Occupation. Benny found cooperating with the Army a pleasant task because of the many senior Army officers, such as General Mueller. I found their wives to be congenial and thoughtful. We next called on the MacArthurs and our immediate senior in the Navy, the Griffins. This was the usual New Year's Day duty in Japan. But we also called because we admired them and enjoyed doing so.

At a party in Hayama given by Colonel and Mrs. McNabb for the senior officers of the First Cavalry, General Bradford's wife told us about the brass piles in Japan. During the war, the Japanese confiscated brass and bronze items for the war effort. This metal was piled ten feet high on vacant lots. One was in Tokyo. There was far more metal than they could ever use and much of this was more valuable as antiques than as scrap metal. Though there were many priceless treasures buried under tremendous mounds, there was no pilferage. We had never heard about brass piles before. For ten cents a pound, Allied personnel was allowed to purchase what they selected. There were drawbacks. The Japanese, not trusting their own government, damaged each piece, usually by driving a hole into each vase or statue. And it was dirty from years of exposure to the wind and weather.

I was most interested, as we needed things to decorate our large unfurnished mansion and also I admired Japanese bronzes. At Lois Bradford's invitation I joined her on a visit to the brass pile in Tokyo. We loved to scrounge. When Lois

214

called for me, I wore my oldest clothes, thick woolen socks over my stockings, sneakers, and a raccoon coat. When I said good-bye to Benny he remarked. "If anything happens to you today, I am not going to claim you." I looked awful. It was a cold day.

At the brass pile there was no one else there whom we knew. It was almost deserted except for the Japanese guard. I immediately spotted a large bronze vase caked with mud on its side in a mud puddle. I put it in the trunk of the car. There were many smaller objects, but you had to dig for them and move many large brass nails, banisters, and cornices from temples. I now realize that I was then looking at an antique collectors' paradise. Most of the small statues had holes. I found several, though, that were attractive. There were many three-foot-high cranes and the six-inch tortoises upon which the cranes stood. These represented long life— the crane, 1000 years, and the tortoise, 10,000! As we were getting colder and colder, as well as dirtier and dirtier, we decided to pay our bill of a few dollars and head for home.

Benny was horrified at my appearance and thought the articles I brought home hardly justified the trouble and the time. I asked Akasawa to clean my trophies while I cleaned myself. Soon the excited servants came into the living room, "Madame, that big vase is Ming dynasty!" As they turned it up, exposing a large seal on its base, "That is the mark of Ming!" Benny had the hole in the large bronze Ming vase repaired, and now it is one of our prize ornaments—with the repaired hole to the wall.

Mr. Konome and Mr. Obashi came to call on us. Mr. Obashi was an expert ivory carver. Benny had wanted some ivory figurines, but all on sale were usually happy gods, small, and not the work of the best artists. There was so little ivory in Japan that Benny decided to purchase "points" in Hong Kong and to have them carved in Japan. The Japanese carvers were yearning to start carving again after years of idleness and would carve a statue out of half of the point, keeping the other half in payment. Mr. Obashi carved five statues for him, of historic or typical Japanese characters. They were Benny's delight and he was so proud of these treasures that he gave his choicest to Jean MacArthur out of admiration for the MacArthurs.

On February fifth, the Takaokas and we went to the Ueno Museum in Tokyo. Mr. Takaoka had arranged for us to be escorted by the director. Benny wanted to see their outstanding netsuke collection, as he had been collecting netsuke for the past year. He did this to learn more about the Japanese thought along mythological and historical lines. By being conversant with their folklore and their religious beliefs, he tried to understand them better. The carving of netsuke was done by artists and by the common people, all of whom seem to have some talent. Here, in the Ueno Museum, there was one of the best collections, but it was not on exhibit. So he was given a private showing. They had a Shusan netsuke in which he was interested, as he had never seen one before. As I went through the museum I was proud of our nation. Here was a museum full of antiques of immense value. There had been no looting by our forces. In other wars by other nations, the conqueror had walked off with the treasures. Here we were shown the wealth of an ancient culture with no fear that we would be covetous.

We then went through the Mitsukoshi Department Store. There was a fabulous display of beautiful silks and lacquers as well as more commonplace necessities. It seemed well patronized by Allied personnel as well as by Japanese, and though the prices were high, the people were buying.

With a group of Army wives, including General Farman's wife, I attended a kabuki play in the Tokyo Theater. Mr. Shimada, who had been in some movies in the states, acted as interpreter. From our box we had an excellent view of the stage. The costumes were gorgeous and the scenery on the revolving stage was effective. We were grateful that we had an interpreter.

With Captain and Mrs. Owsley, we visited the workshop of Hiroshi Yoshida, the famous woodblock artist. Gozo Kawamura, the sculptor who had come to Yokosuka from Karuisawa, was our guide and mentor. We were fascinated by the work of this great artist. His son, also an artist, was present and both the Yoshidas were most attentive. We bought many of their prints and thereafter were always on the lookout for more. Many of their prints were scenes of Japanese mountains, woods, or waters. We found them to be well done and beautiful. Mr. Yoshida was most congenial and instructive. They made a number of impressions as we watched.

They were charming hosts.

On March first, we gave a large dinner party for the Bledsoes with many VIPs including General and Mrs. Eichelberger. Our friend, the sculptor, Gozo Kawamura, had cast Eichelberger's plaster bust in bronze in his new foundry. It was a faithful and strong creation and he presented it to the general with Generals Schilling and Peschkoff, and Consul Generals Alexis Johnson and Archer, witnessing the ceremony.

A few days later Admiral Ramsey and Admiral Salada inspected the base and were most complimentary at a luncheon we gave in Admiral Ramsey's honor. Shortly thereafter, we took Vice Admiral Walter Delaney to the Fujiya Hotel with his staff, Captain Biggs and Dawson. Admiral Delaney had seen the base at the time of the surrender and was amazed at the transition. No sooner was he on his way east than Commodore Keleher and staff arrived. We took them to Kamakura, Misaki, and Uraga.

I attended the graduation exercises of the Yokosuka Girls' High School in Otsu, where I gave the following speech:

"It is a great privilege to have been asked to your graduation exercises and it gives me pleasure to be with you.

"First, I want to congratulate you for the success you have achieved in your studies. This is one of the most important days in your lives and I know that you won't forget it. Graduating from school is like launching a ship. You are just starting out on the voyage called life. Your teachers can be compared to the builders of ships and how you stand the stormy seas of life depends to a great extent on how well they have prepared you for your future. You have so much to offer and I want to wish you much success in the future to help each other. The world has seen so much unhappiness in recent years and it is still upset as a result of the terrible war. Each and every one of you want to improve this unstable condition. Happiness is the true birthright of each and every individual, and you girls can help to bring it about. Now that opportunities are offered to you in every field of endeavor, it is my hope that some of you will take advantage of the new opportunities and assume the new responsibilities. Good luck and thank you."

On March eighteenth, General and Mrs. MacArthur gave

a luncheon honoring Admiral Badger and Mrs. Badger. Also present were Admiral and Mrs. Griffin. Admiral McConnell, Badger's staff; Admiral Griffin's chief of staff and Mrs. Bard; Colonel and Mrs. Huff, and the Deckers. After lunch we saw movies in the Embassy. In the evening, we had dinner with the Griffins. The next day, we met Mr. and Mrs. Barry Faris of INS—International News Service. He had come to Japan to interview the General about running for the presidency of the United States. We had lunch with the general's aide, Colonel Syd Huff and his wife, Kira. The Farises and we all went shopping. We were greatly attracted to Barry, and in later years Benny, for a short time, became an INS correspondent to Korea and Formosa.

The following day, Admiral Badger, Captain Smith, and Commander Anderson were shown about the base. Benny tried to persuade them to use Sasebo instead of Tsingtao for ComTaskForce 31 Base which was being threatened by the communists.

The base gave a splendid Easter party for the children. We had a surplus of baskets which Lieutenant and Mrs. Daniels and I with our capable photographer took to the Japanese orphanage. The children were delighted. They were so polite and grateful, and appreciated those baskets. The Japanese are the most polite as well as grateful of any nationality. Those little children were so lovable. We went through the orphanage and saw the widows making toys, such as auto racers, from beer cans from the base.

26 March 1948

Dear Mrs. Decker,

I have just heard that you visited the Keiai Dormitory yesterday with Easter Baskets for the children. Thank you very much for your kindness. I do not need to tell you how overjoyed the mothers and children were to receive your gifts.

With all good wishes for a joyful Easter.

Yours sincerely,
Toshi Tanaka
President
Yokosuka Women's Society

The orphans receive Easter baskets from the Base.

March 26, 1948

New Chapel Dedicated

With skillfully rendered choir music and a service
reminiscent of our home churches that warmed the
hearts of those attending, the new Base Chapel was
officially dedicated Palm Sunday 21 March (1948) by
Rear Admiral R. S. Berkey, Com Sup Grp.

Prominently displayed at the entrance to the Chapel
was an attractive bronze plaque cast by the Ship's Re-

pair Force commemorating the event and dedicating the chapel to the worship of God. The Chapel was beautifully decorated with palms and cut flowers for the occasion.

The service was opened by the playing of the church call by bugler Schumbacher. The choir rendered as their anthem "Lift Up Your Heads" with Mrs. Hazel Cunningham singing the soprano solo. Lt. Comdr. J. H. Holtom, Choir Director, sang a tenor solo, Fuare's Worshipful Palm Sunday selection, "O'er All the Way". The Scripture Lesson and the act of dedication were read by Admiral Berkey and the sermon was delivered by Chaplain R. W. Ricker. There were over 200 attending the service.

Easter Display

The attention of all hands is called to the life-size Easter Tableau now on display just outside the main gate. The display represents the Resurrection scene of the first Easter morning and depicts the Angel and the two Mary's standing in front of the open tomb. Outfitted in their colorful costumes by Mrs. Mimi Gonzales and Mrs. Isabelle Ricker, the beautiful six foot figures, cast by Gozo Kawamura, well known Japanese sculptor whose work appeared at the New York World's Fair in 1939, make an impressive display.

The Easter display at our main gate—again the work of our sculptor, Gozo.

Another step forward was taken when we initiated an annual affair of a Catholic processional through the main street of Yokosuka, starting at St. Joseph's Hospital and ending at the Mikasa Building on the base (both Catholic activities). Edwina and I, with most of the senior officers of the base, marched with the Catholics, using the station band. Even our Masons joined the parade, for in Japan the Christians were united. Several thousand Japanese marched and many thousands watched from the sidewalks. It is best described by Archbishop Marella's letter:

The Catholic processional.

April 19th, 1948

Captain Benton W. Decker
Commander Fleet Activities
Navy 3923
Yokosuka

Dear Captain Decker:

The impression made upon me by yesterday's beautiful ceremony is far too deep to allow me to let it pass without a word to you to express my profound gratitude for your share in making that occasion so wonderfully successful.

This was the first time that Christians were enabled

to have a procession of this kind in the streets of a Japanese city and the fact that it was not only possible, but was achieved in such an atmosphere of sympathetic respect was due to the inspiration and encouragement you gave the matter as also to your personal participation in it.

This is of course only one more incident in the work of rehabilitation you have been carrying on with such splendid courage and energy during the past three years, but I like to look upon it as a kind of a seal and a mark of consecration placed thereby on all your other works in this country. I am sure that your part in this ceremony must have come as a kind of revelation to the people, showing them the spirit in which all your other works have been accomplished.

May God reward you for all this and grant His choicest consolations to both you and Mrs. Decker and may He and his infinite generosity assist you always in the realization of your splendid endeavors.

In conclusion, allow me to express once again my most cordial sentiments of respect and gratitude both to you and to Mrs. Decker.

Very sincerely yours,
Paul Marella
Archbishop
Apostolic Delegate

Twenty-eight years have passed. When I read the archbishop's letter I feel very humble. At the time I did many things because of my training, and because I believed them right. They all lead to the final goal.

From the Mission Diplomatica Espanola, Tokyo:

April 29th, 1948

Dear friend,

Father Circilo Iglesias came to see me a few days ago and told me that you have been extremely kind to the Missionaries in Yokosuka granting them two bells for the Church and placing at their disposal a site where they can establish that Church and also providing electricity and heating of same.

Father Cirilo Iglesias also told me that you favoured

and gave all your valuable support to the organization of a procession through the streets of Yokosuka which was the first of its kind to be held in Japan!

Considering that the majority of the Missionaries in Yokosuka is Spanish, I take the liberty of expressing to you, as the Spanish Representative in Japan, my deepest gratitude.

Hoping to see you soon and with my respects to your charming wife, I remain

Yours very sincerely,
G. Ojeda

6 May 1948

Dear Friend:

For a wonderful visit and a wonderful time I want to say to you and Edwina a sincere and enthusiastic, "Thank you!" Your beautiful home and most cordial and friendly hospitality will never be forgotten. And Benny without a shadow of doubt you have accomplished one of the finest jobs, and I mean a big job too!, I've ever witnessed. Believe me I have spread the "Gospel of Benny Decker" everywhere.

Sincerely and cordially,
THORNTON C. MILLER
Rear Admiral, Chc, U.S. Navy
Fleet Chaplain

May 11, 1948

Dear Captain Decker:

This letter will not be according to naval form since I have long since forgotten such technicalities of navy procedure. In the past few days I have had reports on the kind of a job you are doing in Yokosuka. The first was in the form of a short squib in the Rome Daily American that is published here which contained a reference to the efficiency and dispatch with which you protected the housewives in Japan who had been victimized by the local racketeers.

The second reference to the great work you are doing was found in a letter that I received from the St.

224

Maur Sisters who have a school in Yokohama. They mentioned that a few days ago they had a dedication service for a new Catholic church in Yokosuka. The church referred to was none other than the former chapel which gave service to the men in my time in Yokosuka. I was formerly stationed at the Marine Air Field near to your activity and was quite familiar with your set up because of a personal friendship with Father McCoy who was your Catholic chaplain at the time.

Congratulations to you on your vision in being able to see the important role that religion plays in the rehabilitation of Japan. If there were more officers like you there would be less occupational problems to deal with. You have my prayers for your continued success.

Sincerely in Christ,
Rev. Francis J. Fleming

April tenth, the anniversary of my assuming command of fleet activities had arrived and once again my officers gave me a big party. The amount of work and care they put into this party more than repaid me for what I could do to make their lives easier and happier. We had had so much to do, that I was limited in making their lives easier. They found happiness in helping others. Certainly I expected much from them, but they always came up to my demands with a smile. This was to be my last command and probably my last duty in our Navy. I was very proud of my officers and men. This anniversary party left a warm feeling in my heart. The following was taken from the *Sea Hawk*, April 9, 1948 issue:

Second Anniversary of
Captain Decker as COMFLTACT

The Staff of the *Seahawk* joins the officers, men, and dependents of Fleet Activities in wishing Captain Benton W. Decker all of the best on the occasion of his second anniversary as Commanding Officer on the Base.

2nd Anniversary Message

Two years mark a short period in the life of an average community, but those of us who have served at Yokosuka during the past two have seen tremendous and invigorating changes in the political and economic fields of the Yokosuka Naval Area. A nearly complete alteration in the physical appearance of the Naval Base had also occurred. This period of growth has been particularly gratifying, both because of the changes wrought in the Japanese outlook and because of the excellent performance made by the Naval personnel of the Base in the accomplishment of their given tasks.

I wish to take this opportunity to express my gratitude and thanks to all who have served with me during this period, and to those dependents who have contributed their cheerful assistance in making this a happy station. Best wishes and happiness to you all during the coming year.

B. W. Decker
Captain, U. S. Navy
Commander Fleet Activities

Edwina describes the party:

The officers of the base gave Benny a dinner dance in his honor, it being the second anniversary of his command. When we entered the Officers' Club we noticed a large, life-size picture of Benny. There was a spotlight focused upon it. In front of the picture the White Hatters were playing our favorite music. The officers gave me two beautiful orchids in a corsage.

After a superb meal and before dessert, they wheeled into the center of the room a 100-pound cake and presented me with a dozen lovely red roses. The top of the cake was a relief map of the base in gorgeous frosting. Every building and every road was beautifully molded, easily identified. Three bakers had worked on it for a week. It was a masterpiece. The most beautiful either Benny or I had ever seen. In cutting it, many officers received their buildings, and their wives received their own houses. It became quite a game. In the middle of the evening, Commander and Mrs. Paton, on the West Coast, called us by radio phone. He had contributed so much as captain of the yard, in making the base what it is now. We were sincerely touched by this grand display of affection from our officers.

We received a thoughtful letter from Admiral Bledsoe's wife, Florence. It always makes me purr to reread such letters telling of happiness and how people enjoyed duty in Yokosuka. She and the admiral were a great help in making others happy. We should be thanking them.

28 March 1948

Dear Edwina & Benny,

I have so many good parties for which to thank you but I particularly want to say how much I appreciate my first party in Japan and my last and I shall always remember what a glorious introduction and send off you gave us. I realize that it was due to your many courtesies and your thoughtfulness that my stay in Japan was one of the happiest times in my life.

Save your money for China—there are many beautiful things to buy and after shopping in Japan—they all seem like bargains. We have enjoyed seeing our friends in Tsingtao, Shanghai, Manila, and Subic Bay. There is just enough time in between ports to get a good rest and the last two weeks from Guam to San Francisco should put us in good shape to fight the Battle of the U.S.A.

We arrived in Guam in a few hours and will stay with the Pownalls. I have spent the morning getting the Easter Bunny's work done for him—which reminds me of the wonderful party we had for the youngsters last year in your garden.

We will be anxious to hear what you are going to do and look forward to a reunion when you return.

Again, thank you for our very lovely coasters—we shall enjoy using them often.

Best love to you both,
Florence Bledsoe

One could not wish for a better relationship than that which existed on all levels between the Army and the Navy. I found myself just as close to my friends of a few years in the Occupation forces, as with those of thirty years in the Navy. A good example of the friendship is that of General Bill Chase, in the following:

Dear Captain Decker:

On behalf of the First Cavalry Division, it gives me great pleasure to request your presence at Camp McGill at 1100 hours, Saturday, the 15th of May.

I also extend to you a formal invitation to become an Honorary Member of the First Cavalry Division, and I plan to induct both you and Adm. Griffin into the ranks at this ceremony.

We in the First Cavalry Division appreciate very much everything you at Yokosuka have done for us during the past two years. We thank you and we hope you will keep our famous Gold Badge as a souvenir of your association with us, and of your services in Japan.

Very sincerely,
Wm. C. Chase
Major General
U. S. Army
Commanding

On May fifteenth, we got up bright and early and drove over to Camp McGill where we were met by General William C. Chase and Colonel Gordon Rogers at the parade grounds. Admiral Griffin and Benny were escorted to the platform. The ladies were seated next to the platform. General Chase gave a talk about honoring Admiral Griffin and Benny in appreciation of the close support given the division by the Navy in amphibious campaigns in the Admiralty and Philippine Islands during the war, and also the close cooperation the Army had received from the base at Yokosuka.

Edwina has reported the close ties I had with the First Cavalry Division. I was honored by becoming a member of this outstanding Army division. This was typical of my Army friends, such as Bill Chase. He was a stalwart friend as well as another Rhode Islander. From then on, when I attended the reviews in Tokyo, I wore, with pride, a large gold cavalry patch on my blue uniform coat. Standing there among the great on the reviewing platform, that gold patch gave me more gold than the Chinese general. The Navy thought there was a change in uniform regulations. All I was doing was stretching a point or two. It certainly made the First Cavalry happy.

Yokohama, Japan
21 May 1948

Captain B. W. Decker
Commander, Fleet Activities
Navy No. 3923
c/o U.S. Army

Dear Benny:

Thanks a million for the grand photographs which I found upon my return from a short inspection trip to Sapporo and Sendai. The sketchings are especially interesting and I am certainly glad to have them.

Congratulations on your having recently been made a member of the great First Cavalry Division!

With renewed thanks and warm regards.

Sincerely,
Robert Eichelberger

From Consul General U. Alexis Johnson:

Yokohama
May 25, 1948

Dear Benny:

Reference our hurried conversation about 10 gals. black enamel. We need it to complete the painting of iron fences, railing, etc. in the Foreign Cemetery on the Bluff. You have already been most generous, but this additional enamel would enable us to complete the work—the Army says they do not have it. As most of the US service men buried there are from the Navy I think that you could justify it, if necessary.

As you know, the Army has assigned one man to full time duty at the cemetery and he has done an outstanding job in fixing up the place until it is now one of the most beautiful spots in Yokohama, which I feel it should be. I have also raised about Y15,000 in the business community here to buy additional shrubs and flowers. I wish you would stop by and give it a look sometime when you are in town.

If you can spare the enamel perhaps you could have it sent up by the Guard Mail, or I could pick it up when I come down Wednesday afternoon to see John Q and Chris off.

Incidentally, I would appreciate a copy of the photo of the Owsleys and Fellers they took Sunday evening. I believe that they took one with just the four of them in it.

Sincerely,
Alex

We had a supply of large searchlight reflectors that I had rescued from demilitarizers who were smashing them with hammers. We used several to decorate our home and, thinking others might desire them, I presented one to Admiral Ramsey. We didn't have many left. It gave me satisfaction to know that Mrs. Ramsey liked hers as much as I liked the one we had.

3 April 1948

Dear Deckers:
There just arrived in my household the searchlight reflector which was sent to us from your Supply Officer at Yokosuka. It is indeed a wonderful gift, and it has brought great joy and pleasure to the Ramsey household. You may be assured that it will be put to very profitable use here.

Please know how deeply Mrs. Ramsey and I appreciate your great courtesy in this matter. She joins me in sending every good wish in the world to you and Mrs. Decker and my good friends and associates of your command.

Most gratefully,
D. C. Ramsey
Admiral, U.S. Navy

Our new dental office opened with five units in its own building, capable of expansion. Commanders F. L. Gonzales, with the excellent support of Commanders C. J. Schork and L. E. Johnson was doing an outstanding job. They used Japanese girls (pretty ones) to clean the patients' teeth. I have never had such soothing attention in a dental chair before! Those dental technicians were capable and careful. Now that the dentists had new surroundings, well designed and equipped. I feared that they would be too popular. We had lost Commander Hal Green, and they did need more dentists. Frank Gonzales suggested that we ask for some junior dentists to relieve the burden from our three senior dentists. Jokingly, I rejected the idea—we were getting along very well with the bosses doing the work. If we got an ensign, he would do the work, and three commanders would do the bossing! Truthfully, our commanders were the best in the Navy and were dedicated to serving the Navy. I was proud of each of them.

And our barber shop opened with beautiful and immaculate tile floors and stateside chairs. Everyone was doing his best to improve the base. All I had to do was sit back and give a bit of encouragement.

Fleet Act was getting publicity by our bowling league. They planned a match between the officers' league and the enlisted men's league for the grand championship of Japan! Those alleys were popular.

The Far East Miniature Railroad was doing well, and other activities were being formed, such as the little theater group, and a hobby shop was being opened under the supervision of Staff Sergeant Sutton. It amazed me how many activities were blossoming on the base under the inspiration and guidance by volunteers. We had no budget or professionals—just volunteers. My people were always surprising me and doing more than their duty required.

The dependent wives were studying flower arrangement under Mrs. Yamamoto from Yokohama and painting at the EM Club, besides lessons in Japanese.

The yacht season was in full swing. Our Star fleet, the first in Japan, was popular. The following was written in the *Sea Hawk*.

Initial Yacht Club Race Sunday

On Sunday, 11 April, at 1400, the 1st official race of the Spring Regatta conducted by the Yokosuka Yacht Club will be held.

Star boats will be underway at that time followed at 1415 by the dingy class. Contestants are requested to register early with the club secretary. Lt. (jg) C. E. Johnson, Jr.

To insure prompt starts, all boats should be manned

by 1300. Results will be published next week. Bring your binoculars and root for your favorites.

Last week's preliminary Star Race indicates some keen competition when all craft finished the 3 mile course within a period of 38 seconds.

Our doctors had tried to help our friend former Admiral Yonai in his final illness, but he died. Our mutual friend ex-captain Yokoyama wrote:

May 8, 1948

Captain B. W. Decker
Commander Fleet Activities
Navy Œ3923
c/o U.S. Army
Dear Captain Decker,

Recalling the visit I made with my wife some time ago I wish to express this belated thanks for the warm hospitality extended to us on that occasion, and also for the pleasant experience of riding back to Tokyo with you in your car.

As you are doubtless aware, the former Admiral Mitsumasa Yonai, on whose behalf you kindly manifested such solicitous concern, finally passed away recently. It is with deep emotion that I recall the occasion of his visit to your quarters a year ago when you did him the honor to receive him with genuine courtesy and warmth.

I met Mrs. Kawabata on the occasion of the first anniversary of his death and was moved to hear from her of all the kindness you have been showing to her and her family. As a lifelong friend of Kawabata, I wish to convey to you my heartfelt thanks. I also heard on that occasion you might shortly be leaving for the States. If all circumstances permit however, I do hope you will be able to remain at the present post to bring to fruition the plan which I know is so close to your heart.

I look forward to seeing you again in the near future. With kindest regards for your health.

Yours sincerely,
Ichiro Yokoyama

The Shinsei Yokosuka Women's Club became politically important. The Governor of Kanagawa-ken, Iwataro Uchiyama, was running for reelection. I liked him very much and thought him an outstanding man. He dropped in to ask for my support.

"I cannot support a political candidate, but I can oppose one!"

"Do you oppose me?"

"Yes. Unless you have on the speakers' platform with you at least one woman." I knew that this was an unusual request and that it required a big concession. He left me to make his campaign talks throughout the Yokosuka area. I had my civil affairs officer report back to me who were his speakers. There was no other man on the platform, but there were three women! He was elected in a landslide.

The General's chief of staff was General Paul Mueller, whom I first met when he was in command of the 81st Division, landing on Angaur Island. He was a good friend. We got along with no difficulty, so when I called on him in Washington after we were both retired, I was surprised when he said, "Benny, you were the only person in the Occupation I could not control!" This had never occurred to me, nor was there any indication of this. I admit that when something appeared wrong to me, I spoke up. The situation was always corrected when I reported it to the senior officer in whose office it had originated. The generals were more than willing to correct matters when brought to their attention. Everytime I had any difficulty it was because of a junior misinterpreting a higher policy.

Here is an example. A signal unit commenced erecting a duplicate signal tower on the base for the control of shipping. It was not only a waste of funds, but it would be confusing to shipping. They could share our tower, but not erect one.

Another example: It was said that I couldn't arrest communists or prevent them from working on my base! I was responsible for the security of Yokosuka, as well as the base, and the communists were not just a political party. They were a threat to my command. And that was that!

The Army authorized a chapel, which was built. Then they authorized a theater. They then reduced the seating capacity. Next they were going to demolish the chapel because we did not rate both a chapel and a theater. At this I stepped in with an emphatic "No!"

Once or twice I had to throw my weight around. A major was signing many directives "by direction." By whose direction was not clear to me. Once I received what I thought was a highly impertinent one, which did not sound like General MacArthur. This was what caused many misunderstandings about the General. I telephoned the major. The major himself had thought it all up and didn't see why I was upset as the Army units were not. "The Navy doesn't do business that way. If there is to be any censoring, we expect the person doing so to sign it." I wanted to talk to his boss about it. "I'm sorry," he said. "Tear it up and forget it," which I did.

116 Ruggles Avenue
Newport, R. I
April 20, 1948

Dear Edwina,

We were so thrilled Sunday to see your pictures on the front page of the Boston "Advertiser"! And such excellent pictures of all of you too. No doubt you will receive scores of copies from your friends, but thought you might want an extra one—and also the full front page—rather than just the clipping.

We think of you all and Japan so often and the wonderful time we had there. How we would love to dash over for a weekend and see all the changes that have taken place since we left. Had a note several weeks ago from Pat Johnson and she said—"Yokosuka looks so different these days—Benny Decker has certainly done a grand job."

What a nice surprise we had last month to receive a money order for the missing coats. Many, many thanks to Sir Captain for so kindly arranging that. It is greatly appreciated and I have been intending to write daily but getting settled here seems to have taken more time than is scheduled.

Much love,
Marian Paton

Chapter X

CHERRY BLOSSOMS

Edwina tells of the beauties of Japan—

It was cherry blossom time in Japan, a beautiful time of the year. Benny recalled with pleasure the arrival of the *Astoria* in Yokohama in 1939 with Saito's ashes. The cherry blossoms were in bloom and Japan was gorgeous, but in 1946 it wasn't. The ravages of war with massive bombed-out areas made Japan depressing. The following year, it had improved and we gave our first cherry blossom garden party in honor of Mrs. MacArthur. Again in 1948, the cherry blossoms were in full bloom and Japan had improved so much. We were delighted to honor the gracious First Lady of the Occupation, but there was more to it than that. We wanted our officers and wives to meet Mrs. MacArthur and for our leading citizens to pay their respects to her. It certainly aided in the build up of the Shinsei Women's Club.

Our garden was beautiful. The Japanese gardeners knew that this was their big day. The cherry trees never looked better. It was Jean MacArthur's day. A delegation of the Japanese leading citizens, people who were democratizing Yokosuka, met her when she arrived at the Tadodai, in the front garden, and presented her with gorgeous bouquets. Cameras clicked and we escorted her to the main garden where our officers and their wives were introduced to her. We had 140 guests.

The wife of our junior officer, presented Mrs. MacArthur with a corsage of purple orchids, and Mr. Carty of Paramount News took movies while Mr. Gory took stills for the newspapers. Each lady received a painted fan and had the pleasure of watching the artists perform. There were luncheon tables set up throughout the garden. The menu was rice and curry with seventeen side dishes, salad, rolls, ice cream with petit fours, and coffee. Our White Hatters played during the luncheon.

Tokyo
April 15, 1948

Dear Edwina & Benny—

I am sure you realized how very much I enjoyed every minute of my Yokosuka Day. You were so thoughtful to plan this again for me and I do thank you. It is always a great pleasure to see you both and to have the opportunity of meeting your delightful friends. Again my thanks and all the best wishes.

Very sincerely,
Jean MacArthur

22 April 1948

My Highly Esteemed Capt. and Mrs. B. W. Decker:

Please permit us to express our sincerest gratitude for your kindest invitation extended to us to a cocktail and dinner party today. We feel it a great honor to be present at the party and we expect to enjoy it to our hearts content.

This invitation will be one of the greatest honors and sweetest memory in our life.

You have always been so considerate to the Japanese hospitals in Yokosuka and have given a kind guidance and assistance for bringing up the standard of the hospitals to the present condition. It is entirely through your untiring effort that our hospitals have shown such an improvement. We shall not reiterate here how grateful we are for all you have done to our hospital as we have expressed our gratitude for your kind favour in our monthly reports.

We have learned through your daily deeds a manly and strenuous living and the manner of business disposition. We understand that you hate men with weak backbones. There are in Japan too many men with weak backbones. We expect to exert a great effort that we may become men of strenuous and righteous workers in the society.

Let us again thank you for your invitation today.

Yours respectfully,
Dr. and Mrs. T. Kawamura

On the twenty-second of April we gave a reception for those Japanese who had contributed so much to the rebuilding of Yokosuka. The guest list is of interest:

Guest List

April 22

The Mayor Ohta
Mr. and Mrs. Okayama (City Council)
Chief of Police and Mrs. Suzuki (Police)
Mr. and Mrs. Murata (Chamber of Commerce)
Mr. and Mrs. Tanaka (U.L.O. and Women's Club)
Dr. and Mrs. Matsuoka (Women's Club)
Mrs. Kawabata (Red Cross)
Mr. and Mrs. Yamazumi (Red Cross)
Dr. and Mrs. Kuwabara (Red Cross and Hospital)
Dr. and Mrs. Harada (Medical Association)
Mr. and Mrs. Tokunaga (P.T.A.)
Mr. and Mrs. K. Suzuki (Charity Board)
Mr. and Mrs. Mabuchi (Women's Club)
Mr. and Mrs. Gozo Kawamura (Sculptor)
Gov. and Mrs. Uchiyama
Dr. and Mrs. Sano (Health)
Mr. and Mrs. Sasaguchi (Diet)
Dr. and Mrs. Kurosawa (Prost. Hospital)
Mr. and Mrs. Takaoka (Liaison)
Miss Ozaki
Mr. and Mrs. Tanikawa (Red Cross)
Rev. and Mrs. Yasumura
Procurator and Mrs. Konichi
Mr. and Mrs. Kobayashi (Oppama Industry Club)
Bishop Breton
Dr. and Mrs. Topping
Rev. and Mrs. Thompson
Father Voss and Father Cullanine
Mother Ernestine and one sister
Capt. and Mrs. Owsley
Capt. and Mrs. Kirten
Comdr. and Mrs. Geise
Lt. Comdr. and Mrs. Ricker
Lt. Comdr. and Mrs. Holtom

Capt. and Mrs. Lawrence
Lt. (jg) and Mrs. Greer
Lt. Hallman
Ens. Jackson

Benny and I went to the most beautiful garden party which was given in honor of the birthday of His Majesty the Emperor of Japan. It was given by the governor of the Kanagawa Prefecture and Mrs. Uchiyama at their beautiful home in Yokohama. The garden was perfectly beautiful, and they had Japanese musicians, dancers, and magicians. As we strolled through the garden from one entertainment to another, it was just romantic. I would say that all the leading people of the Occupation and the prominent Japanese attended. It was a very large affair, and it was just wonderful.

On the evening of May the third, we left for a ten-day trip in two private cars to see as much of Japan as we could. Smith, our driver, took us to the Kirtens' quarters where we met the Fellers, MacDonalds, DeWitts, and Gonzales'. A station bus had been parked near the Kirtens. After toasting to a good trip. we bid good-bye to the Kirtens and servants. We had a bus ride to the Officers' Club where we picked up Captain Fuller, U.S.M.C., who acted as aide, and the Holtoms.

We then went to the Yokohama Central Depot where we waited for our train. It was late because there had been an accident. General Eichelberger's aide had planned our trip and when we boarded our private cars, Benny and I had a large compartment with two lower berths and our private washbowl adjoining. There were a table and two chairs in our compartment. We took one chair out because it was needed in the dining lounge section. There were two or three compartments in that car. Japanese trains are small in comparison with ours, although they are more elaborate. They are not comfortable. They have a single plate of glass for their windows and the coal soot came through. In eleven days we had only three baths, so you can imagine how dirty we felt when we arrived home on the fourteenth.

We arrived at Kyoto early the next morning and were met by a bus for Nara. There, shopping was very disappointing. Since a year ago, prices had gone up five times. We did not buy anything. We returned to the railroad cars for our lunch. Late that afternoon, we left for Toba, where we arrived the next morning and visited Mikimoto's pearl farm. Mr. Mikimoto met us and we were so pleased to see that he was feeling better again. He is such a nice elderly gentleman of ninety and we liked him very much.

After an interesting show put on by the women divers, we went through the workshop. Following that, we had lunch in the guest house on the prettiest spot on the hill. We had lobster, fresh oranges, and when we first sat down, there were two oysters on each plate. When we opened the oysters, we found a perfectly matched pair of pearls, one pearl in each oyster. This was Mikimoto's way of giving each of us a present. After lunch we thanked Mr. Mikimoto and bid him and his secretary good-bye. We went on board a small motor launch that took us back to the mainland where we waited a few minutes for the small electric car. The ride back was beautiful. Flowers were in bloom all over the hillsides and banks, and the rice paddies added to the scenery.

We boarded our train. That evening we had a good dinner and in Japanese money one fish cost fourteen dollars at the fixed exchange of fifty to one.

We joked about it and called it our "goldfish." Needless to say, we didn't get another fish on our trip.

The next morning we arrived at the Kure Naval base in the British zone. Commander Howard Watson, the commanding officer, entertained us with hot coffee at the Officers' Club, after which we were escorted by Commander Raleigh to the dock where we went on board a large motor launch to ride to the island of Miyajima. It was so interesting, as well as beautiful, and the walk along the waterfront, with an ishi dora (stone lantern) every few feet along the way, was romantic. The path led to a temple looking out over the water. The famous Tori (Gate) to the dedicated mariners is one of the most impressive sights I have ever seen. It is located in the water, just offshore.

After a very pleasant day there, we returned to Kure. We enjoyed our ride back with Commander Raleigh, U.S. Naval liaison officer who acted as our guide and the British officer Howard Watson. We went sightseeing around the Naval base. It looked like Yokosuka did when I first arrived. The British

239

had done absolutely nothing, except everything had been numbered and catalogued for reparations. I suppose some things had been sent away, but it looked like an absolute mess to me and it was quite a contrast to our base.

We arrived at the U.S. Naval base of Sasebo the next morning and it was pouring cats and dogs. We were met by Lieutenant Pierce and Commander and Mrs. Carlson, and others and were taken to the Carlsons' quarters. Commander Carlson took care of the menfolks and Mrs. Carlson took care of the women. We bathed and changed our clothes to go to the Officers' Club for lunch, after which we went sightseeing and windowshopping. The U.S.S. *Toledo*, Admiral Berkey's flagship, was in port and Admiral Berkey and officers were present and we returned to the club for cocktails and a buffet supper party. Later, we visited the Army Club where we met Colonel Bing (U.S.A.).

The next morning we arrived at Nagasaki. It was interesting, but a very depressing place. The second atomic bomb was dropped there. Unlike Hiroshima, which has been rebuilt, Nagasaki was just as it was, except the debris had been removed. The people looked whipped. Even the children had no smiles. I saw one poor little boy with half of his face gone. Everywhere else in Japan the children all seemed so happy and smiled in such a friendly fashion that to see this little boy in his pitiful condition and the other children who did not smile at us left a deep impression.

We also saw the early Dutch buildings and homes, which were most interesting.

After our sightseeing trip, we visited the Goldsbys who lived in Madame Butterfly's home. The opera *Madame Butterfly* was based on a true story, except that it was a French Merchant Marine officer and not an American. Pinkerton was fictitious. This French officer was in Nagasaki for about eight months. The house has been added on to by an Englishman who lived there many years. The Goldsbys were very kind in showing us around the place.

On Monday we arrived at Beppu, famous for its hot springs and mud baths, and how we enjoyed our baths! The Nineteenth Infantry Officers and wives entertained us royally at a luncheon at the hotel. The hotel was taken over by our Occupation forces. The cake was in the shape of a battleship.

Colonel Lynch's wife had just arrived a day or two before us and they saved her cake for us. Wasn't that nice? We all went sightseeing before we went to the hotel. We saw the Red Lake, Blue Lake, Green Lake, and several "grotesque" hot springs. It gave the place an eerie atmosphere as hot steam came right out of the "devil's" mouth.

We also saw the famous large stone Buddha. This Buddha does not have the same serene, passive expression as the one at Kamakura. However, it is bigger and interesting.

It rained during the afternoon and we were unable to visit more than one shop. We enjoyed seeing the Army base and a beautiful home which is one of several owned by Nakajima, the Japanese "steel king." Later, we returned to the hotel. Benny and I had the number one cottage, and what a wonderful bath we had there!

On the eleventh, we spent the day traveling on the train and playing bridge. We returned to Kyoto from Beppu. We were there about one and a half hours, enough for a walk.

On the twelfth, we arrived at Kanazawa. We took a bus to the Haka Unro Hotel, which was high in the mountains in back of the city. It was a perfectly beautiful place. The year before there was about four feet of snow on the ground. We had dinner at the hotel, and spent the night there in a lovely suite of rooms. It was the number one suite and had a reception hall as well as a dressing room and a large Japanese bath.

After dinner, the other members of our party joined us. We all sat around the large chow bench in our large living room. Girlie Fellers excused herself and took a bath in our bathroom, as she and Stan did not have a bath in their suite. A Japanese bath is different from ours. You wash from a small bucket and thoroughly rinse off the soap. Then you stop into a deep tank of hot water to soak or relax. This water is used by each person in turn. To change it would require hours of heating the fresh water to bath temperature. Girlie had not been briefed. She rinsed in the large tub. Mimie, following her, pulled the plug and then realized she shouldn't have. She tried to put it back in, but it was too late. The Japanese servants were frustrated. Needless to say, the other women of the party did not take baths in our bathroom. In an hour or so, I was told that the bath water was now hot enough. In the meantime, the rest of the party had gone to their rooms. I enjoyed that bath very much.

After a good night's rest, we went to a temple near the hotel. It was different because it was new, clean, and full of beautiful objects of art.

Benny, Mimi, Stan, and John Holtom went to Toyama to look through a big brass pile. The rest of our party and I went shopping. Benny got some beautiful things at the brass pile and we all returned to the train for a lunch and rest. Soon we were on our way.

We were on the train all that night and arrived in Nikko the next morning about nine o'clock. The splendid lotuses and cherry blossoms were all in bloom. We had a boat ride on Lake Susenchi, and then luncheon at the Nikko Kanko Hotel, after which we rode the cable car to the foot of the mountain and had a visit to the falls. It was perfectly beautiful. We returned by boat on the lake and then went by bus to visit an art museum and store.

We had a pleasant train trip to Yokohama Central Depot, where we were met by the bus and returned to Yokosuka. On the way we sang songs. We had a wonderful time except for the weather. However, when it rained, we were indoors, so it did not dampen our spirits.

May 29, 1948
Dear Captain Decker:

Here is the completed first draft, which will not go to *Reader's Digest* for several days. Meanwhile, will you kindly send me your corrections and suggestions? I'll appreciate a check of first names. I've written in fictitious ones in some instances.

Do not hesitate to suggest changes or additions. I do not want to submit the piece until you feel that it is the best thing yet written on Yokosuka.

My best regards to Mrs. Decker and to Commander Holtom and the others of the staff.

Sincerely,
Blake Clark

On June the sixth Edwina and I went shopping with Dot Casey and had luncheon with her and Pat. Bishop Breton, Father Voss and I picked Edwina up and we went to the

Sofia University where we heard Cardinal Spellman and Monsignor Sheen. The most delightful and unexpected thing happened when we were out in the garden. The cardinal presented Edwina with a bouquet of flowers and said some very nice things to her about the work she had been doing with the Japanese women.

Without Edwina's help and constant interest in the Japanese, as well as in the Americans of the Occupation, my task on the base would have been difficult. It would have been far from the success it has been acclaimed. It might be thought that we attended too many social engagements. We were fully occupied either officially or socially. We did this because we wanted to. We were happy, for we enjoyed people; but also, because we were dedicated to developing goodwill between the Army and the Navy as well as with the diplomatic corps and the foreign representatives. The many visitors from the United States were important as well.

When I arrived in April 1946 I was disturbed that the Navy in Yokosuka was not interested in the Army and had met few, if any, of the senior officers and foreign representatives. It appeared that it was a house divided against itself. The Navy considered its stay temporary and that the Occupation was an Army affair. We had a selling job to perform and Edwina was my top saleswoman!

Even in Italy we had friends, as can be seen by this magnificent letter from the Superior General of our Catholic nuns who were doing so much for us. What we did for them was far short of the great service they were doing in advancing Christianity in Japan. I feel very humble when I read the Superior General's letter.

6th July 1948

Dear Captain Decker,

Since our Sisters went to Nagano and Yokosuka, I have had frequent news of the progress of the work in the schools, and I know how much is due to your never-failing help. I know too, that if it had not been for the interest you have taken and your efforts in smoothing out the difficulties as they cropped up, their work there would never have been possible.

In all the hardships that my missionaries have gone

243

through in Japan, I can clearly see how the Providence of God has been watching over them and the greatest benefit of all has been the help they received from the good Americans who have always been ready to come to their aid whenever there was need.

I feel powerless to express my gratitude for all your goodness to my nuns, but I pray that God may bless you and your family with good health and happiness and prosper all your undertakings. Your name has been placed in the list of the benefactors of our Order as one of the most outstanding.

A new group of missionaries will soon be starting their journey for Japan. With them, I send a small gift for Mrs. Decker which I ask you to accept as a mere token of my very great gratitude for your courteous attention to our Sisters in their necessities.

Yours very sincerely,
Cristine Estrade
Superior General

In a district of Yokosuka called Taura, there was a former Japanese Officers' Club which had been used as a taxi dance hall. This building was turned into a community center by Mr. Everett Thompson, a Methodist missionary. Mrs. Thompson was a great help to her husband. In two short years they had transformed the area from a red light district and a menace to the health and morals of my men into a respectable area of uplifting influence. Chaplain Ricker and his wife had contributed to this successful activity and now that they were leaving for another station in the United States the Community Center invited us to a farewell meeting given by the committee. M. Natsuo was the chairman.

Dear Captain and Mrs. Decker:

On June 24th at 2 o'clock, we are going to have an exhibit of the many articles our Sewing Department has made. We would be so happy if you both could come and see these things. We know how busy you are and we would appreciate the mere privilege of your presence.

We are most grateful for the flags which you so

kindly gave us and we particularly wanted to show you what we have done with them. We have had six women, five of whom are widows with families, working in this department and they have accomplished a lot. They have been directed by a trained sewing teacher, Mrs. Morita. They have been very faithful and ingenious in using up the small pieces of flag cloth. These women all have families and can do only part time work. Some of them have learned to do foreign sewing with us and are now prepared to sew for their families. They come to the Community Center on Wednesdays and Thursdays, and take their work home for the remainder of the week. We have paid them by the piece and most of these six women have made an average between four and five hundred yen a week. In the very near future, we are planning to sell these articles to the people in this section who need them most.

Since the flag material is just about gone, we are looking for some other means of keeping our department going so that these and perhaps other widows can help to support their own families. Our immediate hope is to take in sewing for people who will bring their own materials. We are publicizing this plan very soon and we shall hope for sufficient patronage to keep us flourishing. We also plan to have a foreign sewing school in the form of sewing institutes during the next year. There has been an eager demand for such a service in this community.

While you are here we would like you to peep in at our Day Care Center, and our Library now serving all ages from elementary school to adults.

In our relief department we have just finished some definite projects. One of these was the giving of generous packets of relief clothes to 40 of the neediest families who come to the Welfare Department and we have asked for the names of 20 more such families. We have the ages of all in the family and in making up the packets of the various members of the family. We have recently given a month's supply of vitamins to 55 of the Welfare Department clients who need such help. Mr. Thompson was also able to get from LARA and distribute among the elementary schools in our section, enough santinin for 5000 doses. The school doctor says that almost one hundred per cent of the children need this treatment and he came with the principals of the schools to receive this medicine.

We are all looking forward to having you visit us on the 24th of this month at 2 o'clock.

Most sincerely,
Zora Thompson

The workers took charge of young girls, who were potential juvenile delinquents, and made them into Girl Scouts. Here, they were taught to be useful citizens. The workers also cared for the babies of working mothers, taught English, and set up a children's library. Between five and eight thousand people took part in one or more of these activities each month.

Mrs. Thompson mentioned Satinin. The children as well as many of the people had worms. Even the Occupation became infected. The Russians had a cure, red squill, but only the communists and fellow travelers were given this dewormer. We had to use Satinin. This was a cure, but conditions were so bad that children soon became reinfected.

Our son, Lt. (jg.) Benton W. Decker Jr., U.S.N., arrived at Haneda Airport in General Beiderlinden's plane on three weeks' leave. This made us very happy and we took him with us to the many Army parties. It was part of his education. Please bear with me as Edwina recites a full three weeks of social life. It will give the reader some idea of what it takes to make a successful Occupation!

He met General MacArthur's staff at Colonel Syd Huff's party and at the French Embassy at General Peschkoff's on Bastille Day reception, he was introduced to our friends, the generals who were making history. The next day, Benny had the pleasure of showing Ben about the base. He had last seen it as an ensign when he was a boat officer from the *New Jersey* at the time of the surrender. He couldn't believe what he saw. And then on we went to our nearest friends in the Army, the Second Battalion of the First Cavalry, Colonel McNabb in Hayama. He had a most attractive daughter and it just happened to be an excellent day for the two to go swimming from the McNabb's beach. That evening it was dinner at the Lieutenant Colonel Heles' home in honor of the new commanding officer of our Marines—Colonel and Mrs. Lasswell. The next day it was a trip to the Kawana Hotel. This was a beautiful hotel and golf club on the Izu Peninsula operated by the British.

To digress a moment, this was the club Benny had in mind for the Navy. We had no golf club and should the British withdraw from the Occupation, releasing their many hotels, Benny wanted to take over the golf course and hotel. He planned on staffing it with personnel on leave, rotating the few every thirty days with a continuing staff of Japanese. When the time came, Benny put in his request through channels. The Canadians went direct to the General and got his support while the Navy's request was slowly being processed.

Ben was getting a workout socially. It was typical of our lives in Japan. When we weren't working, we were playing. It certainly made for friendly relations with all services and allies. From Kanawa we went down the peninsula to the Imaiso Hotel. To go into this area required clearance from SCAP. It was readily given and we enjoyed going native. The Japanese were most attentive and friendly. The next day Ben went back to the Kanawa for a golf game with Chick Chen, the best golfer in Japan.

We slept on futons and ate Japanese food. It was a delightful spot. After our visit in Shimoda we returned by sea.

Ben met the Takaokas who had helped us so much in relations with the Japanese. Mrs. Takaoka went with Ben and me to Kamakura for shopping. She was invaluable. The next day we went to the American Club to a dinner party given by General Weikert. And the next evening to the Imperial as dinner guests of General and Mrs. Farman. Next we went to a dinner party at the GHQ given by General and Mrs. Maris for Captain and Mrs. Connolly.

We entertained at lunch the members of the Australian parliament. That evening we entertained at dinner the officers and members of the Masonic Lodge 120 and the head of the Masonic Fraternity in the Far East, having come over from China for the ceremony of inaugurating the lodge on the Naval base. We had received the following invitation, which we were unable to accept:

Backward, turn backward
Oh Time, in thy flight
Make me a child again
Just for the night
Of July 24, 1948 to help Mrs. Casey's
Little Boy Pat celebrate.

Ben went to the Caseys' party with Benny's chief staff
officer. Captain Bill Kirten and his wife, Dickie, Admiral Berkey was Little Lord Fauntleroy! Ben went as a little girl in a
yellow wig and pink dress, and spent the night at the
Caseys'. The next day we picked him up. He was bubbling
over with praise for the Caseys and the entire Army!
We went by train to Sendai as guests of General and Mrs.
Ryder. Commander and Mrs. Bennett, the second in charge of
our public works department, accompanied us. From Sendai
we motored to Matsushima where we spent two nights in the
hotel where the general and his staff lived. It was on the bay
where there were 248 charted islands, and many uncharted.
We cruised among the beautiful islands in the general's
boat. Two days later, we returned to Yokohama in the general's private car. And that evening we attended a Hawaiian
dinner at General and Mrs. Ferrin's followed by a party at the
British Embassy for the commander in chief of the British
Pacific Fleet, Sir Dennis Boyd. The next night our Admiral,
"Count" Berkey, gave a dinner party for Sir Dennis Boyd.
Ben had a chance to see the beautiful Fujiyama gardens
where Admiral Berkey lived. Ben took Sally McNabb, who
was our houseguest that night. And the next night Admiral
Boyd gave a beautiful buffet supper party on board his flagship, the London. August the first, Syd Huff, Colonel Larry
Bunker (Benny's boyhood friend), and Mrs. Gibbens gave a
farewell party for the general's doctor, Colonel Kendricks,
and Mrs. Kendricks. The following day we called on Mrs.
MacArthur and later Benny took Ben to call on the General.
He had asked for five minutes, instead the General generously gave them over half an hour and Ben became a booster
of the General the same as Benny. On the third, we attended
the farewell party for General and Mrs. Eichelberger at the
New Grand Hotel in Yokohama. The Eighth Army did the job
up in style. Benny had hoped that General MacArthur would

be a presidential candidate and that "Eich" would take over the Occupation. We had become fast friends of "Eich and Miss Em"—two splendid people, long to be remembered with affection and love. The next morning Admiral Berkey had us aboard his flagship, *Oakland,* and informed us that we were to get under way in company with his destroyers to watch maneuvers. They circled the USAT *Buchner* in which General and Mrs. "Eich" were leaving Japan. We had bid them farewell at the pier at 9:30 A.M. and now we were to wave them farewell as the ship sailed out of Tokyo Bay. Only Count Berkey could have thought up such a great send-off for such a great general.

Ben's leave was about up and that evening we spent our first night at home—watching a movie. The next morning Ben left Haneda airport in the *Bataan,* the General's plane. Toney Story was piloting. Ben had experienced a cross-section of life in the Occupation. Not a dull moment and everybody a friend. We thoroughly enjoyed showing Ben off to our friends and they were good to include him in their parties. Now Ben would rest on the way home while we carried on.

I went to the hospital for six days. I was worn out.

General and Mrs. Baker and General and Mrs. Casey were at our house for dinner, after which I left with them for Tokyo and spent the night with the Caseys. Early the next morning Dot Casey and I went to Karuizawa by train. We were met by our friends of the press, Mrs. Miles Vaughn, Mrs. Lindsay Parrot, and Mrs. William Costello. We rode in Mrs. Costello's jeep, had lunch with the Parrots, and I was the overnight guest of Inez Vaughn, while Dot Casey stayed with Mrs. Parrot. Five days later, Benny came up by train with the other husbands. We went to the Maida House where we joined General and Mrs. Ned Almond, General Schiller, Colonel P. D. Ginder, and the Bergers.

The Vaughns entertained us that night at dinner, and the next morning we rode to the foot of the Mount Azume, a volcano. We had fun gathering blueberries which reminded Benny of his childhood, gathering blueberries in Bristol, Vermont. Once, he came face to face with a moose, also gathering berries.

The Burton Cranes had us all for dinner. The next

morning Benny and I returned to Yokosuka. It was indeed a pleasant change and we always enjoyed being with the press. These people were an addition to our Occupation hierarchy. Seldom do the services have such excellent opportunity to meet the press socially and to become so attached to them.

Helen Keller came to Japan and was entertained by General and Mrs. Crawford Sams at a tea at the GHQ Club in Tokyo. It was inspiring to meet her. Also, we were invited aboard Admiral Oliver's flagship. The British enjoyed the Occupation and we certainly were pleased to have them visit us. This was to be Admiral Oliver's farewell. September the sixth, the wife of our friend General Paul Mueller arrived in the transport *Breckenridge*. Rear Admiral and Mrs. Womble also arrived. The Muellers had lunch with us. A few days later General and Mrs. Ryder had lunch with us. He went sailing with Benny while Ida Ryder and I shopped in Kamakura. She was well-informed on Buddhism and took me to a temple that I had never visited.

Benny takes over—

For an annual inspection report by ComNavFe, I sent Captain Cutler of Admiral Griffin's staff the following:

Memorandum:
These are the paragraphs you requested for the annual inspection report:

"The smooth operation of this Base depends not only on the morale and good will of the American personnel attached to it, but also on the morale and good will of the Japanese in the surrounding area, the city of Yokosuka.

"In the previous three years labor was improved until now it is reliable, loyal and enthusiastic. There is less stealing here than in any Continental yard. Also less loafing and no evidence of sabotage. Credit for this goes not only to our law enforcement efforts, but also to a planned campaign to better the condition of the people of Yokosuka and to acquaint them with American methods and Christian principles. We have used the former Japanese Naval buildings for the reindustrialization of Yokosuka.

"The following civic improvements are a few of

those that have been accomplished since the surrender—

a. Fifty factories have been opened in buildings of the former Base.

b. Unemployment has been reduced from 40,000 to 4,000 while the population has increased from 241,000 to 271,000.

c. A commercial harbor and facilities have been opened in Naguro Ko.

d. Two Christian hospitals have been established and eleven others have been improved from pest holes into second class hospitals (U.S. standards).

e. Four Christian Schools have been founded, two Christian Churches, and one Community Center.

f. Christianity has increased from near zero to 4,500 school children and over 660 church members. 4,000 paraded in the last annual Catholic Processional.

g. A Chamber of Commerce and two Industrial Clubs are active. A welfare committee, the PTA, and the Yokosuka Red Cross (5,000 members), and a Women's Club (30,000 members), are advancing charity and benevolence in the city. Several kindergartens, an Old Folk's Home, an Orphanage, and thirty-five playgrounds have been opened.

"These activities plus reform in police and schools, and suppression of gangsterism has made the people of Yokosuka staunch supporters of the U.S. Navy and the Occupation. They want us to remain at least fifty years in this Naval Base.

"Labor on the Base is improving. The number has been reduced from 9,000 to 5,000 with increased production. There are three unions and no labor difficulties. The former skilled laborers are returning, and many younger men are rapidly learning American methods. It is necessary, however, to supervise this labor with one American to ten to twenty Japanese. If properly supervised this Japanese labor is equivalent to U.S. labor at a cost of 10%. At present, labor is paid for by the Japanese Government, however, the day is not far distant when labor will be charged to the U.S.

"To obtain satisfactory production it is imperative

251

that the U.S. personnel on this Base be sufficient and of the higher rates for supervision of the Japanese. The average Seamen is of little value while the average Chief Petty Officer obtains excellent results. Every effort should be made to keep the allowance filled with men of maturity and ability as leaders and administrators as well as artisans.

"A request for an increase in allowance of officers and men has been forwarded. This request to increase the officers from 56 to 78 and the men from 601 to 690 is necessary to carry on the increase in work load of the Base."

B. W. Decker

From one of our Navy nurses:

Dear Captain Decker,
    I hardly know how to begin but I do want you to know that I miss you all very much. Since coming to the States I find that Yokosuka was a wonderful place only because we were so kindly and courteously and efficiently taken care of. It does me good to know that I once belonged to such an organization.
    My trip home was wonderful. I had no trouble getting through customs. Duty here is nice—there is much to do—many patients—little help.
    Went to a cocktail party at the Bledsoes'—spent most of the time talking to them about Japan. They asked about you and Mrs. Decker. They would like to come back.
    May I take this opportunity to thank you for all your kindness and I hope that I will again have the pleasure of being under your command. Allow me to say that you are one of my "unforgettables."
    Best wishes for the New York.

Most sincerely yours,
Virginia E. D'Agastino

I received the following letter from my first "boss" in Japan, Vice Admiral Griffin. It was certainly appreciated by me for his good wishes. Bob was a Navy junior—that is, a son of a Navy officer. And I think his maternal grandfather was a famous Naval officer. He addressed this letter to B. C. Decker, which was the name of my father.

16 December 1948

Captain Benton C. Decker, USN (Sic)
U. S. Fleet Activities
Yokosuka, Japan
c/o Fleet P/O, San Francisco
Dear Benny:

Gozo's head of me arrived in perfect condition a few days ago. Many thanks for your part in having it done, and seeing that it was pressed on to completion and shipped.

I think it is quite good, and it received family approval which is an even severer test. I am enclosing a letter to Gozo thanking him, and will appreciate it if you will have it given to him.

How is Yokosuka? I have missed Japan in many ways, chiefly for the friends left there and for the ease of living. Washington I enjoy, and it is fine being with my family again, but the expense of living here is all that it has been reported. To find a place to live we had to buy a house. We spent most of the summer house hunting, and much of the time since getting settled, so that only lately have we been able to live normally and enjoy ourselves.

I was sorry that the recent Selection Board did not pick you up. You have done a fine job in Yokosuka and I hoped that they might do so, though I realize what tremendous odds there were against it.

With best regards to you and Edwina, and other friends in Yokosuka and Tokyo.

Sincerely,
Robert Griffin (Vice Admiral)
P. S. Merry Christmas, if in time!

My new boss was Vice Admiral Russell Berkey, an outstanding Naval officer not only in the war but also in administering the Naval forces of the Far East. I couldn't have had a better superior. We saw eye to eye and he was of great help. The first thing he did was to send me a copy of my fitness report made out by him. It was excellent and I presumed he had in mind that I might again be considered for selection to rear admiral in November. It was the first report that had been shown me by my superior in Tokyo. "Count" Berkey was always considerate of his juniors.

He was also considerate of the taxpayers. When he called me on the phone, "Benny, can you use 3000 barrels of contaminated diesel?" I blessed Berkey and praised the Lord for an admiral who was willing to stick his neck out to save the taxpayer thousands of dollars! It was just what I needed to keep my housing program rolling.

The diesel oil was in a tanker and had had some gasoline mixed in it. It would be either dumped at sea or given to the Japanese. It was not dangerous for use in trucks. My civil engineer, Commander McHenry, was tops. He used it to compensate the Japanese contractors for building additional dependent quarters using salvaged Quonset huts from Guam. The contractors would rather have diesel for their trucks than money. Of course we took steps to prevent hoarding or black-marketing. The contractors had to use all the diesel in their own trucks. We finally received a complaint from the Army. They told us that we should have given it to the Japanese. To prevent a reoccurrence a new rule was promulgated, but we never again expected to receive such a windfall. Those houses cost us nothing and Uncle Samuel can thank Count Berkey for the rents received regularly each month from grateful dependents for the last thirty years!

September 20, 1948

Dear Captain Decker:

The many kindnesses and courtesies extended to our medical group were appreciated by all. There is no doubt you have one of the smartest Navy institutions anywhere due to your dynamic leadership. You command respect and loyalty from all those under your command and all spoke in most adulating terms about you. While visiting General MacArthur he singled you out as one who is doing as much for the rehabilitation of the Japanese as anyone. I know that should please you and it also pleased me.

The dinner at your home I shall long remember.

Do give my best to all those under your command who were so good to us. My best to you and my especial regards to Mrs. Decker. If I ever can be of service to you it would please me.

Most sincerely,
S. W. Swanson
Rear Admiral, MC, U.S.N.

14 October 1948

Dear Captain Decker:

Our visit to Yokosuka was one of the highlights of the trip. It was a great revelation to all of us and more particularly to me as I was able to make the contrast between 1945 and 1948. You are doing a magnificent job. I wish I could have had more time to visit with you, to see more in detail, and to review the past and the present. Some day I hope you and I can sit down and do just that sort of thing.

You showed us every kindness, courtesy and attention. The hospitality extended us by Mrs. Decker and you could not be surpassed. Even yet I cannot get over my disgust that I left your party so early of a Saturday evening. Had I realized it was so early I would have asked the Betheas to excuse me from returning with them to Tokyo and would have sought other transportation. Your party was too lovely to leave at that time of evening and the company too convivial. Your house has a beautiful setting, and I thought the garden before dinner was a most enchanting spot. Of course you decorated it well with beautiful girls.

I can still see your immaculate hennery with those Petaluma chickens.

On the flight into Alaska I read an interesting article about you in *Readers Digest*. I am glad I read it after I had seen your handiwork. It certainly was a delightful pleasure to meet Mrs. Decker and have been meaning to write her a penned note in appreciation for the beautiful

dinner that you both gave that evening.
With best wishes to Mrs. Decker and you, I am
Very sincerely,
J. T. BOONE
Rear Admiral (MC), U.S. Navy
Executive Secretary

27 September 1948

Rear Admiral R. P. McConnell, U.S.N.
Commander Fleet Air Wing ONE,
c/o Fleet Post Office,
San Francisco, California
Dear Bob:

I was very pleased to receive your letter of 21 October in which you commend the performance of duty of Captain Benny Decker. I consider this a very proper representation on your part, for those of us who are going to serve on the forthcoming selection board need all of the good counsel that they can get to assist them in the performance of their duties. Incidentally, I wholeheartedly share of your appraisal of Decker because I have first-hand knowledge of the highly efficient manner in which he has performed his duties over a long period of years.

With warm good wishes to you and Mrs. McConnell.

Ever faithfully,
D. C. RAMSEY
Admiral, U.S. Navy

On October thirteenth, General N. F. Twining, U.S.A.D., Alaskan Command; Vice Admiral John L. McCrea, Deputy CinCPac; and Vice Admiral Russell Berkey, CinCFe held a conference and visited Yokosuka. After the usual briefing and a tour of the base, we entertained them with their staffs and our senior officers at dinner in our house. The maple trees in our garden were ablaze with color, making our home beautiful. It was always a pleasure to entertain such people as John McCrea and Count Berkey. These were close friends of ours.

29 October 1948

My dear Captain Decker:

As you no doubt well know, the paper work has a somewhat nasty habit of piling up during one's absence—which fact accounts in no small part to the lateness of this expression of my appreciation for the wonderful evening you showed us during the recent CINCAL-CINCPAC-CINCFE Conference.

To you, for a most interesting visit to your base and for the many interesting etchings which you so graciously showed us, and to Mrs. Decker for the lovely cocktails and dinner, please allow me to say a very sincere "Thank You." To say that we were all of us intrigued by the evening in question is putting it mildly. Frankly, between Slim Beecher and the lovely Japanese serving girls, and the beautiful furnishings of your drawing room, my head was pretty much in a whirl. I rode home to Tokyo with General Twining and he was most profuse in his expressions of his pleasure of the evening.

Incidentally, you might be interested in hearing that I had dinner last night with Admiral Montgomery, and he spent about five solid minutes describing to all the dinner guests in very glowing terms, the excellence of the job you were doing in Yokosuka. Apparently he was quite impressed.

Yours very sincerely,
N. A. LIDSTONE
(Comdr. USN)

CincPac Joint Staff
c/o F.P.O., San Francisco
2 November 1948

Dear Captain & Mrs. Decker,

I've been home long enough now to get over my cold picked up on our recent excursion to the orient, so I can finally pull myself together enough to try to tell you how very sincerely I appreciate the cordial hospitality you showed to us during our visit to Yokosuka. The trip to your base highlighted my entire visit to Ja-

257

pan. It started with that most interesting briefing in the Captain's office that gave us such a clear, and enthusiastic picture of what we were soon to see. The trip through the yard and installations was illuminating, instructive, and again interesting. Besides the official angle, I'm still rather surprised at myself to find I have to come all the way to Japan to find out how mushrooms are grown. I was most impressed by seeing the facilities that are now available to us at Yokosuka and I can well appreciate the effort that must have been applied to develop the station to its present fine standard.

From a personal stand point I was honored and delighted to have the opportunity of seeing your lovely home and enjoying your most delightful cocktail party and dinner. I enjoyed so much sitting around on the floor after dinner and singing the good old familiar songs—you know Slim Beecher and I have adjacent desks in the office but we don't get much out of him in the way of music during the day. I also enjoyed so much the opportunity of getting together with an old Marine Corps classmate of mine—Red Lasswell—whom I haven't seen for a long time to really talk to. As an additional note, the Captain's use of religion as a means of creating a better understanding of our concept of democracy resulted in a most interesting debate between Jimmy Carter, Slim Beecher and myself *all* the way from Yokosuka to Tokyo after leaving your home—the results of that debate were of course a draw between all three of us.

Thank you once again for your grand hospitality, I only hope I may have the pleasure of returning it in part should you pass through Pearl while I am here.

With best wishes,
Col. Frank Schwable

Christianity is the foundation of democracy. Without it government by the people cannot exist. People must be equal and the voice of the majority must rule. For the Japanese, to shift from a government arbitrarily ruled by a military minority to a democracy ruled by the majority of the people in a few short years, the military and the people had to be educated in Christian principles.

To accomplish this we encouraged Christian missionaries to assist us and using freedom of religion we established Christian schools and hospitals. It was the "soft sell" approach. There was no competition or friction between sects. Nor was there opposition from Shintoism or Buddhism, as these two do not "oppose." Only from Communism, an atheistic political force, did we receive conflict.

The Japanese hated the communists. Anything we did to stop them met with their approval. Japanese lived closer to the problem than the people of the United States. The communists attempted to take over our labor union, but we were alert. We also stopped them on the revision of the school textbooks. We allowed the schools to sing the "Kimigayo" instead of the "Internationale."

My support for Christian leadership in the town was the most effective of all detriments to the atheistic communists. The Catholic parade each spring was a solid blow. The commies came from Tokyo with the announced purpose of causing trouble by parading with all of the frills of blocking traffic, picketing the base, etc. They marched one hundred yards and were stopped. My M.P.s were there in force and the parade without a permit became a disorderly crowd of squatting Japanese. Some, later, complained that they were tortured. The M.P.s had made them squat! They must have been non-Japanese, for a Japanese is most comfortable squatting. This was a confession of imported agitators. Most were put on the next train going north. But we jailed the leaders, including a high-level commie from Tokyo.

The Russian Embassy sent a number of civilians to contact Yokosuka citizens. They were so obviously strangers by their dress and their stolid expressions that there was no difficulty recognizing them. Finally they gave Yokosuka up as a bad job.

I laughingly gave the commies credit for my continued tour in Yokosuka. Normally I should have remained but eighteen months. My predecessors as well as those who followed me all served for less than that. I stayed fifty-one months. Each year they would announce that I was being detached, hoping to get the credit for forcing the Navy to re-

259

move me. Each year I was kept over, I would laughingly say Washington had to leave me or be branded for conceding to the commies. Finally, the last year they said nothing, and I was detached in spite of heavy pressure for my continuing from many important people. I claimed that it was because the commies had kept silent!

Dear Captain Decker,

I have received your very kind letter and it has touched me deeply to see how much you have appreciated the little we did to show you our gratitude.

I really think it is one of our greatest duties to be grateful to you and it is indeed most consoling to us to pray for whom we look upon as a father given us by God to help and protect us. I do not think it is proud to say that you have no more grateful admirers in Yokosuka than the Sisters.

The better I know you, dear Captain, the more I respect and appreciate you, for God tells me that He has put in your heart some of the most beautiful virtues that adorned the Heart of Jesus.

May our Lord enrich you ever more and more with the treasures of His Bounty, and may the people confided to your care know to be ever thankful to you.

Thanking you once more and with kind regards to Mrs. Decker and Lt. Decker,

I am,
Yours ever gratefully in
the Sacred Heart of Jesus
Mother Ernestine Ramallo

Navy Day was a beautiful day with all the ships and clubs open to the public. Admiral Berkey was the honored guest of the Base. At 1315 we held the usual ceremony at Perry memorial monument, and Admiral Berkey placed a wreath at the monument. We then returned to the base where the admiral dedicated our new athletic field. It was named "Berkey Field." I would have liked to have named the entire base after him, he was so well liked. But that was beyond my power. We then witnessed a football game between the Navy and the 138th AAA Battalion. At 1730 we had a good display of fireworks, then KT's at the Officers' Club followed by a dinner dance.

A few days later Bill and Helen Costello gave a cocktail party after which we attended the Correspondents' Club (better known as Number One Shinbun Alley) third anniversary party. I gave a short talk and Edwina cut the cake.

Thanksgiving had arrived with a reception by our Consul General U. Alexis Johnson and his wife in the American Consulate in Yokohama. Dinner was in our home where we were fortunate in having my former shipmate Captain Frank Monroe and a Catholic priest as guests.

Dear Benny,

Florence and I were sorry not to see your name in the recent flag list. Certainly your record and your reputation are such as to justify its being there. However, I know you are able to take the disappointment philosophically and that you will probably live longer thereby.

Please remember me to the Wombles, Kirtins, and any of our other old friends who are still about.

Sincerely yours,
Albert M. Bledsoe
Rear Admiral, U.S. Navy

Edwina tells about Christmas—

Our second son, Ensign Bert Decker, arrived on the fourteenth of November to be with us until after Christmas. We kept him as busy as we had his older brother.

Our efficient supply department had furnished trees and ornaments for Christmas throughout the base and at the main gate our beautiful manger scene made by Gozo Kawamura was attracting many admirers. The life-size figures were realistic and the best I have ever seen. The Japanese placed flowers at the crib. It carried a message to the townfolk.

Over the Administration Building was the lighted star and all the homes, clubs, and ships were dressed in the spirit of friendship and brotherly love. This was to be a happy Christmas for us. We had our son, Bert, with us, as well as so many friends.

Christmas morning we had our Marine orderly, Hicks,

261

and our chauffeur, Galinda, with the servants join us in the front hall for Tom and Jerries. We had bought a large Steinway grand piano that took up space in the living room, so we had to have our beautiful Christmas tree in the large front hall, where we normally set up the bar. In 1946, at our first Christmas, the female servants had tried our Tom and Jerries, and giggled for the rest of the day. Since then, they always refused them, with a smile. But the males thought them the best of the ritual and were more than happy to drink a toast to all. Mr. and Mrs. Takaoka were there to help as we passed our gifts for the servants and for each member of the family. Most of the children attended and were cute beyond description.

That afternoon the Tokyo Symphony gave a children's concert in our EM Club. It was the mayor's party, and we sat with him. When we entered the theater the schoolchildren applauded and gave me a large bouquet of flowers, following the Captain Decker March by Itsuro Hattori. The director joined us. After a splendid concert, Benny went back stage to thank and congratulate the musicians. On his return the children applauded him and he waved back. That brought down the house!

The Tokyo Women's Choir assisted by the Institute of Sacred Music under the directorship of Professor E. Kioka, a well-known Japanese organist, presented the *Messiah* by G. F. Handel on Sunday before Christmas in our chapel. In the evening the Toho Symphony Orchestra presented a program of classical pieces in the EM Club.

Hidemaro Konoyi, conducting, opened with "Captain Decker March" by Itsuro Hattori. These musical gifts were sponsored by the Yokosuka music association, the Yokosuka chamber of commerce, and the Yokosuka industrial club. Unfortunately we could not attend as we had accepted an invitation to the thirtieth wedding anniversary of General and Mrs. Tansey. It was a dinner party in their Tokyo house. "Pat" was an old friend of Benny's. He had won his admiration by his conscientious and brilliant protection of the American taxpayer from a ripoff by our Allies after V.E. Day. We have always admired him and also his cooperation during the Occupation. Benny had heard a rumor that the Japanese were selling the Navy's E.M. Club and Officers'

Club. A friendly Japanese had called upon Benny and casually hinted that this might occur, and after he had left the office Benny carefully went over the conversation and deduced that that was the message his friend was trying to get across. He called "Pat" Casey on the telephone and "Pat" told him he would call back after a hurried investigation. Sure enough, the Japanese were closing the deal without informing us. They excused it by claiming the clubs were the personal property of the Japanese men and officers and that it wasn't of importance to us, for the property would not be transferred until after the peace treaty, when we would be gone! "Pat" agreed that this was most irregular and he had stopped it immediately.

When something of this sort was being done, it was good that he knew the tops and could get such prompt action. No paper work—no fuss.

I was lucky in obtaining a copy of Captain Butler's talk to his Japanese workers in the hospital. He had relieved Captain Owsley as the senior medical officer. We were fortunate in having two such outstanding doctors. I quote in full Captain Butler's message at Christmastime.

Captain Butler gave a Christmas talk that exemplified that spirit of the base.

Christmas Talk

To Japanese Employees   23 December 1948
Dispensary

Prompted by the fact that we have just about reached the Christmas holidays and the New Year. I have requested all of you workers of the dispensary to attend a very short meeting this afternoon. It is my desire to express my deepest appreciation for the fine work and all the effort the Japanese employees of this dispensary have put forth during the past year. This dispensary today shows the results of those efforts. It is clean and neat and orderly and it has aroused the most favorable comments always from all our important visitors. These comments to this effect which I hear so frequently please me very much and I want to pass them on to you who have silently gone about your tasks and have really done the work of making the dispensary so fine and outstanding and to you who really deserve the praise. I might mention the names of a few of the people who have made some of these comments and tell you of some of their remarks:

Captain Decker has time after time told me how clean and neat the dispensary is. I note that he is proud to show the dispensary to important visitors and brings them here whenever he can. He has remarked especially about the fine appearance of the Japanese workers and the Japanese nurses.

Mrs. Decker has joined him in such words of praise. I note that she likes to come to the dispensary to the various shows and events we put on during the year as do all the other ladies of the Base.

Admiral Swanson, the Surgeon General of the Navy visiting here from Washington has said that this is an outstanding dispensary in many respects and as clean and neat as any we have in the States.

Admiral Joel T. Boone, the General Inspector of the Medical Department of the Navy who also visited from Washington and who has been physician to two of our Presidents was lavish in his praise.

Vice Admiral Berkey, the Commander of Naval Forces in the Far East from Tokyo is a frequent visitor to our dispensary and he never goes away without some words of praise of the dispensary which directly reflect credit on the Japanese workers. The last time he was here he specially looked over the uniforms and said something which indicated to me that he thought we had a superior group of Japanese working in the dispensary.

I could name a lot of others and repeat the word of praise I have heard them give. The thing I like most of all is the fact that the patients always have a good word for the dispensary which is sometimes not true in Medical facilities. They notice particularly the fine and prompt way the "chow" is handled, the cleanliness of the galley and dishes etc.

They also appreciate the kind and hard working efforts put forth by the Japanese nurses and our doctors praise the work of the Japanese people who work in the laboratories, the Xray, the operating rooms, out-patient department and wards and elsewhere.

I am pleased to say that I cannot recall a single incident of a breach of discipline or a failure of any of our Japanese attendants to cheerfully carry out instructions or directions given them to the best of their ability since I came to this dispensary.

I cannot fail to mention the fine and outstanding work done by the Japanese in our sanitation department, for their interest in their work, for the intelligence and spirit they have shown in attending their lectures and for the impressions they have made on the sanitary officials of the town of Yokosuka.

It will never be known how much suffering and disease they have helped prevent in their mosquito control, rat control work with DDT and many other jobs they have done in sanitation.

Now as you notice the Christmas decoration going up in the hospital and about the Base—and as you get into the spirit of giving "Presents" which is a sort of contagious spirit. I just want to review again for you what Christmas really means and why we celebrate.

Christmas as you know is the Birthday of Christ, who was born 1948 years ago and whose teachings on Earth were those of peace on earth and good will among men. He taught people to love their neighbors, to be forgiving of wrong doers, to live upright and decent lives and spend their lives doing their best and in using their energies for the good of their fellows.

He taught the Christian principles against greed and malice and stood for the principles on which founded the American concepts of liberty and free speech and brotherly love, and from his teachings stems the "Golden Rule" which is probably one of the best mottos and bases for a Happy Life ever developed—and one which we can all follow regardless of religion or any other differences we may have of any other nature.

The "Golden Rule" is "Do unto others as you would have it that they would do unto you." When we think of Christmas we think of it in the above terms, the Christmas trees and festivity indicate that it is a joyous time and for presents which are exchanged are symbolic expressions of passing on good will toward men.

I want to wish you all a Merry Joyful Christmas and Happy New Year and I accept the gift you put together, and given to me as an expression of your good will and I treasure your good will more than words can say. Thank you very much and a Merry Christmas.

                                                           J. B. BUTLER

Edwina returns the typewriter to me.

Captain Butler was an outstanding doctor and a loyal supporter of my policies. He did an amazingly splendid job of inspiring his subordinates. All of the forgoing is true and to him I give my highest praise. Had I been on his selection board I would have fought tooth and nail to recognize this officer's value to the Navy and our country. Shortly after this the fighting in Korea started and soon the hospital was flooded with thousands of casualties. We shall be ever grateful to Captain Butler, and his predecessor, Captain (the late Admiral) Owsley, and their assistants! And they didn't make Captain Butler an admiral!!!

                              December 30, 1948
                              No. 5, Kagoo-Choo
                              Yokosuka City

Dear Captain Decker:

We wish you a Merry Christmas and Happy New year. Today we have come to express our gratitude for the kindnesses you have done to us.

You have been doing a great deal towards the democratization of our city since you arrived at your post in 1946. It is entirely due to your sympathy for us citizens that our city, which was once being swayed by high-handed militarists and which was once the symbol of the feudalistic Japan, has been reconstructed as a peaceful city of the citizens, by the citizens and for the citizens.

You have proved yourself to have a profound understanding of education and public health by granting disused former military buildings to the citizens and helping them construct various schoolhouses, by dusting D.D.T., and by holding a lecture meeting on the prevention of venereal diseases.

Dear Commander, you are loved and highly respected by all the people of Yokosuka. We believe that there is no one in this city but is deeply grateful for your warm sympathy for the citizens who are suffering from economic destitution, especially from the shortage of food stuffs.

At the beginning of this month you were so kind as to make us a present of "field ration". Each one of us received a water-proof box which contained nutritious food, sweet chocolate, etc. How glad we all were to receive this delicious present of yours! We shall never forget your kindness. In this letter we express our heartfelt thanks for your presents.

At the end of this letter please allow us to tell you about ourselves. We are students of the Kanagawa Prefectural Yokosuka Industrial Upper Secondary School.

Our school was founded eight years ago for the purpose of training good engineers. There are three departments in our school—the Department of Electrical Engineering, the Department of Mechanical Engineering, and the shipbuilding Department of Mechanical Engineering, and the shipbuilding Department. We are now studying very hard, under the sincere guidance of our teachers so that we may become competent engineers in the future.

As the cold winter has come round again and it is getting colder, please take good care of yourself.

Sincerely yours,
Jun Tamura
Dept. of Shipbuilding Engineering
Kanagawa Prefectural Yokosuka
Industrial Upper Secondary School

December 30th, 1948
No. 5, Kugoo-Choo
Yokosuka City

Dear Captain Decker:

We wish you a merry Christmas and Happy New Year.

We thank you very much for your present that you sent to us students at the beginning of December as a Thanks-Giving Day's present.

There has been little warmth felt in our heart since the termination of the war, except for the warmth which is given to our heart by the American Forces.

When the Pacific War ended in the defeat of Japan, we Japanese did not expect that the victors would be so kind and generous to the vanquished. But when the American Forces arrived, we were surprised to find that they were very kind and generous to their former enemy. I think it is no wonder that the Americans are loved and respected in every part of the world.

Now we are devoting ourselves to studying democratic subjects. I beg you will please help us to reconstruct our country as a peaceful and democratic nation.

We thank you for your present from the bottom of our heart.

As it is getting colder day by day, please take care of yourself.

Sincerely yours,
Katsuya Kumazawa
Dept. of Electrical Engineering

On three occasions the base was able to assist localities that had suffered from disasters. A fire in Atami left many homeless, while an earthquake in Fukuoka destroyed many textile mills. A typhoon passing over the Tokyo area dumped inches of rain, flooding the rivers and endangering many lives. In each case the Japanese Red Cross chapter of Yokosuka distributed supplies which we furnished and transported. The leftovers from World War II were not only our rations and some used rubber liferafts but also a great supply of Japanese navy stores. These included blankets, tents, mess gear, cooking utensils, and many inflatable rubber liferafts, of no value to us. We had a building for the storage of such supplies that could be used in disasters. These three emergencies depleted our storehouse, which was then used for other purposes.

In the case of the Fukuoka earthquake we advised the textile industry that we had empty buildings that could be used as textile mills and that we encouraged them to move to our city. At first this was rejected as it would take too long a time to train people to operate their machines. Later, they reconsidered our offer and we gained a number of textile mills, a new industry.

Chapter XI

PROMOTION

On the third of January 1949, Mrs. Mabuchi died. She was the founder of the Shinsei Women's Club, and because of her respected position in the city, as well as her age, she was able to start the club on a grand scale, after which she turned the club over to another one of the founders, which was most unusual and democratic for Japan. We attended her Buddhist funeral on the eighth. As was customary, she was cremated. The funeral was held in the garden draped in black and white bunting. At noon the reading of messages of condolences and citations was begun. There were representatives of all the groups and societies to which she belonged. Each person went forward in turn, and bowed, lighted a stick of incense and placed it in a holder on the altar. I went forward and did the same, bowing in memory of a great woman. I appreciated her help in inspiring women and making Yokosuka a better city. After half an hour we left. From 1:00 P.M. until 3:00 P.M. the ceremonies were opened to friends. She was well admired by all. She and her husband had founded the Deaf and Dumb School years before, helping those who needed it most.

When I returned to Japan years later, I visited her grave with her family and placed some flowers on it, in remembrance of many good deeds she had performed. Land in Japan is limited, so graveyards consist of small tracts covered by many small stones crowded together, each marking the ashes. It is more efficient than our system, and in years to come, when our space is at a premium, this might well become the American way.

269

Dear Captain and Mrs. Decker:

The death of Mrs. Mabuchi, whom we love and respect, has been a great misfortune to us all. We could not believe it when we were told of her death and often thought, on going to school, that we would see her smiling face. However, the funeral on the 8th made us realize that she had indeed passed away and we would see her no more.

Mrs. Mabuchi's funeral was a big affair as if to endorse the virtue of the deceased. Best of all, Captain and Mrs. Decker themselves came to pay homage to the remains of Mrs. Mabuchi and this has given us all so much joy that we have no words with which to thank them. That they should do so much for the people of the defeated nation and pay their respects to Mrs. Mabuchi besides having helped her with her work for the education of deaf and mute persons, fills us with deep gratitude.

I have not been in the deaf school long since the loss of hearing but I have often heard of the kind and numerous assistances and help extended to this school by Captain and Mrs. Decker. Since my loss of hearing, I have realized, for the first time, that a dark world where people are devoid of any pleasures through their sense of hearing. I felt that my loss of hearing was God's will to show me this other world and I have decided to dedicate myself, for the rest of my life, to helping the people in this world of the deaf and the mute. I, therefore, enrolled in the first grade, although I was much older than the rest of the pupils in order to become a friend of the deaf people. I was very, very glad to learn that the American people are understanding and kind to these unfortunate people and have a great concern for their education.

I have taken the pen because of the great surge of gratitude to the Captain and Mrs. Decker.

Sincerely yours,
Mitsuko Takamitsu
(Mabuchi School)

General Headquarters
Supreme Commander for the Allied Powers
International Prosecution Section
215 Imperial Hotel, Tokyo, Japan
3 February 1949

Captain B. W. Decker, USN
Commander Fleet Activities
Yokosuka, Japan
Dear Captain Decker:

Ater the review yesterday, I tried to see you but missed you. I am hoping to come to your office before leaving next week upon completion of duty here. I want to tell you in writing, however, of my deep appreciation of your many courtesies to me and to Mrs. Robinson. We shall always remember with pleasure and pride our visits to your command. No person appreciates more fully than I do the magnitude of your achievements at Yokosuka for the Navy and for the United States. In September 1945, when I first came there, the situation was such that a great opportunity was presented for the judgement and statesmanship and vision and patriotism which you later brought there. I have observed the transformation which you have achieved. My interest and duty assignments in international law and international relations make me particularly grateful to you for providing such an inspiring precedent and example in international statesmanship and in practical service to the United States, to Japan and to all people who value peace and good will in world affairs. Only time and future events will show the full value of your services.

It has been a genuine personal pleasure to have known you and Mrs. Decker here. My wife and I are looking forward to seeing you many times in the future.

With sincere regards and every good wish from both of us to both of you. I am

Very respectfully yours,
James Robinson
Capt. USNR
Director Navy Division (JAG)
U.S. War Crimes Officer

Mr. Royall's visit to Yokosuka was of great importance. It

271

was an excellent example of unification of the services, demonstrating the harmony that exists between the Navy and the Army, with the Army in overall command. Mr. Royall sent for me several days later. He was interested in the costs of overhauling the motor transport of the Army.

We had turned over to the Army our Oppama Air Field in exchange for the air field at Atsugi, as we had no use for Oppama as an air field. The approaches and takeoffs were steep and dangerous. The Army acquired motor transport overhaul shops with an adjacent parking area. From the Pacific Area thousands of trucks and jeeps were arriving to be completely renovated.

We were doing the Navy's motor repairs for less. He wanted the Navy to take over the Army's factory, as it was in the Navy zone. I said I was willing to do so, but explained that the difference in costs was mainly in overhead. We had only two chief petty officers while the Army was doing a much bigger job and had acquired many civilians at great cost from the United States. I would cut the overhead down drastically. Also, while in Yokosuka, he had seen what we did with salvaged Quonset huts. Using a Quonset hut and some wood structures we had made many new homes for dependents at little cost. Mr. Royall had asked the Army to do the same in Okinawa. They asked my opinion, which I frankly gave them. In a typhoon area it would be necessary to anchor the huts with heavy wire in a manner unattractive and, maybe, unsatisfactory. My snap judgment was that concrete houses would stand up better and in the long run be less costly. The colonels were greatly relieved by my answers, and I certainly won friends. I was told that the secretary had sent a lengthy radio to Washington commending me for all that I had done.

The *General Mann*, skippered by Captain Nelson, was soon to sail for the states, taking many of my officers with him. One was Tim Hahne. I had assigned him as officer in charge of the EM Club. Tim had a great sense of humor and whenever he came into my office I always pushed the papers aside and listened.

One day Tim came in with a package, "Captain, I want to give you a present." After I unwrapped it, I found it was a small wooden shovel, the size of an entrenching tool, "Thanks Tim. But what is this for?"

"Captain! By the time I finish telling you my sad tale of woe you will need that to shovel your way out of this office!"

So now Tim was leaving for another station, and I asked Captain Nelson to do me a favor. I reached for the shovel which I kept handy near my desk as a hint to others who were spilling too good a story for me to believe. "Captain, I hate to give up this useful tool, but I know it will be needed by Lieutenant Hahne at his next station. When you are at sea, too far for Tim to swim back, please present this to him with sincerest best wishes for success in his next assignment."

Captain Nelson did a splendid job. He sent for Tim, who was alarmed that the captain was sending for him. The captain presented him with the beribboned shovel. Tim was speechless! He still has the shovel.

I received word in January that I would be retired in June and was informed that I could retire early if I wished. Not me. I needed every day to complete my task, and Admiral Berkey told me that it would be a long turnover.

My senior medical officer, Admiral Owsley, wrote a year later to me, after I had left Japan July 1950:

I need not tell you that Yokosuka was and will always be the outstanding spot that I shall remember of my Navy career. Both Chris and I wished so many times that we could have stayed on out there as long as possible. I am sure that you have heard this same thing over and over again and from many others.

Truthfully though I can't visualize Yokosuka and Japan with you not out there. I just seem to associate the place with you and it would be difficult to adjust to anyone else.

So well do I remember the day I received dispatch orders to Yokosuka. As you may remember I had had command of the big fleet hospital down in Samar and when it folded up I fully expected to return to the States. Shortly before I left I had shoved Margaret Ann Orr, Janie Turner and several other girls off for Japan— never realizing I'd soon be following—I arrived at Atsugi late in the afternoon and at Yokosuka in time for dinner with Tony, Shorty, Tibby and Sam Wilhite. I didn't know you were there until that evening.

I must confess that I was a little confused as to just what we were all doing in Yokosuka and how long we would stay. It didn't take me very long however to realize and understand what you had in mind and what our mission eventually would be. I know now that you had a clear vision, that you had definite fixed ideas of what you wanted and intended to do. It turned out that you were so right, but in the early days there were those who were skeptical—perhaps I was one, but not for long. Yokosuka was right down my alley. It was a big challenge. It took a lot of hard work, but it gave you something to get your teeth into. It was pioneering in luxury with willing hands to carry out your every wish. To me it was lots of fun. You gave me the green light—encouragement and a pat on the back. I must confess that you nudged me now and then, but all of us didn't have your boundless energy. However, I think you and I had a lot in common—we both like to get things done, to see things accomplished.

I was proud of the dispensary as I left it—and wish I could see all the improvements Butler made. He was a good choice for he had been in the planning section of Bu Med for many years and has lots of good ideas, I'm sure he put the finishing touches on where we had done the spade work.

I was pleased recently to learn that the dispensary had now been designated a Naval Hospital with a C.O. exec. and large staff. Sorry I can't go back myself.

I have often thought of the many Japanese friends out there—of the other hospitals that we worked on to clean up. Dozens of people I've seen and have talked to who retired since I left, have all told me of the progress and improvements that were made. Some have told me I'd hardly recognize the place. But then, those who came as I left would hardly have recognized it from the shape it was in when we first saw it.

I know how much you must miss it out there. I don't know of anyone else who seemed to enjoy it more than you did. Certainly except for MacArthur there was no one more well known out there—among the Americans and the Japanese as well.

Everyone feels that you did a swell job—and you did. For my part it was a privilege to have served with you. I won't forget the backing and friendship you gave me. I can truthfully say that without exception it was the most pleasant duty I have ever had. Chris clouds up and nearly cries every time anyone mentions Yokosuka. But I guess for all of us it will be a most pleasant memory.

Chris joins me in very best to you and Edwina.

Sincerely,
John Q. Owsley

John Q was a great officer, doctor, and friend. He deserved his promotion. The Navy was fortunate to have him among its leaders.

Commander in Chief Pacific
and
United States Pacific Fleet

February 14, 1949

Dear Benny:

We have finally returned to Pearl with a score of no casualties or misadventures but with the usual pile of work stacked up that I would expect after two weeks' absence. I do want you and Mrs. Decker to know how deeply grateful I am, and this includes every member of my staff, for the royal hospitality you extended to us while we were in the Yokosuka area. It was really one of the highlights of our whole trip and we will always remember it with deep appreciation.

Everyone that I talked to in the Tokyo area who has any knowledge of your activity and its objectives eulogized you and your leadership to the skies. I share wholeheartedly in this appraisal of your outstanding leadership and I will continue to wish for your welfare and happiness and that of your family throughout all of the years to come.

Be assured of my deep and lasting admiration and regard.

Ever faithfully,
D. C. Ramsey
Admiral, U.S. Navy

From the American Japanese weekly of February 27, 1949:

Capt. Decker, The Father of New Born Yokosuka
Yokosuka City which had been the symbol of Japanese Militarism is now having recovered peace regenerated as one of the most democratic cities in Japan. The wall 8-feet-high, which has been screening the naval port from the people's eyes is now removed and the place has changed to a park from where the Pacific Ocean can be seen at a glance. Citizens are walking along the cleanly paved streets with delight. We can see ambition, welfare, and resolution on their faces. We cannot speak about Yokosuka without remembering Capt. Decker who has made Yokosuka the most peaceful, democratic city and citizens, the happiest citizens in Japan. They unanimously say "Yokosuka will revive as a peaceful city before long, for Capt. Decker is taking much interest in this city, you know. We are very thankful to him."

General Eichelberger, the former Commander of the 8th Army praised him in high terms, writing in his letter to one of his Japanese friends, "I wish such a good man as Capt. Decker would stay long in Japan."

However, Capt. Decker is not just a brave soldier. He has the humor to name his yacht "Suteki-ne". On holidays he goes as often as possible to Tokyo Bay or Izu Peninsula to enjoy hunting and fishing.

Capt. B. W. Decker came to Japan as the commander of Yokosuka Fleet Activities in June 1946. It was not the first time he came to Japan. He had been here once on board the Astoria escorting the remains of Ambassador Saito. Also he had knowledge and understanding about Japan before he came here, because he had many friends in Japanese Navy. One of them was Admiral Kichisaburo Nomura. But he saw at the first glance in Yokosuka stubborn looks of citizens spoilt by the Militarism and miserable orphans wandering about war-damaged buildings. From that moment he began his active work. His idea was reconstruction of peaceful city of Yokosuka based on Christianity. Capt. Decker recently spoke as follows:

"Although systems in Japan were changed in a democratic way, they are not perfect yet in substance. It is necessary to take in Christianity in order to be a really democratic country. When Japan starts her reconstruction on the basis of Christianity, her future will be hopeful in substance as well as in name."

Mikasa Hall was changed into a beautiful white church, which is now the chapel of the Naval Base. Capt. Decker opened it to Japanese also. On Sundays Americans and Japanese gather in this church to offer pious prayers. Perhaps Yokosuka is the only city in Japan where Japanese are attending service with American soldiers in the same church. Though Capt. Decker is a protestant, he joined the parade of Catholics trying to let citizens know the gospel of the Christ. Citizens of Yokosuka are now on their way to regeneration, having regained the once lost spiritual support. The number of the Catholics which was only about 20 in the war-time increased to 300 and is still becoming larger. The bell tolls peace from the former naval buildings where the chorus of hymns is heard. This is a peaceful atmosphere never seen in any Japanese town but Yokosuka.

Rehabilitation of Industry

Promoting peaceful industry in Yokosuka was the most difficult problem to Capt. Decker. The city had no notable industry before the war. The finance of the city was barely maintained by purveyors to the government and public works contractors. But fortunately naval equipments in the city remained undamaged after the war. Capt. Decker opened these equipments to peaceful industries without hesitation. The reason why converted factories in Yokosuka are doing successfully overcoming many financial and material difficulties is that these factories were opened to them promptly. But even after the factories were given to them, they could not get enough electricity and water supply. Capt. Decker ordered Japanese authorities concerned to finish the necessary works without delay. Moreover, he promoted establishment of the Chamber of Commerce and Industry Club to protect and assist converted factories. There are more than 40 converted factories in Yokosuka. The authorities concerned are expecting hopefully that the industry of Yokosuka will be able to support the whole citizens of the city in 3 years.

The City of Schools

Capt. Decker's design of a cultural city appears in the municipal plan of the "City of Schools". At present, Jochi University, Aoyama Gakuen College Industry Sect., Nippon University Agriculture Sect., the Fisheries Institute, Sacred Heart Girls' School and Eiko High School are using the former naval buildings. There are 11 more new system high schools having their own independent school building. There is no shortage of school buildings as seen in every other district of the country. This is another gift of Capt. Decker who opened naval equipments to schools by his prompt decision.

Red Cross

Yokosuka was the first city which had Red Cross service for citizens. Capt. Decker had the Red Cross sprinkle D.D.T. all over the city. As the result, infectious diseases disappeared from the city. It is said that in Yokosuka the number of cases of infectious diseases last summer was the smallest in the country. Besides, water-supply, telephone equipments and distribution of electricity were greatly improved by Capt. Decker's suggestions and instructions. Now citizens of Yokosuka are leading the most comfortable life they ever have enjoyed. Capt. Decker is also interested in protection of the poor. He ordered them to establish Yokosuka Welfare Committee for the purpose of relieving unfortunate people. The finance of the committee is secured by contribution of U. S. Fleet Activities. The total number of people helped by the committee up to today is said to be several million. Capt. Decker brought surplus materials from the south to be used for this work. The committee is also engaged in many other kinds of welfare works such as supply of scholarships, issuing special passes for deaf and dumb pupils and assisting the operation of nurseries.

Women's Movements

Capt. Decker says, "The half of the nation is women. Therefore if men only work without women's help, the half strength of the nation is left unused. Women's position must be elevated first, in order to reconstruct peaceful Japan by all the nation's effort." In this belief he promoted women's movements and helped establishment of Yokosuka Women's Club. Nutritious food given by th Occupation Forces is distributed to the poor through this women's club.

At the same time we must not forget Mrs. Decker's understanding and help. She is working for reconstruction of Yokosuka in cooperation with her husband. For instance, she organized a committee with American Soldier's wives, offered a playground for Japanese children and gave advice to Japanese women on betterment of their kitchen and toilet facilities.

Capt. and Mrs. Decker are to go back to the States in July this year, for which citizens are feeling very sorry. Mr. Goyo Kawamura is now making a bust of Capt. Decker at the request of the Chamber of Commerce and Yokosuka Women's Club. But Capt. Decker tells them to make a statue of the Christ instead of his own, or to be careful not to intrude into children's playground when they place his bust. Some citizens are planning the establishment of "Decker Home", a sanatarium for poor tuberculosis patients. Capt. Decker is much disappointed at his return to the States. Thanking the citizens' cooperation offered during his stay in Japan he says, "Three years in Yokosuka were the happiest time of my life in the navy."

Edwina was as busy as ever with our social activities and in addition was encouraging that which was helpful both in town and on the base. We attended the first meeting of the Japanese Christian fellowship group in the parish house on the base. Edwina gave a short address as follows:

It is a great privilege to have been asked to speak to you this afternoon, and it gives me pleasure to be with you.

First, I want to congratulate you for the success you have had in organizing this Christian fellowship group

279

and to wish you much success in the future. The fundamental reason for organizing, I feel sure, is to help each other. The world has seen so much unhappiness in recent years and is still upset, as a result of the terrible war. Each and everyone of you *want* to improve this unstable condition, and you can. Happiness is the true birthright of each and every individual, *however*, because there is evil in this world caused by *selfishness*, *greed* and *covetousness*, we have thrown away our birthright. We must combat these destructive impulses and there is only one way to do it. We must try to live up to the teachings of our Lord and Savior, Jesus Christ, and practice the lessons we have learned. If we fall short in our dealings with others, we cannot spread the Gospel. Only by setting good examples and attracting others to our ways of thinking, can we improve this world and drive out the evil forces that seem to be working harder to completely destroy all civilization. We owe it to our children and the generations to come, to try to make the world better and make the words of our Lord's Prayer, "Our Father who art in Heaven, Thy will be done, Thy Kingdom come," come true.

We made our annual train trip around Japan in February. Taking a leave of absence and through the courtesy of the Army, I embarked with Edwina and five couples, on leave, in two special cars provided by the Army. The train left Yokosuka at eight in the evening.

Let Edwina tell of our travels:

The Holtoms, the McHughs, the Schorks, the Gays, and the Geises, with our son, Lieutenant A. I. Decker, made up the party. Lieutenant Commander J. H. Holtom was a Japanese linguist and the civil affairs officer. Lieutenant Commander W. W. Gay, Jr. was the base material group officer; Commander C. J. Schork was a dentist on the base; Dr. R. W. Geise was our surgeon; and Captain B. McHugh was the chief of staff for Admiral Berkey. Benny's chief of staff had to run the base in Benny's absence. All of these officers were interested in the Japanese, so the ten days were not only a delightful leave for us all, but added to our knowledge of what was happening in Japan.

The next morning we arrived in Nagoya. We visited the Noritake china factory, where we saw many beautiful pieces of china. Then on to the Ando cloisonné factory. The largest torii (gate) is in Nagoya and we drove through it. Returning to our train we moved on to Yamada, arriving there at 8:46 the next morning we visited the ancient and famous Ise Shrine and were met at the entrance to the beautiful wooded gardens by the head priest and several others. All spoke perfect English. They were indeed interesting and highly intelligent. No one could have been received more courteously or been treated with greater consideration. We were shown several sacred dances at different pavilions. The great attraction to Benny was the house in which the sacred mirror was kept. Ever since the founding of the Imperial Dynasty the three sacred relics necessary for the coronation of an Emperor had been kept in three separate temples under the guardianship of priests. Before us was the temple of the mirror, the emblem of the sun goddess, Amaterasu Omikami of mythology. It was a small wooden building of the exact design of the original temple of two thousand years ago. Every ten years they had built an exact replica and moved the mirror into the new temple. The High Priest in his robes and black lacquered shoes and hat explained that during the war this could not be done. We stood at the gate of the outer fence.

"This is the temple of the sacred mirror. Only the priests and the Emperor may enter, but the Emperor must stop at the next gate. The mirror is in a box on a table in the temple. It was placed there by the Emperor Meiji. The box has never been opened since." Turning to Benny, he said, "Would you like to go up to the next gate?" He escorted Benny through a side gate and up to the next gate where the Emperor would be stopped. "I see no security guards. What prevented our military from violating the sanctity of the mirror, even stealing it?" Benny remarked.

The High Priest replied, "We have no fear. The mirror can look after itself." Evidently he was correct. "No one would dare to touch it!" he added.

This was one of the most impressive days in Japan. In the afternoon we arrived in Toba and once again we visited Mikimoto and his famous pearl farm. We had the usual delicious lunch as Mikimoto's guests, and found matched pearls in the two fried oysters, placed there after the cooking. Mikimoto had this unique and impressive way of giving us presents. The girls were thrilled.

The entourage was fascinated by the process of making a beautiful pearl. We watched the dexterous girls planting a small pearl bead in the mantel and another adjacent to the kidney of each oyster. The pearl divers had brought up oysters from their natural environment for the girls. We were as before amazed by the length of time the diving girls remained submerged. They looked to be in excellent physical condition and it was difficult to judge their ages.

The next day we were in Kyoto, the ancient capital of Japan, and the best shopping area for the Occupation. The store we first entered was Yamanaka's and his museum. We purchased some interesting items and then we went to Hotel Biwako for lunch. The afternoon was spent looking at brocades being woven and on display. We enjoyed seeing damascene being made. In the late afternoon we called on General and Mrs. Coulter and enjoyed their cocktails and interesting conversation. Their garden was beautiful. The rich Japanese had magnificent gardens, even in the middle of the crowded cities.

The next day was Hiroshima. We noted little change in the burned out city. It was good for the officers to see what Yokosuka might have been. It encouraged them in their civil assistance and the renovating of Yokosuka. We boarded a boat and went to Miajima and saw the inspiringly beautiful Mariner's Torii. Lieutenant Commander and Mrs. Adams of the Royal Navy were our hosts, serving us lunch in the boat.

On the twenty-seventh we were in Nagasaki. We revisited the scene of the second atomic bomb drop. It had been greatly cleaned up and some building was being done, but the devastation was still much in evidence. Madame Butterfly's home was most attractive, and the view from the front garden gave us an impressive sight of that great harbor and its former shipyards. Coming down the hill we met the bishop of Nagasaki and had a short talk with him.

Then by train to Tosu, and Unzen National Park. We stayed overnight in a beautiful hotel. It was apparent that this part of the island had felt little of the war, other than the conscription, rationing, and taxation to support it. The next morning we boarded the ferry for Misume. It was a cold voyage, and on arrival the warm train was such welcomed relief.

At 7:49 P.M. we arrived in Beppu from which we rode in three cars to the Sugame Hotel. The cottages were delightful. After a call on Colonel and Mrs. Lynch we returned to our cottage for a marvelously relaxing Japanese bath.

Benny and I took our bath together. First, in accordance with Japanese routine, you wash down and rinse off with water while sitting on a low stool. Then you slide into the large pool of very hot water, slowly immersing, as it is so hot. After fifteen minutes at the most, you leave the bath and dry down. The towels are handkerchief size as the hot water evaporates rapidly. Americans desire larger towels and the Japanese anticipate this need. Benny went to the door to request several; when the door opened a female arm with two towels reached in. Such service! But how did the Japanese girl know we were needing towels at the moment? Clever, these Japanese.

The hot springs were fascinating—all colors and sizes, blue, green, and red. Mostly scalding and all steaming. But the grotesque statues added nothing to nature's attraction. There was a dragon with steam snorting out of his mouth. I enjoyed Beppu more for its baths and Japanese welcome.

In Fukui we visited the silk weaving and dyeing plant with the final washing in the streams, over the rocks. On the third we were in Taguchi, where the snow was deep and the scenery white. We rode in weasels, as cars would have been defeated. From the Akasura Hotel we watched the skiers. We were fascinated by the Japanese children, some about four years old. They were skiing, but their skis were not professionally made. They were barrels staves, and these little chaps were passing some of the better equipped skiers. After dinner we returned down the mountain in weasels, "flown" by aviators trying to be airborne. It was a thrill. They were good drivers, thanks be.

Benny speaks

On the tenth the schoolchildren of Yokosuka put on a "thank you Captain Decker" ceremony for all the things done for them. Typical of the Japanese, they gave full credit to the head man, whereas most of the credit should go to all personnel who did so much for the town of Yokosuka. This was followed by the celebration of the first anniversary of the Japanese Protestant Medical Mission Kinugasa Hospital when addresses were made by me and then by Captain J. B. Butler, our senior medical officer, and Chaplain H. J. Beukema. It was an impressive church service.

I was proud of one of the projects—playgrounds for the Children of Japan. Katherine Schork, the wife of Commander Schork, Mrs. Tanaka, president of the Shinsei Women's Club and Edwina inspected fourteen playgrounds and found them good. We were worried by the lack of playgrounds for children. The little people were being crowded into playing in the dangerous streets. There were many firebreaks available. These would make excellent playgrounds. But the firebreaks were being built upon. If we acted fast, we might be able to stop this building and make the areas into playgrounds. The Women's Club was given this project, guided by Mrs. Schork. They got the Tajimi Company to build the seesaws, swings, and monkey bars. With Japanese steel from the base, the Tajimi Company did a splendid job, all for free. I felt happy that we could use a great deal of former war materials for this purpose. The Women's Club picked the sites. Tajimi built the teeter-totters, jungle jims, and slides as Mrs. Schork suggested, and everyone was happy. The Tajimi Company was allowed to put their name on the equipment, winning the goodwill of the mothers. Later there were more playgrounds constructed by the club.

A Brief Outline
of
Japanese Medical Mission, Kinugasa Hospital

The Kinugasa Hospital had its beginning in August 1947, through the earnest encouragement of Capt. B. W. Decker USN, Commander Fleet Activities at Yokosuka, as the first Protestant Christian Medical Mission Hospital in Japan, sponsored by the Church of Christ in Japan. It is the sincere desire of the staff that the hospital may be instrumental in bringing men and women to the knowledge of our Lord and Savior as they minister to the physical, mental and moral need of the people.

Every member of the hospital staff, doctors, nurses and office helper, is a Christian, and daily duty is done with pleasure and glory in the service. So much so that the average 10 in-patients in our early days grew to be of much larger number within a short time, and now, all 80 beds are always fully occupied. We are hard pressed to care for many others who need medical attention unless the accommodations are greatly increased. Out patients are now averaging 120 to 150 daily. Every patient who comes for admittance, is treated with utmost kindness without regard to social, or financial differences. Maternity room service is deeply appreciated by the citizens of the area as it provides not only "safe birth" at the low cost, but also the ideal nursing habits in the baby room which is found in very few hospitals in Japan.

Although the greatest interest is to serve the physical needs of the patients, the spiritual ministry plays predominant part in alleviating diseases and discomfort. Rev. Nakajima, director of religious department, conducts regular church services on Sunday morning and mid-week prayer services. Each morning chapel service is conducted for all staff and workers on the compounds, as well as the ambulatory patients, ministering words of comfort and of exhortation. Bedside visitation is made daily by the pastor, and a weekly Bible class is conducted for the nurses and ambulatory patients. Since March there have been eight patients who were baptized and accepted to the church. A chapel is to be built within the ground through the kindness of the American Naval personnel.

One of San Diogo's most distinguished and best known pioneer families on visiting Japan, wrote to Edwina's mother:

March 14, 1949

Dear Mrs. Naylor,

I am sure you will be glad to get a firsthand report of your daughter, Edwina. She and Capt. Decker have given us such a good time today and done so many nice things for us. Our ship docked yesterday a.m. about 8 o'clock and at 11 a.m. General Douglas MacArthur's Chief of Staff Col. Huff came for us and for two hours drove us over Yokohama and Tokyo. At 1:30 we were picked up. Mrs. Huff and all four of us went to the MacArthurs' for luncheon and an interesting time. I told Col. Huff that a friend of Ed and Charlie was here and her husband was in the Navy and a high up officer. Her name was Edwina but I could not remember his name. At once he said "do you mean Edwina Decker?" Of course that was it and that I wanted to phone her which we did but they were both out. When we reached the Monroe about 6 p.m., a message from Capt. Decker said to call a certain number which I did and he said Edwina would come with her car and take us to Kamakura at 9:40 today. Right on time she came with a car and driver. It had snowed during the night—the first snow this year and everything was white and lovely. She had on a lovely fur coat, hat and muff and looked very lovely. By the way Mrs. MacArthur said that she is greatly beloved here in Tokyo. We rode till noon when we picked up her husband and son and went to their home for luncheon. They will have beautiful things to bring back to the States. The son is such a nice lad and I understand you have another fine one with you. After lunch, we took pictures in the garden and as the sun was out for an hour I hope they are good, a reasonable hope I think. Its too bad you were never able to go out to enjoy the lovely home in its very choice setting. We drove around the base then dropped Capt. Decker and were taken back to our ship by 3:30. Edwina tells me they will be in San Diego next fall. How happy you will be. I trust your sister is better now. We shall be home late in June.

Cordially,
Mary Fletcher

March 22, 1949

Dear Sister and Brother Decker:

As Master of the Yokosuka Naval Masonic Lodge No. 120, and on behalf of the officers and members of the Lodge, I wish to thank you for the gracious hospitality extended to the Most Worshipful Grand Master Esteban Munarriz, and officers and members of the

Lodge, on the occasion of their visit on March 16, 1949.

Your discussion regarding the base and the aims of the Occupation was described as the most lucid exposition the party had the pleasure of hearing. The luncheon was excellent and the setting beautiful. The Grand Master was greatly impressed by your thoughtfulness, which helped make their official visitation the complete success it was.

Sincerely and fraternally,
Roy T. Powell, Master

During the war the coal miners in Kyushu were Koreans. Being forced labor, they were freed at the end of the war and many were returned to Korea, leaving the mines to flood. Some who refused repatriation had become gangsters and hoodlums.

The judge of our provost court was our Marine colonel, a former Japanese language student. He had before him for trial two Koreans for wrecking a local bar. Both denied being present. The woman owner had identified the two and testified that they had entered by the front door. Whereupon one of the accused blurted out in Japanese to his defense counsel that she was lying. They had entered by the side door. The colonel felt obliged to inform the defense that he understood Japanese. They changed their pleas to "guilty." Colonel Lasswell was a good judge.

Yokosuka
April 16, 1949

My dear Captain Decker,

I want to write to you and to thank you for the scholarship which Mr. Voss gave me in you name. Our new school year began on April the 6th. On that day we had a solemn celebration at the school. On that occasion Fr. Principal called me to the stage, I was very much surprised. What will happen next, I thought. I knew nothing about the scholarship. Then I was given the scholarship, and I was very happy. I never thought that I would receive it. I was especially happy, when I thought of my parents. How happy they would be.

Dear Captain Decker, I want to thank you for your

great kindness to me and to my parents. We are very grateful to you. I have made up my mind to study well and to become a good Eiko boy, because then I shall become a good citizen. Once more, I thank you for the scholarship and also for the many things you have done for us boys at Eiko High School

Sincerely yours,
Francis Tsuneo Kojima

April twelfth, Prince and Princess Takamatsu visited the Eicho High School with us. Father Voss showed us around. The school was developing nicely and had developed an outstanding reputation. The Prince had demonstrated a keen interest in Yokosuka. This was of great importance to the Japanese. We encouraged this delightful couple to visit the town not only because we found them pleasant, as well as attractive, but also because it encouraged the Japanese people.

The following day the affiliation of Women's Clubs in Japan gave a donation tea for the benefit of the Japanese Girl Scouts at the Prince's home, where the Princess exhibited her famous doll collection. Several of our Navy wives accompanied Edwina and were delighted with the display. Edwina was entranced by the dolls representing the royal court. The costumes were exquisitely made and the detailed work perfect. The Princess was a charming hostess and beautiful in appearance.

Easter sunrise service was conducted on the Imperial Plaza. Our friend, Dr. Daniel A. Poling, was the guest speaker. He was not only a most important person but also a splendid speaker. After lunch, with Admiral Berkey, with whom we always enjoyed ourselves, we returned to Yokosuka to receive Mr. Dodge and his party. Mr. Dodge was one of the most important advisors who came to Japan to aid in the balancing of the Japanese budget and to place their economy on a firm footing. He did that in a forthright and positive manner that was effective in making Japan's recovery one of the most rapid and startling in history. Among the Occupation forces he will be remembered for our government increasing the rate of exchange to be a realistic 360 yen to the dollar.

On the nineteenth we entertained ten members of the Diet and the governor of Kanagawa Prefecture and the mayor of Yokosuka as well as our senior officers. I had sent each member of the Diet a pass to the base. I realized that few would use it, but I wanted them to know that they were more than welcome to see what we were doing with the base. It was a friendly gesture.

On the twenty-first, Mother Ernestina and Mother Maria called to bid us good-bye, for they were going to Rome. I was pleased that Mother Ernestina, one of our favorite people, came by to see us. She had not been in our house for several years, as her vows restricted her movements from her school on the base. Evidently this visit to Rome relaxed those restrictions. We expected that she would return, for her good work in advancing Christianity and education in Yokosuka was of great value to me, as well as to the Japanese.

On the twenty-second, Colonel and Mrs. Sid Huff came by bringing Mr. and Mrs. Barry Faris of INS (International News Service). After lunch they continued on to Hayama to have tea with the Empress and Emperor in their summer palace. Barry Faris assigned me my INS correspondent's credentials when I was retired.

After attending the graduation exercises of the Otsu Girls' High School, we were guests of Mr. Uchiyama, the governor of the prefecture, with the mayor, Mr. Ota. We were escorted through the industrial fair. In four years, after reaching the depths of defeat, the Japanese were showing an unbelievable rebirth. I was astounded and very happy to see our friends coming back so strongly.

The twenty-sixth, the prime minister, Shigaru Yoshida, gave a beautiful garden party at the foreign minister's official residence. There were present many of the leading Occupation officials as well as the outstanding Japanese. This affair demonstrated the change gradually taking place in the relationship between our two nations. We were certainly friends. Now we should become allies.

After a luncheon in Hayama, given for General and Mrs. Hodes, the new general in command of the First Brigade of the First Cavalry, we stopped by our favorite shop in Kamakura. It was owned by a friendly Japanese, Mr. Kurikawa. I considered him my art connoisseur. He saved good items for me and advised me on some. One day he saw on my mantelpiece two silver vases with fourteen-petal chrysanthemums, the mon of a prince. He remarked that I, being number one in

Yokosuka, should have vases with the Emperor's crest—nothing less! When I stated I would be flattered to own such vases and that these were the best I could find, he replied, "I'll find you a pair!"

Several weeks later he appeared with two beautiful vases, larger and with the sixteen-petal chrysanthemum embossed on each. I was delighted. He then told me the story—a marshall who had conquered Manchuria was presented these vases by the Emperor—a great honor. But now he was hungry and needed money badly, so he planned to melt them and sell the silver. Mr. Kurikawa told him that Captain Decker needed two such vases and that they would be on his mantel in a place of honor. He asked him if he would sell them. "Yes, providing that my name remains unknown and that the price is no more than the price of the silver!" I have them on my mantel in a place of honor. I tell this story to all, as an example of the Japanese character.

The following is a memo for Dr. Poling:

The Catholics have founded the Eicho High School (Jesuit) of 360 boys and the "Hand Maids of the Sacred Heart" has 1100 boys and girls. The Methodists (Aoyama Gakuen) has 700 students. A Community Center in Taura under the able leadership of Mr. and Mrs. Thompson has an attendance of 8,000 people during the month. The Catholic and Protestant Hospitals also contribute greatly to the Christian influence in Yokosuka. A Catholic Church and several Protestant Churches have been established.

Last year the first Christian Processional in Japan was held and 4,000 people marched. This in a town where in 1945 there were no active Christians!

At Christmas and again at Easter there have been at the Base entrance a display of life size plaster figures sculptured by a famous Japanese artist, Mr. Gozo Kawamura. They portray the birth and the resurrection of Christ. These have proven of great interest to the Japanese who crowd around and read the story, printed in Japanese.

The city of Yokosuka had been a "one business" town—the Navy. Upon defeat, the city was without industry and 40,000 workmen were idle. We encouraged the creation of 80 industries and put to work many machines from the former arsenal. Where there had never been a mill we now have 7 cotton, 2 woolen, and 3 silk mills. The Japanese are no longer hungry and no longer are they in tattered rags. A Women's Club of 30,000 was created. Partial independence of women was assisted by opening mills. The women are learning fast.

Though we inspired the establishment of a Chamber of Commerce; an Industrial Club, a Women's Club, a Red Cross and several orphanages and Old Folk's Homes, it was apparent that charity and benevolence were not fully understood. Therefore, we initiated a Board of Charity. It consisted of Bishop Breton (French Missionary), Mrs. Tokunaga (President of the PTA), Mr. Suzuki and Mr. Murata. These four without pay or any compensation gave their time to distribute charity to the deserving. Old, spoiled, and damaged food or materials were turned over to this committee, who knowing the Japanese better than we can ever know them, saw that the poor and afflicted were assisted. The committee rendered a detailed account monthly. It has been a great influence and guide to the Japanese in demonstrating the real Christian Spirit. The Bishop states it is the happiest committee in town as it is not paid, but works for the pleasure of serving!

All Japan is not so fortunate. With but 2,000 missionaries for all of Japan, Yokosuka's proportion would be but six, far too few to fill the void left by Shintoism's decline and the inability of Buddhism to cope with today's problems. If Christianity doesn't fill the needs of Japan, Communism will take advantage of this void.

A dollar spent on Christianity today is worth ten tomorrow!

Benton W. Decker
Captain, U. S. Navy
Commander Fleet Activities

20 April 1949
Dr. Daniel A. Poling
c/o Colonel Roy H. Parker, Chaplain
Chief of Chaplain Section, GHQ
Hypothetic Bank Bldg. Annex Rm. 307
Tokyo, Japan

CHRISTIAN HERALD MAGAZINE
27 East 39th Street
New York 16, N.Y.

Tokyo,
April 22, 1949

My dear Captain Decker:
I am most grateful to you. You have given me exactly what I want and shall use to really great advantage. I shall send you copies. It was a great privilege to meet and know you.

I am going to Manila tomorrow and may return here late in April.

Sincerely,
Daniel A. Poling

Office of the Secretary of Defense
Washington
May 21, 1949

Dear Captain Decker:
You barely know me, and so I suppose this note is impertinent. Nonetheless, I want to say that Dr. Poling's tributes to you and those of General MacArthur (expressed to us at lunch) would warm the heart of any human. The Doctor did a column on you and is doing a feature in the Christian Herald. What you sent him was, to his mind, historic.

If the whole world could be run the way you are running Yokosuka, it would be virtual paradise.

Respectful regards,
Joy Dow, Jr.
Lieut. Colonel

James Young, a correspondent, told me about Will Adams (Miuri Anjin), a Britisher, and I thought of my good friend the British ambassador, Sir Alvary Gascoigne. He might be interested. He was. I volunteered to assist in the renewal of Will Adams Day, which had been discontinued by the war. Again I quote from the *Sea Hawk:*

The Honorable Ambassador Gascoigne, British Ambassador, accompanied by Captain Decker and the Mayor of Yokosuka, will revive a time-honored memorial service after an eight year lapse. The ceremony is a tribute to William Adams, earliest occidental resident of the Miura Peninsula and advisor to the first shogun. The program will include several short addresses and a laying of wreathes.

Adams, who was born in Kent, England, was shipwrecked near Bungo (Oito Prefecture) in Kyushu, Japan. Although only 18 of his 110 shipmates survived, Adams was extremely fortunate. Taken on as an advisor by the first shogun, Tokugawa Ieyasu, he taught Western gunnery, shipbuilding, mathematics, navigation, and other technical affairs of the Western Countries.

Married to a Japanese wife, he died in 1620 and was buried at the sight of the present ceremonies.

Yearly on 4/14, when the cherry blossoms are at their best, a memorial service is held before the tombs. The Governor of Kanagawa Prefecture, Mayor of Yokosuka and members of the British Embassy and many others attended the service.

Commander Fleet Activities
Yokosuka, Japan

RETENTION CAPTAIN BENTON W. DECKER USN ON ACTIVE DUTY PRESENT BILLET SUBSEQUENT TO RETIREMENT 30 JUNE 1949. APPROVED BY SECNAV FOR FISCAL 1950 X REQUEST CAPTAIN DECKER SUBMIT OFFICIAL LETTER REQUESTING RETENTION ON ACTIVE DUTY TO COMPLETE RECORD.

Vice Admiral Robert B. Carney
Deputy Chief of Naval Operations, Logistics
Navy Department
Washington 25, D. C.
Dear Admiral:

Friday I received dispatch extending my tour in Japan for another year, Edwina and I wish to thank you for your great interest and help in accomplishing this. It is very encouraging to have a friend such as you.

In the coming year we hope to continue to improve Yokosuka. Our plans include more housing for which we shall need some funds for quonsets. We can improve the position of our enlisted and officer dependents at little cost. The savings in rentals will be considerable. I have written a letter through channels asking for $250,000.00 for 50 quonsets. These make excellent temporary housing of two or three bedrooms.

The Japanese economy seems to be the uppermost thought in everyone's mind. No more PD's except in most unusual situations. We were first told we have to pay to crate and ship reparation tools out of Kure. That seems to put us in a less favorable position than the Chinese. Also to get material out of Guam and the Philippines we must pay $350.00 a day for a Japanese LST, property of the USA.

The Admiral has asked to have Captain Burzynski, now on his staff, sent here for our Repair Base. This will be a big help. Also we are gradually building up the repair personnel by cutting other activities.

Bill Kirten leaves May 10th. We shall miss him greatly. Bill is an excellent officer and a big morale booster. Frank Tibbits has taken over with enthusiasm.

Many thanks again.

Sincerely,
Benny Decker

City Hall
May 2, 1949

My dear Captain,

On behalf of Mrs. Ota and myself, I would like to tell you how glad and relieved we both are in reading news in this morning's papers that you will remain in this city for another year.

Having spent nearly ten years abroad, I fully realize that Mrs. Decker and you would rather return home and enjoy civilian life after three years' hard work in Japan. I feel ever more grateful for your decision of staying the fourth year.

I am sure that the next twelve months will be just as happy as the past.

Will you please convey to Mrs. Decker our relief and joy!

Yours sincerely,
S. Ota
(The Mayor of Yokosuka)

The Uraga Dock Co. Ltd.
6 Yato
Uraga, Yokosuka

Commodore, B. W. Decker
Commodore Fleet Activities, Yokosuka

4 May, 1949

Dear Sir,

It is with great pleasure that we hear of your promotion to Commodore and also your staying in Japan for another year.

All workers and staffs of our Uraga Dock Company always appreciate your kind and wonderful administration.

It is not only pleasure of people of Yokosuka area, but also for all Japanese.

It is our duty to work hard for shipbuilding Industry of Japan for reconstruction of Japan to recompense you for your kindness and great aid to our Japanese.

We wish send our congratulation to you again.

Yours sincerely,
Yoshiaki Murata, Director
Uraga Shipbuilding Yard

Kanagawa Prefectural Government
Yokohama
5 May, 1949

TO: Captain Benton W. Decker
Commander
Yokosuka Naval Base

My dear Captain Decker,

I wish to offer you my congratulations on the occasion of the extension of your sojourn in this country for another year.

Since it was published, that you were to return to

295

the United States some time in May, I was one of the many persons who regretted to hear this news, because it would have meant not only the loss of one of the most able high ranking officers of the Occupation Forces, but more than that, we would have had to lose one of the best friends of Japan. It is not the citizens of Yokosuka only who are grateful to you, but I too, as the governor of Kanagawa Prefecture, am filled with a deep sense of gratitude to you for the constant goodwill you have demonstrated for the rehabilitation of Japan throughout the time you have resided in Yokosuka.

I have no doubt whatsoever, that extension of your stay, and of Mrs. Decker who has earned our love and admiration, will bestow well being and a stronger degree of happiness to the citizens of Yokosuka.

Mrs. Uchiyama joins me in renewing our wish, that you will have every success in the execution of your duties, and we pray for Mrs. Decker's and your good health.

Iwataro Uchiyama
Governor of Kanagawa Prefecture

Tokyo
June 30, 1949

Dear Admiral:

I am delighted to address you this way and send you my heartiest congratulations!

I hope that we can have a glass together one of these days to celebrate the occasion.

With best regards,

Sincerely yours,
Cloyce K. Huston
United States Political Advisor
for Japan

May the eighth, Sunday, was the day of the second Christian Processional. As the year before, it started at 2:00 P.M. at Saint Joseph Hospital with the cross bearer followed by dignitaries of the Catholic Church, the Navy band and the representatives of many American and Japanese groups. It was a colorful parade, larger than the year before and watched by larger crowds. Edwina and I, with many of the officers and men of the base, marched while the Japanese choir sang. After blessing the town, it ended at the Catholic Mikasa Chapel.

I wrote to a friend of mine who had been an important member of the Occupation.

We have the communists on the run. One is in jail and one is on trial. The Base Union (OFLU) is having a "free and democratic election" and the communist leaders have all resigned. We feel confident that the people are swinging away from Communism. The Kamakura election showed a reduction in communist votes to 1/3 that of the previous election when the "middle of the road" parties increased a large amount.

In 1947 I had directed my liaison officer, Mr. Takaoka, to have each and every Japanese worker on the base sign a statement that he was or was not a communist. In communist language, this was a "voluntary" statement. If he refused, the workman would be barred from the base. If he admitted he was a communist, he would be discharged immediately. I depended on the other workmen to report any who lied. These would be fired for falsehood. To tighten security on the base each man had to carry his identification card with his photograph on it.

The workmen and the Japanese authorities were elated over this order, as the communists were becoming more brazen every day. I found out that some of the union officials were communists. I ordered them to sign the same statements as the workmen signed. The first reaction was from a foreign legation. The representative stated that, "You cannot refuse to hire communists!" This official later was to commit suicide after being charged with being a communist. A day later the United States political representative, my friend, called on the phone to tell me that there had been complaints. My reply was the same to both, "I am responsible for the security of the base and it isn't secure if there is one communist working on the base, or if the union is controlled by communists."

297

The communists wanted to settle the matter informally. No detente for me—the answer was, "Settle it out in the open where everyone will know the facts." Pete Kalisher cleared the article with me and it came out in the paper that the United Metal Workers of Japan (whoever they might be—not one of three unions on the base!) complained to SCAP that I was demanding the labor union officials sign that they were not "communists, fascists, totalitarians, or subversives." It is true that this statement had to be signed by everyone working on the base. If not, no identification badge, and they could not come on the base. No statement—no work! On the seventh of May, Pete Kalisher broke the story in the papers. That night I attended a dinner party that General and Mrs. Weikert gave as a farewell to General and Mrs. Stratemeyer. Every general and diplomat was there. Everyone congratulated me on the stand I had taken concerning the communists and the security of the base. It was unanimous. If I needed any encouragement to fight, I surely had it from them. I was elated to think that the Army and the diplomats were so united on this subject.

The union officials (self-appointed, so far as I could judge) claimed that they had been elected. They admitted that they were communists. I knew from reports that my workmen were unhappy and that they had suggested a loyalty check. Then the officials claimed that they had been reelected.

I declared this election to be in violation of the Document of Surrender, and said that a secret election would be held during working hours by a truck with a ballot box and officials. It would visit all buildings and conduct a secret election. The result was a quiet and satisfied working force, electing true representatives.

In answer to a request, I wrote the facts to Mr. C. K. Huston, United States political advisor for Japan:

The recent petition submitted to SCAP and the Missions of China, Soviet Russia, and Great Britain was based on a false copy of a letter I addressed to the Yokosuka Labor Management Office (YLMO). Statements in the petition were not true. A certified copy of my letter is attached.

You will readily see the great difference between the two letters. My letter did not direct the Union to follow any action. It did direct the YLMO to have no further dealings with the two communist leaders of the OFLU. And it did recommend a course of action to remove this restriction. I recommended a free and democratic election as set forth in the Japanese Labor Laws.

The reason for my action is based on the security of this Base. I have not a communist working on the Base and I feel that it is just as important that the three Unions on the Base be free from the communist control. Two unions have certified that they are free. The OFLU, however, did not. It is under communist control.

In addition the two officers of this union were continued in office in a most undemocratic election, which was rigged by those in office in such a manner as to perpetuate their positions. The election was announced Friday, April 22. It was held on Sunday, April 24, when the workmen were at their homes, many at some distance from the scene of the election. The election was held in a small building, the capacity of which is 217. There are 3,000 in the Union. The Japanese Government representative was denied admission, which prevented him from observing if the election was free and democratic, as well as secret.

The YLMO has reported the meeting to the Prefectural Office as undemocratic. The Prefectural Office in turn is reporting it to the Central Government in Tokyo. The Central Government has not as yet acted.

The present situation is that the Security of this Base is my responsibility and therefore, I have refused to have any official dealings with communists, either as laborers or as representatives of these laborers. The Japanese Government officials are taking steps to have the Unions hold free, democratic and secret elections. If the new representatives will sign loyalty certificates, I will immediately recognize them. The President of this Union has recently applied for a leave of absence due to poor health.

The petitioners in knowingly presenting a false copy of my letter, so altered as to change the meaning, have opened themselves to legal action against them. I feel that they did this for the purpose of causing dissension and discord among the Occupation Forces, and to challenge my authority to guard the security of this Base.

B. W. DECKER
Captain, U. S. Navy

Nothing further was heard about this. We had established that the communists could not prevent the Occupation from maintaining security.

After the May secret labor elections I asked the newly elected leaders to call on me, thus opening channels direct to the top man. They were most polite and friendly. I expected them to ask for something, but they were happy, maybe because I had defeated the communists. So I asked them if there was anything that I could do. No one spoke up, so I volunteered. "If you insist, we can install hot baths in the repair department for your use after you quit work." This seemed to please them, so my new repair officer, Captain Burzynski, built them a bath house which we opened in September 1949.

On the nineteenth of May we entertained eighty people at dinner in honor of Prime Minister Yoshida and the many Japanese officials, businessmen, doctors, missionaries, and industrialists who had contributed to the revival of Yokosuka. It gave my officers, as well as Rear Admirals Womble and Hermann, a chance to acquaint themselves with these leaders of Japan. The list of guests:

Yoshida, Shigeru	Prime Minister and Mrs.
Ohta (Mayor of Yokosuka)	Mayor and Mrs.
Tanaka (YLO)	Mr. and Mrs.
Yoshikawa	Mr.
Ishikawa	Prosecutor and Mrs.
Suzuki	Police Chief and Mrs.
Kamiizumi	Judge and Mrs.
Suzuki, K. (Wel. Board) & Sagami K.)	Mr. and Mrs.
Murata (Uraga, Wel., c of C)	Mr.

Kobayashi (Opama & Mill)	Mr. and Mrs.
Ogura (Y. land Club)	Mr.
Tajimi (C of C, Foundry)	Mr. and Mrs.
Tokunaga (PTA—Book Stores)	Mr. and Mrs.
Okamoto (Dept. Stores)	Mr. and Mrs.
Noguchi (Red Cross)	Dr. and Mrs.
Tanikawa	Mr. and Mrs.
Kawabata (Kindergarten)	Mrs.
Mabuchi (Mabuchi Gumi)	Mr.
Kawamura, Gozo (sculptor)	Mr. and Mrs.
Harada	Dr. and Mrs.
Kuwabara	Dr. and Mrs.
Sano	Mrs.
Takaoka (Foreign Affair)	Mr. and Mrs.
Koike (Silk Mills)	Mr.
Okayama, K. (Red Cross)	Mr. and Mrs.
Karaki, Valerie (Sec.)	Miss
Kawada (Salvation)	Mr. and Mrs.
Topping (missionaries)	Rev. and Mrs.
Thompson "	Rev. and Mrs.
Voss "	Father
Kurosawa (Missionary)	Dr. and Mrs.
Yasumura "	Rev. and Mrs.
Harker, Rowland "	Mr.
Hermann, E. E.	Rear Adm. Com Cru Div 5
Womble	Rear Adm.
Tibbitts, F. P.	Capt. and Mrs.
Butler, J. B.	Capt. and Mrs.
Lasswell, A. B.	Col. and Mrs.
and others	

Yokosuka Aoyama Gakuin
Inaoka-cho, Yokosuka
May 20, 1949

Dear Capt. and Mrs. Decker,

May I express my gratitude for being included in
your very lovely dinner party last night. It was certainly
an honor to be part of such a gathering. I appreciate
your splendid efforts to bring about a healthy, happy

301

relationship between Americans and Japanese.

Thank you, Captain, for accepting the invitation of our school to come next Thursday, May 26, from 2 to 4 p.m. for the Second Anniversary Celebration of our school. I do hope that Mrs. Decker can join you then.

Dr. Diffendorfer, head of all the foreign missionary work of the Methodist Church in America will be here at that time. I hope that over tea there will be an opportunity for you to impress him with the great possibilities here in Yokosuka for Christian education. We need his backing if we are to get the money we need.

Thank you again for last night.

Sincerely yours,
Rowland Harker
Dean

At the second anniversary of the founding of the Aoyama Gakuin (a Methodist school on the base) Rowland Harker, the dean, introduced us to Dr. R. E. Diffendorfer. He represented the Japan Christian University Foundation in the United States and had sufficient funds to start a new university. I wanted it in Yokosuka where we had already started a big program. Dr. Harker needed funds and this offered him an opportunity, if Dr. Diffendorfer would divert some of the funds to the support of a branch here as well as the major school in Tokyo. There was no doubt that the Dr. Harker considered a Tokyo location more desirable. I failed miserably to persuade him.

On the tenth of June we were invited to the Army Day reception by General Walker at the New Grand Hotel in Yokohama, but we were committed in Yokosuka to receiving His Eminence Norman Cardinal Gilroy and his entourage. We had them for dinner that night. The guests included: His Excellency Bishop McDonnell; Monsigneurs Kennedy, Cronin, Carroll, Freeman, O'Donell, and Scally; Brothers Gannon and Bitter; senior and junior officers of the base; and Lieutenant Edwards and Fathers Mahon and Voss. I attended mass on Sunday and was surprised that many of our men were in dungarees. I apologized and told his Eminence that they would wear uniforms thereafter. He said that he was happy that they attended church in whatever clothes they desired. I issued orders that dungarees were out, feeling that if their religion was so frail, they weren't worthy of being called Christians. There was no drop in attendance. We enjoyed their visit very much and it inspired the Catholics to greater effort.

The Emperor had three sons. We were informed that the two younger lads with a mentor would like to see the base. I was delighted that they were interested. When they arrived in my office, the Japanese gentlemen prompted the lads of five or six years to approach my desk, where I remained seated as desired by the escort. Each lad gave a well-rehearsed greeting in excellent English. I was impressed and welcomed them to the base. I then presented each with a sailor's white hat, as my two sons, when their age, wore sailor hats. I was politely reminded by one boy that they had an older brother who would like a hat also. Again I was happy that they thought of their brother and was glad to furnish them with a third hat. They were most attractive lads, polite and friendly, and reminded me of my two sons when of that age. I then prepared to take them around the base. This was politely refused by the Japanese escort, for he indicated that this was more than expected. I turned them over to my aide.

On the thirty-first of May I received my orders promoting me to rear admiral on the retired list as of thirtieth of June and immediately recalling me to active duty in that rank for another year. Now I was released from Admiral Carney's admonition not to mention the proposed promotion, for there was very high and powerful opposition to it. It had been rumored all through the Navy for over a month, but we had to ignore it. Someone in Washington in a high position had said that MacArthur thought too much of me! Finally, Secretary Johnson had told the Navy, "Stop all this foolishness and make him an admiral!" God bless him!

Looking back on my difficulties with three Selection Boards, I can say that it was all for the best. Had I been promoted by selection I would have had less than a year in command of the base and that would not have accomplished the task I had assumed for myself. There wasn't a better job anywhere in the Navy. As it was, I justified my existence by four years of duty under outstanding and friendly vice admirals, doing what I thought most important for the future of the United States. And I ended up by being promoted, though a little later, and finally retired no worse off than if I had been selected in 1946. I am grateful to all those loyal friends who had faith in me and were not swayed by fear of my enemy, high in governmental office in Washington, whoever he was!

Chapter XII

EDWINA VISITS CALIFORNIA

July first, I was promoted to rear admiral. Captain Tibbetts was no longer my chief staff officer, but now my chief of staff. He organized a celebration to be remembered. At 0800 I arrived at the Administration Building. A full guard and band to render honors to the new rear admiral was standing by. My two-star flag was broken over the Administration Building, as I took the honors. All the heads of department came to congratulate me. And the letters poured in from the states as well as from the Occupation. My officers and men had worked hard and long, and my two stars were the result of their loyalty.

I now rated a "barge" instead of a "gig." It was the same boat, and remained on the wharf out of commission. The crew could be used elsewhere to better advantage. Also, I rated a flag secretary and flag lieutenant, but my chief petty officer, Chief Erickson, an amazingly capable man, could continue to handle both jobs, so these two officers were used by the chief of staff in more important duties.

That evening Mary and Ray Spencer, the Coca-Cola representative, gave me a dinner dance at the Colonial Club in Yokohama, honoring my increase in rank. It was a beautiful party worthy of our Navy's highest rank! Edwina pinned on my shoulder boards. We were fond of Ray and appreciated his ability to do the unusual, such as a wetting-down party for the Navy's junior admiral!

On Saturday, the next day, I reviewed the troops. Colonel Red Lasswell paraded with a band, two hundred Marines, and four hundred sailors past a reviewing stand erected near the city hall, so that the town could see our splendid security force march as well as the junior flag officer in the Navy.

The officers of the base gave me a "wetting down" party. It was a dinner dance. Overhead was an arrangement of blue flowers with two white stars. The huge cake was a beautiful replica of a rear admiral's flag. Edwina was glorious in a mass of orchids. Were we happy!

On the fourth of July we watched the Occupation troops being reviewed by General MacArthur in Tokyo. Our contingent was smart and I was in the stands in my new uniform with the First Cavalry patch on the left arm. It was a beautiful day for all, but especially for me. The American people should have seen the troops pass in review on the Emperor's Plaza. I was proud of the Occupation forces.

That night we had a fireworks display on Berkey Field. It was inspiring. A glorious day for Old Glory. On the seventh, Captain Frank and Mrs. Tibbett gave a large reception in our honor. Edwina was given a beautiful orchid corsage.

In twenty-seven years I have lost, mislaid, or deposited in the Hoover Institute for War, Revolution and Peace, many letters. A few, I quote in the following pages. At the age of seventy-eight I can take an objective view. I ask the reader to do the same. The publishing of these letters is not to satisfy my ego but to share with you the warmth and kindness of the writers. With no possible reward they have expressed their feelings. Their joy at the good fortune of another is the basis for brotherly love. I urge the reader to put me entirely out of mind, and focus his full attention on the writer's thoughtfulness, and share with me the admiration I have for these kinds of people.

From my admiral in Tokyo:

TO REAR ADMIRAL DECKER FROM BERKEY X CONGRATULATIONS ON YOUR BEING RECALLED TO ACTIVE DUTY AS A REAR ADMIRAL X I AM HAPPY TO HAVE YOU WITH ME ANOTHER YEAR

305

General Headquarters, Far East Command
Office of the Chief of Staff

1 July 1949

Dear Admiral:

It is with the greatest pleasure that I send my hearty congratulations on your well deserved and too long delayed promotion to the rank of Rear Admiral of the Navy.

As you well know, I have had great admiration for your accomplishments in the Yokosuka area during the past three years, and this promotion, I feel, is perhaps the Navy's recognition of the fact that it is difficult to keep a good man down.

We are happy to have you with us for another year at least, and if at any time in the future we can be of any service to you here at GHQ, as has been the case in the past we shall always be glad to do so.

Please also convey to Edwina my happiness at your promotion for her sake, and Margaret's best wishes to you both.

Sincerely and fraternally yours,
EDWARD M. ALMOND
Major General, General Staff Corps
Chief of Staff

From Admiral Oscar Badger, NavWes Pac:FOR RADM B W DECKER X HARTIEST CONGRATUATIONS ON YOUR RECENT ELEVATION TO FLAG RANK X WE ARE LOOKING FORWARD TO THE PLEASURE OF RENDERING HONORS TO YOUR FLAG IN THE NEAR FUTURE X OSCAR BADGER

Commander in Chief Pacific
and United States Pacific Fleet

July 3, 1949

Dear Decker:

Congratulations on your well deserved promotion, and looking forward to seeing you again.

I am very sincerely,
W. Radford

306

Dear Benny,

I want to join all your host of friends in sending congratulations to you for this well deserved and long overdue honor.

I am so delighted. Best wishes to you and Edwina.

Most sincerely,
Jean MacArthur

Department of the Air Force, Washington
13 July 1949

Dear Benny:

We dined with the Paul Muellers last night and they told us that you have been promoted to Rear Admiral and will stay on in the Pacific.

Connie and I are delighted to hear this and send warmest congratulations and regards to you both.

Sincerely,
THOMAS D. WHITE
Major General, USAF

From the former general of the Eighth Army:

Department of the Army
Office, Assistant Secretary, Washington, D.C.
1870 Wyoming Avs., N.W.
4 August 1949

Dear Benny:

You and Edwina are in our thoughts so many times, but now especially with the news of your promotion we both want to congratulate you on a very delayed recognition of all the things you have done out there for the Navy and for your country.

Many times I have missed Japan, but I believe if I were given the choice of one evening spent there I would ask for one of those fine Navy evenings with Dickie dancing her one hula and Florence Bledsoe trying out her close harmony.

With renewed congratulations and warmest regards to you both.

Sincerely,
Robert Eichelberger

From the prime minister of Japan:

July 4, 1949

My dear Admiral,
   I am delighted to learn of your promotion to the rank of rear admiral, and hasten to send you my sincere congratulations.
   It is a good news, too, that you are to continue at your present post. Lucky, indeed, is the city of Yokosuka!

Very sincerely,
Shigeru Yoshida

No. 2100, Kugo-machi
Yokosuka City
Kanagawa Prefecture

1 July 1949

Rear Admiral B. W. Decker
Commander of the U. S. Naval Activities
Yokosuka Base
Dear Sir,
   It is with highest respects that I beg to offer my hearty felicitations for your latest promotion reported of late in the Japanese press throughout this country. Indeed, in my humble opinion, it is not too much to say that this sense of congratulations is shared by almost all the citizens of Yokosuka City and its neighborhood, for they are feeling exceedingly grateful for the paternal guidance and valuable assistance which since your assignment to your present post on the Yokosuka Base you have consistently bestowed upon the local Japanese populace.
   Allow me to add, at this juncture, that your paternal guidance in word and in deed is indicative of a fine example of contrast to the tyranical, autocratic self-righteousness of the defunct Japanese militarists who had achieved nothing but thrived on at the sacrifice of the people and by squeezing the people, whereas your

308

deed, please excuse my impudent expression, is likely based on humanity and fraternity, intrinsic reflection of democracy.

Last but not the least, I wish to remark for your personal information that whenever we tell the Japanese compatriots residing outside Yokosuka City that we are living in Yokosuka City, they with one accord would never fail to enviously refer to the good administration you are giving the community of Yokosuka City. This remark I fear may seem compliment, but really it is the truth without least exaggeration. No matter what it may be, it is sincerely hoped your paternal leadership, so long as Yokosuka City is concerned, will not a bit be deviated from its long trodden path.

Apologizing for my impertinent expression and hoping for your invariable benevolent assistance to the masses under your jurisdiction.

I remain, Dear Sir,
Your obedient servant,
Yasuzo Ikeda

1st July 1949

To:
Rear Admiral B. W. Decker
U.S. Navy Fleet Activities
Yokosuka, Japan
Sir;—

I would like to give you most hearty congratulations on being appointed rear admiral in the United States Navy and am hoping your stay here will be as pleasant as before.

Yours respectfully,
Tajimi
President of Tajimi MFG Co., Ltd.

P.S. Also, all members of Tajimi's labor union are jointed wishing you hearty congratulation too.

Dear Admiral and Mrs. B. W. Decker,

On the occasion of your promotion to the admiralty, we expressly offer you, Admiral and Mrs. Decker, our sincerest and heartiest congratulations.

We believe your joy, of course, is exceedingly great indeed, ours, however, is even greater than yours. We have long expected and waited for this happy occasion to come and it has come to a realization.

We pray for your happiness and health and that you continue to be a wonderful "Daddy" of Yokosuka as you have been in the past.

Dr. and Mrs. T. Kuwabara

1 July 1949

Rear Admiral B. W. Decker
Commander Flt. Act., Yokosuka
Sir,

It is with great pleasure that we hear of your honorable promotion to Rear Admiral.

We would like to send our heartiest congratulation to you.

Not only workers of our company but also all the residents of Yokosuka area are happy to hear that because you have done a lot of things to the real happiness of our Japanese.

All workers of our company are working hard to build Norwegian whale catchers and other works which are very important for the rehabilitation of Japan.

And moreover, it is sure we can have a contract to build a French cargo ship before long.

We wish you would continue your favour to our company and to our Japanese.

We wish to congratulate you again.

Yours sincerely,
Yoshiaki Murata
Director,
Uraga Shipbuilding Yard

1 July 1949

Dear Admiral B. W. Decker,

We, the students and teachers, wish to express our sincere congratulations upon your promotion to the rank of Rear Admiral. Upon our celebration of this your happy occasion, we wish to thank you for the many favors bestowed upon us making this school a most pleasant and interesting institution.

We wish you would accept this our humble gift and we all wish you a most happy and prosperous years to follow.

Respectfully yours,
A. Mabuchi
Mabuchi Deaf and Dumb School

And this made me very happy:

To: Rear Admiral B. W. Decker
    Commander Fleet Activities
    Yokosuka, Japan
From: The Base Union President
Subject: Felicitations

Please accept our sincerest felicitations for your brilliant promotion to the rank of Rear Admiral, U.S.N.

Taking advantage of this auspicious occasion, we wish to renew to Your Honor our highest respects, and at the same time to express our heartfelt thanks to your kindness you have been so good as to show towards us in many occasions.

On behalf of all the members,
K. Hanyu
President
The Base Employees' Union

IHS
1-7-49

Dear Captain Decker,

We were not at all surprised to hear that you are to be named Admiral tomorrow, but we are very anxious to let you know how glad we are to hear it!

Those who gave us the news especially emphasized the fact of this honour being due to you very specially, for all the great good you have done in Japan.

You can fancy if we are ready to agree to this wholeheartedly, after all the help we have received from you since we came to Yokosuka.

If our school is today a success and our pupils and students are doing very well, we do not forget that this could never have been, had not the generous hand of you, our great benefactor, helped us to accomplish it.

311

Assuring you that we will all pray very specially for you tomorrow.

Believe me,

Yours sincerely in Christ,

Carmen Ustara

I know that one should not be proud; yet, I am. My promotion to rear admiral was gratifying, but it gave me no reason to be proud. There were many better men still waiting for that honor and reward after years of loyal and capable service. What made me proud was the reaction of my friends. I was most fortunate to have such loyal friends of different nationalities and different callings. It was topped off by the correspondents who feted me at the Correspondents Club in Tokyo. These people had written a splendid recommendation to their liaison in the Navy Department when I came up for selection. This was most unusual and flattering to me. The Navy spends millions to obtain goodwill; yet, the united correspondents voiced an opinion and it was ignored. Now, through the back door, I was being promoted and again the club did the unusual. They feted me at a party that I shall never forget. I am proud of what they did; so I quote the club's release in full.

Admiral Decker Feted at Party

More than 140 persons turned out at the Tokyo Correspondents' Club last evening at a party honoring Rear Admiral Benton W. Decker, in celebration of the latter's recent assignment to remain in command of Yokosuka naval base, and his promotion from captain to his present rank.

A staunch friend of all the correspondents since the early days of the Occupation Admiral Decker received a royal welcome last night, from the time he entered the club's vestibule, where a naval mural adorned the wall proclaiming him in command of the "USS Correspondent", 'til he reached his table embellished by a mammoth birthday cake. Flag festoons adorned the walls; life preservers added a nautical touch, and a bona fide ship's bell announced the gala sea food dinner.

312

Allen Raymond, president of the Correspondents' Club, congratulated Decker on behalf of the members and the Admiral expressed his appreciation to all the correspondents for their support of his career in Japan.

The dinner was followed by dancing to orchestra music, interspersed by vocal "request" numbers, including some old Navy favorites rendered by the guest of honor. Arrangements for the evening were in charge of Julius Zenier, entertainment and mess chairman, assisted by Sylvia Crane, decoration chairman.

The article omitted that I was received aboard by a boson's call and six side boys! Allen Raymond, the president of the Club, greeted me. All of my friends of the Press were there, and I had a great time. Captain Frank Tibbitts and Mickie, his wife, rode up with me to the party. Captain and Mrs. Day went direct from Kamakura.

Edwina had returned to the states to encourage her Aunt and Uncle, Albert Ingersoll, the founder of a pioneer candy company in San Diego. Her mother was doing a good job of helping them in their advanced years, but Edwina thought it her duty to return for a month. She had been away for three years, which is a long absence. I carried on without her for two months, and she was missed. I visited Admiral Madden in the HMS *Jamaica*. We were delighted that his men enjoyed Yokosuka and specially the EM Club. The Britisher is not as well paid as our men so we had to make concessions. They supplied their own beer. It was Japanese and just as good as ours, but far cheaper. It was no trouble to us, and with the British dollar shortage it made life rosier for our friends. Bert, my son, a lieutenant (junior grade), was with me and enjoyed cocktails in the *Jamaica*. The British senior officers in all services are always congenial people.

On the nineteenth of July I was invited aboard the *Jamaica* for luncheon as a guest of Vice Admiral A. C. G. Madden, and on the thirtieth the commander in chief of the British Pacific fleet invited me aboard the *London* for dinner. Several centuries ago, the first *London* had established a custom for the captain to say grace before each meal. He was a man of few words. The same grace has been said ever since. "For this meal, we have eaten, thank God!" Straight and to the point!

We have enjoyed having the British Navy for a visit.

Our yacht club was going well and I had a Star boat and the club had several so we had races frequently. The British are great small boat sailors and of course we enjoyed their keen competition, using our Stars. Though they were unaccustomed to our boats, they did well. On the seventeenth we had twenty knots of wind. One of our sloops sank, one was dismasted, and one British Star had to give up. Bert was my crew in my Star boat, which I had rigged with a minumum diameter mast. We gave the other Stars a thrill. I thought it would go, but it didn't in that race. It only proved fast and that Japanese *hinoki* (cedar) could take the punishment.

With the wind abeam my Star, the *Suteki-Ne* (slang for "Isn't she pretty!"), ran away from the fleet, but to windward she pounded so much that the back stays were slack and the mast threatened to carry away. The mast was acting like a fly fishing pole. We were the only boat to finish! It took a good sailor to handle those sheets, and Bert proved he was the best. His hands lost considerable skin. The mast did carry away the next race.

We arrived late at the Grecco's party, where everyone asked after Edwina. I wasn't the only one to miss her. The party was a singing success with the star performers being General and Mrs. "Pat" Casey. After the night, as the guests of the Caseys', I put Bert on the *Bataan* with Toni Story piloting. Bert was headed for Manila via Guam.

Monday I moved to the club. The Tadodai was to be thoroughly renovated. We had lived there for three years with little improvements because every cent had to go into new houses for our people. But this opportunity created by Edwina's absence made it advisable for me to agree with my competent Commander McHenry to move out and give him a chance to do a complete job. In the matter of a few hours, the place became a shambles. Furniture moved, wall paper removed, and plywood walls erected. The kitchen just vanished and many little rooms became open spaces. All tatami removed, clothes closets installed, bathroom enlarged, porch extended, garden pathways cleaned of white gravel which I had put there in 1946 and replaced with stone slabs. The servants were given three weeks' vacation, and I was to remain at the club until the fifth of August. That public works department was going to do a real job that would be appreciated for years to come, thanks to Commander McHenry.

I had noticed that the outside corner of the living room seemed low. It was measured and found down four inches, but it was impossible to jack up. I guessed that the 1923 earthquake must have done this to our famous home.

My Marine orderly, O'Brian, a loyal soul, complained about the lonesomeness of the house, even with "Cherry," my German police dog.

My social life was not slowing a bit. I was particularly flattered that the Bataan group asked me to a gathering. I was the only outsider. It was a farewell to "Pat" Casey, held in Colonel Syd Huff's quarters. There are so few of the survivors of the original staff of the General: General Willoughby, General Marquat, General "Pat" Casey, Syd Huff, Colonel Larry Bunker, and Colonel Herb Wheeler.

Major General Wm Chase, USA
Office of the Chief of Staff
Fort McPherson, Georgia
Dear Bill:

The last Fourth of July parade was outstanding. They broke out all the heavy guns as well as the light ones. Sixteen thousand men passed the reviewing stand—but we missed you. The First Cavalry is here but the patches are not as "bright" as last year. Since you and Hoffman and Bradford left, the Cavalry has slowed down to normal speed, to that of the other divisions. I miss the Bill Chase enthusiastic leadership! General Devine does not get around as much as you did, probably because of his wife's health.

Thanks to my friends such as you I am now a Rear Admiral, retired and recalled to active duty in the same job.

I am pleased that you should want a picture of me, so I am sending you one that was taken at the Press Club, #1 Shinbun Alley. It was in honor of my promotion.

Many thanks on your congratulations. The Army

315

has been 100% behind me and I appreciate it.
With love to Dorthea and best wishes to you.
As ever,
B. W. Decker
Rear Admiral, U.S. Navy

Herb Wheeler asked me to a party to see the famous Sumida River fireworks on the twenty-third of July. He was looking after Lowell Thomas and Dave Sentner (Hearst special writer); General and Mrs. Stratemeyer got lost in the crowd. We missed them. Mr. and Mrs. Lewis, defense counsel for Tojo; and Mr. and Mrs. Robinson, old friends of the Lowells', as well as Colonel Rizo, Mrs. Court Whitney, and two other couples, formed the party. We had supper as guests of Watanabe, owner of the Toho movie industry, in a most unique restaurant. It was a very old farmhouse moved intact into Tokyo.

The fireworks lasted from 1930 to 2200, and were most extravagant, the best I had ever seen. They were viewed by millions of people, lining the river bank.

On a Sunday I attended two picnics. The Masons and our supply department were getting away from the hot weather by swimming at the Nagai Beach. Then I went sailing with Frank Tibbetts from our yacht club. On my return, Herb Wheeler had brought to Yokosuka Mr. Mathews, owner and editor of the *Tucson Star*. He was most important to the Occupation, so at Court's request I helped out by showing him around for several hours and then we went to Captain Tibbett's for a buffet supper. There he met a small but important and congenial group of our senior officers.

I was asked by Court to escort Dave Sentner and Bill Mathews in the airplane *Bataan* for a tour of Japan. Toni Story was the pilot. Herb Wheeler did the planning and we had Colonel Unger and Major Napier with us. The first night we stayed at the Australian air base at Iwakuni. We went by boat to Hiroshima, where the newsmen interviewed scientists and patients. It was decided that the bomb had left no lasting ill effects, but that the tabulation should continue into the second generation, for genetical changes. Half of the people of Hiroshima had been tabulated and four IBM's were working on the collected data. We talked to the doctors and the sole patient, a mass of keloids. It was explained that he was keloid type and that they were not the result of radiation.

On the way back we stopped off at Iwakuni for supper and lodging. Mosquitoes were bad. The next morning we flew on to Fukuoka, where we caught the train, a special car, and went on to Nagasaki. It was hot. We went on to the bomb site, then to Madame Butterfly's house. By car we went to where we had a marvelous seafood dinner. There we stayed overnight. The beds were hot, the sanitation poor, and the mosquitoes plentiful; yet, the newsmen were good sports and enjoyed the experience. We flew back to Kyoto. By car we traveled to the Biwaka Hotel where they gave me the number one suite. We ate our meals in "my" sitting room. That evening the governor gave us a geisha party. It was in a beautiful Japanese house with the best garden in Kyoto. It was beautiful! The food was excellent and well served. The little geishas were most attractively dressed and cute with their long obi. The older geishas danced. The governor served a new dish to me. It was spaghetti in a bucket of ice water. You fished out a length of spaghetti and dipped it in the sauce. It was delicious. When I made this remark, the woman who had concocted it was asked to come in and I congratulated her.

The weather was hot, as it was all during our trip. I have never had so much attention: meals and special bar service in our rooms, special cars with MP escorts, and guides always at your beck and call. I saw what real VIP treatment was like.

The next morning we visited the fingernail tapestry works, the castle with the nightingale floor, and then went shopping. I added to my netsuke collection. I arrived home after five days of being spoiled, but also seeing a great deal of Japan with excellent companions. We all parted friends.

There were many changes in the command structure in the Far East Navy. The support group was being abolished and Womble would go home on the first of September. Berkey was to be relieved by Joy, and he to relieve Badger on August twenty-eighth. Binford was to be relieved by our classmate Hartman.

I received greetings from Cardinal Spellman by Father Voss who had dinner with me at the club. He was running a summer camp for boys on Kanonsaki. The Catholics were so cooperative and doing much to advance my hopes and wishes for Christian growth in Yokosuka.

U. Alexis Johnson visited the base and I enjoyed showing him around. He was soon to leave for the states. Alex was a devoted public servant with plenty on the ball. I always hoped that he would become Secretary of State. I fail to see why a political appointee with little if any experience in the State Department makes a better secretary than a man who has devoted his life to the job. Alex would have been the best.

Mr. and Mrs. Woods, ex-president of the Santa Fe Railroad, came to Yokosuka, encouraged by Court Whitney; so I showed them around. Then I was the only military man at a party of the Hustons. Mr. Huston had always been thoughtful of me, and I think was trying to help me pass the time while Edwina was in California. I met many interesting people of the diplomatic branches.

On the eighth of August I returned to the Tadodai and slept in my room. I found eighteen things wrong, all because of the Japanese who were trying to please people with entirely different ways of living. But none was difficult to correct. Within a day, everything was perfect. The place was beautiful and much credit must be given to those who planned, as well as those who carried out the plans. It was a better house than the Japanese Navy had for their highest commanders. Our people had even puttied all the windows, stopping the rattling of panes during a windstorm. But there was still much to do to complete all the rooms.

We opened a skating rink with big crowds. It was most popular, but the number of skates limited the number of participants. We opened it one day a week to the Japanese guests of our men. If things progressed as I hoped, we would soon have it open every night to them. This of course opened the base to escorted Japanese girls at night. We found that these girls took their privileges seriously and I expected no lowering of our standards.

Our nurses had moved into a building all their own from the upper deck of the Officers' Club, thus establishing more privacy and also releasing that floor for its first renovating since VJ Day. The Protestant camp on Monkey Island (Sarushima) was proving a big success and Father Voss took his final vows. Mother Ernestina was back from Rome. Our artist, Gozo, was looking much better after his extensive cancer operation. Everything was going my way, except my jewel of a chief petty officer, Erickson, whom all the Army thought most capable, asked to be relieved. He wanted to get back into telephone work. I suspect that some jealousy had inspired other chiefs to look upon Erickson as a "fair haired boy." This had occurred with my previous chiefs. I hated to lose him, but one of my principles was to allow the best officers and men choice of jobs. There is a type of senior who keeps a good man in a job forever, to cover the senior's shortcomings. A good performer should merit quick promotion as a reward and not be penalized for being better than the average.

I wrote this for the *Sea Hawk* on August nineteenth, 1949.

Admiral Berkey will visit this Station on Thursday, 25 August, when he will be the guest of the officers and men of Fleet Activities. He has expressed his desire to thank you all for your support and in particular to say farewell to our enlisted men and the junior officers.

It has been our good fortune to have had Admiral Berkey as our senior naval officer in Japan, for he has not only supported us in our duties, but he has also added a friendliness to our daily lives. His ability to lead his subordinates as well as to coordinate the effort of the Navy with that of the Army and Air Force has brought forth praise from the juniors as well as the seniors in all three services.

Though we deeply regret Admiral Berkey's departure, we are all happy over the honor of his being selected for the more important position of Commander of the 7th Task Fleet. We look forward to his frequent return with his ships to his home in Yokosuka where his many friends will always welcome him with the same sincere friendliness that he has shown us during the past years.

Berkey Day was a great success. He was a most popular officer, and had an unusual personal interest in his juniors, both officers and men. We needed more like him. He was piped into the club garden by a Japanese ex-admiral! The side boys were six beautiful Japanese girls in kimonos. The hors d'oeuvres had tooth picks with miniature three-star admiral's flags. And everyone had a long cigarette holder similar to the one Count Berkey uses. The dining room was decorated as an undersea grotto with paper fishes and crabs. And mermaids. Count rotated, having each course at a different table; thus, we shared him with all hands. After each course he was escorted by the ladies adjacent to him to the next table where there was a vacant chair "Reserved for Admiral Berkey." At 2000 we took the admiral on a tour of the clubs. At the PO Club and the EM Club there were side boys. He gave a talk at four different clubs, all crowded, and he was hailed with cheers and applause and champagne. The ceremonies at the PO Club were conducted by a Negro who did a splendid job. I was proud of him. We had a few songs. I led off with "Auld Lang Syne," then a few of our old favorites.

At the Officers' Club, Count cut his large, beautifully decorated cake and all the ladies cut in on the admiral, giving him a whirl. It was the best night we had ever had for the best guest of honor.

Admiral Berkey had the excellent idea of encouraging yacht building in Yokosuka, not only as a new commercial enterprise, but also to build up the ability to make small craft. He imported teak at a very low price and we encouraged the Azuma Trading Company to make small boats. They needed expert guidance, so "Count" Berkey asked Ted Kilkenney and his wife to come to Yokosuka, as Ah Fong's Yacht Building in Hong Kong had closed down. Ted was their expert. "Count" ordered a motorboat and I, a forty-four-foot yawl. I imported sails and rigging and many other items. Of course we had a few headaches. But we inspired a new industry. It was to pay off in the Korean War.

Labor Day was to be a big affair in 1949. The communists were misleading the Japanese laborers into thinking that May Day, the communist holiday, was also Labor Day and that the Japanese would thus be tricked into supporting the communists. To forestall this I planned on making our Labor Day into a Japanese holiday for the laboring man. Each workman on the base was invited to visit the base with his wife and one child as guests. This had never been done by the Japanese Navy.

The day would start off with the dedication of a new hot bath house for the repair department's laborers. I had promised this to the union leaders some months before. And now it was to be done in style. Also, each laborer would receive a large ten-in-one ration, left over from our war in the tropics. This was not well thought out by me. We gave it to them at the beginning of the day; therefore, it had to be carried wherever they went. And, of course, the women were the ones doing the carrying. But they didn't seem a bit disturbed. Also, we dedicated fifty salvaged Quonset huts combined with a wooden structure into attractive homes for dependents. One we furnished and opened to the Japanese to walk through and see how Americans lived. I had a pretty little Japanese child cut the ribbon. The women were most interested, and it gave them a few ideas.

The laborers walked freely through the base. This the Japanese Navy had never allowed. This gave them a better idea of the complete base. We wanted them to be part of the team, and to think of the base as their base, their home.

We also had a baseball game between Japanese teams; baseball is a very popular sport. There were many other attractions, such as movies, to keep them busy for the day.

A few days before, I was at a party in Yokohama where our plans were being discussed, as a novel subject among the guests. One was Ray Spencer, the Coca-Cola representative. Ray was a good friend of mine and generously offered to contribute to the day by furnishing the Coca-Cola. I thought it too generous, informing him that we needed twenty-eight thousand bottles which would, of course, be out of the question. Not at all! He was happy to furnish the drinks, provided I would do the trucking and return the bottles. Without a thought, I agreed. So each Japanese got a bottle of Coca-Cola.

The surprise was that they didn't drink it. They took it home—bottle and all. And I had to pay out of our store profits two cents per bottle! We lost over five hundred dollars. But the Japanese thought it a splendid gift, for bottles were scarce!

The day was remembered by many. We received so many letters of thanks and Father Voss dropped in to tell me what a brilliant idea to combat communism and win friends. I was quite pleased in spite of the unexpected loss of the bottles. My laboring force was introduced to another American product.

The assistant to the Senior Medical Officer was Lieutenant, later Lieutenant Commander, O. L. Young of the medical corps. He had come up through the warrant grades and had a thorough knowledge of administration and had the ability to get results. After a conference with Captain Butler, I gave Lieutenant Young orders to find us medical supplies to stock a good-size warehouse. There was a large concrete building with an elevator situated adjacent to the hospital. Its location made it useful only as a medical warehouse. But we had no funds and no authority to stock it with reserve supplies. So Young was given two tasks. I gave him orders to fly to Samar and, if necessary, to California.

They were closing many naval hospitals which could be of help to us. Young went to Samar where two Naval hospitals were being closed. He was too late. They had been given to the Philippines. He then went to Long Beach, where he was more successful. A shipload of supplies "for free," arrived soon thereafter, and our storehouse was fully supplied as a reserve. When Korea hit, we were ready.

On the first of September the eye of a typhoon passed over Zushi. The wind was 80 knots with gusts of 105. We lost a number of trees in the garden. The Base lost one Star boat, two wooden buildings, and several roofs. No personnel injuries. Rain was worse than the wind.

We had a splendid berth at Piedmont Pier for ships during a storm. The adjacent hills protected the deck of a carrier from winds of 60 knots or better, outside the harbor, reducing them to 30 across the flight deck.

We were fortunate in having Under Secretary Voorhees (Army) visit the base on the ninth of September. He was accompanied by Vice Admiral Turner Joy, who had relieved Admiral Berkey, as ComNavFE. On the sixteenth, Rear Admiral Chandler (DC) visited the base for five days. I had him to the Tadodai for my first big dinner since the renovation. It was a pleasant occasion and nothing needed changing. Admiral Chandler seemed pleased, as were all of our doctors and dentists.

Edwina returned to Japan in a blaze of glory. Let her tell it from beginning to end of a happy vacation:

When Benny had received orders to stay over another year, he offered me the chance to return home for a month. I had been away from my mother, aunt, and uncle in San Diego for three years, the longest separation we had ever had. Benny knew that they were getting along in years and were not in good health. It was a busy month of planning and preparing for my return to San Diego via the transport *Thomas Jefferson*, which arrived in Yokosuka on July the fourteenth with our son Bert on board. July sixteenth arrived and I was all excited, for I was to see my family in San Diego. Many of the Yokosuka Women's Club and many friends were at the pier to say good-bye. My arms were full of orchids, and there were so many American and Japanese friends to see me off that I had mixed emotions.

But I never forgot that I was also to advance the cause of the Shinsei Women's Club. We had discussed this many times, and it was planned to get the club into the International Federated Women's Clubs, of the United States. The President of the Yokosuka Club gave me a letter to hand deliver to the president of the San Diego Club who was to sponsor their entrance into the Federated Clubs.

8 July 1949

The General Federation of Women's Clubs
San Diego, California

Representing the Shinsei Women's Society and its 30,000 members, I wish to extend to you our most cordial greetings. This Society was formed soon after the surrender and has attained its present position and the prestige it now enjoys in Yokosuka and throughout Japan due to the guidance and aid of Rear Admiral and Mrs. Decker, who have demonstrated to the people of Yokosuka how magnanimous a victor can be and what true Christian kindness is inherent in the American people. We maintain a widow's home, with a factory and day nursery attached, a library, a women's cooperative union and engage in cultural and welfare work.

It is a town where the instant you get off the train and stand in front of the station you feel the atmosphere of amity and unity between the people and the American Forces. The city is clean, the paved streets are well kept and the people go about their every day duties happy and contented. It also boasts of Catholic and Protestant schools, which can match those of our capital, Tokyo.

Yokosuka with a population of 280,000 was formerly the first naval base of Japan. Due to the efforts of Rear Admiral Decker it has become one of the most progressive cities in Japan, with more than 50 re-converted factories engaging in peaceful industries.

Through this demonstration of the true democratic way of life, with its fundamental belief in God and a constitutional government designed to serve the people and protect the dignity and freedom of the individual, I and the members of our Society are determined to become worthy of this way of life and to fight for it, if need arises, for ourselves and for our children.

I ask your kind cooperation towards the promotion of better understanding between the women of two countries by the continental interchange of ideas through all possible channels to help to solve the many problems besetting us today.

Toshi Tanaka
President

Through the efforts of Mrs. John H. Crippen, on Sunday, August twenty-first, a splendid article by Irene Clark was published in the *San Diego Union* concerning my work with the Shinsei Women's Club of Yokosuka. I was quoted as saying in support of the Women's Club in Yokosuka, "We must extend them the helping hand of friendship. . . ."

Mrs. John H. Crippen invited me to be the featured speaker at the fall regular meeting of the county federation to be held in San Diego, at San Ysidro.

Mrs. Bryant, a member of the board of the Federation of Women's Clubs, southern district, as well as the president of the Civic Club in San Diego, called on me. She said that she was so impressed with the article in the San Diego Sunday's *Union* that she was sending it to the chairman of the International Clubs, Mrs. Whitehurst, in Washington D. C. and to the President of the Federation of Women's Clubs in America, Mrs. J. L. Buck.

I hoped that some club would sponsor the Shinsei Women's Club for membership in the International Club. Then Mrs. Tanaka might be able to go to the meeting to be held in Boston, Massachusetts in May 1950.

With my aunt, Mrs. Bess Herrin, I went to this important meeting. I read Mrs. Tanaka's letter and gave a talk about the Shinsei Women's Club. They unanimously approved the plea. The women were very interested and enthusiastic. My speech was well received. Mrs. Crippen, president of the San Diego Federation of Women's Clubs was a great help. I was most fortunate in having such a dear friend of long standing as the president. (I agree, says Benny!) I initiated the campaign to have the Yokosuka Women's Club join the federation.

On September twelfth, I left San Diego to return to Japan. My son, Ben, drove me to San Francisco. I had been most fortunate in having Tony Wong as my roommate leaving Japan, and now I was to have Mrs. Alonzo P. Fox, General Fox's wife, for my roommate returning to Japan. Two better companions could not be had.

I was happy and thrilled to have all of so many good people escort me aboard. I hated to leave Ben, but I was getting homesick for Japan and Benny. My vacation had been a happy one, and I felt that I had served the Shinsei Women's Club well by the publicity and the meeting I had attended on their behalf.

The Army transport *Darby* stopped at Seattle, where Florence Bledsoe and Major "Peg" Moses took us to lunch at the Washington Athletic Club. Later we went shopping! Betty Fox and I enjoyed renewing friendships with these two former members of the Occupation.

The *Darby* was a good ship, but the route to Japan was direct by the northern route. There was fog and little sunshine. There was much wind and heavy seas, causing the ship to roll heavily. One night we had our meals in our rooms and were told to remain there as the deep rolling of the ship made it impossible to serve meals in the dining room. The safest place was in a bunk.

Betty Fox and I sat at the table with Senator and Mr. H. Alexander Smith of New Jersey and Lieutenant Colonel Paulas. We became good friends and enjoyed their company. On the twenty-sixth at nine in the evening, we were in sight of city lights of Yokohama. But the Yokohama pilots didn't work at night. We had to wait until morning to enter the harbor. When we came alongside the pier there were my husband and many members of the Yokosuka Women's Club. They had chartered a bus to come over twenty miles early in the morning, to meet me. The warmth of their welcome made me very happy. Senator and Mrs. Smith were teary-eyed as they witnessed a greeting the likes of which they had never seen before. Leaning over the rail, they were encouraged to believe the Occupation was in good hands for me to receive such a welcome.

I left the ship on my husband's arm. I was surrounded with friends and smothered in beautiful flowers. It was an important day in my life, and the happiest.

Arriving at our home in Yokosuka, the servants met me at the entrance. They seemed happy to see me again. And the house was beautiful. Commander McHenry and his assistants had done a magnificent job of modernizing and decorating. I was in heaven!

The next night Colonel and Mrs. Lasswell gave a dinner in my honor. I was wearing the six orchids, including the one from the Lasswells. I can't remember ever wearing so many beautiful orchids all presents by my friends and Benny. We gave an "At Home" for our officers and wives of the base, then Commander and Mrs. Geise had a dinner party in my honor followed by bridge and poker. And another orchid! We went to three dinners in Tokyo, including one by Vice Admiral and Mrs. Joy, then one in my honor by Lieutenant Colonel and Mrs. Wann, USMC, I was now up to my former social speed. Helen Smith, wife of Senator H. Alexander Smith, wrote:

My Dear Mrs. Decker:

I cannot begin to tell you how much my husband and I appreciated all the trouble you took, to show us around the Naval installations. We were amazed at the extent of it and admired the way the Admiral has over-come so many obstacles!

You are great examples of what can be done if one has the will and the skill and the perserverance.

What fun it must be to work together like that.

We are off at eight o'clock tomorrow morning, on the first lap toward the U. S.

We have had a great adventure. We have learned much, and we have much to think about. I only hope that we can be of some help in the confusion about us.

Our affectionate greetings and a wish that our paths will cross soon again.

Ever affectionately,
Helen D. Smith

Chapter XIII

MACARTHUR'S NAVY

After months of discussions, the Russians were returning the twenty-eight frigates we had lent them under Lend Lease. The war had long been over and the United States had been asking for their return. One had been sunk, leaving twenty-seven. Admiral Joy informed me that I was to receive them and that the Russians wanted to return them in Hokkaido. I immediately asked to be allowed to implement the agreement. He agreed; so, through the Soviet member of the Allied council I said that we could not receive them in Hokkaido, that they must be returned in Yokosuka. As expected, it took more "palaver." We did not have the personnel to man those frigates. Further, they were fortunate that we did not insist that they be returned to the continental United States. The date of arrival was not announced by them. We kept a watch on the agreed-upon frequency, but no information was forthcoming. At 0800 on October fourteenth, nine frigates appeared off Yokosuka. It was a complete surprise. Our boarding officer immediately informed the Russians that pilots were available to moor them at our seawall berths, the most secure in the harbor. Captain 2nd Rank Korovkin refused, though he had previously agreed before leaving Vladivostock. This was the beginning of several conflicts. Captain Boris D. Yashin, the chief of section, Soviet member to the Allied council for Japan, was the liaison officer and was amenable to reason. They finally moored as directed. Our medical teams went aboard for inspections prior to pratique. One ship never completed its forms. We found the ships badly infested with rats, fleas, and lice. Fumigation after the takeover disclosed as many as two hundred large rats in some of the ships. Our Japanese were reluctant to go aboard these frigates, they were so dirty. We insisted upon inspection by departments of each ship. We had received a number of Russian-speaking inspectors from the United States, and with a few of our officers and men we were able to converse freely with the Russian sailors, except when a Soviet official was listening in. In the bilges and other difficult spots we were able to get direct answers. Most Russians wanted to be friendly.

The morning of the fifteenth a conference was held in my office with Captain Korovkin and his staff with Captain Yashin and my officers. I welcomed them aboard and gave them the freedom of the base. I extended to them an open bar at all clubs and offered them the full use of all recreational facilities. I hoped that we could have some games together. We wanted to give them the same welcome that we would give any visiting man-o'-war. Our friendship was rejected. Captain Korovkin explained that some officers might come ashore but that the men were tired from the voyage and that they had far too much cleaning up to spend any time ashore.

I invited twenty-five officers to dinner at my quarters. The State Department had asked me to do this—all expenses would be chargeable to the State Department. The only time in four years that this was done was for the three visits of the Russians. I had never entertained the Russians stationed in Tokyo because of their aloofness, nor had the Soviets ever shown any interest in me except for a few criticisms made by their diplomat in Washington, so I suspected that the State Department thought I might not entertain the officers of the frigates.

328

Captain Korovkin accepted for his officers. He wanted a tour of the base by bus, assuring me that they didn't wish to see anything secret. I informed him that there was nothing secret about our base and that they were welcome to roam around. But I cautioned the bus driver to steer clear of the two restricted areas!

The Russian officers enjoyed our PX. Each was interested in a bottle of "glass" for lady's finger nails and one pair of nylons. Our saleslady advised three pair as more economical, but no, they wanted one pair each.

The men in liberty blues crowded on deck, looking longingly at the base and our people. One of our men, who spoke Russian, asked a Russian sailor to come ashore. He was enumerating all of the attractions such as hamburgers, free beer, dancing, and free movies in all the clubs, when an officer approached and ordered the sailor below. There was no liberty.

The Russian officers didn't trust their men. The few we met aboard were all well-dressed, neat, clean, polite and military. We liked them and regretted that we could not be as companionable with them as we were with all visitors.

The ships had not been used extensively at sea, for their gyros were not all functioning. The radars had been recently retubed, but the antennae frozen. The reciprocating engines were poor, but the bilges were filthy. There were no spare parts for anything aboard. The guns showed they had been fired, but almost all the ammunition was accounted for. The three-inch shrapnel had nose fuses, which had been smothered in preservative grease, thus making them dangerous from muzzle bursts. The depth charges had never been used, and all were inoperative. The watertight integrity was fair, though many bulkheads had wiring holes unplugged. Adequate shoring was not available for the bulkheads. The sick bays were unbelievable dirty and unsanitary. The equipment was almost useless. The galleys had been used to excess. It appeared as if the ships had been used as barracks. The meat blocks were deeply worn, as from years of use. The refrigerators were in poor shape, and the miscellaneous food-preparing machines were inoperative. The ice cream machines had never been used.

We gave, in our house, three dinners, each for about

eighty guests, including the Russian officers, our officers, and their wives. I found the Russians to be pleasant, but at times restrained by the presence of their commissar. As usual, the guests were met at the door by Wah Chan, who would ask the Russian officers, "Cocktail?"

"Niet! Decadent! Whiskey!" This they got—a big glass of straight whiskey. It didn't faze them.

One of our Japanese girls then asked, "Hors d'oeuvres?"

"Niet! Decadent! Sandwich!" After a few minutes Wah returned with sandwiches of thick ham between massive slices of bread. Again without hesitation, they munched on the two-fisted sandwiches while we ate "decadent" canapes.

They were a pleasant group, full of fun, but if the musicians played a verboten tune, they would all stop, put down their drinks or forks, and wait until it was finished, then resume their conversation or eating.

On the base there was a very pretty girl whose husband was in the hospital. Knowing that she was a flirtatious type, I asked her to please attend and help me entertain the visiting firemen. I told her the official photographer would be there and I wanted a full-face of each officer. The Russians buzzed about her like bees about a honeypot—and the photographer was busy snapping pictures. The next day I received the many photos—all showing the beautiful blond full face surrounded by backs of Russian heads!

On the seventeenth the Russians were relieved by our crews and they were mustered before and after marching them into boats to be transferred to a small, dirty-looking transport that had arrived on the sixteenth.

This first group of nine frigates was followed by two more groups of equal number. But we now insisted that they be moored at buoys until fumigated. The next groups were cleaner and cooperated better. They seemed to relax a bit with repetition. But no liberty!

I liked the Russian officers and men, and would have enjoyed making friends. They could have had a pleasant time. I was shocked at the condition of their ships. Of course their first line could have been much better, but no ship I have ever seen was as bad as those frigates. One was somewhat clean, almost up to our standards. This was under the command of an officer whom I complimented at one of our

330

parties, when I was able to speak to him in private. He said that he was a Jew. That the hierarchy had made him change his name to a Russian one, for they needed him. He had to be better than the others to keep his job.

We must refrain from using these ships of 1949 as indicators of the effectiveness of the Russian ships of today. This was the Russian Navy of yesterday. Today they must be vastly improved. I think their officers and men could be excellent men of war, provided more trust was placed in them.

I was invited aboard one of the frigates for luncheon. There were three English-speaking officers and the meal was served at the table in the enclosed bridge. It was an excellent luncheon. Later, I found out that they had twenty dollars to spend in our commissary for special food for the occasion.

I had one luncheon for six at my house. I enjoyed them very much. The conversation was friendly and humorous.

We took possession of the ships, fumigated them, and manned them with token crews of Japanese former Navy men. We used ten men per ship to get them into seaworthy condition, with the assistance of our repair department. These Japanese had civilian titles, such as supervisors, foremen, etc. I reported the availability of the twenty-seven frigates to General MacArthur, who said he might need them. Washington had asked me how much it would cost to put them in a condition of preservation such as our battleships, destroyers, and cruisers. It would have been millions, and I would have been ordered to sink them at sea, or at the best scrap them.

So I answered evasively, stating that I could preserve them for one thousand dollars per ship, for necessary greases and such. We got the money.

Those frigates were not of any value to the United States as they had wartime reciprocating engines. In 1944 the turbine-building capacity of our country was entirely occupied with main drives for larger vessels. Frigates could use reciprocating engines. They were for anti-submarine warfare and had three-inch guns, machine guns, and depth charges.

Before receiving these frigates we had salvaged twenty-one LCTs, each capable of moving 150 tons of cargo at seven knots. These were not on charge and were on blocks in excellent condition—at no charge to the U. S. taxpayer.

Washington had ordered us to ship to China many LCMs capable of carrying one tank each. But besides those on charge we had salvaged 210 which had been abandoned on the beaches of Tokyo Bay. These were overhauled and on blocks and ready to go. All told, my people had salvaged ten million dollars of small craft plus the twenty-seven frigates. In addition there were eighteen LSTs repatriating Japanese. Those would be used later in the Korean War. Assigned to the Western Pacific were two cruisers and two destroyers, not always on station. When Korea burst upon us, we were mighty glad to have those additional few ships in Japan.

I called on the General to inform him of these ships. He immediately said, "That's my entire Navy!" And Korea was but eight months away!

The three-inch AA ammunition coated with cosmoline was reported to the Navy Department as being in less than satisfactory condition. If the grease seeped into the powder train, it might cause muzzle bursts. I was directed to dump the entire lot at sea. I replied that the ammunition was safely stored in our Japanese magazines, under expert Japanese supervision with no danger to us or to property. A few months later the Chinese, after talking to me, requested Washington to sell to them the three-inch ammunition, as they were desperately in need of that type of anti-aircraft shells. It was sold to them for twelve dollars per round, which was its cost to the Navy!

Unannounced, on the twenty-fourth of December, the Russians showed up with the first of three Lend Lease ice-breakers. Being Christmas Eve, I refused to receive it until after Christmas. It was clean but had been used extensively, requiring a major overhaul. It was manned by civilian crews which immediately, after acceptance, went aboard a waiting transport for return to Russia.

The Reader's Digest
Office of International Editions
Pleasantville, N. Y.

October, 1949

Dear Admiral Decker:

The snapshots taken at your home reached me yesterday. They are a delightful reminder of a very interesting evening. It was very kind of you to widen the circle and include me as one of your guests. I wanted to meet you because of the story we published about the wonderful job of reconstruction you did. For the commanding officer of a conquering military force to become so popular that he has had difficulty to avoid being made mayor of a city is something new under the sun. I regret that my stay in Japan was so short that I did not have a chance to learn more of what you accomplished.

May I take this opportunity to thank you for the assistance you have given to the *Reader's Digest* in Japan— Dennis McEvoy tells me that you have always been most helpful. And I want to thank you and your wife again for your hospitality and kindness to me.

With every good wish to you, I remain

Sincerely yours,

Barclay Acheson

Near the end of World War II, I reported from the South Pacific to Washington for duty in logistics. I soon learned that the credit for winning the war went to those in logistics who "thought big." This was done by pencil pushers who moved the decimal point to the right one or two places, or who purposely obtained monopolies for their branch of the military. They got the medals and promotions, while the taxpayer got the bills.

In peaceful Yokosuka the attitude was entirely different. We conscientiously thought of the taxpayer and salvaged everything from the tons of surplus goods dumped on us at the end of the war. The result was our storerooms were full when the Korean war hit us. But no medals—no promotion! I was disappointed that my people, who were so far from Washington, were given so little recognition, especially those in the supply corps.

My supply officer was in charge of the salvaging of over forty shiploads of war surplus dumped in the open on this base after the surrender by ships making a hurried turn around to return to commercial trade. This material in huge piles was scattered over the vacant areas of this base. It was without protection from the weather, which soon erased all labels. When I arrived on April the third, 1946, I was shocked at the waste and the indifference of the officers regarding these valuable supplies. Some of the salvaged material was returned to Hawaii because certain items were in great demand. The remainder was taken up on our books to establish our stock position. At the start of the Korean War these supplies were at the scene at no cost!

My supply officers, Commanders Gray and Spector, accomplished this great task when our personnel was fewer than five hundred men. They trained men, to use Japanese labor, mostly women. This not only saved us money, but also gave work to the Japanese, who were otherwise destitute.

The supply department worked with the Army in the handling of dry provisions and refrigerated stores and disposal of surplus Army provisions. Probably over a million dollars was saved by the transferring to the Army the weight handling and earthmoving equipment that was not needed by the base. We reactivated four million barrels of fuel oil storage on Azuma Island.

Spector was the player coach of the base football team, which contributed greatly to morale. His attractive wife, Ursula, assisted him in civil affairs, such as developing the first playgrounds in town, the reestablishing of the Yokosuka Japanese Red Cross on American democratic lines. The supply department saved the taxpayer millions of dollars, and the time of transporting the goods across the Pacific Ocean.

In 1949 the General wanted me to direct the reconstruction of Okinawa. I agreed, provided I could wear two hats—Commander of Fleet Activities, as well as Commander of Okinawa. We held three meetings in Tokyo with the staff for drawing up the letter of authorization. No one objected to including such authority as establishing exchange rate, taxes, imports and export laws, as well as internal control over the police and election laws, etc. It looked as if the General was to give me all the authority that I had in Yokosuka and that he expected me to accomplish the same results in Okinawa. I was confident with the authority in writing I would be able to accomplish sure results under the General's direct command and his policies. Okinawa was in the same disorder as I had found Yokosuka. I was to have a plane to fly me back and forth. I was confident that Captain Tibbitts could operate the Yokosuka base in my absence.

I was scheduled to fly out in the morning—the plane was to depart at 6:00 A.M. At 10:00 P.M. the night before, General Ned Almond, General MacArthur's chief of staff, called me on the phone and said that the plan had been cancelled. I was never told why, but it was said that *Time* magazine had come out that day with a blast at the Army for not having done more in Okinawa and some thought that it would appear as if the Navy was cleaning up the Army's mess; after all, if I were successful, the General who had selected me for the new task would deserve the credit. Not me. But I feel that someone in Washington had interfered.

Duck hunting on the bay was a popular sport for the Occupation. The Japanese were not allowed to have guns, so the ducks were unmolested. As they flew into the bay by the millions on their way north in the spring they naturally fed on the many rice paddies, doing some damage. The Japanese strung nets on the windward levies and then scared the ducks by beating drums. The ducks flew into the nets and the Japanese obtained the needed meat for dinner. With four hunters in a powerboat, we would slowly approach the raft of ducks. If it was rough, the ducks would be restless and we would get few birds. But in fair weather, out of the millions of ducks we would bring back several dozen. There was no bag limit, but the ducks would take off in clouds well before we got within range. The result was all shots were at long range.

Captain Kirten was our expert hunter. Our parties were made up of friends from Tokyo. Bert, my son, often went with us whenever his ship was in. Miles Vaughn, National Broadcasting Company, liked to go as often as he was free to do so. We got twenty-three ducks one Sunday, but the next, none. We didn't count fish ducks, which we did not eat. We gave them to our servants, who knew how to prepare them.

Miles Vaughn was to go with me one Sunday, but he had to be back in Tokyo in time for the news broadcast to the states, so he called me up to beg off. Instead he had hired a Japanese boat and gone out from Tokyo harbor. It was an ugly day with storm clouds threatening, so we knew that hunting would be poor. We headed back in time to beat the heavy rains and high winds. Our boat was much larger than the boat Miles had hired.

Miles was caught in the storm, his boat capsized, and we

lost Miles, a good friend. The shock was great. He was one of the few correspondents who had access to the General. Men like Miles were so valuable that his loss was immediately felt.

I went to his memorial service in Tokyo and by the many important members of the Occupation, it was apparent the high esteem in which Miles was held.

Nile Temple
Ancient Arabic Order
Nobles of the Mystic Shrine
December 13, 1949

Dear Noble Decker:

It was very nice of you to send me six sets of the photographs taken on the occasion of the visit of Nile's Divan to Yokosuka, Japan.

Our visit to your home was very enjoyable and those who gathered at lunch represented a fine fellowship. What you have accomplished at Yokosuka is a fine tribute to the Navy in peace times. We will long remember our trip to Japan and all of us will continue for a long time to praise every part of the military occupation and the splendid job that is being done by our military people.

As Potentate of Nile Temple, I am highly honored at having you join the Shrine in 1949 and your membership in Nile is a credit to the entire membership.

I have been delayed in my correspondence because of the rush of business matters since returning from our trip to the Orient. Will write again before too long.

Sincerely and fraternally
yours,
Kendall L. Howe, Potentate

American Linen Supply
Company
8th Avenue North and Roy Street
Garfield 8800
Seattle
Air Mail

December 19, 1949

Dear Noble Decker:

After arriving back from Tokyo and sorting out my impressions of the hospitality that you showed us, I am mighty proud of the fact that I know you. Your decriptions of the problems that you had at the Naval Base and the wonderful job that you are doing there, impresses me with the fact that if we had more people like you in charge of our activities, this would be a wonderful world.

I am certainly amused and still can see you with the mop in your hand that tells me that you and the wonderful group of Nobles that were initiated in Tokyo are certainly a very wholesome lot.

I received some wonderful pictures that were taken at your home that Wednesday and I certainly appreciate it. They are going into my Scrap Book which will remind me of the wonderful day spent at your Headquarters.

Wishing you the compliment of the season and the very best the world affords, I am

Sincerely and fraternally,
Charlie Maryatt

Dear Bennie:

I feel, too, that I have had some little hand in assisting you in the success of your venture in Yokosuka; at least I kept the peace and tried to hold the Reds in check, even to the point of jailing them and judging them in our well regulated court. It was a wonderful assignment, the working with a fellow who would and always did back you to the hilt. Sure, I'll never forget one of my most successful and happy years of service, and I have no doubt that the success achieved aided me no little in gaining a star.

Both Girlie and myself, send along the kindest thoughts for grand people so far away, and we sincerely wish and hope for your continued good health and a happiness which you and Edwina are so worthy of—So just from the Fellers to the Deckers: Happiness and security with plenty of luck for the coming year. I know that Christmas will take care of itself, and that even the Yokosuka Japanese will feel the effects of your personal greetings.

Sincerely,
Stan Fellers

10 December, 1949

Colonel Stan Fellers, USMC
Dear Stan:

Never would this job have been so successful had it not been for your energetic and capable handling of the local police and maintaining law and order, not only on the Base but also in town.

The work you did was a tremendous share of the rebuilding of Yokosuka. I realize when they "built up my bust" that I was merely a symbol to receive the credit that was due to the many capable people who did so much for this city and for making this Base a keystone in the frontier of the United States.

Lately we have had three Congressional Committees through here and I believe that we accomplished a great deal in selling them the idea of keeping Yokosuka after the peace treaty.

There is a great trend for businesses now in Tokyo and Yokohama, particularly for these operated by foreigners, to get a foothold in Yokosuka as they deem this place a good risk after the peace treaty.

Edwina is working with the local Japanese, going to various social affairs and assisting me no end in lubricating the wheels of the Occupation.

The Base has been growing in size by the addition of new units and increased personnel. The latest addition was a C.B. detachment. The Oppama Air Facility is now under way and construction started, with the officers being ordered to it. We have a fleet of 27 ex-Russian frigates moored to buoys with no instructions as to their ultimate disposition.

By all means when you come out, our house is your home and we expect you to use it; and if by any good fortune Girlie can accompany you, we would be delighted to have her as a house guest.

Christmas this year will be on a much larger scale than ever before; however, it will never dim 1947 when we had so little and did so much because of the marvelous spirit of the people on the Base. As usual, Mrs. MacArthur opened the Toy Store, and we will have the usual big parties for the officers and men and in addition we will give 100 scholarships to deserving Japanese, for one year in our Christian schools.

The Cross that you had on your hillside is now twice as big and on top of the blockhouse from which point people for miles around will see its lights at night. It recalls to Edwina and me our loyal and good friends, Girlie and Stan Fellers.

As ever,
Benny Decker

United States Pacific Fleet
Cruiser Division Three
c/o Fleet Post Office,
San Francisco, California
24 December 1949

Dear Benny:

This past week I wrote a letter to RADM DuBose summarizing for him my situation out here. In this letter I mentioned you by name and since I am sending a copy of my letter to DuBose to VADM Joy, I thought it best to let you know about it.

"Yokosuka Naval Base. This is a large and interesting base and deserves a word. Decker has certainly done an outstanding job in cleaning it up. All training facilities for us are concentrated here—there are none at Sasebo. There is an attack teacher here which the destroyers are utilizing, small arms range, fire fighting equipment (we must furnish personnel), and a great many training films on gunnery and damage control. The UTU at Yokosuka consists of 7 officers and 14 men—they do the scheduling, assist in instructing, and we have used them as firing and other observers. This base has also made a big effort to provide decent recreation facilities for our personnel—football field, baseball diamonds, bowling alleys, three separate clubs for CPOs, POs and nonrated men, library. In addition, there is an enlisted men's club outside the base which is controlled by Commander Fleet Activities. A real and constant effort is made by Decker to make this a Far East home port for Navy people."

My letter to RADM DuBose was primarily an informal report on our training progress.

Sincerely,
Chick
(Rear Admiral C. C. Hartman)

I was very proud and happy to receive the following:

American Red Cross
Dispensary, U. S. Fleet Activities, Navy #3923

December 1949

To: Admiral & Mrs. B. W. Decker
On behalf of the patients:

We wish to express our sincere appreciation and to thank you for the help and cooperation you have rendered through the American Red Cross Unit of Services in Military Hospitals for the patients at the Dispensary, U. S. Fleet Activities this past year.

And we further wish you a Merry Christmas and the best of New Years.

Marjorie K. Bradshaw, ATFD.

24 December 1949

Memorandum
To: Commander, FltAct
Via: Lcdr. J. H. Holtom
From: Base Union President
Subject: Greetings of the Season

Representing the Base Union, I beg to present to you the Greetings of the Season and to thank you sincerely for the Christmas gifts you have so generously bestowed upon all the members of the Base Union. On the last Labor Day, you were so kind as to give rations to all Base Union members, and now you have been pleased to give each of them very nice Christmas present in the form of rations. We are very grateful for your generosity and wish to express our heartfelt thanks for it, as well as for the kindness shown us by you and LCdr. Holtom and other U. S. Naval Authorities.

We Japanese are now placed in a complex situation both internally and internationally, requiring serious attentions of the nation, in political economic, cultural and other fields of activities. The peace conference seems to be held in the course of 1950. It will be supposed that after the peace treaty this Base will continue to be as important rolls as hitherto. It is our determination to make our best, by firmly keeping in mind the noble efforts by you and other U. S. Naval Authorities, to cooperate and contribute to the reconstruction of Japan under the guidance of the U S. authorities, in order to fully answer your expectations and good will.

In presenting our Greetings of the Season and thanking for the generous Christmas gift as well as all your kindness in the past, I take this occasion to pray for the happiness and prosperity of all the U. S. authorities and families on the Base.

K. Hanyu
Base Union President

Congress of the United States
House of Representatives
Washington, D. C.

January 11, 1950

Dear Admiral Decker:

Permit me to apologize for not having written sooner to thank you for the many courtesies extended me during my recent visit to the Far East. I thoroughly enjoyed touring Yokosuka Naval Base, and appreciated receiving the pictures you sent.

I should like to take this opportunity to commend you on the magnificent job you are doing. I want you to know that, as a result of my visit, I personally feel far better acquainted with the difficult problems confronting you at this time.

If at any time I may be of service to you in any way, don't hesitate to call on me.

With every good wish for your continued success and happiness in the new year, I am

Sincerely yours,

Edward H. Kruse, Jr.

28 December 1949

Rear Admiral John W. Roper, U.S.N.
Chief of Naval Personnel
Navy Department
Washington, D. C.

Dear Johnny:

A happy and Prosperous New Year from Edwina and me to the Ropers! The season here in Japan has been most festive and the Navy at Yokosuka has thoroughly enjoyed as good a Christmas as those in the States. Eddie Ewen and Betty will be our house guests over New Year's and Chick Hartman has found it proper to be in port for the holidays. I would say our morale is high.

We are looking forward to General Robinson's inspection of the Marines on January 8 and Tommy Sprague's visit on the twelfth. Our air facility is just started due to a shortage of yen and no dollars. By June I expect it to be a well established and functioning part of our Far East Navy.

I haven't disturbed BuPers with any problems for several years for things have been operating smoothly. Even though we have no major difficulties I would like to discuss a few minor ones.

Our personnel situation is excellent for ComServPac has kept us over our allowance, thus making it possible to fulfill our mission. My only fear is that a new regime might reduce us to our allowance, in which case the multitude of additional tasks would have to go by the board. Therefore, I have asked CinCPac that our allowance be increased in recognition of our increased missions. But I do not need an increase in personnel over what I have.

This month I lost the services of Lieutenant

Glassman, who was our football coach. I earnestly request that an officer player-coach be sent to us next year, well in advance of the football season. Football in Japan is a great morale booster and a big help in combating VD. The last season was for twelve games, eleven played here on our field. The attendance never falls below 2,000!

Though we expect our boys to practice after 1500 each day and to stand their full watches, etc., we have still been successful in winning 50% of our games against larger Army units where their players are given every inducement such as fulltime assignment to football, officers for full time coaching, and three or four officers playing on a team. The forces afloat do not contribute to our team, as they have more important duties. But our Marines do more than their share.

I do hope you can send us a top notch coach who can play as well as coach.

As ever,
Benny Decker

Edwina continues:

On the sixteenth of November Mr. and Mrs. Suzuki of the Sagami Transportation invited us to see his garden. Benny inquired and was led to believe it was nothing special, just that they wanted us to see their beautiful garden. It was a surprise party in Kamakura. There were many important guests. As we walked through their beautiful garden, the path would turn and there was a hut with a delicacy. One had quail, another duck prepared differently. One had rice birds. These were very small birds roasted whole, less head, foot, and feathers. They were crisp and eaten whole—delicious! We were introduced to many delicacies we had never tasted before. One booth served cold sake, as in the old days from small, unpainted pine wood, square boxes, four inches in size. Drinking from the corner we found the sake of excellent quality, the best I have ever had. It was served as of years past. Now it is drunk hot from china cups.

This was a most unique party and one of the most beautiful. The Suzukis had been so extravagant, but I confess that Benny and I thoroughly enjoyed ourselves.

On the twenty-first of November, the Apostolic Delegate Maxmillian de Fustenberg in Tokyo invited us to lunch. The archbishop surprisingly presented Benny with the medals of the order of the Knight Commander of Saint Sylvester, bestowed upon him by Pope Pius XII. It was most impressive and a complete surprise. Benny was deeply impressed and honored.

On the twenty-seventh of November the citizens of Yokosuka honored Benny by unveiling a bust of him, made by Gozo Kawamura in the park in front of the City Hall. There was a distinguished gathering of Japanese officials and friends plus our officers and men. There were three rousing banzais by the grateful people of Yokosuka.

Program for the Unveiling Ceremony of the Bust of
Rear Admiral Benton W. Decker
Address of Y. Murata, President of the chamber of commerce and industry, at the unveiling of the bust of Admiral Benton W. Decker,

In children's playground before city hall,
Yokosuka, Japan   November 29, 1949

Admiral and Mrs. Decker, officers of the Naval Base, Minister of Foreign Affairs, Minister of Trade & Industry, Governor, Mayor, etc., Ladies, gentlemen, and children:

It is my great honour to officiate at the unveiling of the bust of Admiral Decker by the famous sculptor, Mr. Gozo Kawamura.

Plans to erect this bust to show our appreciation of Admiral and Mrs. Decker's inspiration and guidance were begun last year and we were able to complete our plans because of the great support given us by everyone in Yokosuka. I wish to express my deep gratitude for this assistance.

Miura Peninsula has been very fortunate in having relations with three great men. First, William Adams, who introduced shipbuilding into Japan. Second, Commodore Perry, who opened trade between the United States and Japan. Third, Admiral Decker, who has turned the former naval port into one of the most pro-

The bust of Rear Admiral Decker in front of City Hall.

gressive cities in Japan and has, through his benevolent administration, demonstrated the spirit of true democracy to the People of Yokosuka.

Admiral Decker came to Yokosuka in April 1946 at a time of great confusion. The city had lost its main occupation as a naval port and the future was very dark for the people of Yokosuka. Then, as always, Admiral

Decker led and assisted the people of Yokosuka with deep sympathy and understanding. It is entirely due to Admiral Decker's benevolent administration that this city has revived so quickly and become one of the most progressive cities in Japan.

Among the many improvements begun by Admiral and Mrs. Decker may be noted the new spirit inspired in the Yokosuka Women's Society, the Chamber of Commerce and Industry, the Red Cross Society, the police and the fire service and judicial and governmental bodies.

The Shinsei Yokosuka Women's Society is the first Japanese women's society to become a member of the General Federation of Women's Club, and its president has been invited to attend the 59th annual international convention to be held in Boston next year from May 29–June 3.

A model PTA has been formed in Yokosuka and a Board of Charity established on July 1947 with four commissioners headed by the Catholic Bishop Monsieur Breton. The Board segregates and distributes surveyed food and clothing to hospitals, the poor, and school children. Recently, one million yen was donated by this Board to the City for the building of Oppama Stadium. Moreover, in cooperation with the city and Women's Society, playing equipment for children, such as slides, swings, seesaws, jungle gyms, have been supplied to sixty schools and eighteen children's playgrounds.

Admiral Decker has aided in the establishment of the Seisen Girls School, a branch of the Aoyama Gakuin, the Eiko Middle School, Kwanto Gakuin and Jyochi University, and ninety-seven public schools have received his aid. Hospital facilities have shown a great improvement under the supervision of Admiral Decker's staff and it is hoped the larger hospitals will become among the finest in Japan and in the near future. Nowadays, the patients and especially diseased children have been greatly decreased due to disinfection in the whole city.

It is Admiral Decker's firm belief, which we all share, that the future of Yokosuka lies in her becoming

346

a free port and a tourist centre. Towards this end he has released Nagaura Port and its vicinity, barges & lighters, warehouses, cranes, etc., have been placed at our disposal, while reconstruction of mooring quays have been begun. Moreover, plans are being made to turn the Miura Peninsula into a nationl park and to put into service sightseeing highways from Tokyo to every part of the peninsula.

Furthermore, the Chamber of Commerce & Industry and the Industrial Club have been assisted in establishing peaceful industries, such as manufacture of electric cars, machinery, paper making, spinning, etc. More than fifty reconverted factories have been established and more than 10,000 workers have been given employment and saved their families from starvation.

For all this and much more I take this opportunity to express the gratitude of the people of Yokosuka and my hope that under the continued leadership of Admiral and Mrs. Decker, every effort will be made for the development and improvement of Yokosuka, Japan.

It gives me great pleasure to propose "Banzai" for the health and continued happiness of Admiral and Mrs. Decker. Please follow my call three times.

End

The Foreign Minister's address at the unveiling of Benny's statue:

Four years have passed since Yokosuka City took the first step towards its reconstruction as a peaceful and commercial city after the war.

In spite of various unfavourable conditions, the city is ever progressing towards prosperity. This is a matter of deep admiration and pleasure on my part.

It is to be noted that at this time my esteemed Admiral Decker, as Commander of the United States Naval Base of Yokosuka and as a true friend of the citizens of Yokosuka, has displayed remarkable leadership and rendered generous assistance to both private and public institutions as well as to the citizens of this city. Therefore, it is no exaggeration to say that the present state of Yokosuka is all due to Admiral Decker's efforts.

It is just and fitting that the citizens of Yokosuka should have resolved to erect the Admiral's bust in the center of the city to commemorate his noble personality forever. And it is my great pleasure to participate in this significant ceremony by sending my greetings.

On this occasion I wish for the continued good health of Admiral Decker and expect at the same time that the citizens of Yokosuka will fully strive for the further prosperity and welfare of the city under the guidance of Admiral Decker.

Shigeru Yoshida
Foreign Minister

29 November 1949

A congratulatory message by the minister of international trade and industry:

I am very happy that I can today attend the unveiling ceremony of Rear Admiral Decker who is commanding our utmost reverence and affection.

Thrived once as a seat of naval base and suffered severe war damages, this city, almost crippled at the war's end, was at a loss what to do for some time, suffering difficulties to find a means of its reconstruction.

It was at this time, April 1946, that Rear Admiral Decker arrived at this city as Commander in chief of Yokosuka Naval Base, amid the anxiety and expectation of the citizens. Since then, he, together with Mrs. Decker, Commander Higgins and others, has spared no efforts on a firm and sound guiding principle to wipe militaristic colours out of this city and start it from scratch as a democratic city. It goes without saying that all the surprisingly great achievement be made, overcoming the post war confusion, in relief works, rehabilitation of education facilities, etc., will forever be remembered by the Japanese. However, the matter that impressed me most was his industrial policy. More concretely, immediately followed his taking his office, he showed the citizens how Yokosuka could survive as a peaceful and industrial city, by throwing open buildings and other former military facilities at Nagaura and Oppama to enterprisers, industrial or commercial who, on the strength of this opening, have come to establish more than fifty companies. Through this, not only could above ten thousand persons obtain jobs and were saved from starvation but the citizen came at long last to be able to see the road they should take and look for a bright spot in their future.

For this, with you, of Yokosuka, I should like to extend my hearty gratitude. Cities, once existed for continuing war, are converting into ones to turn abundantly out products for the peaceful Japan. Indeed, it was a sad thing that the nations of the world that should love each other hated each other, broke into war and brought havoc on many places.

It is most heartening for us who have thrown away arms and started as a peaceful nation to have been able to touch the magnaminity and human love manifested by Rear Admiral Decker.

An attempt to dedicate the statue of Rear Admiral Decker in memory of his work is timely one and nothing can make me happier than this.

One chief petty officer exclaimed at the ceremony, "A bust! Imagine that! The old man isn't even dead yet!"

The Japanese Post Office issued a special cancellation on mail that day, showing a picture of Benny's bust.

> Shunkogakuen
> Koyabemachi
> Yokosuka
> December 1, 1949

Rear admiral B. W. Decker

My Lord

I am very much obliged to you for sending us presents the other day. I will repay anothers kindness when I grow up. Japanese had wrong war. In spite of our wrong deeds. You are looking after us. Thank you very much. I should like to do much for the peace with American boys. Please give my regards to American boys.

> Good-by
> Susumu Kasai (15 years old)

Chapter XIV

WE SELL THE BASE

In 1939 I was navigator of the USS *Astoria* which brought the ashes of the former Japanese ambassador from Annapolis to Yokohama. President Roosevelt had planned this to win the goodwill of Japan. When we arrived the Japanese entertained us royally. The Navy gave a party in their Navy club. This building now became the Masonic lodge. My liaison officer, Mr. Takaoka, was present as a member of the Foreign Office. He had saved a picture of the fifty-nine who were present at that time. In memory of Ambassador Saito, we invited the widow and her daughter and son-in-law and some of my officers to a luncheon at Tadodai, and also the Japanese survivors and their wives, which included many notable Japanese. We had about eighty guests. After lunch the new film *Task Force*, a war picture of the aerial fighting with many actual combat shots, was shown. The Japanese admirals were all amazed at what they saw and exclaimed that they never realized things were as portrayed. They all enjoyed the show and were appreciative of the reunion of their friends. And I was delighted to see them once more.

It was difficult for me to realize that these distinguished and well-educated naval officers were our former enemies.

Mr. Kitazawa had escorted Saito's ashes in the *Astoria*. We had grown very fond of him and of course I was deeply indebted to Mr. Takaoka for getting all of these good people assembled in my home.

Mrs. Saito and her daughter and son-in-law, Mr. Kagei, were most delightful company. I enjoyed having them as our guests. In Mrs. Saito's letter she stated "in memory of the *Astoria*" probably inspired by modesty. It was in memory of our friend, Ambassador Saito.

February 5th, 1950

Rear Admiral and Mrs. Decker,

I do not know how to express my sincere gratitude

for the lovely luncheon you had for us as a Reunion in memory of the Astoria.

Ten years seems so long ago, but I shall never forget your kind hospitality. I know my husband was with us in spirit that day, and now joins me in thanking you once again.

Today I received the pictures taken on that day. I will treasure atmosphere of that Sunday afternoon at your beautiful residence. I recalled so vividly in my mind the great honor bestowed on my husband at the time of his death by President Roosevelt.

You may be sure, dear Rear Admiral and Mrs. Decker, those as a memory of the happy Reunion, thank you so much.

Very sincerely yours,
Miyo Saito

Dear Admiral Decker,

My wife and I wish to thank you and Mrs. Decker for your kind hospitality on the 15th January "Astoria Reunion". We have enjoyed your entertainment heartily and we only wished that it had no end. Moreover, it was very impressive for me to have the opportunity of visiting Yokosuka, for I have been the Chief of the Staff of the Yokosuka Naval Station during the late war—from March 1944 to May 1945. I remember the beautiful scene of your garden especially at the time of azalea and cherry blossom. If we could have the opportunity to see your beautiful garden again in spring, it would be beyond our delight.

We cannot thank you enough for your kindness in sending us the pictures which were taken on that memorial day. They will remain as a valuable souvenir to us and a symbol of your kind thoughts.

With our united kindest regards to you and Mrs. Decker.

Yours sincerely,
T. Yokoi

95, 1-chome, Koyamadai
Shinagawa-ku, Tokyo
February 8, 1950
Admiral B. W. Decker
Commander
Fleet Activities, Yokosuka
Dear Admiral Decker:

It was very thoughtful of you to invite me for the reunion of the Astoria and also to send me pictures which were taken at the occasion. Please accept my heartfelt thanks. The party was really wonderful and I enjoyed every minute of your kind hospitality. The movie "Task Force" was very impressive as I had been longing to see it. My wife is very sorry that she missed such a good party. She is all right now. But my third daughter took cold and is staying in bed instead of my wife.

I saw Admiral Sherman at Admiral Joy's room the other day and had a talk with him for a few minutes as I knew him at the Manila Conference in 1945. He said he was deeply impressed with your achievement in Yokosuka especially Navy Yard.

My wife joins me for expressing our thanks for your kind invitation and tendering our best regards to you and Mrs. Decker.

Sincerely yours,
Ichiro Yokoyama

Extracts from a report by the forces afloat:

17 February 1950

There are many other aspects of the material game in Yokosuka which are working to our advantage. Take the matter of canvas—we get canvas work at about one quarter of the cost to us at home which is a considerable saving in funds in itself. Then Yokosuka is doing a big job in overhauling ship machinery which requires periodic breaking down for repair, i.e., pumps, valves, rewinding motors, etc., all of which will save either tender or yard time and money. Then lagging is another item which the destroyers have had accomplished at a big saving in labor. The ships have also worked on

352

tanks and voids—some of this work is usually done at the yard. In addition to the above a great deal of repair work has been done on typewriters, binoculars, clocks, and boats.

Burzynski informs me that each job submitted to him is decided upon on its own merits—that he can only provide limited technical assistance for ordnance and electronic equipment because of its classified nature—but that he can provide unlimited assistance for machinery, structural and sheet metal overhaul. In Burzynski's opinion if a destroyer has a 6 to 8 day availability period at Yokosuka it is comparable to a $10,000.00 U. S. Overhaul. Labor is not charged to our allotment here. I believe that what we accomplish here will result in a direct money saving for our tender and navy yard overhauls at facilities to the utmost and I will see each skipper personally about this.

We have certainly had excellent cooperation from the officers of the Fleet Activities at Yokosuka and their repair department has been most anxious to do all the work we have requested. I have not had a single complaint from any ship concerning the quality or quantity of work being done for us. It has been suggested, though, that we should not build up this base's workload to the detriment of our own Navy Yards. However you specifically mentioned completion of "Forces Afloat" alterations in addition to normal upkeep and I do not see why we need clash with our own Navy Yard boosters on this. I only mention this point as it is another one of those "angles" which was brought up in conference. Further this base will not be useful to us in an emergency unless it is reasonably well oiled and ready to go. Any money saved here can be used at home and will be I'm sure.

U.S.S. TOLEDO (CA-133)

14 January 1950

From: Commanding Officer, U.S.S. TOLEDO (CA-133)
To: Commander U.S. Fleet Activities, Yokosuka, Japan
Subject: Services of U.S. Fleet Activities, Yokosuka, Japan, appreciation of
1. The Commanding Officer upon being detached

wishes to thank the Commander U.S. Fleet Activities, Yokosuka, Japan for the excellent services provided this ship since its arrival in the area in early November.

2. It has been noted that the Ship Repair Unit, the Supply Department, the Underway Training Unit, the Harbor Master services, and in fact, all departments of the Fleet Activities have been very cooperative and accommodating in providing services of all types as they were requested by the ship. This service and assistance has materially aided the ship in meeting its operational commitments and at the same time remain in a good state of upkeep and repair.

3. All the officers and crew of the ship appreciate the opportunity to take advantage of the recreational facilities provided on the base. Many enjoyable hours have been spent in the area both because of these recreational facilities and because of the friendly hospitality offered by the personnel attached to the base.

4. Yokosuka has become indeed our home away from home.

R. E. Arison

Commander Air Force, Pacific Fleet
U. S. Naval Air Station
San Diego 35, California
30 January 1950

Dear Benny and Edwina:

Our visit to Yokosuka, climaxed by lunch in your house, was one of the most unforgettable occasions during our West Pactrip. It was a great experience to have an opportunity to talk to both of you. Not the least of your kindnesses, of course, was to arrange for us to do our shopping under the most favourable conditions. Ev was delighted with the tribute silk, which I must admit was a little surprise to me because I am not a very good picker. Without Edwina's help, I might not have done so well.

Needless to say, I am more impressed than ever with the magnificent job you are doing, Benny. I could kick myself for not having seen your bust in the park, such an abundantly deserved recognition of a great

American. I am still chuckling over the paintings of your ancestors.

Although I hope you will have many years of duty ahead of you in Japan, when you do come home, I hope we will have the opportunity of joining forces with you again. Mrs. Sprague joins me in kindest regards to you both.

Sincerely,
Tommy
(Vice Admiral Sprague)

A Japanese newspaper reported:
BREAKWATER FOR THE RED CURRENT IN ASIA (?)
THE SENSATIONAL PROPOSITION
The proposition to make Yokosuka a base of the U. S. Navy which was made by Rear Admiral Decker. Commander Fleet Activities, Yokosuka created an extraordinary sensation throughout the country. The Naval Base of Yokosuka suddenly appeared in a close-up before the people's eyes. Just then the problem of a military base was being discussed at the Diet in connection with the problems of self-defense and security of the country, and a group of 60 educators opposed to offer a military base to another country and shouted about strict neutrality. They cried, "How Japan, who dreams amity and peace can offer a military base?" But this problem of offering a military base is neither a problem for only America nor a problem for only Japan. It is going to be the only key to the fate of the whole Far East, and also of the two worlds dividing the Earth into two. It is not a mere idealistic theory of the constitution, but a problem of the reality General Bradley said the other day, "Security of Japan after making peace is a problem for Japanese themselves." However, it has no meaning that Japanese people can also decide on the problem of the military base. For, decision of this problem depends on peace, and conclusion of peace treaty depends on the status of international affairs.
"NO EXPANSION OF AREA", ADMIRAL DECKER STRESSES CITIZENS' LIBERTY
Will the plan of Yokosuka Naval Base be

materialized? If so, what will become of citizens of Yokosuka? To these questions, Admiral Decker gave the following answer:

"It is the U.S. Government and Congress that decides whether or not Yokosuka is kept as a Naval Base after the peace treaty is concluded. The United States has always taken such policies that would create warm friendship between America and Japan. So, even after Yokosuka is made a naval base, there will be no change at all in granting liberty to the citizens as in the present. The present U.S. Naval Base of Yokosuka occupies only 10% of the former naval port and 5% of the whole city area, and the other is released entirely for industry and free living of citizens. We have no slightest notion of extending the area of the Base in the future. One Base in Yokosuka will be sufficient for defense of America and the East. Now democratization of Yokosuka is completed. Citizens are enjoying strenuously. I want to add that construction of a naval base is possible only in a really democratic, friendly city."

A Marine unit should be on alert and available for deployment in the Far East, and Yokosuka looked like the correct place, using Camp McGill, evacuated by the Army. I "planted" the idea with General Robinson, knowing that this would cause it to be considered.

Department of the Navy
Headquarters United States Marine Corps
Washington 25, D. C.

6 February 1950

Dear Admiral Decker:

Before starting on the business end of this letter, I want to take this opportunity to thank both you and Mrs. Decker for being so nice to me while I was in Yokosuka. I enjoyed the dinner, to say nothing of the personally conducted tour through your home, more than I can express.

As I remember it there were but two items that you wished me to get answers to for you. Also, as I remember, I guaranteed answers but not necessarily good ones. The first item pertained to relief for Colonel

Lasswell. Attached you will find copies of the answers I received on this question.

The most important item of which you wished information was, of course, your project to have a unit of the Fleet Marine Force stationed at Yokosuka. This item was thoroughly studied by the Marine Corps. In fact, I have the study in front of me and it is several pages long. As it has been classified SECRET I cannot go into detail on the pros and cons. In substance the final decision was along the following lines:

a. The decision to assign Fleet Marine Force units to Yokosuka would have to be made by the Joint Chiefs of Staff.

b. That I should not be given authority to inform you that the Marine Corps would not oppose such assignment until the subject received prior approval of Admiral Sherman as his support would be necessary when the proposal reaches the Joint Chiefs of Staff. Note: I do not know whether the subject was broached to Admiral Sherman before his departure to Japan or not. I am of the opinion that it was, but merely in passing and was not discussed.

c. The Marine Corps' position is not to commit ourselves but to leave the post treaty set up in Japan to the Joint Chiefs of Staff where the decision rightfully rests. In making this decision, the Marine Corps feels that we can be confident that Admiral Sherman will work toward reinstating the Navy in its traditional role in the Far East, which would require our assistance in carrying out. Note: The subject has been considered under a classified status by the Marine Corps. As you originated the idea, however, the decision to maintain it in this classification is, of course, up to you.

If the subject matter was discussed with Admiral Sherman, I would appreciate knowing the results of your conversation.

I am sorry that these answers are not too satisfactory and again allow me to thank you for your many kindnesses.

Sincerely,
Ray A. Robinson
Major General, U. S. Marine Corps

357

U. S. S. TOLEDO (CA-133)

9 February 1950

Dear Admiral Decker,

I desire to express the sincere appreciation of the officers and men of the U.S.S. Toledo for the cordial hospitality and many courtesies extended during our stay at Yokosuka.

The officers and men of the repair facilities of the Commander Fleet Activities were outstanding in their performance of work required by this vessel. All work requests were completed in record time and to the complete satisfaction of the Commanding Officer and the Heads of Departments concerned.

The excellent recreation facilities made available to the Toledo personnel were thoroughly enjoyed by all hands. The various clubs were part of the many outstanding facilities that brought about the high standards of morale maintained by the officers and men throughout our tour of duty in Japanese waters.

While many ports were visited during our tour in Japanese waters, Yokosuka was considered to be our Japanese Home Port by the entire ship's company.

Very Respectfully,
R. F. Stout
Captain, U.S. Navy
Commanding

Edwina interjects:

On the twenty-ninth of January the USS *Boxer* arrived with our son, Lieutenant B. W. Decker, Jr. aboard. The newspaper reported that all protocol was forgotten, because Ben kissed me before he saluted his father. Our son Bert took Ben to Patricia Fox's announcement party in Tokyo when she announced her engagement to Lieutenant Alexander Haig, USA. He is now a general. Patricia was a beautiful blond, like her mother, Betty; she was the daughter of General Alonzo P. Fox.

The next day I took our son Ben to the Tsushima School for the dedication of the new movie screen and curtains. The children were so enthusiastic and happy over the occasion.

Then our son Bert gave a dinner party for Ben in our house, the Tadodai. Undoubtedly a first of that type for that distinguished residence. Admiral Berkey, Ted and Jane Kilkenney, and Benny and I had dinner upstairs while the young folks danced downstairs.

While Benny was in Tokyo at a stag luncheon for the Joint Chiefs given by General MacArthur, Commander and Mrs. Gray of the British Embassy came to lunch, and later Prince and Princess Hiroshi and Princess Lee with Mr. Nakagana and the Takaokas called. On the second of February we went to the Imperial Plaza to witness the parade for the Joint Chiefs of Staff, then to the Press Club and on to Admiral Joy's for dinner with the Joint Chiefs.

United States Pacific Fleet
Headquarters of the Commander Naval Forces Marianas
20 January 1950

Dear Benny:

We will never forget our visit with you and Edwina and our sightseeing, shopping, and partying under the sponsorship of the Deckers. I am sure we have never been guests of more hospitable and delightful hosts.

In spite of the fact that the AirPac party had visited the Philippines en route to Guam, the major part of their conversation while here was in connection with the superb job that you have done at Yokosuka. Tommy Sprague in particular will talk with Sherman about it in San Diego prior to the JCS departure for the Far East in hopes of persuading him, if at all possible, to take the JCS party to your naval base. I just want to put in writing my hearty sincere congratulations upon what you have accomplished during your tenure as king of the naval occupation group in the Yokosuka area.

Please give my very best regards to the Tibbitts, the Butlers, the Lasswells, and the other members of your staff who were so delightful to us during our visit. We both send our love to Edwina and our very warmest to Bert and to you. Our thanks again to your household staff who were so solicitous over our every need. Again with many, many thanks and all best wishes.

Most sincerely,
E. C. Ewen
Rear Admiral, U.S.N.

As an example of the procedure and planning for such a visit I include the routine of the Joint Chiefs of Staff:

COMMANDER FLEET ACTIVITIES
JOINT CHIEFS OF STAFF VISIT TO YOKOSUKA
2 February 1950

1. General Omar BRADLEY, Chairman of Joint Chiefs of Staff, General J. L. COLLINS, Chief of Staff of U. S. Army and Admiral F. SHERMAN, CNO, will visit Yokosuka, Thursday, 2 February 1950. They will be accompanied by the following members of their Staffs—CAPT N. K. DIETRICH, USN, CDR BEACH and LTCOL F. R. ZIERATH, USA.

2. Admiral C. T. Joy (ComNavFE) will accompany them.

3. The following officers will be present in the Commandant's Office to meet the Joint Chiefs of Staff:

RADM B. W. DECKER	ComFltAct
CAPT H. E. DAY	Capt of Yard and Operations Officer
CAPT J. B. BUTLER	Medical Officer
CAPT R. O. BURZYNSKI	Repair Officer
COL A. B. LASSWELL	CO, Marine Barracks
CDR A. B. REED	Supply Officer
CDR F. L. GONZALEZ, JR.	Dental Officer
CDR B. F. SUCH	CO, NAF, Yokosuka

4. The following are invited to attend all or any of the program, and for luncheon with the Joint Chiefs of Staff:

VADM R. S. Berkey	Com7th Task Flt
RADM C. C. HARTMAN	ComCruDiv-3

5. The following itinerary is suggested, based on the Joint Chiefs of Staffs departing from Tokyo at 0800:

0900   RADM DECKER, CDR SUCH AND LCDR BRADY meet Joint Chiefs at border. Drive through Air Facility, Yokosuka without stopping.

0915   Stop at E.M. Club for walk through lower deck.

0920   General BRADLEY, General COLLINS and ADM SHERMAN arrive at Administration Building. Render honors and break 4 star flag. Proceed to Commandant's Office for Orientation and to meet Heads of Departments.

360

0950	Tour base
	Lead car ADM SHERMAN, ADM JOY AND ADM DECKER
	1st car General BRADLEY and ADM BER-KEY
	3rd car CAPT DAY, CAPT DIETRICH and CDR BEACH
	4th car COL LASSWELL and LTCOL F. R. ZIERATH, USA
0955	Visit Command Cave
	Drive through Public Works rehabilitation garage to PO and CPO Club pointing out gymnasium and roller skating rink, into Repair Facility, along Forrestal Seawall. Drive by LSU in reserve. Point out Azuma Island and Russian Frigates.
1005	Drive by Dry Dock #5, net depot DD4 through A49 and A48. Stop and look at foundry.
1015	Drive along Piedmont Pier past Drydock #6 Then drive through Supply Department, J-39.
1020	Drive past Buoy Farm, Signal Tower and Chicken Farm. Point out Ammunition Depot.
1030	Point out ComUnit #35. Stop at Commissary Store, then to Recreation Bay, turning right on First Street. Past Chapel to Snack Bar. Walk through to Gift Shop.
1100	Depart Gift Shop, visit General Mess Hall.
1110	Visit Hospital and Dental Clinic
1130	Visit BOQ and have the rooms on 2nd deck ready
	Refreshments in Fleet Bar

The night before the Joint Chiefs came to Yokosuka we were all at dinner in Admiral Joy's house in Tokyo. Admiral Sherman wanted some publicity for the next day's visit to Yokosuka. Admiral Joy turned to me, and I turned to the telephone. I called the Press Club and got its President on the phone. He assured me that he would have it all arranged. He did a perfect job.

On arrival at the base we diverted to Admiral Berkey's cruiser alongside the Piedmont Pier and, by previous ar-

The Joint Chiefs of Staff visit the Base—*L to R:* Rear Admiral Decker, General Bradley, Vice Admiral Berkey, Admiral Sherman, General Twining, Vice Admiral Joy, Rear Admiral Hartman.

rangements, the forward turret guns were elevated and we posed beneath them. Rosecrans (INS and NBC) arranged the admirals with me on the left. Later I asked "Rosey" why me on the left? "In the list under the picture your name will be first!" It was a great picture published throughout the states and certainly was all Navy. Admiral Sherman was well pleased.

We then went to the Administration Building for briefing. I never objected to the correspondents being present, but Admiral Sherman did, so I cleared the room of the press. They understood the need and made no objection, and later joined us on the tour of the base. I was confident that none would violate security and each would use good judgment in anything reported.

During my twenty minutes of briefing I emphasized that the biggest aircraft carrier ever built was constructed in 1945 in Drydock Number 6. Admiral Sherman came up to me afterwards and congratulated me on bringing out that most important point. I then recalled that there was much discussion in Washington as to the building of a new carrier and how big it should be.

We then toured the base and arrived at my residence for a formal luncheon. Edwina tells the story.

My husband had been working for four years to convince the Navy and the United States that we should keep Yokosuka. There had been great opposition in certain circles, but finally the day had arrived for making the "sale" to our Joint Chiefs. When the inspection was over they had gathered at our house for a formal luncheon. Most of the stars in the Far East Army and Navy were there. Generals Omar Bradley, chairman of the Joint Chiefs of Staff; J. Lawton Collins, chief of staff of the United States Army; Lt. General Walton Walker, 8th Army commander; and Admiral Forrest Sherman, Naval chief of operations; Vice Admirals R. S. Berkey, Commander 7th Fleet and C. T. Joy, Far East naval commander; Rear Admiral C. C. Hartman, and others. There were twenty eight Admirals and Generals, Benny's chief of staff, his wife, and myself. The luncheon was "close the deal."

As usual, I merely told the house manager to prepare luncheon for thirty-four guests and I gave him the seating arrangement. I always left the menu to the house manager as his dinners had always been outstanding, so I dismissed the matter from my mind.

The stars glittered wherever you looked. As we went into luncheon, our pretty little Japanese girls in their dainty kimonos smiled and greatly impressed "the visiting guests."

The courses were served skillfully, starting with a delicious onion soup, then a choice salad, to be followed by the main course with cherries jubilee for dessert. When the main course was served I expected either filet or squab. Instead we got sauerkraut and wieners! I glanced at my husband and I could see that he was at first amazed and then upset. My mind flashed back to a month ago at a luncheon when our VIP guest had said his favorite dish was sauerkraut and wieners and he asked Benny if he didn't like them. Being polite, he agreed. The house manager was standing close by and evidently overheard the conversation. Thinking that he would surprise us with something very delectable and choice, he had ordered from the United States a special shipment. And now with great pride he was serving it at the most important luncheon we had ever given!

My husband was about to apologize to our guests when Admiral Sherman interrupted to say,

"We have been eating chicken, filets, and chicken until we are satiated. Thank goodness one man has sense enough to feed us good old sauerkraut and wieners!"

With much applause and toasting, Benny had become a hero. My luncheon was a success and our house manager was beaming.

Admiral Sherman's sense of humor saved the day. The Chiefs bought the base! And Benny was jubilant. Within six months the good judgment of the Chiefs of Staff would be fully justified, when the war in Korea surprised the world!

The Joint Chiefs of Staff
Washington, D. C.

February 15, 1950

Dear Benny:

Thank you very much for your letter of 7 February forwarding to me your memorandum on propellers available at Yokosuka and photographs of my recent visit to the activities under your command. This visit was most interesting and I greatly enjoyed our brief trip. First hand information on the facilities of Yokosuka and of its potential value is of the greatest help to me.

Our trip home was very pleasant and I appreciate your offer to make any purchases for me which I might desire in the future.

Please remember me to Mrs. Decker and again may I express my appreciation of your courtesies to me and to the official party of the Joint Chiefs of Staff. All hands express themselves as most favorably impressed by the appearance and efficiency of fleet activities at Yokosuka.

Cordially yours,
Forrest Sherman

The Joint Chiefs of Staff
Washington 25, D. C.

14 February 1950

Dear Admiral Decker:

Thank you very much for sending me the group of pictures taken during our visit to Yokosuka. They turned out remarkably well, and I am particularly glad to have them. I know that Mrs. Bradley will also enjoy seeing them and will want them for a scrapbook she is keeping. It was good to see you while we were there, and this note brings with it my kindest personal regards and warm good wishes.

Sincerely,
Omar Bradley

Benny visited Oshima Island where the Navy had a Loran station which he wanted to inspect, informally. It was about twenty miles south of the base at the entrance of Tokyo Bay. The island was famous for those frustrated lovers who purchased one way tickets to the island and hand in hand terminated their earthly problems by jumping into the volcano. Senior Army officers enjoyed hunting quail, dove, and pheasant on this large island. Benny's bird dog, Tomo Dachi, was in heaven. They returned the nineteenth with many birds and also with a good supply of camellia oil for our servants. The girls used it for their hair and also it was used in cooking, but during the war it had become very scarce. Oshima was covered with many camellia trees lining the roads as well as in groves. The red blossoms were dropping upon the dirt roads, making them heavily sprinkled with red petals. The seed pods then grew large enough to harvest and squeeze for their oil.

General Headquarters
Far East Command
Public Information Office

21 February 1950

Immediate Release:

Rear Admiral Benton W. Decker, Commander U. S. Naval Fleet Activities, Yokosuka, will present 546,840 yen to the Yokosuka Kyosai Hospital in a Washington's Birthday ceremony at the hospital tomorrow at 1:00 p.m.

The gift, representing gross receipts from New Year's Eve parties held at clubs at the naval base, will be used to endow one bed at the hospital for a period of two years. A private room has been set aside and will be known as the George Washington Room.

In the room will hang a Gilbert Stuart portrait (copy) of the first president of the United States. On the door of the room will be a plaque in both English and Japanese reading, in part:

IN MEMORY OF GEORGE WASHINGTON THIS ROOM IS DEDICATED TO CHARITY AND ENDOWED TO PROVIDE FREE MEDICAL CARE TO THE UNFORTUNATE FOR A PERIOD OF TWO YEARS AS AN EXPRESSION OF FIRM FAITH AND GOODWILL TOWARD THE PEOPLE OF JAPAN BY THE PERSONNEL OF FLEET ACTIVITIES YOKOSUKA IN RECOGNITION OF THE ACHIEVEMENT AND PROGRESS OF THIS HOSPITAL SINCE 1945.

Mrs. Decker will unveil the plaque. Dr. Toma Kurabara, superintendent of the hospital, will accept the gift on behalf of the hospital.

Edwina continues:

Washington's Birthday was something special. The Navy had collected sufficient yen from many social affairs at the various clubs to be able to endow for two years a room in the Keosi Hospital. The officers and men of the base dedicated it to the memory of George Washington, for charitable cases. After a speech by Benny and one by Captain Butler, the originator of the idea, I unveiled a beautiful bronze plaque. It was a day to be remembered by all.

The next day we attended a Washington Birthday Ball in Yokohama where the Army was celebrating. It was of interest to see Prince and Princess Takamatsu there. They were very democratic and had won our admiration. The Japanese admired them greatly.

We attended, in the Azume Trading Company, the blessing of the boats they were building for members of the Occupation. Four Shinto Priests in elaborate robes performed the ritual.

The boats were Admiral Berkey's powerboat and Benny's Luder's yawl. At last our plans to have a small boat builder were well advanced. Many orders were coming in, and when Korea hit, Admiral Berkey's idea paid off. The company was growing rapidly and was capable of building small boats of all kinds, including landing craft and commercial fishing boats. Benny was happy to have his boat, the *Golden Bird* (Kin no tobi) blessed. Her keel had been blessed in a Buddhist ceremony; now it was blessed by the Shinto; and when launched, the Catholics blessed her. He had protection in all companies!

February twenty-fifth was another day to be remembered. We invited the Prince and Princess Takamatsu, Princess Mikasa (wife of the Emperor's youngest brother), Mr. and Mrs. Murata, president of our chamber of commerce, and our senior officers to dinner prior to seeing *The Mikado* in the EM Club. It was put on by an outstanding Japanese company. The scenery was superb, as were the magnificent costumes. Though we had seen this operetta in the states many times, this was by far the best. In no way could it be improved. Several times an ad lib on the Occupation brought down the house, mostly sailors and officers from the base. The Prince and Princesses had a thoroughly enjoyable time, as they understood the humor and the music was the very best. They said that it was not possible for them to see the show in Tokyo, but in Yokosuka it was acceptable. The cast, audience, and ourselves all had a delightful evening.

February 27, 1950

Dear Mrs. Decker:

I and Mrs. Murata would like to express our hearty thanks to Admiral and Mrs. Decker's kind invitation for the excellent dinner party and also wonderful opera on

367

the last Saturday evening with the American officers, Prince and Princess Takamatsu and Princess Mikasa.

We have enjoyed and impressed very much which we have never been for long years. We, the citizens of Yokosuka, appreciate you very much that you have always led and given us the glorious charity at all times as well as the greatest aid and assistance to the recreation on our lives.

I thank you again from our hearts.

Very sincerely yours,
Hisayo Murata

Our home was always alive with guests for luncheon or dinner. The lunches were usually for eight or ten. Benny had polished an act that caused interest and conversation. It was a show of preparing the salad dressing. Our Chieko would bring in the condiments and with a flourish, Benny would go through a ritual that was most impressive. The guests were always attentive and enjoyed the show. One day Benny was so deeply engrossed in his conversation with his guest on his right that he failed to note Chieko's arrival. After a suitable wait Chieko proceeded to mix the dressing. To Benny's surprise, it was completed and served by the time conversation lagged. And it was just as good as Benny's. Chieko was most capable and immediately was promoted to number one salad mixer!

The students of the Tanaka English School invited us to a musical at the EM Club to honor Mrs. Toshiko Tanaka, who was to attend the International Women's Association.

Mrs. Tanaka, the president of the Shinsei Women's Club, was invited to the United States for the annual meeting of the International Women's Club. Her students in Yokosuka wrote us a letter. We quote part of it.

March 6, 1950

Admiral and Mrs. Decker:

It is the common belief of us her students that her fine personality and high educational background coupled by her fluent English will do a great deal in promoting friendship between the United States and Japan. In order to congratulate her for receiving this invitation, as well as to encourage her, we are giving a great musical concert. Both the orchestra and the soloist are the best available in Japan today.

Yours very sincerely,
All Student of Tanaka's
English School
(representative)
Makoto TAKEDA

The head of the Women's Club made an interesting comment on a news item by Russel Brines.

2 March 1950

I think Mr. Brines is very fair but I think he does not stress sufficiently the important role awakened Japanese women are playing. I firmly believe that the women will tip the scales in favor of democracy when the time of reckoning comes.

Toshi Tanaka

P.S. Women are somewhat like the Communists—they are not displaying all their strength—it would be "undignified" but it is there and can be used when emergency arises.

Department of the Army
Washington

6 March 1950

Dear Admiral Decker:

I should like to express for Colonel Robinson, Colonel Tynes and myself our deep appreciation of the opportunity of visiting the Naval Base at Yokosuka and for the many courtesies extended to us by you and your staff. I feel sure that the day spent with you was one of the most enjoyable of our entire Pacific trip. We were particularly impressed by the efficient manner in which your medical problems are being handled, by Captain Butler and by the enthusiasm which he displays in accomplishing his mission.

I should also like to express for the Surgeon General of the Army our appreciation for the medical service which you are rendering to Army personnel as well as to Army dependents.

I have taken pleasure in reporting my visit with you to Admiral Swanson and he asked to be remembered most warmly to you.

Trusting that I may have the opportunity some time to reciprocate for your many courtesies and with best wishes and kind personal regards, I remain

Sincerely,
George Armstrong
Major General, USA
Deputy Surgeon General

When I broke my Achilles tendon, an army surgeon came to Yokosuka immediately and with my surgeon, Dr. Geise, repaired it. Today it is as good as new. The Army more than repaid me for my efforts to cooperate.

On March tenth Commander Such, the new commanding officer of our air unit and Admiral JOY placed the new unit into commission. It was located in Oppama. We were beginning to grow in size as well as in importance. The commissioning party with wives was then taken to the Tadodai, our house, for lunch.

Rear Admiral T. B. Inglis, Commander of the training Command Pacific, was our houseguest on the eleventh.

United States Pacific Fleet
Commander Training Command
San Diego, California
22 March 1950

Dear Admiral:

Throughout my recent inspection of the Underway Training Element, Japan, I was impressed with the excellent and efficient support furnished to the Element by the Fleet Activities, Yokosuka.

Please convey my appreciation to your officers and men on their assistance. You have made it possible for our organization to raise Fleet training and readiness standards in the Far East.

I consider that the Element's excellent inspection performance record, and high morale reflect the cooperation and understanding of your command in carrying out our common mission of serving the operating forces of the Fleet.

Sincerely,
Thos. B. Inglis
Rear Admiral, U.S. Navy

Edwina reports:

On January eleventh there was a meeting in the Station Theater for the distribution of scholarships to our missionary schools. The four Christian schools were having a difficult time and had informed Benny that they might have to close down for lack of funds. He asked Captain Bursynski and Commander Johnson's wife to be a committee of two to raise funds. Commander Johnson was a dentist. I was told that thirty dollars would pay for the schooling of one child or youth for a year and would include a lunch each school day! He gave thirty dollars for a boy and thirty dollars for a girl, one to be in a Catholic and one in a Protestant school. These two capable people reported that they had raised $5,300.

They now distributed the awards and each youth came forward to receive his or her certificate. It was an inspiring affair and we were informed that the schools would now survive for another year.

Years later Benny received a letter and a beautiful plate from the Catholic boy whom we had sponsored. He wrote, "We have a saying that when danger is over God is forgotten, but I have not forgotten you!"

Judge Advocate Section
Headquarters Eighth Army
APO-343
Yokohama, Japan
24 February 1950
-Personal-

Dear Admiral Decker:

I thought that you might be interested in the enclosed copy of an Oklahoma Newspaper. I recall that I was at Tokyo on the evening that you were presented with this award.

May I say as one 32nd Degree Mason to another

371

that ever since I have been in Japan I have heard more and more people come to realize that your work here is probably the most outstanding work that has been done.

We need more men like yourself who have foresight to meet complicated problems as you have met them, but such men are few.

It does one good to see a spirit and a determination like yours. Congratulations Admiral Decker; you are doing a wonderful job.

Fraternally yours,
Isaiah O. Hagen
Major 0-246742
Judge Advocate Sec.
Hq. 8th Army
APO-343

Ray Spencer, the Coca-Cola representative in Japan, lived in a delightful home in Fujisawa. We stopped to call on Ray and Mary. Much to our surprise, Ray brought out a splendid white horse. He said it was one of the Emperor's thirty-two white horses and was named Snow Ball. It was perfectly tamed and trained by the Emperor's groom. He offered our son a ride, which Bert immediately accepted. He was thrilled and delighted with this unusual opportunity.

Our great sculptor, Gozo Kawamura, died of cancer on March first. Chaplain, Commander Beukema, conducted the service with the Reverend M. Takemoto and the Reverend S. Yosumura. Gozo's death was a great loss, though expected. He helped Benny in elevating Yokosuka's art standards. Our doctors in Yokosuka had done their best, but cancer won. Gozo's wife and daughters carried on his studio successfully. Gozo was a warm friend of all, Americans as well as Japanese. He helped make the world a bit better by his presence.

1870 Wyoming Ave., N.W.
20 April 1950

Dear Benny:

On my return yesterday from a trip to northern Florida and Asheville I found your letter of 5 April. It gives me great satisfaction to know that you were in a position to help Gozo through those last days. Will you please express our deepest sympathy to Mrs. Kawamura and tell her that we consider her husband one of the finest gentlemen whom we have met in many years.

You have many things on the plus side in your life, and your treatment of Gozo is one of the nicest of all the fine things I have known you to do. It seems a shame to take you away from Yokosuka where you have done one of the outstanding jobs in the Far East. I cannot believe that the Navy is so poor that they could not afford the difference between your active and retired pay. Probably neither Secretary Johnson nor Secretary Matthews have any personal knowledge of the matter.

If I were to pick my choice of an evening, I would like to get that old Navy crowd together up in our house in Yokohama or down in your good home in Yokosuka.

Miss Em joins me in affectionate regards to you both.

Sincerely,
Bob
(General Eichelberger)

The Tokyo Chamber of Commerce asked us to a private showing of netsuke. Our Ambassador, Bill Seabold, was an old Japan hand and long-time collector of these unique miniature sculptures of Japanese life. He had convinced Benny that he should collect them and thus learn more about the Japanese. He had an extensive collection, while Benny had a small one. We also visited the Ueno Museum for a private showing of Netsuke, the very best, which were not on public display. They gladly opened their vaults to Benny. There he saw the famous Baron Go's netsuke collection. Later, Baroness Go asked Benny to view what she had left of the famous Go collection, and he was fortunate to obtain one from her.

Chapter XV

SAYONARA

Benny agreed to my flying to Siam. On March twenty-second, I joined Martha Joy, the wife of Vice Admiral Joy, ComNavFe, and her daughter Molly and Nan McEvoy. We were to witness the ceremony of the century, and probably the last of its kind. The King of Siam had died and his cremation was to be an elaborate and national ceremony. En route we were given every consideration and were met at all points by friends and officials.

After arriving in Bangkok we spent hours on the Menan River, the main artery of the city, watching the people and seeing such unique boats as a funeral barge with a large black coffin and six priests. We also witnessed a colorful historical play. *Phra Ruang* at the Silpakorn Theatre.

Mr. Robert Morgan, president of the Northwest Airlines, had generously invited us to fly to Angkor Wat. Admiral Joy had wisely advised his wife not to go because the French were having difficulties. Benny agreed with him as we might be captured, creating an incident. Of course I was disappointed.

Peggy, the wife of Colonel Sheldon, took us to the palace grounds. We were met by Siamese Colonel Shan. In the reception hall we were shown oil paintings of the late king, his predecessors, and his grandfather. The one that interested us most was that of King Chulalongkorn (Anna's protégé in the movie, *Anna and the King of Siam.*). We then went to the Grand Dusit Hall where the royal urn was on an altar. The gold urn encrusted with precious jewels had four large lighted candles. It was dazzling. In the urn was the body of the late King in a fetal position. In front of the urn was a gold statue of Buddha with many lighted candles. The Siamese colonel approached the altar and bowed in respect, after which we did the same, and placed a wreath. We were then seated in the front row where the royal court would be seated the following day. As we looked about the room, we were overpowered by its beauty. The black lacquered woodwork inlaid with mother of pearl with walls of red brocade and a ceiling of gold leaf dominated by the urn made the room memorable. We signed the guest book. In an adjacent area we saw the many gifts from other nations as well as those from the priests. Half-size replicas in papier mâché of an automobile with chauffeur and an attendant, a yacht and a palace were for the use of the king in the hereafter. We also saw in the royal chapel the Emerald Buddha, a thirty-inch-high carving of jasper, enthroned under a gold canopy, on a gorgeously decorated altar. The chapel was of red and gold lacquer inlaid with pearl. The entire picture was beautiful, with the focus upon the awe-inspiring green Buddha.

On the twenty-ninth we attended the cremation ceremony. With excellent seats reserved for us on the photographers' platform, we watched one of the world's most gorgeous parades. It started at 11:00 A.M. with two richly uniformed men on beautiful prancing horses, in step with resonant drums. Next came the PhraMaha Pichai Royal Carriage bearing the urn, escorted by his holiness, the prince patriarch, reading the Abhidama, in a carriage drawn by the military. The bearers of the royal paraphernalia, conch horns and victory drums, Brahmins in full dress, and horses in golden robes, followed the new king. Phumiphon, who was on foot, with the royal family. With minute guns and drums beating, the urn was placed under the umbrella of state, made of fresh flowers, on the cremation pyre, which was two stories high and pyramid-shaped, with the urn at its apex. The officials closed the three royal curtains of gold brocade lined with red. There was one on each side with a pair of pearly gates on the fourth side. His Majesty ascended the steps to the poorly gates, which he opened. He lighted the candles and paid homage to the royal remains, after which he rejoined the royal court and distinguished visitors, in Songdharm pavilion. He then departed in his royal automobile, after which royalty and servants paid homage to the royal remains, while priests chanted the Abhidama.

The ceremony was dignified and memorable. Because of the great heat, we had to leave at noon. A few days later we were back in Yokosuka. It had been a delightful visit and I was thrilled to have witnessed this once-in-a-lifetime ceremony. My traveling companions were most congenial, and we parted with many happy memories.

We had eighty guests for luncheon in honor of the Masonic officials who came from the Philippines to institute the Masonic Lodge F. & A.M. 120, on the base. This was followed by the opening of the renovated dining room of the Officers' Club. The Navy Wives' Club, with Mrs. Koonce and Mrs. Milotta as hostesses, gave a luncheon at which Mrs. Tanaka, president of the Shinsei Women's Club, was presented with a lovely set of luggage for her trip to the convention of the International Federated Women's Clubs in Boston. She was so delighted that it made a happy day for all.

Easter Sunday we attended sunrise service in Seaside Park. Our house guest, Admiral Salisbury, the Chief of Chaplains, officiated at the service.

The officers gave Benny his fourth anniversary party, which would be his last. They went all out to make it a lasting memory. The four-tiered cake was a masterpiece as to size and beauty. Our bakers proved their artistic and culinary ability in this mammoth creation. Admiral Joy and the officers of his staff with their wives attended.

Another party to be remembered was the party on the fifteenth as a preopera affair. *Madame Butterfly* was being given in the Enlisted Men's Club theater. Our guests included Kujiro Shedihara, president of the lower house Naotake Sato, president of the upper house Kuramatsu Kishi, secretary to Shidehara Mrs. Mikozo Tanaka, president of the Shinsei Women's Club Mikozo Tanaka, Bunji Ogura, president of the Industrial Club Kakujiro Suzuki, president of the Sagami Transportation Co.

We spent many afternoons sailing in the *Golden Bird* with friends of the Army and the diplomatic corps. One sail was to be to Misaki. The wind was light and there were many calm spots, so we did not arrive in Misaki until sunset. To our surprise we were met by the mayor with a basket full of lobsters and by the chief of police and others. They told us that this was one of the most exciting incidents of the village.

Mrs. Yoiko Tokunaga was the president of thirty-one PTAs in Yokosuka and was one of twenty-five Japanese educational leaders sent by SCAP to the United States to learn methods useful in the democratization of schools as a representative of 30,900 clubs and 15,660,000 members. She was pretty and charming, and was thrilled to have received from the Navy base PTA a cosmetic case as a going-away gift. She called on Benny in his office to say good-bye.

In 1946 when the first PTA was formed in Yokosuka the parents objected to the name, as they didn't trust the teachers. They had good reason. They called themselves "Parents Association." A change came about gradually as the parents found the teachers' attitude had changed since the VJ Day.

There were as many men as women in the PTA, and they did their part to reduce thefts in 1946. There was no glass in the windows, making the rooms in winter most uncomfortable. We found glass, which was scarce, and these men installed it, only to have it stolen that same night before the putty was hard. The fathers then instituted patrols of the schools during the nights. The women prepared the meals for the children's luncheons. The parents were more involved in their schools than they are in the United States.

Mrs. Tosho Tanaka also called on Benny. As president of the Shinsei Yokosuka Women's Club she was being sent to the United States to attend the International Federated Women's Clubs International, meeting in Boston. She was quite charming, trim-suited, and a soft-spoken lady with a good knowledge of English. She wanted to show Benny the gifts she had received.

Benny was delighted that these two ladies represented Yokosuka. The women had come a long way in four years.

After a week we were pleased to hear from Mrs. Tanaka.

We shall soon leave the ship. Thank you very much for your kindnesses to me before I sailed—especially for the beauty treatment and the beautiful luggage. Everyone thought that I was returning to the United States! I must have looked very smart with my hairdo and my new luggage.

May sixth, Captain Butler and Kay and I went to Tokyo to see Prince and Princess Higashikuni and her doll collection. It was a large and beautiful collection of different periods. It was so different and interesting.

The following day the Catholic procession of the Blessed Sacrament was held, during which the City of Yokosuka was blessed. The Spanish minister and Mrs. Del Castillo marched with us. Prime Minister Yoshida gave a delightful party in our honor the next day and many senior officers of the Occupation including Admiral and Mrs. Joy and many important Japanese, including Governor Uchiyama, attended.

Armed Forces Day, the HMS *Belfast* arrived and calls were made and returned. Then we went to Yokohama for the parade, followed by a reception by Mrs. Walker and General Walton H. Walker, commanding the Eighth Army. Dinner was in Tokyo with the reserve officers at their convention, at which Admiral Joy spoke.

The next day General Fellers and Colonel Davis arrived at Haneda Airport. Stan Fellers was the Marine commander of the Base for two years, and it was such a pleasure to see him again, and wearing the star of a brigadier general. Those in the Navy of the Occupation who were promoted to flag rank were few and far between. They were our house guests.

On Empire Day we entertained at dinner Admiral W. G. Andrewes of the Royal Navy and the officers of the HMS *Belfast*. The British Consul General H. R. Sawbridge wrote:

The Admiral has told me what a tremendously good time was had by all at your house and how much the entire ship's company have appreciated the unfailing hospitality of Yokosuka on the occasion of their visit.

The Kanto Gakuin gave us a farewell party and that evening we gave a farewell party.

The General and Mrs. MacArthur gave a luncheon for Lady and Admiral Brind of the British Navy and for Admiral Radford. Admiral and Mrs. Joy and the Deckers were the other guests. The Commander in chief of the Far Eastern station gave a beautiful party in the HMS *Alert*. We always enjoyed British hospitality to the fullest. Admiral Brind was most gracious. Then General and Mrs. Almond gave the Biederlindens and the Deckers a farewell dinner. All the guests were friends of ours and we again enjoyed ourselves, even though we were saying farewell.

Washington forwarded to me a copy of the most interesting letter from a loyal supporter of mine, as well as a friend and shipmate.

15 April 1950

Rear Admiral C. A. Swanson MC USN
Surgeon General U. S. Navy
Bureau of Medicine and Surgery
Navy Department, Washington 25, D. C.

Dear Admiral Swanson:

My purpose of this letter is to inform you that Rear Admiral B. W. Decker is slated to be detached soon from command of the Naval base here at Yokosuka, Japan, and be retired. Although it may seem quite out of the ordinary for me to write you on this subject it is felt that you will be greatly interested, since it is recalled you wrote me personally after visiting here in September 1948 expressing your feelings of great pride not only as a Naval Officer but as an American, to have noted the unusual accomplishments of the American Navy under his leadership. I wish to assure you that a similar feeling on my own part together with thoughts of the future of the Navy here and the best interests of our country are the sole reasons which impel me to send you the following observations.

It has always seemed that the special interest and support which the Bureau and yourself have extended to the Medical department here may have been prompted to a great extent by the impression you received on the occasion of your visit. This same impression has been widely expressed by a very great number of other prominent Americans who have visited Yokosuka. Actually, it is a well known and established fact, although this is a Navy area of jurisdiction and operation, General MacArthur's headquarters makes a special point of sending all such visitors here to show them results where they may be seen at their very best, as far as the occupation of Japan is concerned.

To such an extent as my opinion may be considered of value after having served at this base for a period of nearly two years and having closely observed and participated in the work of Admiral Decker, I beg to express to you my very strong conviction that the best interests of the Navy and the United States would be served by his retention on active duty as Commander of this base until the peace treaty is signed with Japan. The enclosed newspaper clipping, from the Far East Edition of the "Stars and Stripes," covers in a rather concise way a number of the Admiral's accomplishments which I will not have to enumerate. While these are true enough, they do not suffice in any way to detail or describe certain greater considerations of which you may be aware but which I will try to again summarize for you.

When Admiral Decker came to Japan four years ago he came with orders, undoubtedly well considered at the time by their originators, to destroy and close this base. Truly it was a ramshackle, useless, white elephant of an affair, and may have appeared at that time, in the light of anticipated projects on Guam etc., to be entirely too expensive and perhaps politically too much of a problem, to be of any possible value for practical purposes in the future of the Navy.

From this sort of start, and due to his vision, and grasp of the possibilities by being on the spot, and without expense to the U. S. Government, as practically nothing has been spent, Admiral Decker exchanged scrap and junk on the base, (which was legally of course, our own captured property), for labor and contracting services by the Japanese, and not only cleared away debris, but reconditioned serviceable and useful facilities here until at present we have for all practical purposes, a first class Naval base with all appurtenances in a most defensible, tenable and strategic location. The caves are here, miles of them, which could not be reproduced as well anywhere in the Pacific for what may come. Sometimes I think their potentialities may have been overlooked. We have a 1000 bed modern fire proof hospital by merely moving in the beds, there are first class concrete barracks etc. I do not need to describe expensive dry docks, ship repair activities and other facilities further as you have seen them.

One of the most remarkable things the Admiral has done, (and if not entirely single handed, he has been the originator and moving force), is his work in promoting inclusion of this base for the permanent use of the American Navy, in the Japanese peace treaty. It may be unnecessary to point out, as anyone who gives any thought to its significance can see, that this is a most *important* and *vital* matter. This work is not yet accomplished. The Admiral has not only worked night and day from a public relations angle but he has developed the substantial contacts necessary, not only interservice, but Japanese, American political, and even international, of many of those who must be sold on this before it can be consummated.

Perhaps it may seem superfluous to mention the fact that politically there are many facets and pit-falls in the swinging of such an undertaking. Certainly many advances have been made and ground has been gained, but there would seem to be a *continuity* of effort, and vision, and even inspiration necessary, by someone who knows the answers, right here on the ground, to put this across. I wish to suggest to you that the ramifications of public relations involved in the above mentioned endeavor are multiple and delicate. It would not seem that there could be a great deal gained by changing Commands here in view of this.

In view of the very special and unique situations which I have tried to describe and my very strong conviction, based on the considerations expressed in my opening paragraph, and since no actual orders have as yet been written to my knowledge for the Admiral or his relief, it is hoped that this letter will not be considered out of order and you will understand my sincere purpose in writing you.

It is hoped that you will find an opportunity to visit us again very soon. Since two years will soon have passed you will hardly know the place. I am sure you will be especially surprised and pleased to see our hospital which is now comparable, at least physically, with most of our medium sized ones in the States.

With kindest regards.

Yours very respectfully,
James B. Butler
Captain MC usn

Mr. Melville Bell Grosvenor
National Geographic Magazine
Washington, D. C.

Dear Mel:

I have recieved the copy of the May issue of *National Geographic* Magazine which your organization sent to me and I have read with great interest the excellent article by Vosburg and Roberts. I would like to thank you and (through you) my friends, the authors, for the excellent publicity you gave the Navy, this Base and myself. It has been through such means that it has been possible for us to bring before the American people the importance of Yokosuka. I can well state that if it had not been for the newspapers and magazines, Yokosuka would be unknown to the people of the United States today. I am deeply grateful for this publicity which is in the best interests of both United States and Japan.

I have created here in Yokosuka a yacht building company which built my 44-foot yawl and is now building six or eight other large boats. I named my yawl the "Golden Bird" after the golden bird which landed on Emperor Jimmu's bow and brought to him victories by which he founded Japan. The title appeals to the Japanese and I like the story. So far I have taken the "Golden Bird" to Oshima, into a beautiful little harbor and while there climbed the volcano into which so many Japanese couples have jumped, thereby committing suicide. Next week I expect to sail to Nashima where the girls dive for seaweed and are most uninhibited in what they wear. Then I shall go on to Shimoda where Perry signed the first treaty with Japan.

The workmanship out here is splendid provided it is well supervised. A friend of mine, Ted Kilkenny, has been supervising the construction work and therefore my boat is as well built as any in the United States, and the workmanship, woods and materials are superior. She sails in the lightest of airs and is a very dry boat. I

hope to be able to show the "Golden Bird" when I bring
it to the United States late this summer.
Sincerely,
Benny Decker

5556 Nebraska Avenue NW
Washington 15, D. C.
Rear Admiral Benton W. Decker, USN
Commander, U. S. Naval Facilities
Yokosuka, Japan
My dear Admiral Decker:
On behalf of the members of my party and myself I
want to extend to you our thanks and appreciation for
your excellent briefing on the activities and facilities of
your command, and your cordial hospitality at luncheon
last Tuesday. We all were most favorably impressed.
Our visit to your installation was one of the high
spots of our visit to the Far East Command and will be
highly treasured among our memories.
Sincerely,
R. C. LINDSAY
Major General USAF

Upon the defeat of Japan the policy of the United States
was to destroy the zaibatsu. These were the superconglomer-
ates which gave Japan its industrial power and international
trade advantage. The schemers at home advocated the dis-
memberment of these powerful organizations as a deterrent
to Japan's regaining her status as a world power. The war
had devastating effects upon them. They were broke. Their
factories had been destroyed and what machines they had
were not only obsolete but worn out. But they still had their
managerial staffs, with the knowledge and ability to begin
anew. These were purged, at least theoretically.
On the staff of SCAP was a young civilian who was
charged with the destruction of the zaibatsu. In 1947 he announced that the first of the five giants had been broken up
beyond revival and that within the year the others would
meet their ends. This was unbelievable to many of us, as to

liquidate any of our huge combines at home would require years. I didn't believe it and for that matter hoped it was not true, as they would be needed in the reindustrialization of Japan. I suspected that the purgees were still functioning behind the curtain and that they were forming small companies to act as holding companies for raw materials and salvaged metals. Raw materials would be the wealth of new Japan.

We had some two dozen of the former Japanese industrialists at our home for a highball, then a tour of our repair facility. Commander Higgins, my former civil affairs officer, escorted them about the base and our shops. The point was to show them better management. In their factories they did not have time clocks or job orders or progress records showing where and when work was performed. The result was no accurate costs could be charged for work. On visiting their major plants I had stopped near a large gate valve and asked when it would be completed and how much it would cost. Not only did they not know these answers, but the office didn't know where it was at any particular date—so the invitation for them to visit our establishment and see our cost accounting system.

I had sent to the United States for some old time clocks in store at a Naval base. These we were using. They weren't the best, but were better than nothing.

The Japanese were soon using our system, and probably improving on it.

When they came to my house for a "welcome aboard" and a drink, I noted that the last one to arrive was Mr. Okamo, President of the Mitsubishi Industries. Immediately all the other Japanese fell silent. This must be the number one man—so I took him into an adjacent area where we had a drink. I asked, "weren't you purged?" He said he had been. "Then why did all of these other executives immediately stop talking and pay such respect to you?"

"Oh, they are just my baby vice presidents." I doubted the effectiveness of the purge.

He saw on a table a Japanese tea bowl. Looking at it, he said, "Coney Island!"

"Yes, I agree. It was given to me by a grateful Japanese. Had it been more valuable, I could not have accepted it."

"I am a porcelain collector. I'll give you a piece that is very good."

"I am sorry but I can't accept it, but I assure you that I appreciate the offer."

When I sailed from Japan, there, in my cabin, was a box from Mr. Okamo containing a fine old vase of unusual color.

He had convinced me that the gift he had in mind was a valuable and excellent piece of Japanese ceramics. "Don't sell it or don't give it away. The longer you keep it, the more it will grow on you." He was correct. At first I didn't admire it greatly, but I saw more and more in it, until soon I prized it highly. Today I have it among my most cherished possessions.

Bishop Breton was a valuable help to us all, but typical of the man, he always gave credit to others.

Kamakura

May 18, 1950

Dear Admiral,

News reached me yesterday of the wonderful results of last Sunday Bazaar held at Yokosuka for the benefit of St. Joseph's Hospital. I know the part that you and Mrs. Decker played in the undertaking and I wish to express to you my sincere gratitude. The affair was a success because of the constant encouragement and the material facilities you kindly extended the Committee in charge. Thank you in their name and in mine.

I cannot reconcile myself with the idea that you are going to leave us soon and I keep on hoping and praying for something that would keep you among us, because men of your type are a source of blessing for the peoples and places where they have a chance to work at liberty. However the worst may happen and you may have to go. Before parting with you, dear Admiral Decker, I wish to send you the expression of my deep gratitude for the many kindnesses received at your hands during these last four years you gave me an opportunity to cooperate with your rehabilitation work in Yokosuka. Rest assured that I shall never forget you and until I die, your name and Mrs. Decker's too will remain

385

on the list of my benefactors for whom I have a daily remembrance in my prayers.

The Yokosuka people will not forget you either. I am sure. During your four years of office you have done so much for the city of Yokosuka and its people that your name will ever be remembered and blessed among them. By your example you have taught them how a Christian can love his enemies and his own country at the same time: a combination of love which a non-Christian is unable to understand, still should practice.

Before closing, dear Admiral, I shall make a suggestion. Coming from a real friend, I am sure it will not be misunderstood. When many many years hence, you will knock at the gate of heaven, like everybody else, asking to be admitted ... if you meet any difficulty, just cry out: "O my God have mercy on me. Forget all else, just remember Yokosuka and my Board of Charity." And then I am sure that Christ himself coming forward will utter to you the words he told his apostles, and which contain a real promise: "Come and take possession of the Kingdom prepared for you. For whatever you did for one of these, the least of my brethren, you did it for me."

May God protect you all through the remainder of your life, dear Admiral Decker. May He pour upon your dear self, upon Mrs. Decker and family His choicest blessings and make you all real happy, materially, hearts and souls.

Most sincerely yours,
Albert Breton

I read this letter over and over. It makes me feel humble, and grateful to my friend, Bishop Breton, for his advice! Probably the best advice any person has ever given me. Amen.

Again he wrote:

May 26th 1950

Dear Admiral,

Joined by the Sisters and Fr. Finnerty it is indeed my pleasant duty to thank you, the Officers, men and dependents of the Naval Base for the wonderful work you all have done for us.

That the Bazaar and raffle was such a great success is due to the labor and self-sacrifice of the Organising Committee and the whole hearted cooperation and generosity of the people of the Naval Base.

It was indeed a great pleasure to me to hear of the enthusiastic support accorded the ladies all over the Base especially by the heads of the various departments. To these officers I extend a special word of thanks.

Such great charity and generosity reflects the spirit pervading the Base and is indeed a credit to those responsible for it. It is also an inspiration to those who observe it, Japanese or foreigners.

We only hope and pray that we may be worthy of the trust you all have placed on us by your kindness and generosity. Although there are many difficulties we hope little by little to have an efficient and up-to-date hospital, which will be in years to come be a monument to the generosity and charity of the people of the Naval Base.

May God bless and protect you all in all your undertakings.

Yours sincerely,
Bishop Albert Breton

Dear Admiral,

I have been told by Chaplain Edwards the magnificent success of the Bazaar organized in favor of St. Joseph Hospital. It is to me a well known fact that although a great many of good will have contributed to the preparation of this Bazaar such a result would never have been obtained without your decided and clear-sighted help. In consequence it is a pleasure to me to join my thanks and congratulations to those already given to you Bishop Breton and the Hospital's Sisters, to those also of the poor people who will be able to find their charitable and warm attentions.

I hope firmly to have the pleasure to see you again before your leaving, but it is a real pleasure to me to convey here to you and Mrs. Decker the homage of my respect and gratitude.

Sincerely yours,
R. D. Fumkeubey
Archbishop of Palta
Apostolic Delegate

The British Navy wrote:
at Yokosuka
21st April 1950

Dear Admiral Decker,

I would like to express, as best as I can, the very grateful thanks of all ranks in H.M.S. UNICORN for the wonderful hospitality they have enjoyed from all officers and men under your command whilst at Yokosuka.

Both in the officer's and men's clubs, and in your homes, they have received a welcome that they will never forget. You will yourself know how much that means to us in UNICORN who are so many thousands of miles away from our homes.

It is difficult for us to thank individually all those who have looked after us so well and I should be very grateful if you could publish the sense of this letter to all activities under your command.

Yours sincerely,
H. S. Hopkins
Captain

The British Navy has always been most appreciative of what little we could do to assist them. The foregoing from one of their captains and the following from a Royal Navy admiral are typical of their friendliness.

Flag Officer
Second-inCommand
Far East Station
26th May

Dear Admiral,

Before we leave tomorrow, I am writing to thank you so very much for all you have done for us here and all the trouble you have taken and all the hospitality you have extended to us. We are all very grateful.

Will you please also accept this as my good-bye to you and Mrs. Decker. I know how very much we would miss you if we were to come back to Yokosuka again after you have left. But that I know is nothing to the way that you will be missed by all the people you are leaving behind here. I hear it on every side and I have seen the enormous work you have done.

May I say then how very sorry I am that your time has come to go home and may I wish you every success and happiness.

I do hope that one day our paths may cross again and that once more I may be able to accept your charming hospitality.

I also hope that if ever you come to England we shall be able to entertain you there.

My very kind regards to Mrs. Decker.

Yours very sincerely,
William Andrewes

I did enjoy your party so much.

At our Monday afternoon Brownie Meetings these letters and many more like them were read to the assembled officers and others gathered for the weekly conference. This dissemination of praise played an important part in building morale. No doubt but it encouraged friendship and goodwill.

To unify any group there must be an effective means of communication, up and down, right and left. We had many channels, and always on the alert to create more. Besides this weekly conference between the officers, nurses, teachers and higher echelons of civilians, we also had the base paper, the *Sea Hawk*, which reached the dependents. Also, parties, games, clubs, skating, bowling, athletics, even a golf driving range, besides Masonic organizatons, Holy Name Society, and churches. To all these we give credit.

And now we hope that this book does its part in communicating between Japan and the United States.

Memorial Day I spoke in an LCT on Tokyo Bay to a group of Navy personnel and wives:

We are few and far from home. The great Armed

Forces of the United States have departed, their guns are silent, and quietness prevails on Tokyo Bay. Here, on the deck of the Missouri at anchor, the Imperial Japanese government surrendered five years ago. In humility, without arrogance or pride but with great sincerity in our hearts we commemorate the sacrifices of our brothers-in-arms who gave their lives that the children of the world, regardless of creed, color, faith or nationality, may breathe the free air of democracy and enjoy the manifold blessing of Christianity.

God in his wisdom ordained that certain of us die and others live. We were chosen to live and to carry on the unfinished work for which our late shipmates died. We are expected to perform well our tasks.

We who are standing here today were chosen as soldiers of freedom to oppose the forces of darkness, atheism and immorality, which in this age is called Communism. As long as Communism aggressively and militantly opposes all that we stand for—we cannot remain silent. We cannot give these false prophets the opportunity to destroy our temples and our homes.

Communists and their fellow travellers have long and loudly pointed out that as Christians and believers in Democracy we cannot oppose their traitorous and evil actions. To agree to this line of reasons is to commit suicide. We have the right to survive and we must restrain the communists the same as we would criminals or murderers. If we jail our fellowman for being a menace to society, we should do the same to those who wish to destroy that society. It is the least we can do to support our brothers who died to keep our country free.

When we depart from here today, let us each strive to fulfill our duties the better—let us encourage Christian thoughts and acts and let us positively oppose those who work unceasingly to enslave the world.

R ADM H. E. Baldridge, USN
Director of the Museum
U. S. Naval Academy
Annapolis, Maryland
Dear Captain Baldridge:
Today the representative of the Industry Club of Ja-

pan, Mr. Mototada Nakamura, managing director, came to my office to present me a 4' X 6' painting by Mr. Ogata. The painting is of Commodore Perry landing at Kurihama which is about ten minutes drive from this Naval Base. The Industry Club wishes to present it to me in token of their appreciation for what I have done in Japan for the Japanese and the people of this city of Yokosuka. However I feel this painting is too costly a gift and therefore I have told them that I would not accept it unless the Museum at the Naval Academy would be interested in displaying this picture appro-

Lieut. Albert Decker, Rear Admiral Decker, and Lieut. Benton Decker, in the Alumni House, Annapolis; in rear, the oil painting of Commodore Perry at Uraga.

priately at the Naval Academy. Will you please advise me of your wishes. If you are willing to accept it, I will accept it in my name, then ship it to you on Navy bill-of-lading as a gift from me. In view of my departure from Japan on 1 July it will be necessary for a prompt reply as they will want to present it to me with a certain amount of ceremony.

Sincerely,
B. W. Decker

P.S. Some years ago I presented to the Museum a gold signet ring of the Lawrence family. It would be of interest to me to know if this is still on display and what interest is taken in it. I presume the ring of my father, Admiral Decker, is still on display.

June 8, 1950
Tokyo

Dear Admiral B. W. Decker,

I have much pleasure in presenting this picture to you as a small token of our deep appreciation of your noble and valuable service rendered to the early recovery of our country, especially of Yokosuka thereby contributing to the deeper understanding and better relations between our two peoples.

The scene shows the first landing on June 14 (Lunar calendar) 1853 at Kurihama of Commodore Perry, who is being received by Lord Daigaku Hayashi, the delegate of Shogun, with a Chinese interpreter standing by.

The picture is painted by Mr. Gessan Ogata, a well known contemporary artist, specialized in historical events.

Kumakichi Nakashima
President
The Black Ship Association

17 June 1950

Rear Admiral H. E. Baldridge, USN
Director of the Museum
U. S. Naval Academy
Annapolis, Maryland
Dear Admiral:

I am sending to you on Navy WHIZ bill-of-lading

1130-50 a picture of Commodore Perry negotiating with Lord Daigaku Hayashi, the delegate of Shogun, with a Chinese interpreter standing by, at Kurihama, Japan on July 14, 1853. It was painted by Gessan Ogata, a well-known contemporary artist. Also I am enclosing some photographs of the presentation which took place in my office at the Navy Base at Yokosuka, Japan on 8 June 1950. I am shaking hands with the artist, with Mrs. Decker on my left, and the artist's wife and son on his right. Also in the picture is Baron Kumakichi Nakashima, head of the Black Ship Association, who is presenting the picture to me.

As this picture is far too valuable for me to keep, I am presenting it to you with a copy of their letter that you may place it in the Naval Academy Museum as a gift from me.

Sincerely,
B. W. DECKER

General Willoughby was a stately man with whom I agreed and whom I liked. The CIA wanted to get out of Okinawa in 1949 and wished to move into Japan, but Willoughby insisted that if they did, they must come under him and report through him. This was not the way the CIA operated. Without talking once of this rejection they asked me for a place. It was a case of the right hand not knowing what the left was doing. I was happy to give the CIA an area, which was fenced off, and they had the privilege of entering and exiting without hindrance. But I insisted that on my base they came under my command. Now and then I would inspect their operation by dropping by for a cup of coffee and a chat with the person in charge. I didn't want to see anything they were doing or have them report through me. I was just maintaining discipline. We got along well. They requested a building for their communications. I agreed, provided they fixed up another one for me. I had no funds and they had unlimited funds. This really helped us out. In June 1950 when I was getting ready to go to Korea to take over the command of that Navy, as requested by President Syngman Rhee, the civilian in charge of the CIA dropped in to tell me casually that they had good solid information that the Communists would not attack South Korea. So I passed this word on to the General.

393

"Benny, do you believe that?" I explained that I had no information other than this remark and didn't know how much it was worth. A few weeks later South Korea was invaded and the Korean Navy was sunk. As I looked back on it the General must have had more reliable sources of information. He was a wise man.

Shortly thereafter an interesting, fully unintentional, breach of security occurred. We were shopping in Kamakura, I was called to the phone by General Willoughby. He seemed upset.

"Benny. Why did you prematurely ban the *Red Flag?* That was *secret* and not to be divulged for several days."

"I banned the *Red Flag* many months ago in Yokosuka. We haven't had a *Red Flag* in a parade or seen one flown from a building since January." That was a quick end of the telephone conversation, for it now dawned on him that he had disclosed over a public telephone that the Supreme Commander had ordered the suppression of the Communist newspaper, *Red Flag.* I never breathed a word.

I was deeply touched by the following letter from my first supporters, the Christian missionaries:

Admiral and Mrs. Decker:

On learning of your return shortly to America upon the completion of your duties as Commander of the Yokosuka Naval Base, we planned this simple farewell meeting to express our deep gratitude to you. We humbly requested your kind presence. We count it great honor and privilege and feel profoundly thankful that you have graciously acceded to our humble request and honored us with your presence at this hour when every moment of your time is needed in the preparation of your departure from the country.

It is wholly unnecessary, Admiral Decker, for me to refer to the fact that you have discharged, beyond measure, your most weighty duties as Commander of the Yokosuka Naval Base and have achieved extraordinarily brilliant results from the military point of view. Aside from such military achievements, it behooves me particularly to mention of what you have accomplished for the citizens who have been under your care and jurisdiction; that is to say, the exceptionally remarkable accomplishments have been attained for them in the preservation of the peace and order, in the establishment of social welfare institutions and their activities, in the encouragement and assistance given in the field of education, and in the cultivation and guidance of wholesome ideas during your most distinguished administration. Moreover, very special reference should be made to the great contributions you have rendered toward the fostering and development of the religious, social and educational activities of the Christian organizations in this area. The success of their work is decidedly due to your generous consideration and sympathetic interest. I must not fail to state in this connection what you so kindly did last Christmas for the economically hard-pressed students of our school, enabling them to pay their tuitions in the full, has been remembered by us all with deep sense of gratitude.

On the occasion, Admiral Decker, of my visit with several others to your office, just after the moving of a part of our school to this site at Mutsuura four years ago, you said to us to this effect; "When the United States and Japan with the Pacific Ocean between them shall stand together in the spirit of Christianity and really cooperate in every line of activity, then can the true peace of the world see its realization. So I hope and urge that you will do your utmost toward the Christianization of Japan through Christian education." Never were such words spoken by any Japanese military officer. Upon hearing these words from you, the Commander of the American Navy, I was intensely impressed and I have been endeavoring, to the best of my ability, to carry out their intent and meaning in the work of our school with sincere appreciation to you for the words.

It is not difficult to subjugate a people under occupation by power and by force of arms, outwardly; but they have something in them that can never be subdued by power, armed force, atomic bomb or even by hydrogen bomb; it can be won only by genuine Christian love. The real purpose of the occupation can be truly realized by capturing the hearts of the people under it. Happy are the people of Yokosuka! Their hearts have been captivated and cemented by the superb Christian personality and love of their Commander, Admiral Decker.

Nearly a hundred years ago, Commodore Perry landed with his men at Kurihama Bay. The residents of Yokosuka will remember the event to this day. Unfortunately the people of Japan at that time did not accept all that was offered them by the Commodore; they especially refused the Bible, the symbol of the Christian religion, the spiritual foundation of the Western civilization. They were fascinated by and took in the skeleton of that civilization but refused its fundamental basis. This refusal of the basic factor of the Western civilization was the fundamental cause leading to the recent calamitous war. But I am exceedingly happy to say, Admiral Decker, that we the citizens of Yokosuka area have bountifully received the precious gift of your love based on the spirit of Christianity with our open hearts and we shall remember you and your gift and all that you have done for us with the spirit of endearing Christian love and affection for all time to come.

Now, as to our school, I beg to assure you, Admiral Decker, to reiterate our deepest thanks to you and to earnestly pray that God's enduring grace and abundant blessing may ever be bestowed on you and Mrs. Decker and all who are dear to you as you leave from us.

I humbly thank you and Mrs. Decker for your gracious presence and kind hearing.

> Tasuku Sakata, President Kanto Gakuin University; Ukichi Kawaguchi, Prof. Kanto Gakuin Univ.; Victor Hauson, Luvo P. Hanson, Kiroe Murata, Takeshi Shimizu, Takaaki Aikawa, Takashi Nakae, Mrs. Toshiko Sakata, Mrs. T. Nakai, Mrs. G. Shirayama, Willard F. Topping, Genzaburo Shirayam, Ryukichi Akiba.

June 1st 1950

If I could have done more! The Japanese are the most grateful people. I only regret I could not have served another year in Yokosuka.

Tokyo
May 13th 1950

Dear Admiral Decker,

I believe that Japanese who know you are unanimous in regretting your departure from Japan.

Yokosuka people and ex-Service men whom you have extended sympathy are grateful for your most efficient but very humane administration of ex-naval town and they will feel very sad to say good-bye to you. It was, indeed, a fine model of good administration of a territory of occupied country and they will remember you with great respect forever as a fine and good governor.

I want to express my personal deep appreciation for your and Mrs. Decker's many kindnesses and you will understand that I am unable to reciprocate them. I am going to my native town Wakayama from the 20th inst. for one week. I hope in earnest to see you and Mrs. Decker and your son before your departure to say au revoir and best wishes.

When you see Admiral Turner please be so good as to convey my best wishes to him. I had several contacts with him at Washington and I respect him very much.

With best wishes and respect.

Kichisaburo Nomura

June 2nd 1950

Rear Admiral B. W. Decker,
Yokosuka

Dear Admiral Decker:

It is with a deep regret to learn that, in order to assume an important duty elsewhere, you will be leaving Yokosuka in near future.

During the past four years, Yokosuka has made almost a phenomenal progress on the way to a peaceful, commercial and industrial city and we cannot imagine how this would have been achieved without your kind and helpful hands.

My two companies of Sagami Unyu Co., Ltd. and Tokoyowan Soko Kaisha being engaged in developing the city for a commercial port, I feel especially indebted to your wise guidance and do not know how to express our gratefulness. As a humble token of the heartfelt gratitude, I wish to present a little momento herewith. I shall be very happy if you would kindly accept it.

Your able and benevolent administration here will forever be cherished in our memory, and I pray the Divine grace may always be with you and Mrs. Decker.

Very sincerely,
K. Suzuki

Request for inspection by Admiral Decker

The Misaki Fishery Station of the Yokosuka Ohtsu Prison is situated at the southernmost tip of the Miura Peninsula. It commands the view over Tokyo Bay to the east, the Sagami Bay to the west, and the romantic island of Jo-ga-shima half a mile over the sea to the south. The famous aquarium and Marine Biological Station of Aburatsubo is just nearby. It commands the view over the island of Enoshima and Inushima, above which rises the eternal beauty of Fujiyama. Fifty persons are now boarded at the Fishery Station undergoing training in the fishing work.

It would give us great pleasure if Admiral Decker and other members of the U. S. Navy would visit this Fishery Station and inspect the Station.

Edwina continues:

The people of Otsu, a village south of Yokosuka, wanted to pay homage to Benny for the many things he had done for them. We attended the meeting they held in their club house. The flowers were beautiful and the refreshments delicious. But best of all were the pictures made by the school children of the lower grades. The ceremony was touching and assured us as did all of the manifestations of the Japanese that their friendship was true and lasting.

398

Hisakira Kano of the National City Bank and Ichimoto Naoto, governor of the Bank of Japan, came to lunch. Like all the Japanese they were most grateful and insisted on giving us a gift. It was a beautiful red cloisonné vase which we cherish.

The city gave a farewell and welcoming party for us and the McLeans (the rear admiral relieving Benny). In front of the city hall the ceremony started by a speech, then the "Star Spangled Banner" and the "Kimigayo" was sung by the schoolchildren, then speeches and three banzais. Evelyn and I were laden with bouquets, and so was Benny. We retired to the Chamber of Commerce and the Industrial Club for a buffet reception. The city did itself proud, and we felt that we had many loyal friends in Yokosuka.

Yokosuka Shimbun   5th June, 1950

FAREWELL AND WELCOME PARTY FOR REAR ADMIRAL DECKER AND THE NEW COMMANDING OFFICER TO BE HELD 26th UNDER THE AUSPICES OF THE CITY

Rear Admiral B. W. Decker, Commander Fleet Activities, Yokosuka, whom the 280 thousand citizens of Yokosuka pay high respect as the benefactor to the regeneration of this city, is going back to the States in the end of this month to retire from the naval service.

All the citizens of Yokosuka, whose general meeting petitioned for retention of his office, are very much disheartened at this final news. The city plans to hold a farewell-welcome party for Rear Admiral Decker and the new Commander by establishing a special executive committee. It is unofficially decided to be held on 26th June.

The party is to be attended by the representatives from all parts of the city. From 13·00, at the City Hall Sqaure. Mayor Ishiwata and other representatives are to present farewell and welcoming speeches. Presentation of bouquets and exhibition of fireworks are also scheduled. After that, at the second meeting place which is planned to be the conference room of the Chamber of Commerce and Industry the representatives of the city, government and public offices, Chamber of

Commerce and Industry, Industrial Club, Women's Society, Yokosuka Red Cross Society and other public and private organizations in Yokosuka City will give a toast to the Admirals.

There was the usual bingo game at the Officers' Club, to which Benny's chief of staff, Captain Tibbitts, insisted we attend, something unusual for us. We were unsuspecting until after the first five numbers were called and I had won the only game of Bingo in my life. It was apparent that we had been conned into winning a magnificent silver punch bowl, tray, cups and ladle. And believe me, it was suitably engraved! Benny says, "My officers and their wives were always ahead of me and this evening was no exception. With such loyalty how could I miss!"

179 Zushi
Yokosuka

June 19 1950

Dear Admiral Decker:
    On behalf of the members of the Shonan Area Shinwakai and the Zushi Jusanjo (Zushi Household craft Bureau) I wish to express my deep appreciation of all you have done for our organizations throughout the Welfare Committee (Fukushi Iinkai). All the members are of the firm belief that your most friendly assistance and goodwill will be long remembered with gratitude.
    On this occasion of your departure from this country, the members join in wishing you the best of health and luck.

Most sincerely yours,
Mrs. Chise Furukawa
Chairman

The first paragraph of my order concerning the visit of the Secretary of Defense to Yokosuka

1. Secretary of Defense Louis JOHNSON will visit this Base on Wednesday 21 June. His party will be composed with escorts as follows:

Secretary of Defense
General Omar BRADLEY
Maj General H. Carter
 McGunan
Captain K. D. CRAIG, USN
 (Aide)
Captain Steve Mulkey
 (Aide to Gen BRADLEY)

R ADM B. W. DECKER
CAPT F. P. TIBBITTS
CAPT H. AMBROSE

CAPT J. B. BUTLER

LT COL R. C. BURNS, USMC

During the tour of the base by the secretary of defense we entered the headquarters cave. There were many generals with the party and all were interested in what we had done with the large Japanese cave from which the Japanese air defense was controlled. The large control room showed visually all gun stations throughout the area and all sightings of enemy aircraft. Reports were mechanically reported and as much as two minutes were required from sightings to orders to open fire. It was a cumbersome system.

The former emergency ventilation system as a battery of man-powered bicycles with a belt drive to the blowers. Several diesel generators were for standby use. A 1,000-bed hospital underground had been burnt out by the first landing parties. It had been complete.

We gunited the main cave, cemented the floors, and installed running water and electric lights as well as telephones. This was done to prepare for the worst, should we need cave shelter. We had even considered it for General MacArthur. But to justify the expenditures for improvement, we had to have a use for it during the interim.

Captain McNeill, USMC, had dropped by the office to show me a large mushroom he had grown, saying that it was a hobby of his. He bought the spore from New Jersey and obtained the manure from the Army, and in a cave with constant temperature and humidity he grew a few pounds.

"Captain, you are just the man I need. I want to justify fixing up the command cave. You are now in charge of our mushroom farm. Welfare will finance it and you'll have Japanese labor. I want tons of mushrooms a year!"

He did a splendid job as he had with our general mess. With manure from the adjacent First Cavalry at Camp McGill and three enthusiastic Japanese women he had an efficient farm going in about six months. The sailors and marines were enjoying mushrooms with their steaks! And the commissary was selling them to the dependents. When it became self-supporting we turned the operation over to the supply department.

As the inspection party consisting of several generals was leaving the cave, the secretary asked for an example of unification of the services. I couldn't resist the chance for a laugh.

"Mr. Secretary, this mushroom farm is an excellent example of unification. We give the Army mushrooms and they give us manure!"

Actually we couldn't grow mushrooms without manure and the Army was doing us a real favor by supplying us with enough for our purposes.

We then proceeded to the hospital where we came to a ward known as "boys town." I had assured the secretary that the Army used our hospital, and we were glad they did. Our maternity ward was popular with them. So when he arrived in this ward and saw a number of men in khaki standing by their bunks, he jumped to a conclusion. "Why this is a real example of unification. Admiral, I congratulate you on having so many Army men in your hospital. And what ward is this?"

"Mr. Secretary, this is the VD ward!"

A general promptly jabbed me in the ribs. "Go on, Benny, tell him the truth—they are Marines!"

As we passed through the hospital he asked about a recent order of his to close some of the wards in each hospital to save money. "Yes, Mr. Secretary we closed that ward which you can see is locked."

"How much did you save?" he inquired.

402

"Nothing, Mr. Secretary, for we depend on Japanese help, which is charged against reparations. And our staff remains the same. It really makes no difference to us, for, if we have another epidemic, like last year, we would unlock the door."

Within a few months we were to have 3,700 patients from the Korean War and my successor was using every building possible for wards. During that war a total of 47,000 patients passed through the Yokosuka Hospital! The two senior medical doctors responsible for building up our capacity were Admiral Owsley and Captain Butler. They saved many lives.

The Secretary of Defense
Washington

June 30, 1950

Dear Admiral,

Our visit to Yokosuka Naval Base was most interesting. I was particularly glad to see the naval installations while there and know the capabilities of such a station. I congratulate you on your excellent performance of duty in your interesting and successful effort in improving the Yokosuka Base to its present standard.

I wish you every success in your new retired life.

With kind regards, I am,

Sincerely yours,
Louis Johnson

From Rear Admiral Kitts:

Dear Benny:

I cannot tell you how sorry I am—for the Navy and the Nation—that you are coming home; nor how strongly I feel your loss is going to be the Navy's where ways are still incomprehensible to me. You did the best job in the service from the standpoint of real importance, and no one is going to fill your shoes.

My kindly regards to Edwina, best wishes to you both—and let us hear from you.

Sincerely,
Bill

Edwina takes over

The parties were coming thick and fast, Captain and Mrs. Tibbitts had a large dinner party for us to which the base officers and wives were invited. This was followed by many others. The officers' wives gave a luncheon for me and presented me with a silver jewel box and lovely jade ring which recalls fond memories. The unique decorations on each table were the Edwina dolls in my likeness with blond hair, in kimonos. They were beautiful and showed not only originality but also deep affection from the wives. I have my doll, a twelve-inch-high beautifully dressed "Japanese Edwina." After the luncheon Benny and I left for Kyoto and Giffu for three days, where we spent out twenty-ninth wedding anniversary. On our return we stayed overnight at the Fujiya Hotel with General and Mrs. Courtney Whitney and the John Gunthers, the author and his wife.

On the twenty-fifth of June we went to Tokyo to leave by train for Nikko with the Whitneys and the Gunthers. Court had asked Benny to help brief John Gunther on the Occupation, as John was writing a book. Court looked worried and told me on the side, "The Russians are up to something, and the General doesn't want me to leave Tokyo." We left in a special car without Court.

In Nikko we had luncheon at the hotel and had left when Benny was called back to the telephone. He was told that the South Koreans had invaded North Korea. It was unbelievable. We didn't know the truth until we returned to Tokyo, where we were informed that the North Koreans had invaded South Korea.

Benny asked John Gunther, who was leaving Japan, "John, you have been here only two weeks. How can you write your story when there is so much more to learn about the Occupation?"

He replied, "If I stayed much longer I wouldn't be able to write the story."

When the book came out, Benny was upset and disappointed by the attack on the Occupation. Also, he was alarmed at the two glowing paragraphs about himself. He wrote to Court from the States, who replied on the twenty-eighth of February, 1951:

Things are going much better in Korea now that we were able to entice the Chinese Commies away from their Manchurian sanctuary where we can get a good whack at them. The results have given Mao much to think about. The fight will be hard and long, however, unless and until our hands are untied and we are able to employ the full potential of our air and sea power.

It is obvious now that John Gunther was writing to order. Had we realized at the time that he was employed by Look Magazine, we might have suspected the slanting and coloring which was to follow, however I think he did himself more harm than he did the General as people are fed up with such petty sniping.

Court

General MacArthur sent Benny by dispatch: "I wish you were here." So did he! The Gunther book had not changed our friendship.

Kyung Mu Dai

June 20, 1950

My dear Admiral Decker:

I am writing to ask you if it is possible for you to pay us a visit before you return to the United States. I wrote to General MacArthur requesting him to extend our invitation to you. However, a direct invitation may have personal appeal and I am sending this note to the Korean Minister in Tokyo who will personally transmit it to you. I have something in mind, which may interest you when I have an opportunity to explain in person, I hope.

With sincere wishes and best personal regards.

Sincerely yours,
Syngman Rhee

President Syngman Rhee asked me to serve in his Navy upon retirement. The Korean minister and another representative called on me. I said that I would want assurance of no politics (!) and that I would like to return to Washington to get the cooperation of officials in our government. A plane was to pick me up on July first to fly to Korea. The week following, the Communists sank the Korean Navy and the United States was involved. I disappointedly concluded that my services were not needed, and nothing further developed.

The General wanted me to remain in Japan as a civilian. To do this, the law required me to be retired for physical disability. I knew of none, though shortly after retirement my hearing was found to be impaired. The year before, the Nationalist Chinese wanted me to serve in Formosa with their armed forces. This I rejected as I had heard throughout the years of the political storms that centered around those jobs. I knew I was not capable of dealing with political intrigues. When Admiral Carney asked me in 1949 to stay on, I gave the Chinese no further thought.

To our great surprise and joy, we were asked if we would like to be received by the Emperor. We had never dreamt that this could be arranged, and certainly never hinted or expected it. This was indeed a great honor and more so because it was volunteered.

We were asked a few logical and reasonable questions and received a form from SCAP. We appeared at the time set. Mr. Matsudaira, who received us, was most polite and asked us to do certain reasonable things. We agreed. Would we arrive in the audience chamber before and leave after the Emperor and Empress. Would we please wait for him to offer to shake hands and please remain standing until he asked us to be seated. If it pleased us, the Emperor would initiate subjects to be discussed and he would terminate the audience. All of these were most reasonable and expected.

Matsudaira escorted us into a room with a few chairs and a settee. Soon the Emperor and Empress with an interpreter appeared. They were most friendly and immediately put us at ease. Shaking hands, he invited me to be seated near him, and Edwina near the Empress.

He asked about Yokosuka and what we were doing. "Do you think the Japanese were handicapped by their size?" I assured him that their size might have been an advantage under certain conditions, that they lost the war for other reasons. "Would the Japanese grow taller?" I thought they were already taller because of a change in diet, and said that they would be several inches taller in the next generation.

After forty minutes we were asked to exchange places and I talked to the Empress, for a shorter period.

The Empress talked to Edwina about Yokosuka, the Women's Club, playgrounds, orphans, toys from beer cans, etc. Edwina liked the Empress very much.

They arose and, saying good-bye and wishing us happiness in retirement, they left the room. Then we left, having enjoyed our audience with two such democratic and likable people. It was a notable day for us.

I called on the General to say farewell. He said, "Benny, Yokosuka is the only part of the Occupation that has not been criticized." I felt that much of this was due to the cooperation of the Japanese people in Yokosuka. Americans and Japanese were working together and getting results. He also remarked, "No matter how high you climb in the service there will always be some bitterness, when you retire." I think he was trying to warn me of a common reaction. His father was treated badly after he had reached high in the service. He had shown some bitterness. His warning alerted me to overcome any such reaction.

Letter of Gratitude

20 June 1950

Rear Adm. Benton W. Decker

Dear Sir:

Since assumption of office as commandant of the Yokosuka Naval Base, you have extended over this Prefecture, especially to Yokosuka, your superior guidance and kindest assistance in various phases of industry, culture, education and so forth. It is really of great achievement you have done towards the rehabilitation of Japan through your excellent character and profound judgement, which fact will, we are sure, remain eternally alive in our minds.

We wish you will keep good health, for your contribution to the establishment of the world's peace and, at the same time, your esteemed help in the recovery of new Japan is most earnestly desired by our people.

Availing ourselves of this occasion of your returning home, we, every member of this Prefectural Assembly, wish hereby to express, with unanimous vote, the deepest gratitude for your kindness and guidance.

Respectfully yours,
Masaru Kamijo
Chairman,
Kanagawa Prefectural
Assembly

To: Rear Admiral Benton W. Decker
Dear Sir,

With your great insight and aid the former Japanese Naval Base of Yokosuka, has today become a city teeming with industries pursuing peaceful aims, and this former fortress is now a city of peace.

Our company is one of the many which has been established there and is now manufacturing export textiles since the past two years. Young boys and girls who had never before known the art of weaving have become very proficient in this art and are now able to produce quality textiles.

At this time on the eve of your departure for your homeland, this honour and pleasure of presenting as our token of appreciation for all you have done for us, the textiles woven by these young boys and girls, is not only my own but the happiness and pleasure of all who had done the work.

Sincerely yours,
Kakehi Koike
Tokyo Textile Co.

Sir,

It is a great grief for us, seven hundred officials working at the Police in Yokosuka, to bid farewell to you whom we have admired as the greatest benefactor of the rehabilitation of Yokosuka.

The happy life now enjoyed by all the citizens has been given by you who have lead us with a warm heart for the revival and welfare of the citizens during these four years and a half since your arrival in Yokosuka.

After war, we, all the citizens of Yokosuka, had been panting under a feeling of social unrest such as the confusion by the defeat, deficit in food, the occurrence of criminal cases and the prevalence of infectious diseases, but your policy that the foundation of the rehabilitation of Yokosuka must consist in the maintenance of public order and the improvement of public health, enabled us to have the present Yokosuka as a peaceful city with great future having improved sanitary arrangements and public order.

Your efforts for the rehabilitation of Yokosuka have been too numerous to be mentioned and we have long expected the time to come when you would be able to see the citizens leading a happy life for themselves without troubling you any further.

But what a pity to hear that you should go home soon in spite of our eager desire not to leave us before you take a look at the bright life of the citizens in future.

However, we firmly believe that you will remain in our mind forever as the symbol of the city and all of the citizens. We will be able to think of you by the bronze statue in front of the City Hall as Americans call Washington's distinguished services to the State to their mind by his bronze statue.

In conclusion we hope you will come again to Yokosuka in the near future and also we promise you we shall bear your instructions in mind and devote ourselves to the duty of protecting all the citizens.

Yours Respectfully,
Masuo Suzuki
Chief Police Headquarters

24 June 1950

Rear Admiral B. W. Decker
Dear Sir;

May I take the liberty to express my deep gratitude for the great merits you have accomplished, and the distinguished services you have devoted to the reconstruction of democratic Japan, especially to the rehabilitation of Yokosuka.

I, as a president of a Japanese industrial organization, have been working in this Yokosuka area since 1948, and ever since it was my great pleasure to work in this area.

So many things have been improved and elevated

by the great exertion and kindness of you, and the present prosperity of Yokosuka is completely attributed to your effort. Not only the citizens of Yokosuka, but all the Japanese had and will have a great respect to you.

Now a sad news came to us that you, the father of Yokosuka, have to leave for the United States, it is really a great regret that we have to see a great man leave from Japan, but at the same time, we heartily hope to see you back again.

As a token of my deep appreciation, it will be my greatest honor if this piece of picture be accepted. This picture was embroidered by a famous embroiderer in Kyoto, and it is desired that this will be kept as one of your souvenirs.

Your bon voyage and health is heartily wished, I remain

> Yours very truly,
> Souji Yamanoto

27 June 1950

To: Rear Admiral B. W. Decker
> Commander Fleet Activities, Yokosuka
From: Shige Kita, the Director of Shonan
> After Care Society
> A Letter of Appreciation

Sir,

I, the Director of Shonan After-Care Society, have the honour of expressing my hearty thanks for your kind assistance and encouragement to the medical care and sanitary arrangements of this city.

With this greatest assistance, there has been a great improvement in the public health of the city.

It is our great regret that in spite of so many tuberculosis patients in this country, medical treatment thereof and the count-measure are in a state of their infancy.

Recognizing these facts, you gave a great assistance to the establishment of Shonan After-Care Society, the first private organization of this kind in Japan.

In addition to the said assistance, in the beginning of this year, you were so kind enough as to donate to this Society out of money collected from Naval and Military personnel in Yokosuka. With this donation we could set up a cooking room in the rear office of the Society.

The patients are suffering not only from bodily and mentally but also economically. But with the establishment of this organization, their misery will no doubt be mitigated in future.

I, as the Director of Shonan After-Care Society, and in behalf of the patients wish to express my hearty thanks for your distinguished service, as an apostle of God, given to this Society.

I wish also that you will take the trouble of conveying our sincere gratitude to your staff and men for their donation.

Yours respectfully,
Shige Kita
The Director, Shonan After-Care Society

I received a letter addressed to me:

It is a great sorrow to hear that Your Excellency is going to retire and go back to America. We really do not know how to express our gratitude, when we recall all the generous help and support you have given to the education of youth in Japan. We are especially grateful for the aid you have given to our Eiko High School since you arrived here as Commander of Yokosuka Base.

It is our desire to commemorate in some way the kindness you have shown in giving birth to our school. We know that it is Your Excellency's desire to build up Eiko into an even better school. Therefore we have raised a fund of 500,000 yen in order to help towards the completion of the auditorium, thus to perpetuate the memory of Your Excellency at Eiko forever.

We promise Your Excellency that in the future we shall do our very best to carry on with the same spirit the work that you have so splendidly begun.

In closing this address, we all pray for your future happiness and health.

June 27, 1950
Eiko Parents' Association
Yujiro Watanabe, President

411

Yokosuka Chapter No. 1
Order of the Eastern Star
Yokosuka, Japan

28 June 1950

Dear Brother Decker:

The officers and members of Yokosuka Chapter No. 1, Order of the Eastern Star wish to let you know how deeply we regret your leaving us. You have been our friend at all times and it would be impossible to count the number of things you have done for our Chapter. Everywhere we look in our Chapter room there is a reminder of something you have helped us acquire. We hope you will not forget us when you are in the United States as we cannot and will not forget you or Sister Edwina.

Bon Voyage Admiral and Mrs. Decker, it was a pleasure having you aboard, your departure will sadden us all and leave us with fond remembrances.

Sincerely and fraternally,
Betty J. Schremser
Secretary

The Resolution

June 21st, 1950

The citizens of Yokosuka, two hundred and eighty thousand in population, are very grateful to His Excellency the Rear Admiral Benton W. Decker, thinking that he has given greatest help and guidance in promoting the welfares of citizens of Yokosuka and also in reconstructing Yokosuka City ever since his appointment to the Commander, Fleet Activities, Yokosuka.

At the repatriation of His Excellency the Rear Admiral Benton W. Decker, the Yokosuka City Assembly herein tenders its heartfelt gratitude for his merciful government by passing this resolution without a dissenting voice.

The Yokosuka City Assembly

412

Kanagawa Prefectural School Board
Board of Education
Kanagawa Prefecture, Japan
26 June, 1950

Dear Admiral Decker,

Since you took up your post as Commander of the USA naval base, Yokosuka, Japan, you have looked busying yourself always with your duty. Nevertheless, having been kindly interested particularly in culture, and education of the locality, you have been so gracious as to, with your profound knowledge and high intelligence, make an unspeakably great contribution, sparing some of your precious time, to the advancement of CULTURE and the promotion of NEW EDUCATION not to only in Yokosuka City but also in the whole part of this prefecture. That has proved really conducive to a sound and speedy growth of newly-born democratic Japan. Words cannot express our heart-felt thanks. We shall never forget your kindness and graciousness.

The present Board of Education hereby expresses its sense of deepest gratitude respectfully to you in accordance with the resolution it has passed unanimously, hearing you are going home shortly.

Please be kind enough to send us continued warm help in our striving for democracy in this country. Be ever more careful of your health in home and may we wish you ever more successful naval years.

Sincerely yours,
Hyohzoh Minoshima
(Chairman)
Shoh-ichi Kawada
E-iji Katoh
Junsaku Kubota
Shiroh Kurotsuchi
Tsuneko Hirano, Mrs.
Se-i Yoshida, Mrs.
    Board of Education
    Kanagawa Prefecture
Shinichi Nakamura
Superintendent

413

Bishop's House, 44 Bluff
Yokohama
27th July 1950

Dear Admiral Decker,

A thousand thanks are not sufficient to show my appreciation of your letter! You have no idea of the wonderful impression your zeal left on the people of Yokosuka—a zeal which showed itself in the establishment of schools, hospitals, and other institutions. Your assistance at the magnificent Procession of the Blessed Sacrament effectively aroused an interest in Christianity. As a living example of love and peace you have shown that there is no other spiritual chain by which all nations can be united. The people continue to talk of you with admiration and gratitude.

I was very sorry I could not see you off on the day of your departure, as I had to preside at a Convent ceremony. Yesterday I visited Yokosuka and the sight of your good work once again aroused my deep gratitude. This letter is to express that gratitude, and to assure you that I pray most heartily that Our Lord's blessing may be ever with you and your family.

Sincerely yours in J.C.
Thomas Wakita
Bishop Yokohama

Admiral Joy asked that I stay over in spite of several refusals by the Navy Department. Both the General and Admiral Joy had sent several dispatches and the answers were negative. I had removed my household effects several times from the Navy Transport. On June thirtieth Admiral Joy called me on the telephone again to ask me to stay over and I explained, "Admiral I would like to very much, but all I am doing is causing you embarrassment and the best I can do is to leave and clear the the air. If the Navy Department reverses itself, I'll fly back immediately and be happy to serve under you in any capacity."

Had he actually had a plan or a job in mind I would have stayed, but to drift about Japan without a job and in disobedience of orders could cause trouble.

I certainly wanted to stay. The lowest point in my life was when I was forced to retire, and now I was being forced to reretire when my services could be of help. If only I had known that a few hours after my transport had sailed, all personnel in Japan was to be "frozen," I could have let Edwina and our effects continue while I remained behind. Admiral Joy would have been faultless and I might have been kept on in some capacity.

TO COMNAVFE (ADMIRAL JOY)
IN LEAVING YOUR COMMAND I DO SO WITH REGRET X YOUR THOUGHTFULNESS AND STRONG SUPPORT HAVE MADE MY TOUR UNDER YOUR COMMAND PLEASANT AND PRODUCTIVE X PLEASE EXPRESS MY FAREWELL THANKS TO YOUR OUTSTANDING STAFF X DECKER

TO CINCFE (GENERAL MACARTHUR)
AFTER FOUR YEARS OF THE HAPPIEST AND MOST PRODUCTIVE YEARS OF MY NAVAL CAREER WHICH WERE SPENT UNDER YOUR COMMAND I DEPART WITH REGRET THAT THEY MUST BE INTERRUPTED X MAY YOU AND YOUR FAMILY CONTINUE TO ENJOY GOOD HEALTH AND HAPPINESS AND THOSE ABLE MEMBERS OF YOUR SUPERB STAFF LONG HAVE YOUR LEADERSHIP AND GUIDANCE X DECKER

Edwina brings the story to a close—

On July the first, following breakfast, Bert, Benny, and I were whisked away to the pier in Yokohama where we boarded the Transport *Gaffey*. On the dock was the Navy band and crowds of Yokosuka Japanese and American friends, and Navy and Army, diplomatic and press corps, who had come all the way to say good-bye. Our friends in Japan had become very dear to us. Yokosuka was as near heaven as I could ask. I had been happy in Japan. As the ship pulled away from the pier we saw Nan and Dennis McEvoy dashing down the dock. They were late but wanted to wave us good-bye, and we waved back with a tear in our eyes.

When we went to our cabin, we found it full of flowers, fruits, and gifts. And we had our son as an aide returning to a new duty station in the Naval Academy.

Sayonara, Japan!

EPILOGUE

Two hours after our departure all personnel was frozen. Bert's ship, the *Partridge*, was sunk in the Korean War.

Admiral Kichisaburo Nomura, the ambassador to the United States at the time of Pearl Harbor, wrote:

> 15 September 1950
>
> Just about the time of your departure, the North Koreans invaded South Korea, against everyone's anticipation. Your government moved decisively and quickly. Japan has been saved by your move. We should do our best efforts to cooperate with the U.S.A.; in more diplomatic way, the U.N.
>
> Russia has wanted Korea for a long time. Before the Russo-Japanese War, she wanted it and now just the same. She does not change her mind with time and circumstance.

Captain Butler, the senior medical officer who had built up the Yokosuka Hospital for two years before the Korean War, wrote the following letter, quoted in part:

> December 16, 1950
>
> You should see the hospital at Yokosuka—here is today's census—2787 patients in the hospital, 914 at the annex in Otsu and 661 in Barracks B. The Hospital received 650 patients yesterday. Remember it was amusing to contemplate how the Japanese crammed 2000 patients into the hospital? You would never believe the place could hold so many.
>
> Now they have a large number of base personnel stationed over at McGill, others at Oppama, etc., some 6000 or so all told. Even have an old exliberty ship in use as a barracks.
>
> All your thoughts, and work, and effort, on the importance of Yokosuka as a base for the Navy in the Far East have been borne out by the events that have come to pass. In my concentrated interest in the medical situation I have not kept abreast of all the ship repair and

commissioning work, etc., that has been done there. Needless to say the volume has been terrific, I have heard very little mention made of the way you paved the way for the base to perform this service—but of course, that's the way of life is. . . .

Very sincerely,
Jim and Kay Butler

Testimonial

June 24, 1950

Dear His Excellency Rear Admiral Benton W. Decker,

All social welfare groups in Yokosuka are very grateful to His Excellency Rear Admiral B. W. Decker, because the present status of improved and reformed social welfare is greatly due to Admiral Decker's special concern and earnest assistance supported by not only by his spiritual guidance but also by his material assistance towards social welfare facilities.

At the departure from you we wish to tell you our resolution that we will continually put our efforts to push the remarkable works you left behind so as may prosper as ever.

At the end we pray God may bless Admiral's and Mrs. Decker's health.

Kenzo Akiyama	Shonan Hoikuen
Shunko Hashimoto	Asahien
Seisan Kanaya	Kinugasa Aijien
Takusaburo Higuchi	Shunko Gakuen
Toshiko Tanaka	Keiai Hoikujo
Yu Yonezawa	Keiai Boshiryo
Kurakichi Abe	Kyorakuso
Kurasaku Abe	Kyorakuso
Kurakichi Abe	Hinode Hoikusho
Takeo Ishida	Nagai Hoikuen
Suye Haraikawa	Heiwa Hoikuen
E. W. Thompson	Zenrinen
Senko Kawabata	Shinaisen Hoikujo
Michiko Fukuda	Sanwa Hoikusho
Toragoro Yamada	Fukudakai Zushi Bunin
Kako Miyata	Sano Hoikuen
Benkai Tamki	Choanji Joikuen

Heikichi Hirota	Gyokusei Hoikuen
Fusa Takeuchi	Yokosuka Boshiryo
Kimi Koike	Futaba Hoikuen
Kyoku Mochizuki	Numama Aijien
Chiyono Hangaya	Shirahatoen
Ryunen Mitamura	Tachibana Hoikuen
Yuko Kawashima	Taura Hoikuen
Hideo Hirasawa	Funakoshi Hoikuen
Take Takahashi	Ohgusu Aijien
Misao Amano	Hayama Kodomoen
Akino Tsukahara	Oppama Hoikuen

Yokosuka Christian Community Center
82 2-Chome, Taura
Yokosuka, Japan

November 1, 1966

Admiral Benton Decker
1086 Bangor
San Diego, Calif., U.S.A.

Dear Admiral Decker:

TWENTY YEARS AGO this month you challenged Christian leaders in Tokyo to do something socially constructive with a disreputable dance hall in Taura which you had closed down. As a result, Mrs. Thompson and I were asked to serve here and have continued here except for furloughs in the States.

From the very beginning we were able to establish COOPERATIVE WORKING RELATIONS with the Yokosuka City Hall—the Welfare Department, the Police Department, the Educational Department—and with local schools and hospitals and with neighboring private agencies.

Our DAY CARE CENTER AND NURSERY has been giving all day care and guidance to 120 children of working parents each day. These range in age from six months to six years. Our trained Christian staff members have always maintained a close relationship with the parents, guiding them to better understand and help their own children. Among the graduates of this Day Care Program may now be found college students, young business men and young mothers sending their own children to us.

Our WELL BABY CLINIC has over the years offered the consultation of Christian doctors and trained nurses to several thousand parents, sharply decreasing the post war infant mortality rate in and around this neighborhood.

Our CLUBS for CHILDREN, and for YOUNG PEOPLE, and for their PARENTS, and for their GRANDPARENTS have offered constructive use of leisure time on various levels. When the demand for children's clubs far exceeded the time available to our limited staff, we have given professional direction to the parents' self help program for conducting their own children's clubs.

The SEWING SCHOOL at the Community Center has for years been graduating skilled young women who could readily find employment in high grade tailor shops, and—better yet—turn the same taste and fitness to the creation of clothes which they have been proud to wear.

The evening ENGLISH CONVERSATION SCHOOL was first set up, as you will recall, to meet the needs of Navy Base interpreters, housed across the way. This school soon came to meet a wider need. For years it has conducted conversation classes on five different levels of ability, meeting three nights a week—fifteen classes a week. Volunteer Navy personnel continue to play an important part in this school. Many young officers of the Self Defense Forces have studied English with us before going to America for graduate studies.

An ORGAN PLAYING SCHOOL, and ABACUS SCHOOL, regular assistance with HOME STUDIES from public schools, rehabilitation services for CRIPPLED CHILDREN and a home for WIDOWS and their DEPENDENT CHILDREN are among other activities of our Center.

Out of the varied contacts of our Christian staff with the non-Christian community has come an INDEPENDENT TAURA CHURCH, part of the interdenominational United Church of Christ in Japan. This church has always paid its own pastor's salary in full and is now regularly contributing to Christian work in pioneer spots in Japan and in a half a dozen foreign countries—Brazil, Nepal and others.

419

At least six other Christian Community Centers have come to us for inspiration and standards as they have begun their work in scattered places from Nagasaki to Aomori. From our staff, Christian workers have gone out to establish Christian social work of their own in a dozen different places, so while our work continues to grow in Taura, it is multiplied in *daughter institutions elsewhere.*

With sincere gratitude for all that you have previously done for the people of Taura.

Respectfully,
Everett W. Thompson